Lowell L. Bennion

LOWELL L. BENNION

TEACHER ❖ COUNSELOR HUMANITARIAN

BY
MARY LYTHGOE BRADFORD

WITH A FOREWORD BY
EMMA LOU THAYNE

DIALOGUE FOUNDATION
SALT LAKE CITY

To my husband,
Charles Henry ("Chick") Bradford,
1928-91

Printed in the United States of America.

For information, contact Dialogue Foundation, P.O. Box 658, Salt Lake City, Utah, 84110-0658.

Book and cover design by Warren Archer II.

Library of Congress Cataloging-in-Publication Data

Bradford, Mary Lythgoe.
Lowell L. Bennion: Teacher, Counselor, Humanitatian
/ by Mary Lythgoe Bradford
p. cm.
Includes index.
ISBN 1-56085-081-7 (cloth)
1. Bennion, Lowell Lindsay, 1908- . 2. College teachers -- Utah -- Biography.
Mormon authors -- Utah -- Biography. I. Title
LA2317.B376B73 1995
378.1'2'092 -- dc20
[B] 95–40866
CIP

CONTENTS

vii	Foreword	
ix	Introduction	
xiii	A Thank You Note	
		PART 1. FOUNDATIONS
3	Chapter 1.	Heritage and Home Life (1908-28)
25	Chapter 2.	Marriage and Mission (1923-31)
44	Chapter 3.	Honeymoon and Heartbreak (1931-34)
		PART 2. THE SANCTUARY
63	Chapter 4.	Institute Beginnings (1935-39)
85	Chapter 5.	An Adventure All the Way (1939-50)
105	Chapter 6.	The Heyday of the Institute (1950-60)
126	Chapter 7.	The Unified Church School System (1953-62)
154	Chapter 8.	Leaving the Institute (1962)
181	Chapter 9.	Recovery and Renewal (1963-70)
197	Chapter 10.	The Teton Valley Boys Ranch (1961-85)
		PART 3. HALLS OF IVY
223	Chapter 11.	Calm Center in a Storm (1962-74)
243	Chapter 12.	Personal Convictions, Public Issues (1962-78)
		PART 4. THE "REAL" WORLD
265	Chapter 13.	The Community Services Council (1972-88)
286	Chapter 14.	Private Lives (1962-88)
311	Chapter 15.	The Lowell L. Bennion Community Service Center (1978-94)
331	Chapter 16.	The Teacher's Voice (1978-92)
349	Epilogue	
357	Appendix A.	Lowell L. Bennion's Writings
366	Appendix B.	Honors
369	Appendix C.	Interviews
375	Index	

FOREWORD

To write about the influence of Lowell Bennion is to try to capture the wind in the trees of a canyon. More fruitful is to look instead at how the touch of his life is alive in the 9,000 students volunteering themselves through the Bennion Center at the University of Utah to tutor homeless children or design a better wheelchair as an engineering project or—as Lowell has done all his life—paint the house of a widow and make sure she has food for the week.

Again the influence might be found in a classroom or discussion group—for more than fifty years I've been in on both—where new ideas are welcomed or on a page where old ones are explored. Mostly he is where neither is condemned—nor their proponents.

Lowell Bennion has traveled our lives by moving among us with the stride of an athlete and the grasp of a huge hand and an even bigger spirit. "Relationships," he says, "are what matter," as he delivers goods from his garden or talks from a pulpit or counsels from an office, never not in touch with the divine or unaware of the human in each of us. He is as compassionate as he is passionate.

His religion is as practical as it is consistent as he "never lets the things that matter most be at the mercy of the things that matter least." What has mattered to him are faith, hope, and charity, each manifesting the other in a reversing of order: charity equals hope equals faith. He offers as much charity to a stranger facing a firing squad as to a member of his church facing excommunication. His door is open to a student wondering whom to marry or a couple fending off divorce. Issues and events, youth and age, male and female like and unlike him in conviction or experience, varieties on the theme of being human he addresses with equal sanity, good humor, vision, and obvious affection.

Beauty he embraces in a Teton forest or a Beethoven symphony or a philosophical discussion with a fourteen-year-old learning to fence a pasture. Scripture is as alive to him as leaves returning in spring or the comfort of a helping hand. "To action alone have we a right—not to its fruits" is his motto, good works incorporating the body, mind, and spirit. The connectedness of a universe to all creatures and a loving God is as real as his expectations for his garden or his intuitive concern for the well being of a friend.

One day last winter, when I was adrift in the fever of pneumonia and a bewildering infection of my eyes, ears, nose, and sinus, worse even, the revved-up non-focus and sleeplessness of steroid cures and the loss of access to my inner self, I picked up the phone by my bed to hear, "Emma Lou, this is Lowell. Call me any time. And get better. We need you."

For months, years really, Lowell Bennion's physical voice had faltered. Parkinson's disease and arthritis slowed his speech and fettered his arms. Talking or using a phone were precipitous at best. Making a call was near impossible. Yet his connectedness transcended impairment or distance. He knew of my need. And he acted on his knowing. In a clear, unhalting voice he offered what he always has—himself. Charity. Healing by the grace of knowing how.

It's time that his life be seen in its entirety. True, his own writings, prolific and profound, will continue to lift and persuade us; his Community Services food bank will feed hungry bodies and souls; and the center in his name will send goods and goodness via another generation moved as he has been moved to befriend in broad and pinpoint strokes those needing a friend. His family and close associates will carry him into their daily lives. But his life story will be him, a handbook of integrity in action. With the intrepidity of Job and the loving kindness of Hosea, to say nothing of the twinkle of the Bennion sense of the world, Lowell will be like the wind in the trees—a presence, a reason to stay alive and well, a blessing both earthly and eternal.

I love this man. Thousands do and will. His life is his message and gift. Now it can be a resource in these pages brimming with him.

Emma Lou Thayne

Introduction

"I just want to be remembered in the lives of my students," said Lowell Bennion when I first broached the subject of writing his biography. It is true that his students, the children of his students, and countless others remember him with more than nostalgia. Many of them chose their careers, met their spouses, and rethought their religion within his sphere of influence. His classes and books provided a safe place to explore both doubts and convictions.

Now eighty-seven, he is a living legend. People trade tales—"Remember when the bushel of apples appeared on our back porch and we opened the door in time to catch sight of a battered truck speeding away?" "Remember when we looked out to find our garden newly weeded?" "Remember when a group of students showed up to paint our house or repair the roof?" They tell of mysterious food boxes and Christmas caroling and many another task performed miraculously overnight. One elderly woman tells of the year Lowell gave her the mattress off his own bed.

He spent twenty-seven years at the LDS institute of religion across the street from the University of Utah. He broke new paths during the stormy decade of the 1960s as Associate Dean of Students and Professor of Sociology at the University of Utah. For twenty-five years he directed the Teton Valley Boys Ranch, where he taught city boys how to work, and for sixteen years he directed the Community Services Council in downtown Salt Lake City, where he taught a community how to serve. In his LDS ward he served as bishop. As a writer of LDS religious curriculum he produced instructional manuals that are not only respected but read, then went on to produce a series of nine "little books" that succinctly explored issues of ethical living.

With everything else, he was a gardener, growing fruit and vegetables on two to four acres near his East Millcreek home in the Salt Lake Valley. The produce fed family, neighbors, and the hungry in his community. Solitary garden-weeding deepened his serenity. Combinations of conversation and tomato-picking continued his informal teaching, and his dedication to service expanded to meet the needs of the underdeveloped side of society.

He has been called "the conscience of his people." Mormon to his very bones, devout but never dogmatic, he is seen by those of other religions, or no religion, as a universal figure whose influence extends beyond the place where he was planted. A slight figure now stooped with Parkinson's disease, he still visits the aged and infirm, ignoring his own age, his own infirmities. He serves on various boards aimed at helping the aging, the handicapped, the poor, the hungry.

Honored and embarrassed by the Utah State Legislature with a joint resolution in 1992 and by the Caring Institute in Washington, D.C., as one of the most caring souls in all humanity, he says, "I wouldn't mind being honored for writing a book, but not for doing what everybody is supposed to be doing." His books also perform a humanitarian service. While his food baskets feed the body, his books feed the mind and spirit. An intellectual who works with his hands, Lowell Bennion radiates a serenity that ministers to the whole rational, moral, spiritual self. "To action alone hast thou a right, not to its fruits," is his paraphrase of the essence of the *Bhagavad-Gita.* Through a superior education, he prepared himself for any professional position he might have desired, filled each day with his best efforts, and turned to the next with no regrets. His brand of service depends on a quiet charisma that thrives on anonymity.

Lowell Bennion's networking skills mobilized a community. He seldom asked for money. He simply presented his case, made phone calls, and volunteered himself. No task was beneath him. This appealed to those with social consciences and money. His ability to focus on problems one-on-one, his ability to show people how, and his gifted teaching skills equal success.

With one honor he was especially happy, even though he blushed at its name: The Lowell L. Bennion Community Service Center at the University of Utah, founded in 1988 to perpetuate his brand of volunteerism among students, faculty, and the larger community. Suspicious of institutions—"institutions have institutional goals"—he nonetheless gave himself to religious, educational, and community institutions. His influence moved horizontally, spreading in ever-widening circles that reach the individual.

I was one of the thousands of students "Brother B." touched and transformed during his twenty-seven years in the LDS Church Education System. I signed up for all the institute program had to offer—the wholesome social life at Lambda Delta Sigma (the LDS fraternity/sorority), the religion courses that delved deeply into the philosophy of Mormonism, the history of Christianity, other world religions, and the sacred nature of worship itself. I became part of the world of introspection and action he created with T. Edgar Lyon, George T. Boyd, and Marion D. Hanks at the University of Utah in the 1950s. "Brother B." instilled in me an edge-of-the-chair desire to volunteer for whatever he suggested: caroling (though I had no talent for singing), visiting the sick (though I felt tongue-tied in their presence), and cleaning (though I disliked it).

His influence was deeply personal. He had a way of focusing on me as a mirror of the self I hoped to become. He allowed me to try my wings in leadership roles, presiding, speaking, and performing. As a fledgling editor and writer, I was given the opportunity to practice on him. He asked me to critique his classic *The Religion of the Latter-day Saints* and then to edit *Religion and the Pursuit of Truth.*

He gave the gifts of self-worth to all of his students, while his teaching and counseling worked a powerful magic. In fact, I was part of a charmed time in Utah's educational history. The "Toot," as we called institute, was a home away from home, a bridge between religion and the university, a safe place to be, a laboratory in human relations. It was here that I began to understand that no church needs to fear its own history, that it is safe to be honest, safe to speak out about problems and fears. I also shared in another of his laboratories—the Teton Valley Boys Ranch—when I sent my son there in the early 1970s.

In 1978, when I was part of an LDS church education week with Lowell as the memorable closing speaker, I asked him about a possible biography or autobiography. He answered, "I'm not ready yet, but when I am, I'd like you or Dennis [my brother, Dennis Lythgoe] to do it." He said he was still too busy living his life to record it.

The time for making such a record arrived in 1986. Emma Lou Thayne gathered funds from Lowell's friends and family to buy him a new station wagon, with enough left over for a start-up grant for his biography. I began research in earnest that year, and the writing began in 1989 even as the research continued.

I have relied heavily on the words and memories of Merle and Lowell themselves. Merle's memory was so clear that I found myself wishing that she had accompanied him to his work each day! I was aware of the dangers of creating a plaster saint, so I probed for disappointments, failures, and sorrows as well as successes and satisfactions. Lowell and Merle, anxious to avoid the brush of the whitewasher, candidly described intimate sorrows and passions.

Still, strength and joy predominate. They lived remarkably seamless and uncompartmentalized lives. Lowell's students married and sent their children to learn from him. Neighbors became colleagues in many community and church endeavors. Students grew up to be fellow workers in various projects, and Lowell's long life allowed him the special joy of seeing "how things turned out" with many of his programs and the lives of his friends.

Lowell has lived in the powerful belief that "every human being should be allowed to craft his or her own destiny." He has crafted his own. After retiring from three different careers, he continued to visit the sick, sharing his garden's harvest, and sitting on numerous church and civic boards. He enduringly counseled youth and former students. He outlived the season that removed him from the job he loved best; he has outworn the voices that spoke against his activist brand of theology; he has traveled beyond those who doubted his influence on youth. In summing up his philosophy, he said, "If you have integrity and love, you have all the great virtues."

Lowell L. Bennion is a remarkable Mormon in an era when Mormonism itself is changing, a community-builder at a time when his community was torn between outreach and inward-turning, a voice of conscience and liberalism when forces of narrow-mindedness and intolerance were strong. Sometimes checked but never defeated, Lowell Bennion stands steadfast for the finest principles of human decency. When a full history of Mormonism in the latter half of the twentieth century is written, it may well be that the quiet voice of "Brother B." will be heard above the rest.

A Thank You Note

Lowell and Merle Colton Bennion devoted their lives to people. Not surprisingly, then, this book is filled with people whose generous memories, opinions, and documents have shaped it. From each phase of the Bennions' lives, I selected interviewees who represented literally hundreds who might also have been interviewed. In fact, when a mutual friend asked Lowell that fearsome question, "How is the book coming?" he responded, "Slowly. Mary is interviewing everyone who has ever breathed in the same room as me." I plead guilty as charged, and my debt is enormous to friends, acquaintances, and strangers who shared their love for Lowell and Merle.

Unfortunately, Merle did not live to see the manuscript published. On September 23, 1994, five days after her sixty-sixth wedding anniversary, she departed this life. I salute her—my best source, my mentor, and my generous friend.

Their five surviving children—Lowell Colton ("Ben") Bennion, Douglas Colton Bennion, Steven Don Bennion, Howard Wayne Bennion, and Ellen Jean Bennion Stone—and their spouses—were courteous and generous in sharing memories and documents, welcoming me to family reunions and other gatherings.

I was welcomed into the homes of Merle's sister, Ethel Colton Smith, now deceased, and Lowell's siblings: Claire Bennion Jones, also deceased; Milton Lindsay ("Lynn") Bennion and his wife Katherine Snow Bennion; Maurine Bennion Folsom and Leonard Folsom (both now deceased); Ione Spencer Bennion, widow of Wayne Bennion; Grant Madison Bennion and Marjorie Ralph Bennion; Frances Bennion Morgan and Elmo Morgan; and Vaughn Lindsay Bennion, and Lyle Cornwall Bennion.

I deeply appreciate the kindness of other kin who were interviewed: Sterling Colton and Eleanor Ricks Colton, Alice Colton Smith and Whitney Winslow Smith (now deceased), John Bennion and Sylvia Lustig Bennion, Barbara Folsom Mecham, and

Ralph Mecham, Anthony Morgan, Kent Morgan and Lynn Cannon Morgan, Paul Bennion Cannon, Alice Cannon Schmidt, Lora Bennion Nebeker, grandson Lindsay Bennion, Dolly Lindsay Ward, Richard Lindsay, and "Uncle Teddy's" great-granddaughter Carolyn Bennion Burns-O'Brien. Merle's cousin, Eleanor Colton, interviewed Merle's uncle, Hugh M. Colton, before his death. Janet Bennion Cannon assisted me in early research on the Bennion pioneers, as did Eileen B. McKean.

Interviews with other family members supported and clarified the work. Among the hundreds I could have interviewed, I picked those colleagues and friends whose experiences seemed representative, ranging from casual contacts to long-term relationships throughout Lowell's three-pronged career. (Unless otherwise noted, all interviews and oral histories I and others conducted or conversations cited in the text and notes exist as tapes and/or transcripts or notes and are in my possession. See "Interviews" at the back of this book for a complete list.)

Linda Sillitoe reviewed each chapter as I drafted it. I am grateful for her insightful comments and criticisms and her willingness to enter into my creative process with sensitivity and caution. She also interviewed some of Lowell's former colleagues at the University of Utah and at the Community Services Council.

Emma Lou Thayne, loyal friend to me and the Bennions, has acted as agent and go-between. With her help, the Bennion biography project was funded through the Lowell Bennion Community Service Center at the University of Utah. She read and critiqued the manuscript and wrote its foreword.

Douglas Jensen of the University of Utah Development Office and Irene Fisher, director of the Bennion Center, dispensed the funds that helped defray my expenses during the first five years of this project. A long list of Bennion, Colton, and Bradford friends contributed to this fund with Sterling and Eleanor Colton and Jack and Renee Carlson as its driving force.

My network of friends in the Washington, D.C., area gave me not only financial support but also constant encouragement during trying times: Renee Pyott Carlson and Jack Carlson, Belle Call Cluff, Mark Cannon, Kay Atkinson King and Robert King, Diane Ramsey Lloyd and Kent Lloyd, Alice Pottmyer, Marlene Jones Payne and John Payne, Esther Peterson, Jalynn and Gregory

Prince, Carolyn McDonald Shipp and Royal Shipp, Stephen Stathis, Maida Withers, and Teddie Wood.

My family embraced the project as their own: my husband, Charles Henry Bradford, who died before he could read the finished manuscript; my sons Stephen and Scott and their wives, Jane MacArthur and Sharon Aldous; my daughter Lorraine and her husband, Marc Gravallese. Even my children's in-laws offered financial support and room and board. In 1990 Mary Ellen and Thomas MacArthur gave me a quiet writing "retreat" at their Oregon home; LaRee Baird Aldous and Richard Aldous gave me a serene room in Salt Lake City; and Kathryn Christensen Gardner and Delworth "Del" Gardner provided space for me in their home in Provo.

Other Salt Lake City relatives and friends supplied writing space, computer time, financial support, and editing advice. My brothers, Thomas Mitchell Lythgoe and Dennis Leo Lythgoe, both read the manuscript and gave me advice based on their experiences as writers, historians, editors. My husband's siblings also stood ready: Rhea and David Allen, Phyllis Bradshaw, Clive and Leila Bradford, Afton and Howard Bradshaw, and Gwen and Jack Goaslind.

I am grateful to Barbara Redford Cook, Annette Sorenson Rogers, and Jack and Linda King Newell, who gave me rooms and computer time. Linda also acted as an agent with publishers. Alice and DuWayne Schmidt put me up at their home near the Bennions and shared their memories and papers during the early years of my research. Elaine M. Castleton, a friend and former student of Lowell's, acted as appointment secretary and chauffeur on some of my numerous trips to Utah.

I have been further supported in Utah by Gene and Charlotte England, Elouise Bell, Philip L. Barlow, Garr and Joan Cutler, Margot LeVitre, Frank McEntire, Curt Bench, Sam Weller, Dale LeCheminant, Hardy Redd, Cherry and Barnard Silver, Richard K. Winters, and Helen Candland Stark. Alida Woolley Tyler of Salt Lake City assisted in researching Lowell's University of Utah years. In California I was lovingly received into the homes of Lowell's lifelong friends, William (Bill) and Olive Moran. In Alaska Marie Jones interviewed Yvonne Welling Cassity, Lowell's former secretary at the institute, and LaRee Baird Aldous interviewed Orlene Jones Paulson. In Tucson, Arizona, Gigi Doty and Dick Butler interviewed Bartley Cardon.

Lisa Newey Stringham, a student at Brigham Young University, was adept at interviewing and word processing. Other volunteers who gave secretarial and research services were Sabra Hardy, Rebecca Reid Linford, Carolyn Miller, Boyd and Zina Nibley Peterson, Margot Van Orman, Stephanie Terry Wallace, and Caroleen Nord.

The suggestions, records, and mentoring of several historians have been indispensable: Maureen Ursenbach Beecher's fine oral histories of Lowell and Merle, and Leonard Arrington's early advice; David Whittaker and Thomas G. Alexander guided me in some of the necessary archives; and Laurel Thatcher Ulrich, Claudia Lauper Bushman, and Helen Z. Papanikolas supplied motivating encouragement and advice, as did Sylvia Beech Cannon, Davis Bitton, Richard L. Bushman, Susan Larson Paxman, and Jan Shipps.

I appreciate the help of the following archivists: Kirk Baddley, Stan Larson, Greg Thompson, and Robert Miller at the University of Utah; Dennis Rowley, Harvard Heath, and David Whittaker at Brigham Young University; Robert Parsons at Utah State University; Linda Thatcher, Gary Topping, and Jay Haymond at the Utah State Historical Society, Division of State History; and Delmont Oswald and Linda King Newell at the Utah Humanities Council.

I express particular gratitude to the sons of T. Edgar and Hermana Lyon for permission to read personal letters from their parents and to see their parents' papers at the LDS Historical Department archives, where Ronald Barney was extremely supportive. Laurie Newman DiPadova Stocks researched professional literature on Max Weber and sociology, aiding immeasurably in my understanding of Lowell's contributions to that field. She also reviewed the entire manuscript.

I am deeply indebted to Eugene England for his research and writing on the life of Lowell Bennion, which greatly enhanced my own. He also reviewed the entire manuscript. Lavina Fielding Anderson is the midwife who helped me ready the final manuscript for the press, and thanks to Martha Dickey Esplin for proofreading and typing.

I am also very grateful to my son, Stephen L. Bradford, to the editors of *Dialogue: A Journal of Mormon Thought* (Martha Sonntag Bradley and Allen Dale Roberts) and to the Dialogue Foundation for so willingly and ably reviewing and proofreading the final manuscript and making the necessary business arrangements for publication.

This catalogue of names is an honored roll call, reminding me of my great debt to others. How appropriate for a biography of Lowell Bennion! For all interpretations, conclusions, and errors, however, I alone am responsible.

"My career divides naturally into three parts:
the Sanctuary of the Institute,
the Halls of Ivy—and the University of Utah—
and the Real World of the Community Services Council."

—LOWELL L. BENNION

PART ONE

FOUNDATIONS

Lowell in Zurich, Switzerland, on April 21, 1931, where he served as district president.

CHAPTER 1

HERITAGE AND HOME LIFE (1908-28)

I like Goethe's statement,
"What from your father's heritage is lent,
earn it anew to really possess it."
– LOWELL L. BENNION

On July 26, 1908, Lowell Lindsay Bennion entered this world, in the words of his father, as a "well-rounded, well-adjusted, smiling baby."[1] His first portrait captured the blond sunniness and glint in the eye that announced a family trait—the "Bennion independent streak."

Lowell's earliest memory of himself is as a four-year-old reluctantly en route to the Salt Lake City railroad station and "kicking up a terrible fuss until they let me take along my toy rooster." This same spirit manifested itself when his father administered a light slap for some infraction. "Hit me again, you big bully!" was five-year-old Lowell's response.[2]

He came by his independence genetically, the son of Milton Bennion and the grandson of John Bennion, both hardworking and intelligent men with an unusual respect for their children's capabilities. His mother was Cora Lindsay Bennion, Milton's first cousin, once removed, who lived to be one hundred years and seven months old. Cora's grandfather, Samuel Bennion, was John Bennion's older brother. The family saga of their conversion to Mormonism in England, beginning with John in 1841 and Samuel seventeen months later, and their immigration to the American West via Nauvoo, Illinois, continues to speak to generations of Bennions.

Lowell's respect for Grandfather John is based not only on family stories but also on his reading of the self-educated ancestor's diaries, short autobiography, and letters to relatives. They track the dailiness of a hard-scrabble existence made manageable by strength, good humor, and cheerful devotion to the "calls" of his church. John and Samuel braided their polygamous families together in a tough strand, committed to each other, their faith, and their community but often displaying the "Bennion independent streak."

The Bennion brothers were reared on a twelve-acre tenant farm in Harwarden, Flintshire, North Wales, where their father, John Bennion, raised grain, vegetables, and hay.[3] The passion of present-day Bennions for gardens and orchards may well have germinated in this green and misty spot, just over the border from Liverpool on the River Dee. The farm held scant promise, however, for energetic young men seeking their fortunes. The four children's mother, Elizabeth Roberts Bennion, died of "dropsy" and a stroke in 1830, when young John was ten. Samuel, two years older than John, was apprenticed that same year to his uncle, a Liverpool baker. At fourteen, John was apprenticed to a boilermaker. Finding his Methodist membership "burdensome," he began spending Sundays "with my comrades in home fun." One Sunday he and his friends, accused of poaching rabbits, were brought before a local magistrate. Innocent and indignant, John avoided a trial by leaving for Liverpool, boarding with former neighbors, and working at the Vauxhall Boiler Works.

Searching for more than a job, John joined the Christian Society at Aiken Church. There he and Samuel heard the preaching of one of the first Mormon missionaries in Britain—John Taylor. Taylor told how fourteen-year-old Joseph Smith had prayed for divine guidance in a grove near his home in Palmyra, New York, in 1820, John's birth-year. Puzzled by "a war of words and tumult of opinions," he was searching for the truth, as John was. In the grove he saw a vision of God and Jesus Christ who comforted him but warned him not to join any existing church. Later an angel named Moroni led him to an ancient American record engraved on golden plates that he translated with instruments called Urim and Thummim, an echo from the Old Testament. It was published in 1830. A year later Joseph Smith founded the Church of Christ (later Church of Jesus Christ of Latter-day Saints).

This heady story of burgeoning revelation and new scripture disturbed Liverpool listeners, and twenty-one-year-old John feared he would "get caught in the snare." He avoided further meetings until his former Sunday school teacher, now a Mormon convert, explained "the plan of salvation as taught by the ancient apostles." The message was "too plain and scriptural for me to resist," John recorded. He was baptized May 2, 1841, and, ablaze with his newfound faith, proselyted fervently in and near Harwarden. Samuel, an independent Liverpool provisioner since age twenty-one and married to Mary Bushel, a lady's maid of good education, accepted Mormonism on September 30, 1842.[4]

Gathering to Zion was an expectation of the new religion. Purposefully, John went to Liverpool "to get me a wife," vibrant Esther Wainwright, his landlord's daughter. Friends tried to dissuade him from emigrating, but "the more they talked, the more intent I had to go ahead." On February 14, 1842, John and Esther were married by a Mormon elder. About a week later they boarded the *John Cumming* and sailed for New Orleans with two hundred other Latter-day Saints.[5] A river steamer brought them up the Mississippi to their American Zion—Nauvoo, Illinois—on May 7, 1842.

Within the month John had purchased land and a house and soon wrote eagerly to Samuel, urging migration, praising Joseph Smith's preaching, and zealously explaining that the "patriarchal order [plural marriage] is already entered into by many families in the city" because "the Lord wants increase." By age thirty-seven, John would be the husband of three wives. Lowell's father was the youngest son of the third.

In 1843 John penned a short discussion of "perfection" that would influence Lowell's thought on the same theme: "I would say if they were coming here looking for perfection they must not forget to bring plenty with them, for this plant does not grow spontaneously here. . . . We have to cultivate it with care or it will not grow at all but the soil here is fertile and plenty of room for it to grow."[6] John's commitment to Mormonism remained high as Nauvoo rose around him, even when Mormonism's fortunes suffered a brutal blow in the 1844 assassination of Joseph Smith and his brother, Hyrum.

Sisters Mary and Elizabeth married and reared families in England. John's father, together with Samuel and his wife, Mary Bushel Bennion, reached Nauvoo on May 3, 1845. In Nauvoo's barely finished temple on February 7, 1846, the two couples—John and Esther, and Samuel and Mary—received a rite that would "seal" their marriages beyond the power of death to disrupt them, according to Mormon beliefs. Almost simultaneously John wrote his in-laws that the Saints planned to go to "some good place between the Rocky Mountains and the Pacific Ocean where we will be clear from partial and corrupt government."[7] The Bennions joined the Mormons' half-planned, half-forced exodus in 1846.

John's father died en route to Utah in Garden Grove, Iowa, where Esther gave birth to a third child, Ann, who also died. Two other children were born to John Jr. and Esther in Nauvoo, Samuel Roberts in 1842 and Mary in 1844.[8] In July 1847 the first company of Mormon pioneers, led by Brigham Young, reached the valley of the Great Salt Lake in what would become Utah. In October the Bennions arrived.

Two years later John wrote enthusiastically to his Wainwright in-laws that the purported wilderness had already grown "thousands of bushels of grain a plenty to supply the people who are here and plenty to sell to those who come this season." His faith also flourished. "That thing called Mormonism which eight years and six months ago caused me to leave my native land, where my kindred and friends dwelt and where lay the bones of my ancestors for generations back, is as dear as it ever was to me."[9]

John built a first house near the central fort but in 1848 moved it to the "Five Acre Survey" at 5th East and 17th South, a neighborhood that would later be developed as Forest Dale, Lowell's childhood home. Brigham Young "wanted the lots occupied by the Bennion brothers and others adjoining them for a church farm," summarizes the family history, so they moved "with good will and actually found in their new location more room for a livestock business."[10] Their willingness to accommodate Brigham Young's request reflected a lifelong loyalty. Recalled one Bennion descendant, "If Brigham Young had told them to eat a bale of hay, they would have done that."[11]

The new location was "over Jordan," west of the Jordan River and south of 33rd South. In the summer of 1849 the two brothers and their families moved upriver to what became known as Taylorsvillle, which boasted "some of the finest grazing land in the territory." The Bennions herded cattle for Mormon leaders John Taylor, Wilford Woodruff, John M. Bernhisel, and others.[12]

Over the next twenty-eight years the Bennion brothers, still maintaining their Taylorsville homes, also opened "Mountain Home" at Vernon, a ranch at the south end of Rush Valley watered by Bennion Creek. They fought crickets, grasshoppers, disease, and adverse weather but raised flourishing herds of cattle and sheep. The bond between the two brothers remained unbroken during their lives and continued into the next generation. Children and grandchildren were born close together in time and location; wives shared with and cared for each other, and cousins circulated freely through the homes the brothers built together. In 1857 John was ordained bishop of their ward in North Jordan and later served as one of the twelve high councilors of Salt Lake Stake.[13] John also saw service in the Nauvoo Legion during the aborted but threatening Utah War, 1857-58; he was assigned to colonize the "Muddy" in what would become Lincoln County, Nevada, in 1864, but sent a substitute; and he was called again in 1868 and obediently relocated there with part of his family, while the others stayed in Utah.[14] In November 1872, not long after John returned from his mission to the Muddy, Brigham Young sent him on a six-month genealogical mission to England and Wales. His relatives in Hawarden were "amased to see me turn up," he wrote home. He met "premier Gladstone" while he copied parish records, and Gladstone's wife Princess Glynn "asked me how I was suited to my American home" and invited him to dine at her nearby castle, where his cousin, Susannah Catheral, worked. He marveled at the 20,000 books in the Gladstone library. He also was reunited with Esther's sister, Hannah Berry, who saved his letters, archival treasures today. In London he bought a complete set of John Milton's works.

When John returned, the Muddy Mission was closed and he resettled his families in Vernon and Taylorsville (also known as "Jordan"). He helped build Taylorsville's first school, a one-room rock structure, that doubled as a meetinghouse and the only public building in the community. Daughter Hattie, educated at the University of Utah, taught in this school.

He also took two more wives. In 1856 he persuaded the ambitious and hard-working Esther that another wife would "lighten her burden." By then Esther was thirty-nine and had borne eight children, the six survivors ranging from fourteen years to one year old. She gave birth to three more children in the next six years, also adopting her sister's child and a Native American boy.

Esther Ann Birch, a studious woman, had been designated as a "good wife for John Bennion" by Brigham Young when he met her working as a domestic. Young performed the marriage in his office on July 20, 1856, two weeks after introducing them.[15] In the next nineteen years Esther Ann gave birth to nine children. Lowell grew up with the family tradition that the three wives were "completely compatible, supportive of each other,"[16] but John's diaries show that the two Esthers were not congenial before the addition of Mary Turpin, the sixteen-year-old sweet-tempered third wife (Lowell's grandmother), whom John married in 1857 when he was thirty-seven.[17] Mary gave birth to eight children in twenty years and also raised Effie Lenore Cooper, the baby daughter of her sister, Hannah Turpin Cooper, who died in 1886.

Lowell's father, Milton, was Mary's fifth son, born June 7, 1870, at Taylorsville. From his settlement on the Muddy, John wrote farsighted congratulations: "We have a number of boys engaged in farming and livestock operation. Now I think it is time for one of them to become an author, so we will name this one Milton after the poet John Milton and see if he will not be inspired to become a writer."[18] Thus was Milton anointed to scholarship and education.

Milton's first memory of his father combined qualities of fairness and mercy. "As a young child . . . I started to run across the meadow toward the Jordan River. Father called to me to come back, but I kept going at top speed. He overtook me and brought me back to the house. I was not punished."[19]

John was severely injured while mounting a horse on August 31, 1877. He died the next day at age fifty-seven.[20] Milton's last memory of his father was his dying counsel, "Follow in my footsteps," which Milton interpreted as "Adhere to the faith."[21] Mary, pregnant with another son, suffered a double bereavement when the child died of heart problems at six months. (She lived in a lean-to against the Jordan home with the three youngest children until her older children built her a new home.)

For Milton's future wife, Cora Lindsay Bennion, John Bennion's funeral was one of her earliest memories. Cora, the three-year-old granddaughter of Samuel Bennion and Mary Bushel Bennion, remembered "the long stream of white-tops [buggies] going over the hill to the Salt Lake Cemetery" to her great-uncle's funeral.[22]

Cora was born December 9, 1874, in a log cabin in Jordan to Joseph Shanks Lindsay and Emma Bushel Bennion Lindsay. Her father plucked the banjo at ward dances "with his eyes shut and foot tapping." She showed an early interest in music, taking guitar lessons, playing the organ at church, and singing in the choir. After graduating from public school, Cora attended the fledgling LDS College in Salt Lake City for a time and then the University of Deseret for three years. She then returned to her former schoolhouse as a teacher and to her strict father's supervision. He brooked no card playing, criticizing of church leaders, or flights of independence from his children. "Mother told me in later years how cruel he was if she came home from a dance later than the set hour," one of Cora's daughters recorded.[23]

Lowell, born after the deaths of both grandfathers, enjoyed visits to his devout and warmly hospitable grandmother, Emma Lindsay, but has fewer memories of Grandmother Mary, who died when he was six. Her death was impressive for its order and discipline, even in the impressively disciplined Bennion family. Milton wrote: "Mother survived to the age of seventy-four, apparently without thought of death until the day of her passing. Then she announced that her time had come. In the afternoon she talked freely, bid goodbye to each member of the family and grandchildren who was available. . . . About nine p.m. she . . . sank back on her pillow and passed away quietly without a struggle."[24]

Milton was educated in Taylorsville's one-room schoolhouse until, in 1885 at age fifteen, he entered the University of Deseret. John R. Park, president and one of the institution's five faculty members, inspired him to study English grammar and composition, arithmetic, elocution, and penmanship. Park's readings from the Bible during chapel services stimulated Milton to read

Mormon theologians like Parley P. Pratt and Orson Pratt. He aspired to a career in medicine but left the university after his first year to take care of the family farm and work for his brother Heber. He trained and rode horses, drove teams, milked cows, hayed, hoed, and irrigated. At eighteen he owned six horses, helped care for twenty-six others, and accepted a schoolteacher's job back in the rock schoolhouse now enlarged to two rooms. Among his students was fourteen-year-old Cora Lindsay. "We began to look on each other with favor," wrote Milton, "like Jacob and Rachel of old."[25] Also like Jacob, he waited a long time for his love.

That same year he enrolled in the new LDS College where James E. Talmage's classes in chemistry, astronomy, and domestic science absorbed his attention. During the third week of the 1889 term he was surprised by a letter delivered to him in class: a call to the New Zealand Mission. His mother was even more surprised—and alarmed, too. Why had church leaders snubbed her four elder sons for the "teen-aged home chore boy?"[26]

Dutifully, Milton left school and Cora in November 1889 for three years in New Zealand that confirmed both his intellectual curiosity and his religious commitment. Entrusted with leadership responsibilities, he supervised missionary activities over a two-hundred-mile area. He struggled against heavy rains, floods, and coastal mountain trails with only a "horse too weak to carry more than my blankets and books." Trapped for ten days alone in a grass hut during a storm, living on water and potatoes, he learned the value of meditation and prayer. Like his father, he kept a detailed journal.

He left New Zealand on December 31, 1892, and traveled for the next five and a half months to: Australia, Ceylon, across the Red Sea and into Egypt, Palestine, Syria, Italy, Belgium, France, Germany, Holland, and England. Landing in New York, he visited historical sites in the East then stopped at the Chicago World's Fair before reaching home in June 1893. Along the way he passed through a chain of Bennions, beginning with brother Edwin serving a mission in Holland. In England he met Yorkshire kin. In New York he was greeted by his brother Alfred and wife Eliza. In Chicago brother Heber and wife Susie were working on the Utah exhibit for the World's Fair. And at home Cora Lindsay was part of the surprise welcome-back party held for him at the chapel. A week later they were engaged. His next older brother Edwin, who had already married Cora's sister, Mary Elizabeth Lindsay, coined the term, "Bennion double-cross" for this alliance of cousins. Cora was now nineteen, but she and Milton decided to wait five years to be married because he was determined to get an education.[27]

Milton spent the summer of 1893 again working on Heber's farm and entering the newly renamed University of Utah. Interested in education and ethics, he edited the student newspaper, earned a B.S. degree in social science, and gave the commencement address for his class of 1897. He then accepted the position of founding principal of the university's teaching training branch in Cedar City[28] and at the end of the school year in June 1898 married Cora in the Salt Lake temple.

Two days later the newlyweds joined schoolmates Eva and Howard Driggs on the train to the University of Chicago, where they shared a furnished apartment above the clattering "El" (elevated train). They took its intrusion lightly and would "get to laughing so hard when the train passed during dinner, that they could not get through the blessing" on the food.[29] While Cora and Eva took vocal lessons, the men attended summer school. Milton took courses in philosophy and education from John Dewey and social psychology from James H. Tufts—a stimulating introduction to Progressivism. Milton and Cora returned to Cedar City during the winter of 1899-1900, where Milton served as principal and teacher of history and geography. They welcomed the first of their ten children, Claire, on July 15, 1899.

In 1900 the Bennions moved to Forest Dale in Salt Lake City at the urging of Milton's sister Zina, who had settled there with her husband, John Cannon. The Cannons were caring for Milton's and Zina's mother, Mary Turpin Bennion. During that summer Milton left Cora, who soon gave birth to daughter Maurine (born October 18, 1900), while he spent a year at Columbia for his master's degree. There he studied with some of the nation's foremost educators: Nicholas Murray Butler, James E. Russell, Frank McMurray, Franz Boas, and M. McKean Cattell. Cattell directed Milton's thesis: "Testing Eye Sight of School Children," which drew on his insights in social psychology.

In September 1901, M.A. in hand, he became assistant professor of pedagogy at the University of Utah, his academic home for the next forty years. In 1913 he was appointed dean of the School of Education, a position he held until his retirement in 1941. During his last academic year he also served as vice president of the university. In addition, Milton edited the *Utah Educational Review* (professional) and *The Juvenile Instructor* (Mormon). Known for his *Citizenship, An Introduction to Social Ethics* and *Moral Teachings of the New Testament,* Milton became an intellectual force at both the university and in the LDS church's Sunday school, where he served on its general board for forty years (1909-49)—as its assistant superintendent from 1934 to 1943 and as general superintendent from 1943 to 1949.[30]

Between 1902 and 1921 Milton and Cora became the parents of eight more children: Milton Lindsay ("Lynn"), Wayne Lindsay ("Pat"), Lowell Lindsay, Ruth, Grant Madison, Frances, Margaret, and Vaughn Lindsay. Ruth, born in 1911, and Margaret, born in 1917, each died at age three months, but the eight survivors grew up near cousins in the friendly neighborhood of Forest Dale, a rural suburb of Salt Lake City eventually extending from 21st to 27th South and from 5th to 11th East.

Lowell remembers his mother, only five feet tall, as a serene influence in their home. Not demonstrative but consistently loving, she was "very conscientious about family prayer and seeing we got to church clean and neat and on time. She was devout in a quiet way." She loved vegetables and "would cook seven in one meal." Famous for her cakes and pies, she baked often but resorted to hiding them from her brood until supper time. Lowell summarizes, "She was very hospitable. A modest, hard-working lady with eight [living] kids and no help, a very good housekeeper, cook, laundress. And she never complained."[31]

Once when Cora was in her eighties, Lowell took her to the spartan accommodations at his boys' ranch in Idaho. Even he was surprised when, without a murmur, she not only slept in an unheated log house but got up early to help with chores. When she was ninety-five, a widow for more than twenty years and living alone, the power went off in her apartment. Anxiously daughter Maurine offered to come for her. "No," Cora said, "I'll light a candle and play my guitar."[32]

Cora's influence on Lowell was "not so much intellectual but just plain human." She "didn't express herself very much" at the dinner table that often hosted academic dignitaries from Milton's world of professors and ideas; but when the family was by itself, she "listened to debates about the church with father and the rest of us, and while others were skeptical, she was very cautious and considerate, and always right down the line."[33]

Knowing the intensity of his parents' love for each other, a puzzled young Lowell once asked Milton why he wasn't publicly demonstrative. Milton answered, "That is not for public show."

Cora joined the university Women's Club with other wives of professors and served a term as president. She spent nineteen years (1921-40) as a diligent member of the LDS church's Relief Society General Board then another thirteen as an ordinance worker in the Salt Lake temple. According to Lowell's wife, Merle Colton Bennion, Cora "did quite a lot of speaking" as part of her Relief Society assignments and "prepared very well," but Lowell seldom heard her because few men attended those all-women events. Her family achievements were honored in 1952 when she was chosen "Utah Mother of Year."

Merle Bennion would call Cora "the perfect mother-in-law: She would talk things out with me, but she never interfered." After Milton's death in 1953, Lowell often brought Cora home for the day, where she would placidly "sit and mend all day for me." A visible sign of her devotion to her grandchildren was her thoughtful gifts at Christmas which included a carefully economized five-dollar bill.[34]

Cora's children followed her lead in many ways. Claire, her firstborn, was a motherly and responsible older sister, playing Santa Claus when family means were straitened. "She bought me a football for Christmas," Lowell recalled. "I found its hiding place and played with it considerably before being 'surprised' Christmas morning."[35] Claire taught him to drive her Model-A Ford. Devoted to academics, she earned a teaching certificate and M.A. from the University of Utah and Utah State Agricultural College in Logan, with a summer's course at the University of California at Berkeley. She taught school in Cedar City, married a local farmer, William Lunt Jones, and reared a family of three sons and one daughter. She earned a local reputation as a "saint" for her open-handed generosity and quick service, but her personal maxim was the "eleventh commandment" that Milton had taught her as a teenager: "Don't take thyself too damn seriously."[36] Claire died in 1989 at age ninety.

The second daughter, Maurine, graduated from the University of Utah in 1923 in literature and dance, then attended the Juilliard School of Music in New York City. Lowell remembered, "She tried to spark my cultural and intellectual interests." She took young Lowell to hear legendary violinist Fritz Kreisler at the Salt Lake Tabernacle and the most memorable play of his youth, *Robin Hood,* at the Salt Lake Theater.[37] Maurine was also interested in women's rights. Cora would listen to her views and then send her to Milton, who also listened patiently and remarked, "Well, sometime you will understand. A teenager finds it hard to understand what it means to be a mother."[38] This satisfied her. She married Elry Leonard Folsom in 1928, and his engineering career took them to Chile, where they reared two daughters and a son, finally returning to Utah to settle near Lowell and Merle. Maurine was a club woman and local Relief Society president, bright and convivial, contributing her literature, painting, and music to community and church gatherings. She died in 1993.

Milton Lindsay (Lynn), born in 1902, was so mischievous that Cora once begged Milton to spank him. Milton refused.[39] Lowell remembers Lynn, five years his senior, as occasionally "bossy" but a fine example "of initiative" and "tremendous drive all his life." He fearlessly tackled new jobs like running a tractor, planting wheat on the desert to contribute to World War I production, and delivering *The Salt Lake Tribune* with the help of the family pony, Black Beauty.[40]

Lynn attended Utah Agricultural College (later Utah State University), served a church mission in Missouri and Oklahoma under Uncle Samuel O. Bennion, then attended the University of Utah where he joined Sigma Chi fraternity, was a teaching assistant to E. E. Ericksen in the philosophy department, and graduated with honors and a teaching certificate. He also earned a master's degree in education from the University of Utah and a doctorate from the University of California at Berkeley. He began his teaching career in the LDS Church School System (later Church Education System) under his cousin Adam S. Bennion, administrator. He became LDS seminary superintendent in 1935. Ten years later he began a twenty-four-year-long career (1945-69) as a visionary and sometimes controversial superintendent of the Salt Lake City School District. He married his college sweetheart, Katherine Ellen Snow, also a teacher, and they became the parents of Annette, Carolyn, John, and Rebecca.[41]

The fourth child of Cora and Milton, Wayne Lindsay, was quickly nicknamed Pat, thanks to the combination of red hair and the date of his birth—March 17, 1906. Milton described him as peaceable, quick "to see what was needed in the way of service." As a young boy, he would uncomplainingly help his mother prepare for dinner guests.[42]

At age seven Wayne took over the family chicken business and, with Lowell, milked cows and sold milk to neighbors, finally selling the cow "at a good profit."[43] Wayne served a mission to Hawaii and earned a business degree at the University of Utah and an M.A. in business administration at Stanford University. He became an associate professor of business at Utah State University and married Ione Spencer. Unloading boxes at the train station as a wartime volunteer, he was fatally injured when a heavy box fell on him, and he died three weeks later at age thirty-six. His untimely death remained one of the great sorrows of Lowell's life. He left no children.

Lowell, born July 26, 1908, was named for the Boston intellectual family. "Close in age and spirit" to Wayne, as sister Frances recalled, they formed a team and were "everybody's favorites."[44]

The next surviving child, Grant Madison Bennion, was born in Madison, Wisconsin, where Milton was studying philosophy, on January 2, 1913. Grant resembled his older brothers in scholastic ability, sense of humor, and his love of horses and basketball. Pronounced "an enterprising child"[45] by his father, he bored easily, dropping out of kindergarten and skipping class in grade school. When his parents transferred him to the Stewart Training School at the University of Utah, he rose to the challenge, became a good student, a singer, an artist, a basketball star, and, in college, student body president, basketball star, and a popular fraternity man. Graduating with a teaching certificate, he taught briefly at Granite Junior High School and then, at Lynn's recommendation, was hired by Ginn and Company, an educational publishing house. He retired after a career as president and chief executive officer in 1975. He and his wife, Marjorie Ralph, a Montana native and schoolteacher, are the parents of Deanne and Robert.

Frances arrived May 21, 1915, and received the nickname "Tiny" because she was "very small and especially slender, but very active both mentally and physically."[46] She remembered that Lowell often went to "choir practice" (a chiropractor) for his persistent and violent headaches (they turned out to be allergy-caused) and would perform operatic arias while washing dishes, making up in gusto and gestures "any lack in voice and training."[47] A bright student with a large circle of friends, she sang, danced, and played the piano like her sister, Maurine, and attended the University of Utah where she frankly enjoyed the natural advantage of being the dean of education's daughter. As a missionary, Lowell urged teenage Frances to forego makeup like the "natural" German girls. She declined: "I wanted to please him but I didn't want to be different."[48]

When she joined the high school newspaper staff, Lowell wrote her of his own experiences as a journalist. Frances graduated with elementary school certification, married Elmo R. Morgan, and they became the parents of Kent, Anthony, and Nancy. Elmo became vice president of the University of Utah in the 1950s, and one of their three children, Anthony "Tony" Morgan, served as a university vice president during the 1980s and 1990s.

Milton and Cora's ninth child, Margaret, born in 1917, was "stolen by whooping cough" at three months. When the baby died, Cora "threw herself face down on the bed, overcome with grief. 'It was so cruel. We may never have another baby,'" she wept.[49]

She was comforted, however, by the birth of Vaughn Lindsay, born April 25, 1921, when Cora was forty-six. She pronounced him their "most affectionate child" and recorded that Vaughn was so charming that he even "won over Grant's Airedale."[50] He "made friends quickly, spent money with abandon, [and] took to sports without restraint."[51] Vaughn served in the marines, married Lyle Cornwall of Forest Dale, and became an executive with United Airlines. They reared Richard ("Ricky") and Kristin.

Lowell summed up his family life in these words: "We were creative and energetic and innovative and unafraid of life—all of us!"[52] In later life Lowell attributed these traits to his mother's love and attention and to his father's trust, tolerance, and love of freedom.[53]

Milton's approach to discipline was noncoercive. Lowell remembers learning Christian and ethical principles from Milton's discussions of Proverbs, the Psalms, and the New Testament. When five-year-old Lowell grew bored with kindergarten in Wisconsin, Milton "respected his wishes" and left him free to "roam the open spaces and to take care of our rabbits." Milton recorded this incident as evidence that Lowell was perfecting his own version of the "Bennion independence streak."[54] Once Wayne showed the same streak, refusing Milton's request to ask a blessing on the food because he had "done more than his share"; Milton simply called on another child, admitting, "I forgot to count, I guess."[55] When six-year-old Lowell was showing off for a girl, he poked Black Beauty who kicked him in the face, leaving a permanent scar under his eye. Milton, instead of rebuking Lowell, bought a halter for the animal.[56] When Lowell threatened to run away from home, hid in the barn, then sneaked up to bed, Milton effectively short-circuited future flights by offering to pack his bag.[57]

In their discussions Milton was scrupulously fair, listing the pros and cons of an issue but seldom offering advice or a definitive answer. He wanted his children to learn to think for themselves. But his example was unflinchingly Christian. At the height of the German hysteria of World War I, Otto and Karl Buehner, neighbors for twenty years, saw ward members shun their children. Lynn remembers how Milton quietly took him by the hand and led the entire family over to sit by the Buehners in church.[58]

Lowell's physical environment was almost as important as family. Family, ward, and neighborhood united in the deeply stabilizing environment of Forest Dale. Next door lived Milton's sister, Zina Bennion Cannon, and brother-in-law, John M. Cannon, with their large family. Milton and Zina's mother, Mary Turpin Bennion, lived with Zina between 1897 and her death in 1914. Other descendants of Mormon pioneers lived nearby—Spencers, Youngs, Woodruffs, Loves, and Merrills. Forest Dale was a town by itself in the geography of Lowell's childhood: "Only a streetcar connected us with Salt Lake City," he recalled, "and we seldom used it."[59]

Forest Dale had its beginnings in 1889, when George Mousley Cannon, nephew of George Q. Cannon of the Mormon church's First Presidency and son of Angus Cannon, president of Salt Lake Stake, bought the Forest Farm House and its environs from John W. Young, who had inherited it from his father, Brigham Young. George M. divided the land into building plots, naming it Forest Dale after the beautiful walnut, locust, and fruit trees planted by Brigham. He settled his first wife, Marian Morris Cannon, and their children there and invited other friends and relatives to do the same. A civic benefactor, he furnished the Forest Farm House, which successively became a town hall, the Pleasant Hours Club, and finally the Forest Dale Branch Meetinghouse. He paid a large bonus to secure electric street car services beginning in 1890. In 1903 the ward dedicated a chapel across the street from the farmhouse. An individualistic statement among today's standard-plan chapels, it still stands below the freeway (I-80) which swept away the Bennion home at 2385 S. 700 East.

In Lowell's youth this meetinghouse had a circular dome over the center of an essentially square chapel with a row of clerestory windows immediately under the hemisphere dome. The entrances were framed with columns, and columns also appeared on either side of the rostrum.[60] Brigham Young restored Forest Farm House, and it now occupies a prominent place in Salt Lake's Pioneer Trails State Park.

Forest Dale Ward played an important part in Lowell's spiritual development. At age twelve he was ordained a deacon in the Aaronic priesthood, an event to which he attached considerable significance. One of his first responsibilities gave him a taste of being misunderstood. He was sent, like other twelve-year-old deacons, to collect fast offerings from adult members for the poor. After "fouling up" a few pages in the receipt book, he tore them out. The next day at Sunday school the bishop asked for an explanation. "I guess some thought maybe I'd taken the money—but the bishop put his arm around me and said to the other brethren, 'I'm sure Lowell is telling the truth. Thank you, my boy.'"[61]

This understanding bishop was Elias Smith Woodruff, who served for most of Lowell's youth—sixteen years. When Lowell, a shy teenager, raised his hand during a planning meeting for a new cultural hall and asked for basketball hoops, he was gratified that his question commanded the same attention as those of the adults. Lowell loved Bishop Woodruff's "simple reverence" and considered his boyhood "very religious . . . but not piously so."[62]

Academically, Lowell "got along fine in school, . . . was a whiz in arithmetic and did all right in everything else."[63] An early I.Q. test placed him in the "genius" range, probably accounting for his family reputation as "the smartest"; and Milton was so proud of Lowell's prowess that he wrote in his memoirs: "Before he was of school age he became a juvenile prodigy in mental arithmetic. He could do wonders in addition and multiplication and without any training."[64] In third grade Lowell transferred from Forest Dale Elementary to Columbus School on Fifth East, skipped fifth grade, and maintained high marks through Irving Junior High.

As the fifth of ten children, he learned the negotiation skills of a middle child. Enticed by neighborhood friends to smoke cedar bark, he first refused then struck a bargain: "If you promise to quit, I'll smoke with you this once." The experiment ended as the boys realized the corral was on fire and the flames were approaching the hayloft.[65]

Forest Dale was a healthy setting for vigorous family life and a flourishing community. The Bennion children slept on screened porches for fresh air, and the family was astonishingly self-sufficient. Their food chain, according to Grant, was "anchored by cows, calves, chickens, rabbits, pigeons, and a large garden which was marvelously productive because our own fertilizer plant operated around the clock just inside the corral fence."[66]

At home, recalled Grant, "Lynn, Wayne and Lowell took their turns at housework before graduating to outside jobs where character-building was supplemented with a little spending money. Lacking cash, Father substituted pride of ownership. He christened one cow 'Wayne's Delight' and another 'Lowell's Pride.' Father knew how to press the right buttons." Ruefully, Grant recalled that Lowell did, too. Grant had leaped at the opportunity when "Lowell generously offered to enhance my social standing in the family by teaching me the skills of milking."[67]

In the fall of 1923 after two years at Granite High School, Lowell spent his junior year at LDS High School in downtown Salt Lake City where he studied German and English, skipped his senior year, and graduated at age fifteen. Guy C. Wilson, principal of LDS High School, was the first person Lowell remembered as teaching "religion and theology and Mormonism all together."[68]

Milton's brother Edwin (Ted) hired Lowell and Wayne to work on his ranch near the Utah-Nevada border when Lowell was fifteen and sixteen. Lowell returned from tent living, cold showers, and dawn-to-dusk labor, calling it the "best summer I've ever spent . . . in terms of influence on my values and my life."[69] On Wayne and Lowell's first trip they "got stuck in the mud and spent two days and a night, cold and without food."[70] They also cleared off ten acres of sagebrush in a day to match the record Uncle Ted told them another boy had set the previous summer.[71]

Uncle Teddy enhanced Lowell's self-confidence by remarking, "Lowell, I wish I were as young and handsome as you are. That scar under your eye just makes you look all the more distinguished." "I believed him," Lowell admitted.[72]

When Lowell wrenched his back, he kept it to himself, afraid of being sent home, but "promised God that if he would heal me, he would not regret it because I would serve him. My trouble disappeared and never returned." Much later in life Lowell reflected on his boyish bargain: "I have tried to keep my promise, although for more important reasons."[73]

Lowell also enjoyed sports. Too young and small to match his brothers' success, he played on Granite's "midget" basketball team and, with Wayne, played guard on the Forest Dale Ward basketball team that won an all-church tournament in 1925. "We had little finesse, practically no coaching, but lots of fight and good coordination," he summed up.[74]

A significant friend was Angus S. Cannon, son of George M. Cannon by a plural wife who lived in Centerville, Utah. Angus shared Lowell's love of basketball and philosophizing. Lowell, who saw Angus as mature and thoughtful for his age, recalls spending "an exhaustive time" analyzing the nature of "being." When Lowell began to read Will Durant, Angus gave him advice he never forgot and seldom failed to follow. "Now don't just read the book. Write down some questions: What is the ultimate nature of reality? What is the good?—and look for answers as you read." Angus later described Lowell as "impersonal" in his desire to learn. "You find a lot of guys who try to learn something in order to give themselves airs. Lowell didn't have any of that."[75]

Both young men, "enamored of ideas," sought answers to questions about their faith, reading such books as William James's *Varieties of Religious Experience.*[76] They began to realize that different approaches to religion can challenge provincial thinking.

Finally the pair agreed to test the promise in the Book of Mormon "to see if we could get confirmation of its truth," as Lowell put it. They read it separately then met on a hill near Angus's home overlooking the Great Salt Lake. Like young church founder Joseph Smith, they knelt and prayed. Lowell remembered that they waited, half expecting "Moroni to come and verify the book; but he didn't." Both were disappointed by the lack of a revelation[77] But while Angus eventually left the church, Lowell's belief in Mormonism continued to grow, building on "the joy and satisfaction I'd had in Forest Dale and in my family life."[78]

From that foundation he took two important steps simultaneously in 1928: he married a "beautiful girl" and, a month later, left on a mission to Germany. He would not return to Utah for over five years.

NOTES

1. Milton Bennion, *Memoirs of Milton Bennion* (Salt Lake City: Milton Bennion Family, 1966), 116.

2. Ibid., 116.

3. Information on Lowell's family background comes from two volumes of family history: Mary Bennion Eyring, *The Bennion Family of Utah, Volume III,* published by the Bennion Family Association, which includes John Bennion's diaries from January 1855 to 1877, John Bennion's letters, illustrative materials and maps prepared by Howard S. Bennion, and other family materials, most of which is housed at the Utah Historical Society, Salt Lake City; and Ruth Winder Rogers, writer and editor, *Bennion Family History, Volume IV: John Bennion Family* (Bennion Family Association, 1990), which contains most of the material in previous volumes plus John Bennion's 1868-70 diary of the Muddy Mission and 185 family letters.

4. John Bennion's conversion story comes from "The History of John Bennion by Himself," in M. Bennion, *Memoirs,* 97-102.

5. The *John Cumming,* named for an American shipbuilder, was a 721-ton, full-rigged ship, one of seven prominent in the systematic and well-

organized Mormon migration from British ports. Conway Sonne, *Saints on the Seas: A Maritime History of Mormon Migration, 1830-1890* (Salt Lake City: University of Utah Press, 1983), 50.

6. John Bennion to Samuel Bennion, 4 June 1843, in *Bennion Family of Utah,* 3:511.

7. John Bennion to Edward Wainwright (Liverpool), 24 Dec. 1845, in *Bennion Family of Utah,* 3:512.

8. Samuel and Mary were eventually the parents of ten; Samuel's plural wife, Rhoda Jones, whom he married in 1868, bore six children.

9. John Bennion to Edward Wainwright, 15 Oct. 1849, *Bennion Family of Utah,* 3:513.

10. Foreword, *Bennion Family of Utah,* 3:vii.

11. Mary Elizabeth Lindsay Bennion, speaking in "Interview with Mrs. Milton, Cora Lindsay Bennion, and Her Sister, Mrs. Edwin Bennion," interviewed by Desla Bennion and Lora Bennion Nebeker, n.d., audiotape, Utah Historical Society; copy of tape in Bradford's possession.

12. Glynn Bennion, "A Pioneer Cattle Venture of the Bennion Family, *Utah Historical Quarterly*, reprinted in *Bennion Family of Utah,* 3:560.

13. A Mormon ward is a congregation presided over by a bishop and two counselors; a "stake" consists of a number of wards—ten or so—which is governed by a stake president, two counselors, and a high council of twelve men.

14. *Bennion Family of Utah,* vol. 4, contains John's diary and correspondence from the period. For a history of the Muddy Mission, see Andrew Karl Larson, *I Was Called to Dixie* (1961; rprt. ed., n.p.: n. pub., 1979). Reasons for closing the mission included exceptionally arduous conditions, hostile native tribes, and heavy taxes from Nevada.

15. Lowell L. Bennion, Oral History, 27. In February 1857 John and Esther Ann were sealed in the Endowment House.

16. Ibid.

17. See *Bennion Family of Utah,* 3:35-36, 4:29.

18. Ibid., 4:60.

19. M. Bennion, *Memoirs,* 1.

20. Ibid., 2.

21. Ibid.

22. "Interview with Mrs. Milton, Cora Lindsay Bennion, and Her Sister, Mrs. Edwin Bennion."

23. Frances B. Morgan to Mary L. Bradford, 12 Apr. 1989.

24. In *Bennion Family of Utah,* 4:94.

25. M. Bennion, *Memoirs,* 70.

26. Ibid., 6.

27. Ibid., 112.

28. Program of the Homecoming Alumni Banquet at Southern Utah University, Friday, 23 Oct. 1992, copy in Bradford's possession. At this event Milton Bennion was inducted in the SUU "Hall of Honor."

29. Frances Bennion Morgan to Mary L. Bradford, 12 Apr. 1989.

30. Roald Campbell, *Nine Lives: Leadership and the Graduate School of Education at the University of Utah* (Salt Lake City: Graduate School of Education, 1990), 59.

31. Lowell L. Bennion, Oral History, 19.

32. The reminiscence about both the ranch and Cora's candle are in ibid., 19.

33. Milton Lindsay Bennion, *Recollections of a School Man: The Autobiography of M. Lynn Bennion* (Salt Lake City: Western Epics, 1986), 27.

34. Merle C. Bennion, interviewed by Mary L. Bradford, 19 Sept. 1989.

35. Lowell L. Bennion, Oral History, 21.

36. Claire Bennion Jones, interviewed by Mary L. Bradford, 10 July 1988.

37. Lowell L. Bennion, Oral History, 35.

38. Maurine Bennion Folsom, interviewed by Mary L. Bradford, 12 July 1988.

39. M. Bennion, *Memoirs,* 113.

40. Lowell L. Bennion, Oral History, 7.

41. Their only son, John, became superintendent of the Salt Lake City School District in 1985 after an impressive career as superintendent of schools in Provo, Utah, assistant superintendent of schools in Elgin, Illinois, and superintendent of schools in Rochester, New York, and Bloomington, Minnesota.

42. M. Bennion, *Memoirs,* 113.

43. Ibid., 113.

44. Frances Bennion Morgan to Mary L. Bradford, 10 May 1988.

45. M. Bennion, *Memoirs,* 114.

46. Ibid., 122.

47. Frances Bennion Morgan to Mary L. Bradford, 10 May 1988.

48. Ibid.

49. In M. Bennion, *Memoirs,* 123.

50. Ibid.

51. Vaughn L. Bennion, interviewed by Mary L. Bradford, 9 Feb. 1988.

52. Lowell L. Bennion, Oral History, 23.

53. Ibid., 26.

54. M. Bennion, *Memoirs,* 113.

55. Ibid.

56. See Grant Madison Bennion, speech at family reunion in Salt Lake City, Aug. 1989, typescript in Bradford's possession; Lowell L. Bennion, Oral History, 17.

57. Grant Madison Bennion, speech at family reunion.

58. M. L. Bennion, *Recollections of a School Man,* 43.

59. Lowell L. Bennion, Oral History, 28.

60. Richard Jackson, "Meetinghouses of The Church of Jesus Christ of Latter-day Saints, 1830-1980," unpublished manuscript, chap. 6, p. 23, privately circulated.

61. Lowell L. Bennion, Oral History, 28.

62. Ibid., 39.

63. M. Bennion, *Memoirs,* 116.

64. Ibid., 116.

65. Lowell L. Bennion, Oral History, 27.

66. Grant Madison Bennion, speech at family reunion.

67. Grant Madison Bennion, interviewed by Mary L. Bradford, 29 May 1989.

68. Lowell L. Bennion, Oral History, 34.

69. Ibid., 9.

70. Ibid.

71. Ibid., 36.

72. Ibid., 37.

73. Ibid.

74. Ibid., 8.

75. Angus S. Cannon, interviewed by Mary L. Bradford, 6 July 1988.

76. Ibid.

77. Lowell L. Bennion, Oral History, 40.

78. Ibid., 41.

CHAPTER 2

MARRIAGE AND MISSION (1923-31)

I kind of concentrated on this little Merlie.
She was a beautiful girl and
enraptured me, as it were.
— LOWELL L. BENNION

In 1923, during theology class at LDS High School, fifteen-year-old Lowell vigorously debated philosophy and unknowingly attracted the attention of a slender, dark-haired seventeen-year-old girl. She thought he was a "quite handsome young fellow with reddish golden hair and rosy cheeks."[1]

"I also caught him looking at me," she said. He was too "shy and modest" to actively pursue a social relationship with Merle Colton, who was, according to Lowell's cousin, "the most beautiful girl in Forest Dale."[2]

Merle was a transfer student from Salt Lake City's East High School where she had spent her sophomore and junior years. Though much loved by her relatives, Merle was an orphan, moving frequently between Colton homes on Mormonism's rough-and-tumble outposts where education was often catch-as-catch-can.

Merle was born on March 31, 1906, in a bedroom dubbed "the incubator" in the Colton family home in Maeser, Utah. Scotswoman Nancy Wilkens Colton, Merle's paternal grandmother, was an unofficial midwife with "healing hands" and a history of meeting challenges. Born in Provo, Utah, in 1853, two years after her Canadian parents crossed the plains, Nancy married Sterling Driggs Colton, the son of Michigan converts who settled in Provo, where Sterling was born in 1851.

After marriage in 1870, Nancy and Sterling left Provo for Mona, Utah, in arid Juab County, and established what a grandson would call a "legacy of toughness."[3] After six years of farming they took another step toward the ultimate frontier—northeastern Utah's Uinta Basin.[4] There Sterling took up freighting, herding, mining, and mercantiling.

Territorial governor Brigham Young had deemed the Uinta Basin too hostile a landscape for colonization, and in 1861 Abraham Lincoln established the Uintah-Ouray Reservation for Utah and Colorado Utes. In 1877 Mormon farmers and ranchers began settling lands east of the reservation. Ashley Fork Center (now Vernal), established permanently in 1878 on Ashley Creek, welcomed Sterling and Nancy Colton and their four children the next fall. Other families followed, and Uintah County was organized in 1880. Sterling Colton became a civic officer, serving as sheriff (1880-95), justice of the peace (1891-92), and county commissioner (1893).

As sheriff, Sterling earned a reputation for courage when he dispatched an outlaw in a *High Noon*-style shootout in a local saloon.[5] In 1905 the government opened more than a million acres of reservation land to homesteaders. In 1911 the Coltons moved to Vernal, the county seat, where Sterling served as bishop and mayor. In 1922 he and Nancy retired to Salt Lake City and later purchased a home in Forest Dale near the Bennions.

Ten children were born to Sterling and Nancy Colton between 1872 and 1901: Flora Elsie, Sterling LeRoy ("Roy"), Don Byron, Frank Edwin, Warren Alfred, Charles Henry, Lewis Lycurgus, Nancy Fern, Zora Maria, and Hugh Wilkens. All the Colton children distinguished themselves as professionals and as founders of good families. Don, Merle's favorite uncle, became a congressman and LDS mission president. Indomitable first son, Roy (LeRoy), was Merle's father. The family history records that when one horse in the team gave out as the family was leaving Provo, seven-year-old Roy rode "the best horse for help." The others waited—all afternoon, then all night. "Early the next morning, they heard whistling. He had returned with two fresh horses."[6] This fearlessness Merle interpreted as a willingness to tackle hard work and to serve those in dire straits.

In 1897 Roy married Lula Camp in the Salt Lake temple. Lula

was born in Wallsburg, Utah, in 1878, to Richard Cecil Camp, an Iowa-born lawyer and teacher[7] and Sara Jane Glenn Camp, a "sweet and lovely" woman from Manti, Utah. Sara Jane and Richard left the Mormon church after "some unhappy dealings with Brigham Young." After Richard's death, Sara Jane became a Christian Scientist and settled in San Francisco. One of Merle's few memories of her maternal grandmother is of Sara Jane nursing her through whooping cough when she was still living in Utah.[8]

Roy and Lula settled in Vernal where he and his father ran a store. They had four children: Mildred, born in 1898, who died of whooping cough; Roland, born in 1899; Lula Ethel, born in 1902; and Lela Merle, born in 1906. The Vernal store failed, and the family took over a government store in Whiterocks on the Uintah-Ouray Reservation, then moved in 1908 to Bluff, Utah, near the beautiful LaSal Forest where Roy became a forest ranger. The young mother died of cancer in 1912 when Merle was six. Roy left his three children with his parents, returned to Bluff, and died suddenly of tetanus after a tooth extraction in 1914.

This double loss was deeply disorienting to Merle. She gazed into a mirror at a blond girl who resembled neither her dark-haired mother nor her red-headed father and wondered who she was and where she belonged. As she matured, her hair darkened like her mother's, and Roy's red hair appeared in two of her children. But as a young orphan, her bewilderment lay too deep for words.

Merle had few memories of her gentle mother. "Mother was always reading to you," Ethel told her years later. Merle couldn't remember, though when she entered first grade, she already knew how to read and had a strong appetite for the written word.[9] In her early teens Merle found her mother's elementary school report card bearing a teacher's notation, "Excellent in every way." "I can't tell you what that did for me!" she exclaimed. "I just waltzed around the room, saying, 'My mother's excellent!' It inspired me all my life."[10]

Within a few months after these grandchildren joined the household, sixty-one-year-old Grandmother Nancy had a nervous breakdown. Her youngest and tenth child was thirteen-year-old Hugh. Nineteen-year-old daughter Zora, who married George

Melvin ("Mark") Poulson that year, assumed Merle's care, even taking the little girl along on their honeymoon to Kenilworth, Utah. There the three shared a tent while Mark, an engineer, built a tunnel for the Union Pacific Railroad. Roland went to live with Nancy's daughter, Flora Colton Collett, in Roosevelt, Utah, then with his Uncle Lew Colton in Maeser, near Vernal. Twelve-year-old Ethel stayed home to help her grandmother.

Nancy soon recovered enough to resume care of Merle who, anxious to please, was "a good little girl" who "didn't get into any mischief." She ran a mile home for lunch, gulped her meal, and provided another pair of willing hands for the seemingly endless chores. Nancy, who served fifteen years as president of the Uintah Stake Relief Society, "had an insatiable hunger for helping others," as Merle put it.[11] "Relief Society was the medium through which [she] exercised her gracious, hospitable nature." Practical and down-to-earth, Nancy considered it an advantage that men did not attend the women's meetings "to argue about the things that nobody knew anything about anyway, as they did in Sunday school." Merle often gave up her bed to a guest or a convalescent and frequently found Nancy asleep under the dining room table, her own bed taken by a night-time emergency case. Merle was dazzled when Nancy hosted the pioneer general president of the Relief Society, Emmeline B. Wells (1910-21), a "frail-looking, lovely little lady."

At age ten Merle went back to Zora ("Aunt Zoe") in Laramie, Wyoming, where she tended a baby son and did weekly laundry. This two-year sojourn was not unhappy, but she longed for adventure. From her post in the sandy plains she often waved to the "elegant" passengers in the brightly lit dining cars in passing trains. "Every time I'd hear a train whistle, I'd want to go someplace."[12]

When elder daughter Flora protested that Zora was "working Merle too hard," Nancy brought Merle back to Vernal. Genuinely attached to Mark, Zora, and "their darling little boy," Merle left reluctantly. She also gave up the attentions of a Laramie boy who took her to the Episcopal church, where she listened happily to the organ. Her religious education to that point had been haphazard. Though instructed to say her prayers, "nobody ever prayed with me," and there was no Mormon meeting house within walking distance of the Paulsons' tarpaper shack.[13]

Back in Vernal Nancy and Sterling sent Merle to the LDS church, where she was absorbed into the "Beehives," a program for girls ages twelve to fourteen, a peer group that assuaged her loneliness. In Vernal she also had her "first spiritual experience." Mormon apostle Melvin J. Ballard, attending their stake conference, stood illuminated in sunlight, his white hair "almost like a halo," and sang "I Know that My Redeemer Lives." Responding with deeply reverent feelings, Merle for the first time "really believed that there was a Savior."[14]

An insatiable reader, she found her father's copy of Shakespeare's works at age ten and, largely uncomprehending but "fascinated," picked her way through the plays. Nancy learned to keep an ear attuned for the clatter of dishes and the swish of the broom when Merle was doing chores. When these sounds faltered, she called, "Merle, are you reading again?" Merle's academic aptitude anchored her intellectually, and Sterling gave her developing self-esteem another boost. Noticing that Merle and Ethel often sang and pretended to play the piano as they did their chores, he purchased a Kimball piano, paid for lessons, and, beaming with pride, introduced Merle and her repertoire to guests.

In 1922 Sterling and Nancy sent sixteen-year-old Merle to Salt Lake City where she lived again with Zora and Mark at 1435 South 10th East. Merle's twenty-year-old sister, Ethel, also a member of the household, was attending the LDS Business College.

Merle entered East High School where she met Mildred Spellman, an English teacher with a broad command of world literature. Merle became so excited about *Canterbury Tales* that she composed "a modern pilgrimage." She reencountered Shakespeare as an old friend, memorized long sections of Sir Walter Scott's *The Lady of the Lake,* thrilled to the intricacies of nature in biology, and fell in love with history. She also took music from East High's celebrated Lyle Bradford.

Her dark prettiness and quiet charm attracted a University of Utah student who led a dance band that played for home parties. Merle became its pianist toward the end of her junior year at East. But Sterling and Nancy, who had purchased a home in Forest Dale, disapproved. The young man was four years older and

Presbyterian, so her grandparents moved her to their home and insisted she transfer to LDS High School in the fall of 1924.

"I must have been a problem to my grandparents," Merle mused later. "They were good people who wanted to do the very best for us . . . and I did things that weren't very good." Yet her "badness" actually amounted to little more than normal adolescent resistance to rules. For instance, in Vernal at fourteen, she had secretly arranged to meet a boy at a dance; when Nancy decided to drop by, Merle "skipped out and got back home before her."[15]

Forest Dale was a good neighborhood, a good ward. Merle joined Luella Ferron Sharp's chorus of twelve girls, singing with the group until she was in her early twenties. And there was Lowell. Despite his shyness, he began calling regularly, with Nancy's and Sterling's approval, usually bearing welcome gifts from his garden. Once when Merle sat anguished by the telephone, trying to summon the courage to invite him to a girls' dance, Nancy asked playfully, "Does your grandmother have to call him?"[16] In spite of her approval, Nancy waited inside the front door for their return after a date. If Merle's step did not sound on the porch within a short interval, Nancy flickered the porch light.

"I was always comfortable with Lowell," Merle said. Talking brought them together—conversations at the kitchen table, on walks, during long drives in Lowell's tin lizzie on crisp fall afternoons in the canyon where they could sit on a log with a sack of apples. Their engagement emerged so naturally out of that ongoing dialogue that neither could remember exactly how it happened. Lowell's version is that they were sitting on the granary steps at his Grandmother Lindsay's when "I said something that she interpreted as meaning, 'Will you marry me?' and she agreed." He was eighteen, she twenty.

While Lowell took another year at LDS High School (which became LDS Junior College), Merle attended the University of Utah. To pay tuition, she became "a flunkie" for Uncle Mark and Aunt Zoe on a road-building project in Kemmerer, Wyoming, during the summer and fall. She cooked, baked, and cleaned for thirty-five men for five months without a day off. After that single winter quarter, her Grandmother Camp sent a hundred dollars for a year at LDS Business College. This training landed her a job in the spring of 1926 as a general clerk, typist, and teller at the Sugar House Bank.

Meanwhile, Lowell "had a hard time deciding on a major," finally choosing history and political science when he transferred to the University of Utah in 1925. Instructors who admired his father took an interest in him. Elbert D. Thomas, a future United States senator, sparked Lowell's interest in political science, as did George Emery Fellows in history. Geology brought Lowell his first exposure to the theory of evolution. His professor, Frederick G. Pack, "a very faithful, active LDS person," didn't "get into Darwin very much," but found no reason to question the geological age of the earth.[17]

In sociology Arthur Beeley "really opened my mind to the scientific approach to human problems." After classes in criminology and mental hygiene, Beeley hired Lowell to spend one summer "tracking down boys and girls and studying their recreational life." Lowell saw in Beeley's class the provocative possibility of connecting "the two fields, religion and social science." It was his first awakening to the "limitations of institutions and how [they] develop institutional goals instead of . . . the ethical ideals of religion." As a result, "I decided to take full responsibility for what I think and feel and do," attempting to understand others accordingly.[18]

Milton Bennion, a Socratic teacher both in the classroom and at the dinner table, remained Lowell's greatest influence. His ethics lectures, Lowell said, were "very, very profound."[19] Milton Bennion took a low-key but principled stand for academic freedom in 1911 when controversy flared at church-owned Brigham Young University in Provo. Two sets of brothers, William and Ralph Chamberlin and Joseph and Henry Peterson, came under attack for teaching elements of higher biblical criticism and organic evolution. The church's Board of Education passed a resolution that "teachers in the church schools must teach gospel subjects as taught by the first presidency and apostles" and pressed Ralph Chamberlin and both Petersons into leaving.[20] As editor of the *Utah Educational Review,* Milton summarized the BYU controversy, acknowledging the "right of the trustees to . . . say what shall be taught" but advising church educational leaders to "promote the intellectual and moral advancement of the students without interfering with their religious beliefs." He asked, "Will the placing of restrictions upon teachings, especially in scientific subjects, promote or hinder the discovery of truth?"[21]

Young Lowell quietly absorbed his father's open-minded attitudes, laying the groundwork for his own position as a teacher of LDS university students. Milton, personally acquainted with the leaders of the church, was never afraid to voice his opinions in person or in print, retaining his good standing with Mormon authorities throughout his long career.

Lowell earned a secondary teaching certificate, practice-teaching at the Stewart Normal School where his father had once been principal. Without having taken world history, he "taught it anyway," with his younger brother Grant as a student. Grant distracted Lowell during lectures by gesturing that his shirt-tail was hanging out.[22]

On August 1, 1926, Uncle Israel Bennion pronounced upon Lowell the "patriarchal blessing" traditional for Mormon youth. Such blessings typically trace a lineage as the Lord's "chosen" and promise blessings predicated upon worthiness. "The gospel is clear to you," this blessing told Lowell, "by reason of your faith and works in a former life, so that you were prepared to take part in the work of the Lord." He would marry and rear a posterity "that will serve the Lord and ever stand in their place in the Holy Priesthood." Lowell would "preach the gospel at home and abroad, with power from the Lord in miracles and in the discerning of spirits," and it promised that he would achieve "high and responsible positions in the church and the nation" if he remained faithful.[23] Lowell took this blessing to heart. After his graduation in 1928 he "was determined to be married and go on a mission both," he said simply. "So we did."

Married male missionaries of all ages were the norm, but the custom of calling only young, unmarried men was growing. In Lowell's own family Uncle Teddy Bennion had married Aunt Mary Lizzie before his mission to Holland. Lowell later could not recall considering any option besides virtually simultaneous marriage and mission. Both families gave their blessings.

He was delighted when he was called to the Swiss-German Mission as he had hoped he would be, having studied German for years. Lowell and Merle set their wedding date for September 18, 1928, six weeks before he was scheduled to leave, because Lowell needed to work as long as possible to pay for the ring and for his journey.

Merle joyfully anticipated Lowell's mission without fully envisioning the pain of parting for so long and so soon after the wedding. Splurging on "a beautiful maroon dress with matching hat and shoes" to wear to the temple on her wedding day, she was accompanied by her grandmother, whose temple clothes she wore, and by Lowell's mother. Lowell was escorted by his father and brother Wayne. Officiating was Apostle David O. McKay, a longtime associate of Milton on the Deseret Sunday School Union Board. All were impressed with the apostle's "twinkling brown eyes" and admonitions to "trust each other" and "live within your means." A modest but jolly wedding breakfast followed at the Colton home, prepared by Aunt Zoe and Merle's sister Ethel.

Duly feted, dragging strings of tin cans, and escorted by tooting horns, Lowell and Merle drove to Weber Canyon for a ten-day honeymoon at the family cabin of Merle's friend, Ione Spencer, later Wayne's wife. Lowell repaired three tire punctures as they spiraled up the switchbacks. Their first dinner—fried chicken—was purchased, live, en route. Lowell killed the fowl; Merle dressed and fried it.

Their honeymoon was "very peaceful and nice" with time for serious planning. Doctors had warned Merle that childbearing would strain her heart. So seriously did Merle take the warning that one day before the wedding she offered Lowell the chance to change his mind. He refused, but they decided not to risk pregnancy. Their honeymoon was, therefore, a romantic but sexually unconsummated idyll whose memories would strengthen them in the lonely months to come. "We were so idealistic," they recalled later.[24]

When the ten days ended they reluctantly returned to the Coltons while Lowell entered the Missionary Home in Salt Lake City for a week's orientation and training. He made a habit of "sneaking away" and visiting Merle during the evening hours.[25]

Merle's uncontrollable tears at the train station blurred her last sight of Lowell's hand, lifted in farewell. Lowell would have the advantage of distractions brought by new sights unassociated with Merle; but for Merle, every room, street, building, and event in Salt Lake City called up fresh associations of Lowell. "I'd get through the day because I had to work and I could keep my mind busy," she said, "but then I would go home and I'd be so lonesome." She looked back on their few weeks together with their blithe assumption that the waiting would be endurable. "Unbelievable!" she recalled later. "We were so naive."[26]

In fact, Merle felt orphaned again, cast adrift for the next thirty-two months. She moved in with Ione Spencer's family when Ethel married Elwin Smith a month after Merle's wedding and their grandparents left with Aunt Zoe for California's mild climate. Later she rented a room from Agnes Huish, a family friend whose husband was a travelling coffin salesman.

She continued her secretarial work, taught Sunday school in the Emerson Ward, and then became Granite Stake Gleaner president, working with teenage girls in the church's Mutual Improvement Association. When her landlady's husband injured himself and returned home, Merle accepted an oft-extended invitation from Milton and Cora Bennion to move into Lowell's childhood home.

It was a comforting decision. She found herself compatible with Lowell's siblings: teenaged Vaughn, "a very friendly and affectionate boy" who "really liked me"; Grant, a student at the University of Utah; and Frances, a vivacious high school student at LDS High School. They all welcomed Merle as a sister. She joined the dinner discussions with visiting university professors, even though she was "scared to death" of the Bennions because they were "so bright." Milton and Cora asked her to call them "father" and "mother," praised her unstintingly in their letters to Lowell, and "made me feel one of them," Merle recalled gratefully. "They never made me feel I was intruding, that I shouldn't have been there." Milton was "just as good and kind as he could be. So I grew to love him, and he was a real father to me." She was "still frightened to converse with him because . . . I hadn't grown up in that atmosphere [of open-ended discussion] at all."[27]

Cousin Mera, Don and Alice Colton's daughter, was also a cheerful friend. When her grandparents returned from California, Merle moved back in with them but continued to migrate between the Colton and Bennion homes, summer and winter, never unwelcome but always missing Lowell.

For his part, as the train pulled away, Lowell described the parting as "the hardest break I ever made in my life. . . . I spent the night thinking of Merle and . . . I realized that Merle was indeed my better half—that I love her with all my heart."[28] Mission rules were less strict then, and Lowell traveled without a companion. Elias S. Woodruff, president of the Western States Mission and Lowell's former bishop, met him in Denver for a two-hour visit. Cousins Angus Bennion Cannon and Hugh Bennion, missionaries in Independence, Missouri, took him to visit sites of the Reorganized Church of Jesus Christ of Latter Day Saints. Friends showed him around Washington, D.C., and New York City until he boarded the *Leviathan* whose social director, a fellow Mormon, greeted Lowell and two other missionaries.

The *Leviathan,* formerly the German *Vaterland,* was the largest of the magnificently furnished "floating palaces" awarded the United States at the end of World War I as part of German war reparations. It became a troop ship in World War II, carrying up to 9,000 soldiers. During the six-day voyage the missionaries modestly skirted the sumptuous promenade decks and the luxurious restaurant, admiring the ballroom splendor from afar. The romantic dance music made Lowell homesick for Merle, as did the moon over the night sea. The swimming pool was off-limits to missionaries, so he took brisk walks around the deck. He visited the massive boiler room, immaculate kitchens, bakeries, butcher shop, and the kosher galley and occasionally struck up conversations with fellow passengers.

When the ship docked at Rotterdam, the missionaries boarded a train that took them through lush countryside to Cologne, where Whitney Winslow Smith, who later married Uncle Don Colton's daughter, Alice, taught at the church's missionary school. For three weeks the Americans were drilled in basic German in the mornings, then sent tracting in the afternoons. "In the evening," Smith quipped, "people would show up and ask, 'Who were those two nice young men who brought us this tract, and what were they trying to say?'"[29] This school represented the church's first formal effort to improve the elders' effectiveness. Given Lowell's maturity and his background in German, Smith hoped aloud that Lowell would one day return to teach there.

Lowell's mission president, Fred Tadje, was a native-born German who had lived in America. Both the Swiss-German Mission he oversaw and the German Mission were supervised by European mission president John A. Widtsoe, who had received his doctorate from the German University at Göttingen. The baptism rate was high during the early 1920s but leveled off as the Great Depression tarnished Utah's image as the promised land.

Lowell experienced the mood swings normal to missionaries. At his first district conference he "enjoyed a good spirit and was encouraged greatly" after feeling "quite down beforehand."[30] His first companion, Harold J. ("Hap") Carlsen from Ogden, Utah, was a good partner and, like Lowell, "determined to work hard and live right."[31] They visited the "lone Saint" in the quaint village of Siegen near Cologne, a city with 286 Mormons, then were assigned to begin proselyting in Bonn, which had neither members nor missionaries. Bonn was very expensive, very Catholic, and very windy. Lowell was discouraged by the weather, the coldest since the time of Frederick the Great, and by his own fumbling German. He was also "terribly lonesome for a dance with Merle."[32]

Reading provided much solace. He balanced his scripture study with philosophy texts, current events, and German classics, reading Will Durant on Herbert Spencer in combination with Alma in the Book of Mormon "for my spiritual pleasure."[33] Weekly he attended the movies, a medium Germany was perfecting. Charlie Chaplin had become the epitome of the "little man" and *The Blue Angel* that of Weimar troubles. Though Lowell was only dimly aware of trends, the fading Weimar Republic was producing a final flourish in the arts as Richard Wagner's son directed the Wagner festivals and the legitimate stage bloomed under Max Reinhardt. Thomas and Heinrich Mann, Remarque, Brecht, and Rilke remade literature while Max Weber shaped sociology, Friedrich Meinecke influenced history, Albert Einstein revolutionized physics, and Sigmund Freud redirected psychology.

Proselyting required both determination and ingenuity. Mormon missionaries had tracts to give away and copies of the Book of Mormon to sell but no preplanned introductions and lessons. "You adjusted to different attitudes," Lowell said of his door approaches. "I had one for the Catholics, one for Lutherans, and one for non-believers. . . . They let us in quite a bit because they were curious about America."[34]

A stirring experience was addressing twenty-two "free thinkers" who had broken from the Adventists. "I bore my testimony through the Holy Ghost, and I didn't recognize my voice, nor did Hap," he recorded, filled with "joy and gratefulness" at this modern experience of "the gift of tongues."[35]

After three months in Bonn and Siegen he was transferred to Bielefeld in Westphalia in February 1929 where an active branch of Mormons immediately made him welcome and taught him "faith, humility, [and] hospitality."[36] Shocked by the unemployment and poverty, he initially blamed it on the "blackness of the Catholic Church," which kept the people "without hope."[37] Later he could see that the whole country was sliding toward the economic collapse that made Hitler's message an appealing one, and it softened his view of Catholicism.

Lowell's second companion did not enjoy tracting, so Lowell went alone, despite his struggles with the language. His third companion, Kenneth Huber, a prize fighter from Arizona, proved a more willing worker. "I like the way I preach the gospel better than my partner," Lowell observed. "I go from what we agree on to something else instead of hitting up a debate right off." He recorded one success story in his diary. "One fellow at first wanted to kick me out and ended up buying a Book of Mormon. Another lady knew all there was to know about religion and she told me it all. I'm a good listener. I let them talk until they are embarrassed for want of something more to talk about, and then I put in a word."[38] It was a method retained all his life.

Many wanted to argue about polygamy. Lowell usually disarmed them by candidly announcing himself as the grandson of a polygamist who "would neither shame myself nor apologize," then explaining the former Mormon practice as a combination of social "conditions, the spreading of good blood, and true knowledge as it was done through Jacob and Abraham."[39]

In September 1929 Lowell ended his first year as a missionary by transferring to nearby Minden as branch president. His companions, Floyd Cannon, "an honest, realistic fellow," and Billy Morrell, an "eager beaver, anxious to learn," kept him company.[40]

With an intellectually inclined seamstress, he debated how resurrected beings could have children with spiritual bodies, why no Heavenly Mother was mentioned in scripture, why Adam fell, and how the atonement of Jesus Christ operated. Lowell admitted he couldn't "find these things in church works as yet" but enjoyed the discussions because they made him think and made "the whole gospel seem clearer to me." He promised her: "Someday I'll see you in heaven and we'll continue this conversation."[41] After a lively discussion with a thirty-seven-year-old college-educated philosopher about Kant, Aristotle, and Schopenhauer, Lowell penned himself a private and prophetic note: "I felt the need of a book in the church for such good honest philosophers. . . . If no one will write such a tract, I'll try."[42]

Other members treated him to meals and complimented his excellent accent. He broadened his cultural horizons by studying opera, Plato, and Pappini's *Life of Christ*. One member took him to Beethoven's "Ninth Symphony," thus beginning his life-long love of Beethoven. After he and his companions had spent the day hiking up the mountain for "a beautiful view of [the Pied Piper's] Hamelin," he commented guiltily: "The joy of a mission comes in work, and I would trade all trips for one good gospel friend."[43]

Not all experiences were positive. On Merle's birthday when he was consumed with homesickness, a man refused to believe he served "without pay. I felt almost angry that a man should call me a liar in my face." That evening, after a bitter argument about a program in the branch, he recorded dolefully that one member "hates me like poison." The next day he and his companion were "accused of being rich by a gang of road workers, chased out by one old modern Cicero; and met a great deal of curiosity and indifference." To end the day his companion fell in a ditch. He recorded, perhaps melodramatically, "I have lost all false pride."[44]

During his entire stay in Germany he saw almost daily the effects of unemployment and poverty. One man had lived on two white biscuits a day for two years. Other family men had not worked in eleven years.[45] This opened his eyes to suffering in a way that he had not experienced before. He also suffered frequent pain in his eyes, ears, and abdomen, largely because of what he diagnosed as allergies, particularly to chocolate, and "chronic appendicitis."

He was seasoned timber by June 1930 when he was transferred to Zurich as district president. "Brother Tadje told me they needed a spiritual leader here, a preacher, said I was the man," Lowell recorded, adding wryly, "he is certainly off." Feeling unequal to the task, he promised to live a "humble, clean hardworking life and trust the Lord to help us out."[46] A few days later he defined that task succinctly: "Well, sir, it looks to me as though everything here needs changing. The problem in life is not to choose between good and evil but to choose within the realms of righteousness. The Lord help us."[47]

One predecessor, a former German army officer, had excommunicated thirty-two members in the district, often for trivial reasons. A missionary became mentally disturbed after fasting over the "devil that was loose in Zurich."[48] Warning himself "for all time" against the dangers of fanaticism,[49] Lowell released certain officers, organized a tracting schedule, strengthened leadership, streamlined programs, and counseled members with candor and warmth. When a man accused his wife of being "possessed of the devil," Lowell "saw her condition as a result of her physical weakness" and gave her a blessing.[50] Lowell felt his baptisms were sparse—only eleven "and somebody came along a year or two later and excommunicated them."[51] He coped with unruly Boy Scouts, matched scriptural references with a Protestant minister, and pondered the significance of grace in the gospel.

Throughout this period of rapid spiritual growth he judged himself harshly whenever he did less than his best. Life as a district president was hectic. He frequently ran for trains and sometimes missed them. When this happened he purchased his favorite lunch of hazelnuts and figs and read until the next train. One Sunday he rebuked himself for giving "a poor speech" on "the Reformation and the better teachings of Joseph Smith. . . . Not enough faith, I guess." He wrote that "I made a fool of myself trying to talk about 'false' teaching of churches and I was faint and the Lord left me very much alone. I guess I wasn't worthy of his spirit—felt like two cents afterward."[52]

Thanks to Milton's generosity, Lowell joined the other missionaries in seeing the Oberammergau Passion Play, which he greatly enjoyed, although he concluded with innocent chauvinism, "I'm sure our church could put on something better."[53] His father was also the link to acquaintances with interesting people, especially Cavendish Cannon, a relative of George Q. Cannon, then United States vice consul for Zurich. Cavendish had become disaffected from Mormonism because he disliked the "familiarity of the members" and the church's predilection for "taking all his free time." Lowell admired him, appreciated his frequent and generous hospitality, but parted company with his philosophy: "I have a good deal more faith in idealism."[54]

As Lowell continued his intellectual growth, he read Dante and Buddha and bought a complete set of Schiller's and Goethe's works for twenty Swiss francs (four dollars for twenty-three books). These would become a lifetime consolation, with Goethe exemplifying the best of the German spirit.

On Christmas Day 1930 he assessed his progress: "I feel very responsible to other people and not quite as selfish as I used to. My heart really goes out to the poor and needy and sick. I hope the Lord will see fit to lead me in paths of enlightened service for my fellows. I wish I could increase the faith of other people in God."[55]

Homesickness and longing for Merle dampened his spirits during the whole thirty-two months, but they warmed his letters. "You are the most distinctive, original, and *the only one* more than ever before," he wrote, looking at Merle's photograph.[56] He wrote nostalgically of "the days when we held hands under my coat."[57] Remembering their first half-year anniversary, he wrote, "Tonight is six months married and I wouldn't trade them for my whole life beforehand. . . . I love you, dear, and I'll still think you're perfect when I have to live with you, as you put it."[58] Repeatedly he promised, "You will certainly get all the love and affection from me you can stand—incidentally, I could stand all you have with a thrilling joy."[59]

On September 18, 1930, a matured Lowell wrote: "Two years ago this morning, Merle and I got married. We were happy, in love, full of faith in each other and a supreme being. . . . My happiness is enriched with gratitude and appreciation, which could only come with the experience of the last two years. I certainly love Merle and imagine what a brave girl she has been these two years. Some day I hope to make it all good."[60]

As Lowell's release was set for April 1931, Milton offered to support him in Ph.D. studies in Germany, stipulating that Merle could join him. Lowell was happy and "stimulated with this thought."[61] Merle had lost her job when her bank failed during the Depression, so European study seemed practical to her.

Lowell made inquiries and collected letters of recommendation for use in applying for scholarships—from Elbert Thomas, G.

E. Fellows, and Arthur Beeley. He finally decided on the University at Erlangen in Bavaria.

Lowell's release came on April 9 amid a flurry of sorrowful farewells from weeping members and missionaries. He felt "punk . . . about leaving my friends."[62] Later he declared himself permanently influenced by "the language, the thinking, the music, the culture, the scenery, the simple values of life in Germany and Switzerland, the cleanliness, the order."[63] But now he had a new and delightful task—to prepare for Merle's arrival.

NOTES

1. [Lela] Merle C[olton] Bennion, interviewed by Maureen Ursenbach Beecher, 1985, typescript, 6, in James Moyle Oral History Program, archives, Historical Department, Church of Jesus Christ of Latter-day Saints, Salt Lake City; copy in possession of Merle Bennion.

2. Paul Cannon, interviewed by Mary L. Bradford, 22 May 1987.

3. Lowell Colton [Ben] Bennion, untitled essay, photocopy in Bradford's possession; Merle C. Bennion, interviewed by Mary L. Bradford, 19 Sept. 1989.

4. *Uinta* is the spelling of geographical terms like Uinta Mountains and Uinta Valley; *Uintah* is administrative: country, reservation, stake, and ward.

5. Ray Haueter, "Early Law Enforcement," *Utah Peace Officers Association Magazine,* 22-24, undated article in Bradford's possession.

6. Miriam C. Perry, ed., *The Historical and Biographical Record of the Sterling Driggs Colton Family, Descendants and Related Families* (Logan, UT: S. D. Colton Family Organization, 1977), 3.

7. Merle C. Bennion, interviewed by Mary L. Bradford, 19 Sept. 1989.

8. Ibid.

9. Merle Bennion, "150 Years of Relief Society: Do We Have Anything to Celebrate?" audiotape of panel at Sunstone Symposium, Aug. 1992, in Bradford's possession.

10. Merle C. Bennion, Oral History, 3.

11. Merle's memories of Nancy are from "150 Years of Relief Society."

12. Merle C. Bennion, Oral History, 3.

13. Ibid., 3.

14. Ibid., 5.

15. Merle C. Bennion, interviewed by Mary L. Bradford, 2 Feb. 1988.

16. Ibid.

17. Lowell L. Bennion, Oral History, 45.

18. Ibid., 45.

19. Ibid., 46.

20. See Gary James Bergera and Ronald Priddis, *Brigham Young University: A House of Faith* (Salt Lake City: Signature Books, 1985), 134-38.

21. Milton Bennion, "The 'Evolution' and 'Higher Criticism' Controversy at the Brigham Young University," *Utah Educational Review,* Mar. 1901, 10. He called "the disagreement that has arisen between a group of teachers at the Brigham Young University and the authorities to whom they are responsible" the "most significant happening in recent Utah educational history" (9).

22. Lowell L. Bennion and Merle C. Bennion, interviewed by Mary L. Bradford, 25 Jan. 1990.

23. Israel Bennion, patriarchal blessing on the head of Lowell L. Bennion, 1 Aug. 1926, typescript copy in Bradford's possession.

24. Merle C. Bennion, interviewed by Mary L. Bradford, 17 May 1987.

25. Ibid.

26. Ibid.

27. Merle C. Bennion, Oral History, 10.

28. Lowell L. Bennion, Diary, 18 Oct. 1928. Lowell kept a missionary diary from 18 October 1929 to 23 May 1931, holograph in his possession; photocopy in Bradford's possession. For the first six months he wrote his diary entries on stationery which he sent to Merle as letters; on 14 March 1929 he began writing separate letters to Merle and keeping his diary in a leatherbound book. Both forms are cited as "Diary."

29. Whitney W. Smith and Alice Colton Smith, interviewed by Mary L. Bradford, 20 Sept. 1989.

30. Lowell L. Bennion, Diary, 1 Dec. 1928.

31. Ibid., 8 Dec. 1928.

32. Ibid., 4 Jan. 1929.

33. Ibid., 3 Jan. 1929.

34. Lowell Bennion, Oral History, 60.

35. Lowell L. Bennion, Diary, 9 Jan. 1929; Lowell Bennion, Oral History, 55.

36. Ibid., 18 Nov. 1929; Lowell L. Bennion, Oral History, 55.

37. Lowell L. Bennion, Diary, 14 May 1930.

38. Lowell L. Bennion to Merle C. Bennion, 8 Mar. 1929.

39. Ibid., 22 Apr. 1929.

40. Lowell L. Bennion, Diary, 23 Sept. 1929.

41. Ibid., 17 Apr. 1930.

42. Ibid., 19 May 1930.

43. Ibid., 17 May 1930.

44. Ibid., 31 Mar. 1930; 1, 2 Apr. 1930.

45. Ibid., 20 Mar. 1930.

46. Ibid., 9 June 1930.

47. Ibid., 16 June 1930.

48. Ibid., 17 June 1930.

49. Ibid.

50. Ibid., 20 Oct. 1930.

51. Lowell L. Bennion, Oral History, 60.

52. Lowell L. Bennion, Diary, 17 Aug. 1930.

53. Ibid., 6 July 1930.

54. Ibid., 14 Sept. and 14 Mar. 1930.

55. Ibid., 25 Dec. 1930.

56. Ibid., 28 Feb. 1931. At this point he was keeping a leatherbound diary and also writing letters home to Merle, but he frequently addressed Merle in his diary. Sometimes he sent letters to Merle from his diary.

57. Ibid.

58. Lowell Bennion, Diary, 19 Mar. 1929.

59. Lowell L. Bennion to Merle C. Bennion, 18 Sept. 1930.

60. Ibid.

61. Ibid.

62. Lowell L. Bennion, Diary, 9 Apr. 1930.

63. Lowell L. Bennion, interviewed by Mary L. Bradford, 22 Sept. 1990.

CHAPTER 3

HONEYMOON AND HEARTBREAK

(1931-34)

I got interested in the philosophical approach to sociology and social philosophy too. I reveled in it. I took courses in philosophy, as well as sociology and economic theory. I took courses in religion. In Europe one didn't have to be as specialized in his study as we are here [in America].
—LOWELL L. BENNION

As her rendezvous with Lowell in Europe drew near, Merle, who had never been east of Denver, now traveled by train to meet the same ship that had carried Lowell away thirty-two months earlier. Her companions were Emma Mosher, whose family Lowell knew in Switzerland, Emma's friend, Aseneth Smith (a daughter of former LDS church president Joseph F. Smith), and Vera Calder, a friend from Vernal, whose brother was also finishing a Swiss-German mission.

In parting, Ione Spencer presented Merle with a small leather-bound diary inscribed, "For our benefit write the places you go/ The things you've seen/ So that we might appear less green." Merle made her first entry on May 22, 1931: "Left Salt Lake. Grandfather, Grandmother, Ethel, Elwin, Aunt Zora, Uncle Mark and kiddies . . . and innumerable friends" sent them off at the station. Through "Uncle Mark's tunnel" in Wyoming she ate the lunch prepared by Mother Bennion and contracted "an intense headache" from Nebraska's heat but was delighted with "Ole Man River," the "immense city of Chicago," and her first glimpse of the Potomac River. Relatives and friends took her sightseeing in New York until she boarded the *Leviathan*. She was "thrilled as the huge ship pulled away . . . supremely happy at the thought of meeting Lowell in Paris."

The four young women, none of them seasick, shared a stateroom and entered enthusiastically into ship life. Merle observed the other passengers keenly, attended LDS services, enjoyed the "delicious meals," and met Apostle John A. Widtsoe and Leah Dunford Widtsoe who were returning to supervisory duties in the European missions. Like Lowell, she paced the decks and watched moonlight on the ocean.

The ship docked at Cherbourg, France, and Merle took a train to Paris where Lowell met her on June 2, 1931, after an absence of two years and eight months. "The dear boy!" she wrote. "He hasn't changed in his love for me." Their two days in the Hotel de France found the young couple talking "nearly all night . . . I surely love him." They left for Erlangen, twenty miles from Nuremberg. In this university town of 35,000, 10 percent of them students, they selected an apartment on Kaiser Wilhem Platz near a forest and stream, where even the least elegant houses boasted flower boxes. It was their first home, and Merle wrote that she was "in Lowell's arms and in heaven."[1] It seemed like an endless spring—opera in Nuremberg, participation in the local branch, long walks in the blossoming countryside.

Lowell first learned about this university from Professor Max Haenle, who had visited Utah in 1927 to study the relationship between religion and economics and had become fast friends with Lowell's father. Lowell had driven him sight-seeing through southern Utah while Haenle urged Lowell to "get his feet wet" in a small German university before fixing on a specialty. Erlangen was in Bavaria, not far from Haenle's hometown of Tübingen. Lowell's father strongly supported this choice.[2]

Lowell had a vague ambition to study political science and perhaps become a "senator from Utah," but his favorite class was political economy from Hero Moeller. Here he began to understand "Germany's terrible economic plight—loss of the war, followed by inflation, then the depression, large numbers out of work for years."[3] Lowell did not know that Moeller was affiliated with the Nazi party; but he began to understand that Erlangen was one of Adolf Hitler's centers for mobilizing students against academics and that Nuremberg was a center for Hitler's ceremonial "cultic tradition" based on racism. Since the nineteenth century, Romantics had focused on German traditions and the city had long symbolized the national culture.

Some of these connections would come clear in 1933 when Hitler rose to "chancellor," Germany withdrew from the League of Nations, and the students of Germany burned their books in one wild Berlin night. Lowell attended a student rally in a packed hall. He chilled as the crowd shouted, "Heil, Hitler!" and realized, as the speaker promised to drive all Americans from Germany, that he was the only American in the room. Years later he would berate himself for not sensing "more keenly than I did where it would all lead."[4]

Lowell read to Merle as she cooked, and she to him as he ironed his trousers. They exercised together, exchanged "hair rubs," and enjoyed their excursions to the bath-house. They celebrated Lowell's first examination paper, marked *fast gut* (almost good) except for limitations of language. Lowell gave Merle informal German lessons, which she practiced diligently. She typed his notes, sometimes attended classes with him, or waited peacefully for him in the botanical gardens. They marketed together, wrote detailed letters home, and absorbed each other. "Can't get over the wonder of his loving me," Merle recorded in her journal. The modest language of a religious young woman breathes the magical sense of their shared fulfillment, "good old loving" mingled with laughter and hours of conversations that never palled.

When Lowell finished his seminar at the end of July 1931, Milton recommended that they travel to Geneva for six or eight weeks and generously sent them money. As a regrettable space-saving measure, they tore up most of the letters they had exchanged during Lowell's mission.

In Geneva they rented a one-room apartment with access to a kitchen so dirty that they took turns drinking milk from the bottle rather than using a glass. They liked their perch above a square where musicians serenaded every night and streetcars ran on an elevated rail over Lake Geneva on the Rousseau Bridge.[5] Merle noticed that Swiss fathers "aren't ashamed to take the baby out for an airing" while "German men won't even push the baby carriage." They took one hot meal a day in a restaurant, "then we would buy this wonderful alpine milk and cheese, and the brötchen, these crusty little rolls."[6] They saw their first movie together, visited museums, read the libretto of *Tristan und Isolde* in the evenings, and attended the local LDS branch with a congregation of forty.

While in Geneva, Lowell attended some pivotal League of Nations meetings as an observer. Only a few months before his death French foreign minister Aristide Briand gave a powerful plea for peace on September 12: "Let them say clearly in this decisive hour—no more war! We will not in any case, for any cause, or in any circumstance, allow war, which we have nailed to the pillory as a crime, to break loose with impunity."[7] With the U.S. Secretary of State, he had developed the Kellogg-Briand Pact for the renunciation of war in 1927-28 and had earlier facilitated the entry of Germany into the League of Nations.[8]

While Lowell attended meetings, Merle walked by the lake, read in the sun, and characterized Geneva as "the city where all the shops close for two hours at noon, where the people take enormous bites, and there are no good-looking men."[9] Their third anniversary on September 18 was a private celebration of the wonder of their love and a turning point in world politics. On September 21 Lowell was shocked to learn that Japan had invaded Manchuria. Moved by the Chinese delegate's plea that the league take a stand against Japan, Lowell was disappointed by Lord Cecil's "evasive and diplomatic" reply. As the Chinese delegate walked out, Lowell thought, "Here's the downfall of the League."[10]

The league meetings confirmed Lowell's uneasiness, and he decided to continue his studies in Vienna. They went to Austria by way of Lowell's beloved missionary branches, where "Merle made a fine impression," then on to Berlin, Dresden, Leipzig, and Prague, arriving in Vienna—city of Beethoven, Mozart, and Freud—in October 1931.[11]

An LDS nuclear physics student helped them locate an apartment with a "beautiful bedroom and living room and a real bathtub."[12] The forty Mormons in Vienna, a "rich mixture of Austrians, Poles, and Czechs, . . . did not get along very well," observed Merle, regretfully.[13] Merle, who played the piano and organ in their rented meeting room, frequently acted as peacemaker as well, while Lowell taught Sunday school class and translated for Apostle John A. Widtsoe when he visited the branch. "Lowell not only translated every word, but he mimicked Widtsoe's gestures too. . . . It was a scream!" Merle recalled.[14] A conversation between Lowell and Leah Widtsoe grew somewhat heated when Lowell asserted that the church should scale down its labor-intensive programs for the struggling European branches while the apostle's wife insisted that all programs must be kept intact and afloat.

Lowell and Merle visited museums, splurged on a visit to one of Vienna's famous coffeehouses, and attended the opera where Lowell bought Merle a twenty-five-cent seat then stood behind her for fifteen cents to hear the hundred-piece orchestra conducted by Johann Strauss, namesake of his famous grandfather. Lowell studied at home "until money arrive[d] for his tuition" at the end of October.[15] "Our finances are pretty low," Merle admitted, "but we are planning some rigid economy. It's a great life!"[16]

Lowell studied jurisprudence under Victor Verdross, "a wonderful teacher . . . who traced the idea of the good from the ancient Greeks down to contemporary German philosophy."[17] Lowell wrote a paper on Kant's *Critique of Pure Reason*. Under the influence of dynamic young Eric Voegelin,[18] Lowell switched from political science to sociology and social philosophy, or the study of human behavior in groups and in society. This attempt "to explain human behavior" introduced him to the work of Max Weber, whom Lowell described as "the most creative, expansive mind I ever met."[19] A decade later, Weber would take his unshakable place as one of history's greatest thinkers, his ideas discussed in almost every university department. But at the time he was practically unknown in America.

Lowell directed his youthful idealism toward reform, but Weber suggested that social science as a science had to meet a high standard of objectivity. It "should be free from value judgments. . . . It should simply describe the nature of things." Determining whether those facts were "good" or "bad" was a value judgment made "not by science, but . . . from our total human experience" including "ethics and religion."[20]

This philosophy spoke directly to Lowell's already strong need to find balance and harmony between personal and professional values. If reality is constructed from experience, history, and observation, then the task of the intellect is to construct pure models of that reality, "more pure than anything that exists," and then "shift gears" among the various levels of abstraction—but "to know when you are shifting."[21]

This model gave Lowell a way of approaching his earlier questions about science and religion. Each inhabited its own sphere. Reason and morality made parallel demands, which a human being could meet by exercising creativity. The creative thinker took what was real, analyzed it, and then applied it to a value system. For a religious person this exercise produced religious values and creativity. Weber also viewed science and history as open-ended, a harmonic fit with the Mormon concept of eternal progression and its expansive view of truth. Weber's observations of bureaucracy and its institutions gave Lowell insights into the routinization of charisma and the distinction between the "priestly" and the "prophetic" that helped him better understand Mormon history. All of these concepts became part of his conceptual mapping of the world, to be shared with hundreds of students in science, religion, economics, and politics.

In February 1932 Lowell and Merle began thinking about transferring to Strasbourg, just across the German border in France. Lowell was doing well at the university, and a speech he gave at the Old Hapsburg Castle on "*Was ist das Mormonismus?*" was reported the next day in a newspaper,[22] but the university frequently closed because of student disturbances. Lowell was dismayed when starry-eyed Othnar Spann, an apostle of National Socialism, spoke to an "enthralled" Nazi audience.[23] Although some professors denounced the Nazi persecution of Jews, the anti-Semitism repelled and frightened Merle. At the university Lowell would hear thuds and cries in the hall and go out to find "blood on the floor."[24] Lowell and another American escorted a Jewish friend between them "to prevent a gang of Nazis from kicking him down the front steps."[25] Lowell remembered this as "one of the few occasions I had to display courage as a student."[26]

Soon they had an even more pressing reason for seeking a calm environment. On March 5 Merle recorded, "Food doesn't appeal to me these days! Funny feeling!" In a few weeks they were certain of her pregnancy. Despite occasional queasiness during the first few weeks, Merle was relieved that she experienced no heart symptoms.[27] They decided not to inform their families, no doubt staving off an avalanche of concerned advice and demands, and they spent the summer in the country, traveling serenely through Italy and spending a month in Zurich where they renewed Lowell's missionary friendships. Reaching Strasbourg in early October 1932, about a month before the baby's birth, Lowell asked Elise Kayser at the Mormon branch meeting if she could recommend a good obstetrician. "*Warum?* [Why?]" was the confused reply. According to Lowell, Sister Kayser "nearly fainted" when he explained that Merle was eight months pregnant.[28] The doctor reassured her when he pronounced both mother and baby well.

They changed apartments twice, studied French voraciously (the language in which classes were conducted), tutored in English, took long daily walks, ate "good little dinners," and wondered "what the little dear would look like."[29]

Lowell studied, finished a paper he was writing for Voegelin, translated articles for *Der Stern,* the German LDS magazine, and was almost immediately appointed president of Strasbourg's three-family LDS branch, since American missionaries had just been expelled. Lowell did well academically, stimulated by the power of Weber's ideas and mentored by Dr. Maurice Halbwachs, professor of sociology and a disciple of philosopher Henri Bergson and sociologist Emile Durkheim. In an early interview Halbwachs hospitably offered beer, wine, and cigars. When Lowell refused all three, he inquired, "Bennion, don't you have any vices?" Gracefully Lowell replied, "I have so many I can't afford yours."[30]

On November 13, 1932, when Lowell got home from Sunday school, Merle was in the beginning stages of labor. About 9 p.m. they left for a private clinic. With Lowell beside her, Merle gave birth the next morning to Laurel Colton Bennion. Lowell described her as "a queer, striking baby girl with golden hair and a fair, rosy complexion, weighing 7 lbs., sucking her little fingers as though it were an old habit."[31] Lowell rushed to post his previously written air-mail letters to their families.

For Merle, giving birth "was a very spiritual experience. I felt at one with our maker," recipient of a miracle.[32] After the medical warnings, this birth did seem miraculous. Lowell fussed over the baby at every visit, marveling at her "small pretty mouth, . . . a nose like her parents, a crooked little head, which promises to straighten out in a few months time. Who ever dreamed of a little girl resembling her Dad? Her large hands and feet certainly do. We were mighty happy and thankful to see our most original, questionable looking little daughter."[33]

After the two weeks deemed necessary for Merle's full recovery, they brought her home and hovered anxiously during the first night. Laurie slept placidly until morning. Merle's sister sent ten dollars and Milton sent a very welcome one-hundred-dollar check. Congratulations and presents arrived from friends in Switzerland, Germany, and Austria. Paul Kayser of Strasbourg rode his bike seven miles to their apartment to take the laundry home for his wife to do "with a plunger." When Lowell objected, "they with tears said, 'Look what you do for us.'"[34]

That winter and spring, as Lowell read Albert Schweitzer's works describing "reverence for life," Laurel continued to grow, a happy, healthy, and rosy baby. Lowell recalled that "Merle took wonderful care of Laurie. As it turned out, we were too cautious."[35] To protect her from drafts, they fastened her blanket to the mattress with giant safety pins. Hearing her cough one evening, they discovered that she had swallowed an open pin. They rushed her to the hospital where the pin, lodged upside down in her esophagus, was removed. Mission president Francis Salzner gave her a blessing, but she died of infection three days later on May 17, 1933. The penicillin that could have saved her had not yet been discovered.

Lowell felt comforted in his grief by a "kind of spiritual experience" that brought peace and acceptance.[36] Merle, with her longer history of bereavement, was disconsolate. "I can't take it," she told herself. "I can't go through it. I've already lost half my family, mother and father and a little sister. It's just not fair. I just can't stand it."[37] For her healing came as the members of the little branch gathered around them, confused at "why the Lord would let anything happen to dear Brother and Sister Bennion's baby." In trying to shore up their faith, Merle found the depths of her own. After a few days of praying "mightily," she "had the feeling that my mother was going to look after my baby. It was almost as if her presence were there."[38] This sense of comfort cradled her, as if in the arms of that long-lost mother. Lowell and Merle explained to their friends that the death had been an unfortunate accident and could be blamed on nobody, especially not God.

Although spiritual comfort eased the sting, nothing else was easy. They moved to another apartment, sent Laurel's body home in a sealed coffin with a returning missionary, and pored over the newspaper accounts and family photographs of the grave-side service. They were comforted by the bouquets generously heaped on the tiny grave.

Both called on a core of discipline. Lowell determinedly studied and wrote on his dissertation, while Merle typed drafts for him, studied French with him, took a course on Goethe's folklore, and walked for hours with Anna Kayser along the Rhine.

Lowell had planned to write his dissertation in German, but Halbwachs encouraged him to write in English, probably to introduce Weber's thought to a broader audience. In September 1933 they went to Paris so Lowell could immerse himself in French, preparing for the oral defense of his dissertation. (There were no written exams.) Merle typed new drafts and spent her free time in the Louvre. Lowell defended his dissertation in Strasbourg in December, responding to questions from professors in four different fields. At one point vigorous arguments among the professors convinced him he was failing; Halbwachs later assured him they were arguing among themselves over Weber's ideas.

Merle thought that he was probably speaking in a language only she could understand: "He'd written his dissertation in English, he'd done all of his studying in German, and he had to defend in French."[39]

On December 11, 1933, the twenty-five-year-old Lowell was awarded the degree of Docteur D'Université de Strasbourg, *avec mention honorable.* As was customary, Lowell published his dissertation, *Max Weber's Methodology,* in a very limited edition of 100 copies with Les Presses Modernes of Paris, "after many delays and promises and with a rich sprinkling of errors."[40] At that point the only English work available on Weber was a translation by Talcott Parsons, later one of the United States' most influential sociologists and its foremost Weberian. There is no question that Lowell's work was both sound and important—not only because it was the first book-length analysis of Weber, but also because it was the most lucid and complete explanation to date of Weber's methodology. Weber had never described his methodology in a single place, instead sprinkling it throughout his prolific writings. Lowell's assembling of his methodological concepts was a seminal contribution destined to be cited with respectable frequency in the literature of sociology.[41]

Kimball Young, a descendant of Brigham Young and professor of sociology at the University of Wisconsin, requested a copy of Lowell's dissertation in September 1937. Lowell wrote back, "It would be a pleasure to send you a complimentary copy in the hope you might have sufficient interest and patience to critique it. Alexander Von Schelting and Professor Becker have corresponded with me about it. Utah sociologists, as far I know them, are too engrossed in other fields to give Max Weber more than passing notice."[42]

Kimball Young had learned of Lowell's dissertation from his colleague in Wisconsin's sociology department, Howard Becker, who had written Lowell on February 4, 1935, encouraging him to prepare a 10,000-word treatise on Weber for Becker's three-volume *Social Thought: From Lore to Science,* coauthored with Harry Elmer Barnes (1938). It became a classic in the field and Becker became one of the major interpreters of social theory. He and Young were at Wisconsin in the 1930s and 1940s. Although Lowell sent his dissertation to Wisconsin, he had not responded to Becker's earlier invitation. It was a decision according to priorities of the moment and pressing demands on Lowell's time; but if he had written the article, it may well have drawn him into the network of influential American Weberian scholars.

With the exception of this preliminary correspondence about possible articles, Lowell chose not to follow up on his dissertation's possibilities. It was thus a happy and belated recognition of his contribution to Weberian studies when modern scholars "discovered" his work in the early 1990s.[43]

Practical considerations no doubt played a role in Lowell's choice. A longing for home and family made relocating in Utah more immediately appealing than shopping for a prestigious university post. Personal poverty and the grinding national depression meant that Lowell needed to find a job as quickly as possible. With Merle and Lowell's European idyll over and with foreshadowings of global conflagration, they started for home in December 1933, visiting the newly installed Netherlands mission president

T. Edgar Lyon and his wife, Hermana Forsberg Lyon, a friend of Merle. It was the first meeting between Lowell and the man who would become his partner and close friend in the church's institute of religion program.

Lowell and Merle sailed into New York City in time to spend Christmas with Merle's Uncle Don and Aunt Grace Colton. (Don was presiding over the Eastern States Mission after being defeated in his bid for the Utah Senate.) Other relatives greeted them in Utah, shocked by their poverty-stricken appearance. Brother Grant "took one look" at Lowell's spats and "hand-me-down coat (from a Zurich Saint) and laughed, 'You Look like a Swiss goat-herder.'" Merle's eighty-year-old grandmother, Nancy Colton, took her aside and made her promise to borrow a coat from her. Milton Bennion immediately gave Lowell a hundred dollars to buy clothes.[44]

It was January 1934 and the United States was still struggling desperately against the Depression. Lowell and Merle moved in with Milton and Cora, and Lowell, for five dollars a day, began scraping paint from the windows of a house Ethel Colton Smith and Elwin Smith had just built.

Lowell applied for college teaching positions throughout the state and also for the Civilian Conservation Corps (CCC), newly created as part of Franklin D. Roosevelt's public works program. In March 1934 he became a CCC education advisor with the charge "to assess the men's interests, find teachers on the staff and in the community, and teach them what they wanted or needed." In May they moved with Lowell's unit to Salina in central Utah then to Soapstone in the Uintah Mountains. Lowell liked this "free-wheeling" job that allowed him to organize courses in shorthand and typing (occasionally taught by Merle), English, German (taught by Lowell himself), music, and auto mechanics.[45] Classes numbered about forty men ranging in age from eighteen to forty. According to the CCC mandate, a successful education advisor needed to "develop powers of self expression, self entertainment and self culture . . . with habits of health and mental development, . . . [to] develop a sense of humor, a desire to help others, and [to] have spiritual qualities without being a sissy, . . . [to] refrain from being a stool pigeon, be broad-minded and possess initiative and financial integrity."[46]

Lowell interviewed each man, building his educational program around their individual interests. He used books from his own library, borrowing others from his father, from the public schools, and from his cousin, Captain John B. (Jack) Cannon, who was part of the U.S. Army unit managing the camp. Lowell organized a male chorus and quartet as part of a weekly musical program, often inviting talent from nearby communities. He arranged for religious services and recruited teachers from the nearby school district. University of Utah instructors taught geography, geology, and even prospecting. Lowell's July report states that "10 men learned how to pan gravel."[47]

Accommodations were spartan. Lowell was assigned sheep wagon lodgings. Merle did all the laundry by hand, cooked on a "monkey stove," a miniature iron, wood-burning stove, took long walks over the hills, and gratefully endured nausea from her second pregnancy "because I wanted a baby."[48]

She remembered this experience as a very pleasant summer with one frightening close call. On the way down a mountain Lowell swerved to avoid a truckload of firefighters only to find his car teetering on the edge of an embankment, balanced by trees and underbrush. A truck full of CCC men behind them stopped, gingerly pulled Merle and Lowell through the windows, and hauled the car back onto the road with chains. "We thought we were goners," Merle recalled.[49]

At the end of August the unit moved back to Salina and Lowell rented "an old house with a real bathroom." Merle scrubbed its filthy walls, accepting Lowell's help with the cooking and housework. They were grateful to have each other, another baby on the way, and job offers from Branch Agricultural College in Cedar City and from Owen Horsfall, president of Snow College in Ephraim, Utah. No sooner had Lowell and Merle accepted Horsfall's offer to teach economics, German, and sociology, than Lowell received a call from John A. Widtsoe, newly returned from Europe and newly appointed LDS Church Commissioner of Education.[50] He offered Lowell the chance to join the church's institute of religion program at Moscow, Idaho, where J. Wyley Sessions, formerly professor at Utah State University and mission president, had founded the first institute in the fall of 1927.[51]

When Lowell described his reluctance to move to Idaho,

Widtsoe countered with a more tempting offer. Would he found a new institute at the University of Utah? It didn't take Lowell long to realize that this opportunity could combine intellectual stimulation with community service, wholesome recreation, and spiritual nourishment for a fine sample of Mormonism's young people. It might have been possible to maintain parallel interests in Weber scholarship, but Lowell chose not to. Despite his impressive credentials, he felt that he was not "properly schooled in contemporary American sociology" and therefore shrank from promoting himself in the United States as a Weberian scholar.[52]

Perhaps Lowell was also resisting a fate common to those who follow genius—a possibility articulated by Professor Arthur J. Vidich, of the New School for Social Research in New York City: "If you read and thoroughly understand Weber, you can ask yourself, What else is there to do? Or put another way, Can I ever be as good as that? Every Weber scholar has to ask these questions for him/herself. The ones that stay in Weber and never get out . . . have the worse fate."[53]

Since Lowell had already accepted the position at Snow when Widtsoe called with his offer, Lowell was candid about his desire to accept but refused to break his word to Horsfall. Widtsoe then offered to negotiate with Horsfall himself. After an interview with church apostles Charles A. Callis and Joseph Fielding Smith, Lowell and Merle made plans to move to Salt Lake City to open the church's fourth institute of religion in the winter of 1934-35.

This move heightened Lowell's sense of homecoming. He was home from his mission, home from his studies, a full-time husband, a prospective father, and at last a teacher. The classroom had so long been the second home of the Bennions that his decision to enter "the sanctuary of the institute" seemed exactly right.

NOTES

1. Merle C. Colton, Diary, 2 June 1931, photocopy in Bradford's possession.

2. Lowell L. Bennion, Oral History, 62.

3. Ibid., 63.

4. Ibid.

5. Ibid., 64; Merle C. Colton, Oral History, 12.

6. Merle C. Bennion, Oral History, 12.

7. *New York Times,* 12 Sept. 1931, A1.

8. See Maurice Baumont, *Briand: Diplomat and Idealist* (Gottingen: Musterschmidt, 1966). Paul Claudel, French poet and ambassador, wrote Briand's epitaph: "The day Europe took leave of its common sense, Briand took leave of life." In Frances P. Walters, *History of the League of Nations* (Oxford, Eng.: Oxford University Press, 1952), 467.

9. Merle C. Bennion, Diary, 10 Sept. 1931.

10. Lowell L. Bennion, Oral History, 64.

11. Merle C. Bennion, Diary, 31 Oct. 1931.

12. Merle C. Bennion and Lowell L. Bennion, interviewed by Mary L. Bradford, 16 Sept. 1990.

13. Merle C. Bennion, Diary, 7 Nov. 1931.

14. Merle C. Bennion, interviewed by Mary L. Bradford, 19 Sept. 1989.

15. Merle C. Bennion, Diary, 22 Oct. 1931.

16. Ibid., 4 Nov. 1931.

17. Lowell L. Bennion, Oral History, 65.

18. Eric Herman Wilhelm Voegelin was born in Cologne, Germany, in 1901 and received his doctorate from Vienna in political science and law in 1922. He taught and studied at Harvard, Wisconsin, and Heidelberg universities with Karl Jaspers and Alfred Weber, Max's brother. During Lowell's stay in Vienna, Voegelin was part of the intellectual "Vienna Circle," one of whom described him as "perhaps the greatest living political scientist." Eugene Webb, *Eric Voegelin: Philosophy of History* (Seattle: University of Washington Press, 1981), 53. Fired by the Nazis in 1938, he escaped from the Gestapo, became a U.S. citizen in 1944, and enjoyed a long and productive career until his death at Stanford, California, in 1985. Lowell heard him lecture at the University of Utah in the 1970s. Like most of Lowell's major influences, he was a wide-ranging and broadly-based scholar on political, scientific, and historical issues.

19. Lowell L. Bennion, Oral History, 65.

20. Ibid.

21. Ibid., 75.

22. Merle C. Bennion, Diary, 25 Feb. 1932.

23. Lowell L. Bennion, "Memories," 27, photocopy in Bradford's possession.

24. Ibid., 27.

25. Ibid.

26. Ibid.

27. Merle C. Bennion, Diary, 19 May 1932.

28. Lowell L. Bennion, "Memories," 28.

29. Merle C. Bennion, Diary, 13 Oct. 1932.

30. Lowell and Merle Bennion, interviewed by Mary L. Bradford, 19 Sept. 1989. Described as "a sensitive and humane scholar whose works are among the most important in the sociology of the first half of the twentieth century," Halbwachs, a Jew, died in Buchenwald. George Friedmann, "Halbwachs, Maurice," in *International Encyclopedia of the Social Sciences*, ed. David L. Siels (New York: Macmillan/Free Press, 1968): 6:304-306.

31. Lowell L. Bennion in Merle C. Colton, Diary, 14 Nov. 1932.

32. Merle C. Bennion, Oral History, 14.

33. Lowell L. Bennion, "The 'Little Fellow' Arrives!" chap. 2 in a baby book Lowell kept on Laurel, 1932, photocopy in Bradford's possession.

34. Lowell L. Bennion, Oral History, 79.

35. Lowell L. Bennion, "Memories," 33.

36. Ibid., 68.

37. Merle C. Bennion, Oral History, 15.

38. Ibid., 15

39. Merle C. Bennion, Oral History, 16.

40. Lowell L. Bennion, Oral History, 75.

41. The first reference, in 1938, is Howard Becker and Harry Elmer Barnes, whose three-volume sociological text, *Social Thought: From Lore to Science,* was still in print in its third edition in 1961 (New York: Dover Publications, Inc.). They footnote Lowell's dissertation, misdated as 1931, as "an excellent elementary presentation" and lament that "only a few copies are to be found in the United States" (2:lvi, n. 35). Talcott Parsons footnoted Lowell's dissertation in his major text, *The Structure of Social Action* (Glencoe, IL: Free Press, 1949), in *Essays on Sociology Theory* (1949; rprt. ed., 1954); and *Essays in Sociological Theory, Pure and Applied* (New York: The Free Press, 1949), 169, where he called it "one of the most comprehensive secondary accounts in English." Julian Freund, *The Sociology of Max Weber,* trans. Mary Ilford (New York: Pantheon Books, 1968), 302, cites Lowell's book in the bibliography. Raymond Aron, *Main Currents in Sociological Thought, Vol. II: Durkheim, Pareto, Weber,* trans. from the French by Richard Howard and Helen Weaver (New York: Anchor Books/Doubleday, 1965; paperback reprint by Anchor Books

1970), 338, also includes Lowell's work in its bibliography. Thomas Burger footnotes Lowell several times in *Max Weber's Theory of Concept Formation: History, Laws, and Ideal Types* (Durham, NC: Duke University Press, 1976).

42. Lowell L. Bennion to Kimball Young, 29 Sept. 1937, copy in Bradford's possession.

43. Renewed attention to Lowell's dissertation came late in his life when Laurie Newman DiPadova, Department of Public Administration and Policy, State University of New York, had one chapter from Lowell's dissertation published as "The Business Ethic of the World Religions and the Spirit of Capitalism," *International Journal of Politics, Culture and Society* 6 (Fall 1992). Arthur J. Vidich, professor at the New School for Social Research's graduate faculty of its political and social science department in New York City, edits this journal.

44. Lowell L. Bennion, Oral History, 82.

45. Ibid. Lowell's unit of the CCCs was Fort Douglas District, Company 960. The government provided room and board and paid each man a monthly wage of about thirty dollars. Their work was supervised by the Forest Service and the camps were managed by Army Reserve officers.

46. Kenneth Baldridge, "IX, Education in the Camps,"in "Nine Years of Achievement: The Civilian Conservation Corps in Utah," Ph.D. diss., Brigham Young University, 1971, 25; see also his "Reclamation Work of the Civilian Conservation Corps, 1933-42," *Utah Historical Quarterly* 39 (Summer 1971): 270. Baldridge notes a number of educational advisors who joined the program with master's degrees but overlooked Lowell, possibly the best-educated man to teach for the CCC in Utah.

47. Civilian Conservation Corps, Company 960, Soapstone Camp F-6 at Kamas, Utah, 25 July 1934, Record Group 35. This report bears Lowell's signature. The report is filed, not with CCC records but under Record Group 12, Records of the Office of Education, Civil Reference Branch, National Archives, Washington, D.C.

48. Merle C. Bennion, interviewed by Mary L. Bradford, 16 Sept. 1989.

49. Ibid.

50. Widtsoe succeeded Apostle Joseph Merrill, former neighbor of Lowell in Forest Dale and the first Mormon to earn a doctorate degree. Merrill had succeeded Adam S. Bennion, a descendant of Samuel Bennion.

51. The second institute opened in 1928 at Utah State Agricultural College in Logan, a third at the University of Idaho Southern Branch in Pocatello in 1929. See Leonard J. Arrington, "The Founding of the L.D.S.

Institutes of Religion," *Dialogue: A Journal of Mormon Thought* 2 (Summer 1967): 140.

52. Laurie Newman DiPadova and Ralph S. Brower, "A Piece of Lost History: Max Weber and Lowell L. Bennion," *The American Sociologist* 23 (Fall 1992): 37-51.

53. Arthur Vidich to Laurie DiPadova, 31 Aug. 1992, photocopy in Bradford's possession.

PART TWO

THE SANCTUARY

Lowell about 1962.

CHAPTER 4

INSTITUTE BEGINNINGS (1935-39)

Many students have in one way or another been disillusioned about life and religion. This is based on an unwise teaching of religion and the wrong conception of the fruits of religious living. Students no longer involved in church activity have not enjoyed the true religious experience. Religion has just not been integrated into life and thought.

—LOWELL L. BENNION

On January 2, 1935, Lowell walked three blocks uphill from his rented home on Twelfth East in Salt Lake City to the University Ward chapel of the LDS church at 116 University Street. It was the first day of registration for classes at the University of Utah and for students at the church's institute of religion adjacent to the university. Later he would refer to the institute as "the sanctuary," a Utopian society largely of his own making that embraced family, students, and faculty. Paradoxically, the sanctuary would become the setting for the most intense phase of his career.

In 1935, though, with a promised salary of $1,800 a year, the twenty-six-year-old teacher felt only excitement as he was greeted by a colorful tile mosaic of an open-armed Christ. Fittingly, its inscription read: "And he went up to the mountain to teach them." When Apostle John A. Widtsoe presented Lowell with his contract, Lowell asked, "What should I teach?" Widtsoe answered with another question: "What can you teach?"[1]

Together they planned a two-month survey of the university for an institute site, interviewing Mormon professors and preparing courses. John Ballif, dean of students and Sunday school superintendent in the University Ward, promptly called Lowell as a Sunday school teacher. He also shared student lists that enabled Lowell to visit four hundred out-of-town Mormons in their dormitories.

Relations between Mormons and non-Mormons on campus were prickly at first. Earlier, severe conflicts had arisen between the University of Utah and church-owned Brigham Young University, forty miles south in Provo. George Thomas, president of the University of Utah, was determined to keep relations on an even keel; therefore, he had little desire to see an institute for Mormon students that would give religious affiliation a higher profile than it already had. As dean of education, Milton Bennion kept Lowell informed of administrative politics, advising him not to seek university credit for institute courses. In a note to Lowell in 1937 he wrote: "Just now, Pres. Thomas is not opposed to religious education, but he does not want to stir up a Mormon versus Non-Mormon fight in the Board of Regents & Faculty by bringing up the question of credit for this work. He thinks it is OK to carry it on as you have been doing."[2] This issue was especially touchy since the university had only recently stopped giving credit for work through "outside agencies" on the advice of accreditation officials. Lowell was founding a program with no campus standing and no on-campus advertising privileges.

He also encountered some resistance from LDS professors and their families, who, inordinately proud of the University Ward chapel, feared that students would damage it. Its leaders had contracted for a dignified building modeled after the Gothic-style Rockefeller Chapel at the University of Chicago.[3] Its design deliberately omitted a central foyer to discourage friendly but irreverent chatting.[4]

David O. McKay, then second counselor to church president Heber J. Grant, telephoned his friend Milton Bennion to suggested that Lowell call on him to chat about his new job. An educator by profession, McKay had headed up a new Church Commission of Education under Heber J. Grant in 1918 and he appointed Adam S. Bennion superintendent of church education to replace

Horace H. Cummings. (It was Cummings who had forced the resignations of BYU professors over evolution in 1911.[5])

Lowell remembered the meeting with McKay as a sort of intellectual swearing-in. "He sounded me out as far as my attitude on various things. Then he said, 'I don't care what you do or what you draw upon, but be true to yourself and loyal to the cause.' This was wonderful advice to a young man, . . . a guide throughout my church career."[6] Perhaps Lowell had this incident in mind when he later wrote, "Integrity is the first law of life. I learned that I would have to define what it meant for me to be loyal to the cause because men, even the Brethren, differ on what this means."[7]

It seemed a good time to join the Church Education System. LDS scholarship was developing some intellectual muscle. Lowell's older brother, M. Lynn, finished his doctorate in education at Berkeley and in 1935 became supervisor of the church seminary system. Widtsoe, the second Mormon Ph.D., had already been president of two universities. In late 1935 the new Church Commissioner of Education, Dr. Franklin L. West, a physicist at Utah State Agricultural College (later USU), had been Widtsoe's assistant commissioner, had studied at Stanford University, and had received his Ph.D. from the University of Chicago.[8]

Lowell felt at home among church leaders and educators who seemed united in a quest for intellectual excellence. Many of these leaders and thinkers had gathered around his family dinner table, and others had worked with his father in church and university positions. That first quarter he attained high visibility by teaching, not only in the ward Sunday school, but in the youth program (MIA) of the church as well, and he sometimes officiated in priesthood meetings. These were all directed toward out-of-town students.

Lowell acquired a small office just inside the front hall and outfitted it with a desk, a filing cabinet, a telephone, and a bookcase. He labored over an inviting brochure to be posted on church bulletin boards and mailed to out-of-town students. The brochure outlined four purposes of the institute:

1. To discuss with students, freely and frankly, individually and in

> groups, questions of their religious thinking and problems pertaining to their philosophy of life;
>
> 2. To broaden their understanding of life by acquainting them with the great role that religion and religious leaders have played in the formation of our civilization;
>
> 3. To increase their knowledge and appreciation of the position of Mormonism in the religious thought of the world, and thereby to strengthen their belief in the truth of the restored gospel of Jesus Christ;
>
> 4. To offer them pleasant social contacts and stimulating recreational activity; to be a social center for LDS students, especially out-of-town students.[9]

Lowell's goal was to create a program that would be a "magnet not a net."[10] Hoping to attract the curious, he scheduled three classes with intriguing titles: "Comparative Religions," "The Position of Mormonism in the Religious Thought of Western Civilization," and "Religion and the Rise of Our Modern Economic Order." Weekly seminars featured "questions and problems of religious thinking and living raised by students." Each Thursday evening the institute sponsored an "open evening" with informal entertainment and instruction from "some of the best talent in the vicinity." Lowell invited church leaders and other prominent people to lead discussions on pertinent questions of the day or to review important books—a tempting menu for eager young minds.

The brochure introduced Lowell as "young, well-trained in American (Utah) and European (Erlangen, Vienna, Strasbourg) universities," a returned missionary "well able to appreciate the student's point of view," and "keenly interested in the spiritual and social well-being of students and very desirous of serving them." He also maintained an open-door policy and kept himself available for consultation six days a week for half a day.

On the evening of January 2 Lowell opened a black ledger and recorded proudly: "Sixty-five students . . . a very encouraging beginning." By the next day 140 had registered. The most popular course was the "Position of Mormonism in the Religious Thought of Western Civilization." By week's end it had enrolled thirty-five graduate students and other "downtown friends. Even the daunting title "Religion and the Rise of Our Modern Economic

System," based on his Max Weber studies, attracted "thirty mature students."[11]

For the first open discussion on January 15 Lowell started with the topic "How to Verify Religious Experience." Three young women, stimulated by an evening lecture, came by for an hour's discussion on what constituted true morality. He listened to their concerns, then suggested they consider this proposition: "True morality is not a standard of conduct or an economic-social condition, but . . . rather the acceptance of a standard voluntarily ahead of absolute necessity." From this nucleus sprang a Friday morning discussion group.[12]

Before the first month had ended one young woman was investigating requirements for baptism, and David S. King, later a lawyer, a Congressman from Utah, an LDS mission president, and president of the LDS temple in Washington, D.C., considered with Lowell his philosophy professor's view that natural laws of cause and effect led inexorably to a conclusion of no free will.[13] King recalled Lowell's persuasive argument: "One of the strongest proofs of the existence of both free agency and a conscience, is the fact that human beings universally have such a strong feeling that both of these attributes do in fact exist."[14]

Thursday evening firesides[15] featured such visiting speakers as general church authorities John A. Widtsoe, Stephen L Richards, Levi Edgar Young, Melvin Ballard, and Charles A. Callis, and such dignitaries as John Henry Evans, author of the first professional biography of Joseph Smith,[16] and Father Dwyer of St. Mary's of the Wasatch school. Topics included individual versus institutional responsibility to aid the poor, church history, leadership, human origins, temples and covenant-making, Joseph Smith, the Holy Ghost, and the Word of Wisdom (the Mormon health code). Lowell also introduced a seminar on "Fruits of Religious Living," based on a list of topics that "disturbed" and "perplexed" students: the Adam and Eve story, organic evolution, the divinity of Jesus Christ, the reality of Joseph Smith's first vision, an anthropomorphic God, and birth control.[17]

Neither Merle nor Lowell tried to keep home separate from institute. Lowell brought his beloved opera records from home and played them at noon on his Magnavox record player at the institute, instilling a love for classical music in at least one student.[18] Lowell brought students home to dinner, held evening discussions there, and welcomed drop-ins almost any time. Glenn Schwendiman, a transfer student from Ricks College in 1933, met his future wife, Helen Snow, in Lowell's institute class. Their courtship really began when Lowell loaned Glenn his car so he could take Helen to an institute dance at the Old Mill in Cottonwood.[19]

Merle enjoyed city living with the downtown bus only a few steps away. She took a class in English grammar from Dr. Louis Zucker, a respected Jewish professor at the University of Utah, and declared herself "stronger than I have ever been" despite the pregnancy. On May 7 redheaded Lowell Colton ("Ben") Bennion arrived, weighing a hefty nine pounds six ounces. Nothing could have been a healthier antidote for grief than this robust child. Merle, laughing at herself, put away Laurel's clothes embroidered in pink but took baby Ben for his daily perambulator strolls under a pink carriage robe her sister Ethel had made for Laurel.[20]

She became fast friends with neighbor Grace Adams Tanner, wife of Obert C. Tanner. They created a mild sensation by promenading their redheaded babies.

To keep intellectually active, Merle helped organize the Bennions' first study group, which included Lowell's cousin, Paul Cannon, a lawyer, and his wife, Oa Jacobs Cannon, a student couple, Louis and MaVonne Moench, and an older student, Bill Moran. The group enlarged and thrived. At first they studied Greek mythology, Russian authors, and English literature, with members taking turns leading the discussion. Merle especially enjoyed *The Flowering of New England*, by Van Wyck Brooks, and Edith Hamilton's *Mythology*. The group's reading supplemented a course on Shakespeare she was taking from Dr. Sherman Neff, head of the university's English department. Merle also kept up a lively visiting schedule with Ethel and Aunt Zoe.[21]

And Merle energetically became a "meticulous housekeeper" for her family and their student boarders, who, for eighteen dollars a month, enjoyed not only rooms but meals and laundry service. They let an upstairs bedroom to a "very poor boy from Hunter [Utah]," Paul Jones, who was soon joined by a friend and a cousin. "We spent more on their food, electricity, and hot water than they paid us," Merle admitted,[22] but she and Lowell never considered ejecting them. Augmented with produce gardened from a shared plot and an orchard in the Mount Olympus area of South Salt Lake, Lowell's salary seemed to go a long way.[23]

One snowy morning a student named Verna Swann burst into Lowell's office in tears. The professor who employed her as a domestic had made unwelcome advances. "You'll just have to come home with me," Lowell said, and the Bennions acquired a fourth boarder.[24] For the next year Verna made her bed on the couch and did household chores for Merle, who remembered her as "full of faith, and so vivacious and wonderful, with a beautiful singing voice and lots of dates."[25]

When Verna met a rising young accountant, Richard Johnson, she brought him home for the Bennions to meet. She and Lowell arranged a signal. If Lowell approved, at the end of the visit he would shake hands good-bye; if not, he would simply show them out. As it turned out, a hearty handshake signified his complete approval. Verna and Richard subsequently married and maintained a lifelong friendship with the Bennions.[26]

Edward L. Hart, a lonely student from Idaho, often dropped by the Bennion home to talk and to babysit. One midnight he drove to the Mt. Olympus garden with Lowell for an irrigation turn. An economics major, he confessed his desire to write and asked Lowell's advice. Lowell, perhaps playing devil's advocate, pointed out that making a living would be easier if writing were a "free time" activity. Hart did not take this advice. He changed his major to English and became a Rhodes scholar, an honored poet, and a BYU English professor.[27]

With institute classes in full swing during the winter and spring of 1935, Lowell retained his position as Sunday school and MIA teacher in University Ward, spending almost as much time preparing those lessons as he did on his institute classes. He had already written his first study manual, *What About Religion?* in late 1934 for the General Board of Mutual Improvement Association. It inaugurated what could be called a lifetime of "manual labor."

Although he was comfortable with the freewheeling format of the Thursday evening discussion sessions, he preferred to focus on a single theme or concept. He was not a lecturer but a Socratic teacher, using provocative questions. Ed Hart described Lowell's teaching style as "thinking all the way around [a principle] to discover its meaning, following its roots to wherever they go." With only a blackboard for a visual aid, he kept students on the edge of their seats, ready to respond. "Anybody with any intellectual imagination goes through the experience of wanting to fit what you are learning with your religion," reminisced Hart. "He . . . helped reconcile our intellectual and spiritual beliefs. . . . Everyone respected him both as a religious leader and as an intellect." He summed up Lowell's morally authoritative role for hundreds: "For those years he was a dominant influence in my life."[28]

Another of Lowell's teaching strengths was his insistence that scriptures, "though inspired, were nevertheless clothed in human language rather than in celestial language."[29] This approach insisted on interactive involvement with interpretations of the scriptures. He urged students to develop a multi-faceted philosophy composed of self, everyday experiences, the arts, science, philosophy, reason, and religion. "To leave any one [approach] entirely untapped is to go through life with limited vision," Lowell advised. "To tap each source—to know its flow of knowledge and inspiration—is to live most fully."[30] Students hungry for a role model saw "Brother B." as a father figure, "a person who could think and still be a good Christian."[31]

When Glenn Schwendiman was called to the Swiss-German Mission in the fall of 1935, he found himself floundering in his attempts to teach the gospel without the help of modern "standardized teaching programs." He wrote Lowell for help, and Lowell sent him a mimeographed class syllabus of a recently developed missionary course that "helped me to develop an intellectual as well as a spiritual testimony of the Restored Church, of Joseph Smith, and of the Gospel of Jesus Christ."[32] Lowell had developed that course in June 1935[33] with Whitney Winslow Smith, Lowell's mission friend and grandson of two apostles, who had married Alice Colton, Merle's cousin. Whitney and Lowell outlined a series of lessons that taught gospel principles systematically. Whitney took it to his cousin, George Albert Smith, apostle and future president of the church (1945-51). Although the apostle was pleased, he explained the political realities of such a project to them. According to Whitney, he said,

In order to get something done with this, you boys must decide, do you

> want the credit for this? If you want to be recognized as the authors of this, I am afraid I can do nothing for you; but if your real interest is for the church only, then . . . I'll arrange for each of you to meet with the Missionary Training School committee. They will listen and make a few comments and they will dismiss you. And you will hear nothing on earth about it. But if you keep your eyes open, you will see that many of the things you suggested will be adopted.

Whitney, no stranger to church administration, recalled that his cousin's prediction was correct.[34] Lowell used the course for his missionary classes, a form of training which certainly made its adoption in the field much easier.

During the second year enrollment increased steadily, at least partly because Lowell had received permission to "advertise" in the student newspaper, *The Daily Chronicle.* Among his other obligations and ongoing interests, he added a class on "Mormon Doctrine, History, and Philosophy," held biweekly meetings at his home "to discuss Gospel subjects," and continued his open-door policy of individualized counseling.[35]

Lowell also began an innovation that would become his hallmark—community service. A student complained, "I'm tired of just passing sacrament and ushering. Why don't we do something worthwhile?"

"Why don't you meet me Saturday at one o'clock, wearing your work clothes, and I'll have something for you to do," Lowell responded.[36] This became the first of many service projects to assist the elderly and lonely. At Christmas students caroled for the widows of professors and homebound ward members, branched out to hospitals, and added sub-for-Santa projects.[37]

By the end of the school year Lowell, who had been concerned as early as January by student reports that some faculty were attacking the Book of Mormon, decided: "There is need of a careful study and fresh presentation of the [external] evidence for the Book of Mormon."[38] At his father's suggestion, he registered for summer school classes in anthropology, sociology, philosophy, and religion at the University of Washington, loaded Merle and Ben in a precarious Oldsmobile, and drove to Seattle. He began with the assumption of a strong match between archaeological evidences and Book of Mormon patterns, but unflinchingly realized as the quarter wore on that it was not that easy. "I made a list of all the things in archaeology that I might be able to relate to the Book of Mormon," decided that "a person has to be an archaeologist to be able to use scientific data judiciously," and concluded: "The Book of Mormon is not a scientific work. It is not history nor a geographical treatise. It is not even a theology text." Rather, it is a "profoundly religious record, relating religion to life." At that point Lowell abandoned any ambition to "prove" the book to his students through external evidence, deciding the book is what it announces itself to be: not a "full account" but writings of "the things of God" for the purpose of persuading people to "come unto the God of Abraham, the God of Isaac, and the God of Jacob, and be saved."[39]

Steady and moderate, Lowell withdrew faith in external evidences without postulating that their absence would prove the Book of Mormon false. Through prayerful textual study that summer, he became converted to the Book of Mormon in a way that had eluded him when he and Angus Cannon had climbed a hill in Centerville as teens. He felt he could now present the book as "an honest, true-to-life reporting of human experience" that was filled with insights "concerning our relationship to Jesus Christ." It was a position of intellectual and spiritual peace that he recorded as "time well spent."[40]

The 1936-37 school year opened with CES's first directors' convention. John A. Widtsoe and four institute directors—Lowell, George Tanner, Wyley Sessions, and Thomas Romney—spent the day discussing objectives, working assumptions, and courses of study for the next year. Lowell recorded plans for an experimental "course in Mormonism" as the principal and introductory non-credit course, with outlines going "to the other men in the field."[41] Students flooded the institute—50 percent more than the previous year. The most popular classes were "Mormonism: An Interpretation and a Way of Life" and "Religion and Modern Thought."[42] For Lowell's students, perplexities about the historicity of the Book of Mormon were less relevant than identifying with a Mormon community.

When a group of returning male students wanted "more than classwork" to help them "be brothers," Lowell invited them to his house where they spent Sunday afternoons for the next few weeks hammering out spiritual, intellectual, and social goals embodied in a constitution. In October twenty-six male students united in a simple ceremony, extending the "right hand of fellowship with our minds and hearts in accord." They called themselves the Alpha Chapter, but had no name, no symbol, no slogan, and no authorization except Lowell's. In deliberate distinction from Greek fraternities, which had stung too many students with their emphasis on snobbery and materialism, members pledged themselves to accept willingly any male student who promised "to promote LDS ideals and purposes, to develop the institute, to promote intellectuality, fellowship, leadership, and culture."[43]

Rheim Jones, a sixteen-year-old with "an extra need for guidance," which he found through institute classes and counseling with Lowell, helped write the constitution and design a pin. "Many of the things I have done since," Jones said years later, "have been in an effort to repay [Lowell]."[44]

By late November the young women students asked, "Why can't we have a sorority?" Lowell answered, "You can." The women started Omega Chapter at the other end of the alphabet, swiftly adapted Alpha's constitution and adopted it at a December 3 meeting in the Bennion home.[45]

Student Ardith Moore suggested that the chapters jointly call themselves Lambda Delta Sigma, to provide the acronym LDS. Sally Cannon, an art teacher at the university, perfected the pin design using the Egyptian ankh or crux ansata, the symbol of eternal life, with the five ideals of Lambda Delta Sigma — truth and light, eternal progress, revelation, (sacred) knowledge, and priesthood — symbolized by a cross bar of pearls. Lowell called it "the prettiest pin I've ever seen for a fraternity."[46] It was produced by his friend O.C. Tanner, who had recently founded a jewelry design business. Frank West, Church Commissioner of Education, presided at its 1937 spring formal.

Lowell and Merle regarded the new organization with pride. "Lambda Delta Sigma became a laboratory for a lot of things. Service projects, leadership experience, real brotherhood and sisterhood," Lowell later mused. "It was a marvelous thing to have these men and women chapters together in the same organization."[47] Even during summer the Omega chapter met every two weeks.

While these LDS students were shaping a collective identity of sociability, spirituality, and service, the institute curriculum was expanding and encountering some opposition from some church apostles. At a winter conference of seminary and institute teachers on January 23, 1937, Lowell and A. C. Lambert of BYU presented "Problems of Religious Thinking of College Students, a Course on Mormonism," while W. W. Henderson and Heber Snell, institute teachers from Logan, spoke on "An Approach to the Old Testament."[48]

Despite their neutral titles, the courses were potential bombshells. Snell had studied with William Henry Chamberlin at BYU and E. E. Ericksen at the University of Utah. After teaching education and psychology at Snow College (1923-36), Snell opened the institute at Pocatello.[49] Snell's paper, "Criteria for Interpreting the Old Testament to College Youth," summarized some of the contemporary biblical higher criticism that questioned the literalness of biblical narratives, their authorship, and their traditional dating.

In early March 1937 Frank West and Lynn Bennion, now supervisor of seminaries, received a letter from Joseph Fielding Smith, apostle, official LDS church historian, and head of the church's Literature Committee. He sharply criticized the Henderson-Snell papers, then declared: "If the views expressed in the papers by these men . . . are the views being taught in our Church School system, then I am in favor of closing our schools and seminaries . . . and for the good of the youth of Zion, the sooner it is done the better."[50] After typing out three single-spaced pages of scriptures denouncing the learning of men, Smith, who charged that reading Old Testament narratives as anything but strictly literal would weaken students' faith, concluded that questioning Old Testament historicity would force people "to reject all that has come through Joseph Smith, for if he found difficulty in interpreting the word of the Lord and made so many mistakes which the scholars have detected, then what is there left that we may rely on for a belief in him and his inspiration?"[51]

This censure shocked West and Lynn Bennion, who had been proud of the conference. They hoped for high-quality church education texts from an increasingly well-educated body of instructors. Lynn, who took his own doctorate at Berkeley, wrote in his memoirs: "I remember that Daryl Chase, Russel Swenson, Wesley Lloyd, Sidney Sperry, and Antone Cannon were among those who went to the University of Chicago's Divinity School with Dr. [and LDS apostle Joseph] Merrill's blessing. . . . The idea . . . was to encourage these men to lead the LDS seminaries and institutes in the finest religious education program in America. This was a bright day for the educational program of the Mormon church!"[52] But the Snell controversy turned out to be the first volley in an escalating conflict between intellectual and literal approaches to teaching Mormon students.

Lowell took no position on higher criticism, focusing rather on presenting religious studies in a practical way that would make a difference in the daily lives of students. "More and more I sense the need of centering religious instruction in the life experiences of the students," he wrote in a reflective moment.[53] He concentrated on the scriptures, studiously avoiding "becoming the authority to which they might come for the last or latest word in one limited area." He was not tempted to explain the whole of the gospel according to a single idea or belief, to "elaborate the unknown" or dwell "on things which God has only touched on lightly." He shunned the tendency of many religion teachers to "specialize too early and with too little breadth."[54]

For relaxation during these intensive months, Lowell entered a bee-keeping partnership with Bill Moran, with a salary paid in honey. Estranged from his Catholic father, Bill lived a few blocks from the Bennions, supporting himself and his former nanny with bee-keeping, despite intermittent hospitalization for osteomyelitis. Generously, Bill trained teenage boys to fit hives and harvest honey, apprenticing them for a future trade and giving them spending money.

Lowell's expeditions with Bill were a chance "to get away from the phone and write." While Bill checked the bees, Lowell spread out his papers on a small table in the orchard.[55] But Lowell was also an indefatigable worker. Bill recorded gleefully: "Phd friend Lowell Bennion going through hives with me all morning. He asked me a hundred questions while we worked. I answered two hundred" and "I had Lowell Bennion, doctor of philosophy, dribbling granulated honey into a melting tub all morning. It was sticky work but he insisted on doing it."[56]

Bill groped to define Lowell's magic: "I always come away from Dr. Bennion feeling wholesomely bigger than I did when I entered his presence. He doesn't exactly teach and inform me with facts but with his friendly sympathetic appreciative attitude."[57] For his part, Lowell appreciated having a friend his own age with whom he could enjoy relaxing labor and frank conversation.

In July 1937 Frank West surprised Lowell by asking him to open a new institute in Tucson, Arizona. T. Edgar Lyon, recently released as president of the Netherlands Mission, would run the Salt Lake institute in Lowell's absence. It meant a raise—$2,600, up from $1,800. When Frank assured Lowell that he could resume his position as director of the Salt Lake institute after two years, he accepted.

Lowell approached the new assignment as an adventure. So did Merle after the first shock of having to move again had worn off. In late September 1937 they drove to Arizona where Merle fell instantly in love with the "beautiful little building just being finished."[58] The LDS branches in Tucson and Binghamton numbered 128 students of eligible age, nearly all of whom registered. They included LeVan Kimball, oldest son of Spencer W. Kimball (later an LDS apostle and church president), Stewart Udall, later Congressman from Arizona and Secretary of the Interior under President John F. Kennedy, and some of the nine children of Irena Cardon, granddaughter of early church leader Parley P. Pratt and plural wife of Louis Cardon in the Mexican colonies. Lowell immediately impressed Edward Kimball, younger son of Spencer and Camilla Kimball, "as humble, soft-spoken, and very spiritual."[59]

The Bennions lived in a small apartment on the top floor of the new building. "We were just one big family," Lowell remembered happily, even though ping pong games kept five-month-old Ben awake. Students might appear in the doorway at any hour needing anything from a conversation to a meal, and the Bennion table had company around it "almost every night."[60] Still, Merle, pregnant since October, was determined to see everything as "fun." The institute had its own Sunday school, MIA, and chapter of Lambda Delta Sigma. At mid-year the University of Arizona agreed to give credit for institute courses on the Bible, an achievement Lowell attributes to Franklin West. "It looks as though some few non-Mormons will join us" for classes, he wrote jubilantly to a sister.[61]

In his spare time Lowell typed drafts of lessons on courtship and marriage, sending them to his sister, Frances B. Morgan, in Salt Lake City for her critiques. He also wrote a series of articles commissioned by British Mission president and editor of the *Millennial Star,* Apostle Richard R. Lyman, who complimented Lowell on his "fine, clear, interesting way of presenting matter." Lyman requested further submissions and concluded, "You are a great credit to your excellent father and your remarkable mother."[62] Much encouraged, Lowell enthusiastically completed articles on "Religion and Life in the World," "How Can a Man Be Saved?" "Whence Religion?" and "How God Speaks to Man."

When Bill Moran was hospitalized again, Lowell and Merle invited him to join them in Tucson's healthy winter climate. Bill arrived in January 1938 and stayed until April. "Lowell is being swell to me," he wrote in his journal. "He's feeding me and giving me the run of his $50,000 building. He's driving me around town as faithfully as he would the Pres. of the Church."[63] Lowell frequently took Bill and baby Ben, clad only in "his shoes and his smile"[64] for desert sunbathing, a popular therapy then.

After this successful year the Bennions returned to Salt Lake City where they rented a home. Douglas Colton Bennion, a "big, broad baby," arrived on July 4. The image of Lowell's baby pictures, "he would just sit there and beam at people," Merle recalled.[65] Lowell hired Melissa Farr, an institute student and returned missionary, to plan meals, shop, clean, and care for Ben while Merle rested and nursed the baby.[66]

Lowell began attending a two-month "convention," from mid-June through mid-August, sponsored by the Church Educational System for institute directors and instructors in BYU's Aspen Grove in Provo Canyon. The training session—the first to involve all of the ninety or so instructors—had been planned to showcase the scholarship of the best "institute men." President Heber J. Grant, whom West referred to as "quite a liberal man," had delegated curriculum to West who in turn had asked Lynn Bennion to develop "the finest [program] in the country in terms of nurturing moral and spiritual ideals and commitment to the Church and its heritage."[67] This stimulating and progressive agenda exploded on the last day when J. Reuben Clark, first counselor in the LDS First Presidency, denounced church educators who were teaching "philosophies of the world, ancient or modern, pagan or Christian." He warned, "Any Latter-day Saint psychologist, chemist, physicist, geologist, archeologist, any other scientist [who attempts] to explain away or misinterpret or evade or elude or, most of all, repudiate or deny the great fundamental doctrines of the church . . . can have no place in our church schools or in the character-building and spiritual growth of our youth."[68]

Frank West and Lynn Bennion heard him announce that seminaries and institutes were an experiment "of doubtful procedure" that "might be discontinued at any time."[69] He bore "heavily . . . down," as Lynn Bennion recalled, "that we should all the time be teaching the doctrines of the church, presumption being that we were not doing it."[70]

It stunned West that a man of Clark's knowledge and experience should criticize education and intellectual prowess, but Clark made no secret of his uneasiness with abstract thought. One of his biographers observed, "Despite the brilliance of his mind and speech, he shrank from the complex and abstract . . . in a lifelong estrangement from those he referred to as 'so-called intellectuals.'"[71] Equally as perplexed as West, Lynn Bennion later recalled the implications of Clark's rebuke:

> [Clark] emphasized that ours is the restored gospel; that it is revealed; and that he knew exactly what it meant! He enjoined seminary teachers to faithfully direct the young people according to the revelations of the church and to be definite about it . . . not to raise doubts but to solve doubts.
>
> This was a powerful speech from an orthodox or doctrinal point of view. . . . The truth is known, is well-established, and should be clearly expounded by teachers. That's why they were hired: to make good Latter-day Saints! And "good" in his opinion, was to be a conforming LDS—conforming to the rules, regulations, and doctrines of the church.[72]

Coupled with Joseph Fielding Smith's earlier attack on Snell, Clark's speech chilled some of the young scholars planning careers in church education and "had a crushing effect on our efforts and programs." Within the next few months several seminary teachers and administrators departed and a number of "attractive personalities who possessed fine personal and professional resources" declined to work for CES.[73]

It was impossible for Lynn not to take the criticism personally. As director of LDS seminaries, he and Frank West had worked together preparing "problem-solving" lessons in which students were challenged to think. They had field-tested these materials with seminary teachers, eagerly gleaning their responses. West had drawn on his experience as a physicist, chemist, and student of religion, and Lynn had applied religion to human experience. Both men made a "conscientious effort to relate [the lessons] to the interests and needs of youth." The teacher's manual, *The Old Testament and the Problems of Life*, reflected their approach. West wrote in his introduction to the manual: "The curriculum that is here presented has been developed in harmony with a sound philosophy of education which puts the child at the center and guides and controls his experience. It takes into account his interests and needs and guides him toward lofty religious goals."[74] Lynn Bennion eventually left CES to become superintendent of Salt Lake City Schools in 1945.

Lowell missed Clark's speech because he was preparing to leave for Tucson but, like Lynn, based his lessons on student needs. It was fruitless, he maintained, to try to prove scientifically that such stories as Jonah and the whale had actually occurred. When a freshman girl came to him in tears because her professor had called the Old Testament "a bunch of myths," Lowell shared his own perspective: "It's not all factual. But a balanced view is that great ideas in the scriptures comfort us and give us perspective in life."[75] He thought he could coexist with Clark's philosophy.

Meanwhile, Lowell's young institute was in good hands. Enrollment was holding up, Ed Lyon's Doctrine and Covenants courses were well received, Hermana Lyon's willingness to open her home to students continued Merle's tradition of hospitality, and the students enjoyed the Lyons' four sons: David, John, and twins Jamie and Laurie. Ed's scrupulous management of the building and his bookkeeping skills put Lowell's mind at ease. His only reservation was the elaboration of Lambda Delta Sigma's simple pledge ceremony into an initiation ritual complete with spotlights, robes, and candles. He protested in vain to West, who had imposed the changes.[76]

Lowell and Merle returned to Arizona for their second year—a year of warm family life, close friendships with students, and welcome writing time for Lowell.

NOTES

1. As quoted in Peggy Fletcher, "A Saint for All Seasons: An Interview with Lowell L. Bennion," *Sunstone* 10 (Feb. 1985): 7.

2. Milton Bennion to Lowell L. Bennion, 14 Sept. 1937, photocopy in Bradford's possession.

3. T. Edgar Lyon described this chapel on Kenwood Avenue as a limestone structure with side aisles, nave, cruciform design, and an elevated pulpit. The Gothic window at its rear featured beautiful colored glass but no images. T. Edgar Lyon, Oral History, interviews conducted by Davis Bitton, 1975, typescript, 144, James Moyle Oral History Program, archives, Historical Department, Church of Jesus Christ of Latter-day Saints, Salt Lake City, Utah. I used copies in possession of Lowell L. Bennion and Ted Lyon, son of T. Edgar Lyon.

4. Ibid., 144.

5. Gary James Bergera and Ronald Priddis, *Brigham Young University: A House of Faith* (Salt Lake City: Signature Books, 1985), 50.

6. Lowell L. Bennion, Oral History, 125.

7. Lowell L. Bennion, "Memories," 43, photocopy in Bradford's possession.

8. Franklin L. West, Audiotaped Reminiscences, n.d., Archives and Manuscripts Division, Harold B. Lee Library, Brigham Young University, Provo, Utah; transcript in Bradford's possession.

9. "The General Board of Education of the Church of Jesus Christ of Latter-day Saints Announces the Opening of the Salt Lake City L.D.S. Institute," 2 Jan. 1935, University Ward Chapel; brochure in possession of Lowell L. Bennion, photocopy in Bradford's possession.

10. Douglas D. Alder, "Lowell L. Bennion: The Things That Matter Most," in *Teachers Who Touch Lives: Methods of the Masters,* comp. Philip L. Barlow (Bountiful, UT: Horizon Publishers, 1988), 27.

11. Institute Record, 11 Jan. 1935, 2, photocopy in Bradford's possession.

12. Ibid., 18 Jan. 1935, 3.

13. Ibid., 24 Jan. 1935; 27 Feb. 1936, 15.

14. David S. King, "Some Impressions of Dr. Lowell L. Bennion," letter to Mary L. Bradford, 1 Apr. 1988.

15. Lowell has been credited with founding the "Fireside" as a Mormon institution. See "Some Things Uniquely LDS," *Church News,* 15 Jan. 1992, 10: "According to the recollections of current and former members of the Salt Lake Institute of Religion, firesides were begun in 1935 by Lowell L. Bennion, the founder of the institute. On Sunday nights he would invite students to come into a room with a fireplace and discuss the gospel." These were Thursday evenings, however.

16. John Henry Evans, *Joseph Smith: An American Prophet* (New York: Macmillan Co., 1933). In 1946 Deseret Book Company reprinted it with Macmillan's permission.

17. Institute Record, 24 Jan.-15 Apr. 1935.

18. Edward L. Hart, interviewed by Mary L. Bradford, 7 July 1988.

19. Glenn Schwendiman to Mary Lythgoe Bradford, 10 May 1988.

20. Merle Colton Bennion, Oral History, 33.

21. Ibid., 36, 39.

22. Ibid., 37.

23. Ibid.

24. Verna Swann Johnson, telephone interview by Mary L. Bradford, 24 Jan. 1989.

25. Merle C. Bennion, Oral History, 37.

26. Ibid.

27. Edward L. Hart, interviewed by Bradford.

28. Ibid.

29. David S. King to Mary Lythgoe Bradford, 12 July 1988.

30. Glenn Schwendiman, class notes for "The Place of Religion in One's Philosophy of Life," taught by Lowell L. Bennion, 25 Mar. 1935, institute of religion, University of Utah, photocopy in Bradford's possession.

31. David S. King to Mary Lythgoe Bradford, 12 July 1988.

32. Glenn Schwendiman to Mary L. Bradford, 18 May 1988.

33. Institute Record, 4-5 June 1935, 13.

34. Whitney and Alice Smith, interviewed by Mary L. Bradford, 29 May 1988.

35. Institute Record, events recorded for 1935-36.

36. Lowell L. Bennion and Merle C. Bennion, interviewed by Mary L.

Bradford, 26 Jan. 1990.

37. Lowell L. Bennion and Merle C. Bennion, interviewed by Mary Lythgoe Bradford, 3 Feb. 1990.

38. Institute Record, events recorded for 1935-36.

39. Lowell L. Bennion, "I Gained New Light on Christ's Relationship to Our Sins," in *Converted to Christ through the Book of Mormon,* ed. Eugene England (Salt Lake City: Deseret Book Co., 1989), 158.

40. Ibid.

41. Institute Record, 4-5 Sept. 1936, 64.

42. Ibid., 22 Oct. 1936, 65.

43. Ibid., 11 Oct. 1936, 66. Lowell added, "This meeting was inspirational and is the beginning of a plan to place the institute students (both boys and girls) on a high and dignified social level during their collegiate days. We visualize all of the advantages of any other social unit plus the religious and idealistic inspiration born of our religious heritage expressing itself in group life." The original members were Paul Jones (the first president), Edward L. Hart, David S. King, Wendell Jones, Morris Christensen, Steve Hatch, Elwood Haynie, Barton Howell, Clark Russell, Brit McConkie, Paul Lyon, Verden Bettilyon, Frank Freeman, Reed Beckstead, Ray William, Eldon Romney, Rheim Jones, Bruce Jones, Joe Hatch, Harvey Hatch, Robert E. Lee, Cyril Fullmer, Ben Wallace, Earl Cox, Joe Miller, and Knight Kerr. "History," *National Handbook, Lambda Delta Sigma Fraternity* (Salt Lake City: n.p., 1936), 4.

44. Later a physician, Rheim became president of the Idaho Falls temple. Rheim Jones to Mary Lythgoe Bradford, n.d.

45. On 22 January 1937 they elected officers: Frances Salzner, Gladys Moore, Mary Ruth Chapman, Ardith Moore, and Lue Cheever. Officers for 1937-38 were Verna Swann, Beth Bennett, Pat Richards, Florence Dale Woolley, Jean Layton, and Knell Spencer. "Lambda Delta Sigma Notes—from December 1936-May 1941," 7 May 1937, Lambda Delta Sigma minutes, institute of religion, Salt Lake City; holograph copy in Bradford's possession.

46. Lowell L. Bennion, Oral History, 89.

47. Ibid.

48. Institute Record, 23 Jan. 1937.

49. Snell was institute director at the University of Idaho for eleven years, during which time he spent some summers in graduate work at the University of Chicago. He received his doctorate in biblical studies in 1941. In 1947 he became director of the new institute at Utah State

Agricultural College. In the fall of 1948 he published *Ancient Israel,* a scholarly work that West liked but refused to publish as a departmental project or recommend for course work because of its potential for controversy. Richard Sherlock, "Faith and History: The Snell Controversy," *Dialogue: A Journal of Mormon Thought* 12 (Spring 1979): 28-29.

50. Joseph Fielding Smith to Franklin L. West, 11 Mar. 1937, Sterling M. McMurrin Collection, Marriott Library, University of Utah, Salt Lake City; photocopy in Bradford's possession.

51. Ibid.

52. Milton Lynn Bennion, *Recollections of a School Man: The Autobiography of M. Lynn Bennion* (Salt Lake City: Western Epics, 1987), 87.

53. Institute Record, 6 June 1936, 83.

54. Lowell L. Bennion, "Memories," 44.

55. Bill Moran and Olive B. Moran, interviewed by Mary Lythgoe Bradford, 18 May 1989.

56. Bill Moran, Diary, 9 May and 14 Nov. 1936, notes in Bradford's possession.

57. Ibid., 1 Apr. 1936.

58. Merle C. Bennion, interviewed by Mary L. Bradford, 29 Oct. 1992.

59. Edward Kimball and Bee Kimball, interviewed by Mary Lythgoe Bradford, 10 May 1988.

60. Merle C. Bennion, interviewed by Mary L. Bradford, 29 Oct. 1992.

61. Lowell L. Bennion to Frances B. Morgan, 10 Feb. 1938, photocopy in Bradford's possession.

62. Richard R. Lyman to Lowell L. Bennion, 26 Nov. 1937; photocopy in Bradford's possession.

63. Moran, Diary, 2 Jan. 1938.

64. Ibid., 10 Jan. 1938.

65. Merle C. Bennion, Oral History, 42.

66. Ibid., 44.

67. M. L. Bennion, *Recollections,* 104.

68. In Bergera and Priddis, *Brigham Young University,* 61.

69. Ibid., 106.

70. M. L. Bennion, *Recollections,* 104.

71. D. Michael Quinn, *J. Reuben Clark: The Church Years* (Provo, UT: Brigham Young University Press, 1983), 163.

72. M. L. Bennion, *Recollections,* 106.

73. Ibid., 108.

74. In M. L. Bennion, *Recollections,* 101.

75. Lowell L. Bennion, Oral History, 87.

76. Lowell L. Bennion, "Memories," 123.

CHAPTER 5

An Adventure All the Way (1939-50)

Instead of trying to harmonize science and religion, I tried to talk about the essential elements of the contributions of each field to life, along with their limitations. I tried to show their contributions to our total view of life and our total living and thinking.
—Lowell L. Bennion

Lowell returned to the Salt Lake institute in September 1939 to a congenial partner. Ed Lyon was six years Lowell's senior. "It didn't bother him a bit to be the associate director to a younger man," Lowell remembered. Ed "was a great story teller, a fascinating teacher, and a very likeable man with an encyclopedic memory." Lowell could see that "students liked him very much and got a lot out of his classes." Ed was particularly successful in combining impressive scholarship with faith. He was "a superb role model for students."[1]

In fact, Lowell declared the two friends to be "David and Jonathan—we had a wonderful feeling for each other."[2] Ed provided a sprightly complement to Lowell's low-key approach to administration, and Lowell encouraged the students to consider them equal in authority. Not only could Ed keep books, he was also skilled in building maintenance and logistics. His experience as mission president gave him added resources for classes in missionary training. Their rapport was built on mutual respect, shared values, and gentle teasing. When a young woman told Lowell she wanted "to write on the history of the three degrees of *immorality*," Lowell, with a straight face, replied, "Oh, that's Brother Lyon's area of expertise."[3]

The challenges of the institute made them comrades in arms. Four hundred University of Utah students were enrolled in institute of religion courses for 1939-40, and Lowell, who had brought his family back to Salt Lake City in June, teamed up with Ed to negotiate for expanded quarters. The University Ward Sunday school, with Bennion and Lyon alternating as teachers, had expanded into nearby Thirty-Third Ward; but space for institute classes was a must. Their proposal was to take over the top floor of University Ward. A reluctant bishopric yielded only when Apostle Joseph F. Merrill came down firmly on the institute's side.[4]

For seventy-five dollars a month, the institute offered a classroom for 80-100 students, with the library doubling as a smaller classroom. Lowell and Ed each had an office, and they shared a part-time secretary. A seldom-used space in the corner of the top floor became a cozy lounge, luxurious with new carpeting, couches, a record player, and even a fireplace.

Some ward members were scandalized: "Imagine having young, unmarried people associating in the lounge all day long."[5] Lowell and Ed assured them that at least one director would be present. Besides, most students were too busy to frequent the lounge "all day long."

Lowell and Merle gratefully accepted Milton Bennion's offer of the down payment for a home at 352 University Street, just two blocks from the institute and across the street from campus, where Ben attended pre-school at the Stewart Training School and where Merle enjoyed plays, operas, and lectures. The university campus then consisted of ten buildings with just under 3,000 students.

Lowell stayed home with the children one afternoon a week while Merle took the bus to town or studied in the library. Both parents were proud of Ben's early and enthusiastic scholarship. "I can see that little kid opening our big, glass-enclosed bookcase," Merle reminisced, "and pulling out one of those *Britannica* encyclopedias, and lugging it up to the couch where he would sit by the hour and copy the letters."[6]

They reknit their social interests quickly—their study group, Lowell's beekeeping activities with Bill Moran, family reunions, and other visits with German/Swiss friends who had emigrated or were attempting to do so. Since life was difficult in Germany and even Switzerland, Lowell actively recruited sponsors for emigrants.

Despite J. Reuben Clark's earlier stand, as far as Lowell could tell, church education was healthy. Franklin West defended his employees well, negotiated social security benefits and contracts for new buildings, and dealt deftly with criticism from those who distrusted education. He retained the support of church president Heber J. Grant and, thanks to his assignment on BYU's board of trustees, saw that institute courses were also taught at the church university.[7]

During the summer of 1939 West organized a brain trust at his cabin in Logan Canyon. For ten strenuous days institute directors joined him in curriculum writing sessions. So they could concentrate fully on the task at hand, they hired a man to cook meals and divided the costs among them. Each morning they arose at 6:00, ate breakfast, and took turns reading aloud what they had produced for the group's critique and brainstorming. After lunch and a second intensive session, they shared an hour and a half "to play softball . . . and hike or go fishing." Out of this crucible emerged twelve original courses. "It was hard work," Ed Lyon recalled.[8]

In addition to such predictable topics as Mormon Doctrine, Book of Mormon, The Scriptures, LDS History, Christian History, World Religions, directors were free to create their own courses. Lowell contributed outlines on "Restoration: The Nature and Mission of the Church," Joseph Smith, and his favorite, "Sources of a Personal Philosophy of Life." This class was an exercise in synthesizing a personal philosophy from "science, art, philosophy, religion, and everyday experience." He also created classes on courtship, marriage, and family life, church leadership, missionary training, and Mormonism and the arts. "It was great training in how to make things interesting enough for people to come back," he summarized.[9] In 1939 he also finished writing his first version of an institute text, *The Religion of the Latter-day Saints,* and an MIA manual, *Youth and Its Religion.*[10]

Both Lowell and Ed admired Frank West, a well-organized, creative advisor. Although Lowell did not share West's gymnastic, wrestling, and equestrian skills, he respected the manifestations of a sound mind in a sound body. West was wholeheartedly committed to church education. Initially reluctant to leave his secure post as chemistry/physics professor at Utah State Agricultural College, he decided to give his "own people" his unqualified attention, refusing other attractive offers.[11] A gifted leader, West defended his young CES faculty and trusted them—trusted them to be creative, mature about criticism, and responsible in relating to students. He created a colloquium of equals—"an open, free, stimulating relationship," Lowell recalled.[12]

Lowell appreciated both West's difficult position and his loyalty to the institute program when some general authorities "misunderstood their approach." Lowell dedicated *The Religion of the Latter-day Saints* to West, calling him "a constant source of loyalty and encouragement in this work."[13]

When Pearl Harbor was bombed on December 7, 1941, thirty-three-year-old Lowell reported to his draft board as ordered but applied for deferment. "I didn't want to leave my family nor did I want to fight my German friends," said Lowell.[14] As the United States became an ally with Britain, France, and China against the Axis powers of Italy, Japan, and Germany, Lowell and Merle saw Nazism and fascism wash across their beloved Germany. Male students enlisted "by the hundreds," leaving the young women to take up "knittin' for Britain," roll bandages at the Red Cross, or dance with soldiers at the USO in the campus fieldhouse.

One of Lowell's students, Yvonne Welling, noticed that the turmoil of war triggered intense relationships. She recalled at least twelve proposals from young men either leaving for or returning from the war. Some began, "Brother Bennion told me I should tell you how I feel." When she asked Lowell why he kept "setting me up" since she was not interested in marriage, Lowell, hiding a smile, shifted the responsibility back to her: "That's your message."[15]

Institute enrollment remained surprisingly stable during the war years, largely because of the increased number of young women taking institute classes. During the four years of the war Lowell emphasized self-improvement, service, and leadership. When Lambda Sigma Delta interchapter president Clinton Miller was drafted, vice president Louise Livingston organized students to register for Red Cross courses in first aid and to join work parties that cleaned and painted houses for needy neighbors. At Christmas the Lambda Delts sewed nightgowns for the children at the Primary Children's Hospital and repaired, painted, and delivered toys, with Lowell in a Santa Claus suit.

With a greater need for spiritual moorings, young women gathered for study classes, music hours, and fireside chats. Lowell and Ed spoke at memorial services for the dead and counseled the living. They sat on the floor with the students, eating and talking in the refreshment sessions that always ended work and service projects. Lowell also had the sobering responsibility of launching young couples onto the seas of matrimony. "I haven't kept track," Lowell mused later, "but I guess I've married a hundred couples in my day."[16] He worked hard to make such ceremonies positive, dignified events. In late 1939 when Bill Moran married Olive Belnap, one of Lowell's student editors, Lowell performed their wedding in the institute lounge before a blazing fire. "The wedding was brief and simple and ever so beautiful," recorded Bill. "I'll never forget the way Olive looked into my eyes as we stood there clasping hands."[17]

Another innovation was an unusual half-hour monthly worship service, exactly thirty minutes long, on Thursdays. Many students, grateful for a peaceful space in which to meditate, considered it "what all sacrament meetings should be."[18] It focused on a single theme, from organ prelude, scripture readings, and musical numbers to short talks and a single prayer. Each number was timed, and only the best musicians performed. These meetings encouraged meditation and religious worship in ways that the business and bustle of weekly sacrament meetings could not.

Lowell heard about a "vesper service" at the Pocatello institute, so he decided to enlist a committee of students to work with him. "We'd get the best musical talent we could find. We had no announcements. We'd write the program on a slip and hand it to each person on the program. No one conducted, no business. Sometimes we had two prayers, but often just one, maybe in the middle. Sometimes we'd have a talk, sometimes a scripture reading, anything to put over a feeling and an idea." One student told him that he came home from the war an atheist, but after attending worship services he came back to the Mormon church.[19] Arguing for "more reverence" in LDS sacrament meetings, Lowell felt the best talent in music should be presented. "Let the kids practice in youth groups, but not in sacrament meeting. . . . Cut down on anything that doesn't contribute to the spirit of worship."[20]

Lambda Delta Sigma, already a healthy co-ed fraternity, with chapters at new institutes in Utah, Idaho, Wyoming, Arizona, and California, took on wartime duties, corresponded with servicemen, mailed out a quarterly newsletter to other chapters, sponsored the first national convention of Lambda Delta Sigma (1941), published a yearbook, *The Argus,* and a national handbook in 1947 with information on all chapters, membership, songs, and news. That year the national membership of Lambda Delta Sigma reached 2,500.

The size of the women's chapter became unwieldy, but its members vetoed Lowell's suggestion for dividing it during 1939-40. He therefore met quietly with a group of twelve women. "One was a little girl with a built-up shoe; another was on crutches . . . a brilliant girl!" Soon this second group of twelve had multiplied until he asked it to form "the second [women's] chapter of Lambda Delta Sigma. And he managed to do this without offending the other girls."[21]

The war years became prime teaching years for Lowell. Between 1941 and 1945 his students had special reasons for seeking the stability that came from principles and values. With six years of teaching behind him, he was able to give his top effort to perfecting the classroom synergy that he never lost. His intellectual curiosity made him a generalist with a broad background. When he decided to teach a class on world religions, he began with Max Weber's theory, then, he said, "I got the best books and dug out for myself."[22]

Scrutinizing male-female relationships, Lowell set up a typology of dating systems as a means for discussion in his courtship and marriage classes: (1) The search for the "one and only," a popular holdover from Victorian sentimentalism, he believed, limited one's circle of friends to people too much like oneself without enough variety for meaningful comparison, too-early choices, and too-high expectations of romantic fulfillment. (2) Another troublesome custom was the "staccato method," popular among returned servicemen and missionaries, which involved dating a different person each time. He was appalled to learn that one young man had charted 176 women in a notebook with an evaluation code! (3) Lowell also deplored the popular habit of going steady. It took young people out of circulation too quickly and promoted intense physical affection before the relationship was mature enough to handle it. (4) The ABC method, his favorite, required dating two or more friends at a time, getting to know them well, then dropping one if it didn't seem to work out and adding another, while continuing to date those with whom the relationship was progressing. He thought this method kept associations creative, prevented too-early and too-intense physical involvement, created better judgment about character and personality, and allowed happy and successful friendships to ripen into equally happy and successful marriages.[23]

Weber-like, he made a clear distinction between the "ideal type of marriage" and the reality of marriage, encouraging prospective couples to consider compatibility in health, economic security, even "ample living quarters," and age compatibility—none of which he and Merle had considered in their own courtship and marriage. His outline reflected the unconscious sexism of the 1940s. "Girls" should be versed in housekeeping, nutrition, cooking, and home decoration. "Fellows" should be "cooperative in the home" with various "household abilities" and hobbies that would contribute to a happy home life. Certain "disturbing factors" should be absent, including in-law troubles, economic dependence, social and moral dependence on others. There should be no conflicting loyalties to another person, to sports, or to other interests.

Students observed his example closely. Yvonne Welling remembered that Merle was gracious and quiet, "always let[ting] him be the focus."[24] For young men and women looking for a model of their own future, "Lowell and Merle had an ideal family . . . that made marriage look appealing," as Ed Hart put it.[25] Lowell's esteem for Merle appeared in teaching that "every woman needed a day off once a week" and insisting that the stay-at-home mother was "earning the man's salary equally with him."[26]

Ed and Hermana Lyon, now the parents of six, including two sets of twins, were equally idolized. If Lowell and Merle had a model supportive marriage, Ed and Hermana had a model romantic one, and Merle, though uncomplaining, sometimes longed for their intense closeness. It was not unusual for Ed to call home four or five times a day, and he seemed to find time for his own family in ways Lowell never mastered. Lowell, both blessed and cursed with unusual energy and vitality, had a mind "constantly churning" with ideas for the institute.[27] Even when he was home, part of his mind was elsewhere. Merle's wistfulness was never voiced, nor was there anything but the best of feelings between her and Hermana, or between Lowell and Ed.

Lowell's discussion of "love and affection" in his courses acknowledged the need for physical affection and eschewed "extreme religious attitudes." Sexual relations were a "natural, normal, desirable part of married life."[28] Sex was neither good nor evil in itself but should be expressed in ways that would build stability and joy in family life. He pointed out the power of sex to preserve physical, mental, and spiritual health, to build friendship and love, and to enhance "a good family life."[29] By placing sex in the context of the good life, Lowell gave it a wholesome reality for students.

Lowell was progressive about birth control, believing that all forms were all right if they were "healthy." In his introductory interview with David O. McKay, Lowell had broached the subject then explained his own view about the importance of self-control in sexual relations. "President McKay gave me the feeling that we were thinking together, that he was incorporating my reflections into his own." This gave him confidence in teaching these ideas.[30]

A student during the 1950s recalled Lowell's taking the position, with which McKay would have certainly agreed, that "A woman should be queen of her body. A woman is more than a machine for turning out children."[31] Such respect logically leads to thoughtful planning of families. He spoke disapprovingly of one husband who insisted his invalid wife continue to endure repeated pregnancies when she was unable to care for the children. One student remembers Lowell explaining, "He taught us that it was all right to use birth control for the health of the mother and the child. . . . This was a brave thing . . . to talk about in a class."[32]

In 1942 Apostle John Widtsoe had allowed abstinence to be a "natural method" that "violates no principle of nature," and President McKay wrote in 1947, "When the health of the mother demands it, the proper spacing of children may be determined by seeking medical counsel, by compliance with the processes of nature, or by continence." Both Joseph Fielding Smith and J. Reuben Clark in 1949 took the more common and oft-repeated stance: "The purpose of sex is to beget children."[33] In 1969 McKay's First Presidency issued a formal statement affirming that the church teaches healthy couples should not "curtail or prevent the birth of children," acknowledging that the mother's health should be conserved and that a husband's duty is consideration for his wife. Married couples should "seek inspiration and wisdom from the Lord that they may exercise discretion in solving their marital problems."[34] According to historian Lester Bush, the statement placed the topic "above ecclesiastical review" by shifting responsibility "from the church to the individual member."[35]

And Lowell emphasized family goals based on the "sacredness and eternal nature of human personality," with the home as the "greatest personality-building institution." He guided his classes through the "relative merits of temple and civil marriages," the advantages and disadvantages of a large family, the obligation of parents to children and children to parents. Should parents, for instance, endure unhappy marriages for the sake of the children? In making room for religion in the home, he recommended an early version of what developed during the 1950s and 1960s into a regular weekly "Family Home Evening."

In 1945 Lowell wrote McKay, now president of the Quorum of the Twelve Apostles and heir apparent as church president, a carefully worded letter confessing that he was having trouble defending the church's position of denying priesthood to worthy black men. How, he asked, should he present it to young people?[36] He felt no need to make a *cause célèbre* of the issue, but neither could he imagine himself looking into a black man's face and explaining that he had "not been valiant in the pre-existence" or that he belonged to the cursed lineage of Cain.

McKay's response graciously acknowledged, "I know of no scriptural basis for denying the Priesthood to Negroes other than the verse in the Book of Abraham (1:26)," but that posed a logical dilemma: "If we have faith in the justice of God," then somehow the deprivation must be "merited."[37] Perhaps humans of various races have chosen "parentages for which they are worthy . . . by the operation of some eternal law with which man is yet unfamiliar," he suggested, affirming that "in God's eternal plan, the Negro will be given the right to hold the Priesthood."[38]

Although Lowell found the explanation inadequate, he was

heartened by the possibility of dialogue and anticipated a brighter age for church education as McKay, a professional educator and firmly committed to programs for youth, moved toward the presidency. Lowell began in the late 1940s but did not finish an article titled "Race" in which he declared, "Having read the first five books of the Bible, . . . I can find absolutely nothing that pertains to race directly." He also denied any scriptural support for the concept that the "mark of Cain" was a black skin. "Most people fall for this because it sounds good and appeals to their imagination. But, as an argument, it has no foundation and should not be used."[39] When the subject came up Lowell said, "I just don't know. I can't answer that." His muted bewilderment was, in itself, a message.

Nor was the black policy the only example of Lowell's open-mindedness. When he could not in good conscience explain a doctrine or policy, he was unwilling to pass it off with a general appeal to faith, even though he knew such an attitude displeased the successors of J. Reuben Clark, who died in 1961. For example, when Lowell addressed a weekly brown-bag luncheon of medical and pre-med students, he expressed his opinion that artificial insemination might be a "pure way of letting a woman become a mother. I saw no moral issue, lust, or infidelity involved." Instead of challenging Lowell in person, one student reported him to Apostle Mark E. Petersen, who editorialized anonymously in the *Church News* against the practice. When Lowell wrote to the newspaper asking for clarification, he received an unsatisfactory reply.[40]

Ben was six and Douglas three when dark-haired Steven Don was born in August 1941. Three months earlier Ed and Hermana Lyon had moved to East Millcreek, a rural suburb southeast of the city. Lowell, who had long aspired to own a farm, reminded Merle, "I don't want to raise boys on a city lot."[41] As they drove to the hospital for Steve's birth, he asked her to promise that they could move if the child were a son. Merle quietly agreed.

In early spring of 1943 the Lyons pointed them toward four acres and a rundown house above 27th East at 35th South. The house, heated with a coal furnace and lacking hot running water, was filthy. Merle was dismayed, but Lowell could see only the barn, the cow, and the generous garden acreage. He concluded the sale quickly in May 1943, and their city home sold speedily. Merle, pregnant again, exhausted herself cleaning the city house, then started on the country house. One hideous day, alone with baby Steve and three-year-old Doug, cramps warned her of miscarriage. Since the bedrooms were torn up, she lay down in the living room and waited until Lowell returned with Ben, who was still attending Stewart School near the institute.

Lowell drove to a neighbor's to telephone the doctor, who briskly counseled, "If she isn't hemorrhaging, you don't need to bring her in." Merle endured a night of such unremitting pain that she awakened Lowell: "I think I'm dying." He sleepily soothed her, "Don't worry, dear. That would be the last thing you'd do." Merle just "had to laugh."[42]

But she miscarried, and Aunt Zoe took Merle home with her. Sister Ethel took Steve, and Lowell's parents took Doug for the next ten days. When Merle returned, still feeling "emotionally drained and not well," she found the living room full of seed potatoes Lowell was getting ready to plant.[43] Even for a usually uncomplaining woman, it was a hard spring.

Merle's loneliness on their little farm overwhelmed her at first, but she steadfastly adjusted. Only one family with small children lived nearby; but within the next few years Obert and Grace Tanner moved in down the street, and Gordon and Marjorie Hinckley, with a son Steve's age, built on the old Hinckley farm on 27th East. Merle made the ward her extended family, patiently managing alone with the children each Sunday while Lowell was at the University Ward. She simply "accepted the fact that this was Lowell's life's work and that's what he was going to do."[44]

The boys adjusted easily to a new school and a new ward, thriving in the out-of-doors. Merle read to the children a great deal, an activity they enjoyed. She asked each child to bring an unfamiliar word to the supper table each evening for an impromptu quiz. She enforced table manners and welcomed friends and cousins. She served in a variety of church positions over the next twenty years but arranged to be home when the children returned from school. She found it rewarding to immerse herself in her children. "I wasn't strict enough at times with them," she confessed, "but I loved them, and that was my role, the role I had chosen to follow."[45]

Ben was diligent and punctual about homework and household duties, an excellent student, a bird watcher, and a hiker. Doug and Steve, though not irresponsible, had active social lives and were "intent on having a good time." They would sometimes wait till the last minute to complete a school assignment. [46]

Much later Lowell reflected, "I committed myself maybe too much to the church, to the institute, and not enough to my family. As I look back, I should have spent more time at home."[47] But Lowell was not negligent either as a husband or a father. He continued to relieve Merle at home one afternoon a week, which she would sometimes spend at a movie matinee, taking the bus to town. She attended institute functions, "cook[ed] yards of spaghetti and cookies by the gross," and turned out three nourishing meals a day at home: "I baked bread . . . I made butter. I made sure vegetables and fruit were available. I was busy keeping four hungry boys fed."[48]

Lowell basked in country living, writing with satisfaction to his sister Frances, after Christmas in 1943: "They got skis and . . . Sunday morning they were out an hour before daylight on a back hill. The country is the place for boys!" Since spring they had also made significant progress on the house. Merle decorated the living room in "soft wild-rose-oyster-gray." Lowell continued, "We have installed cupboards, patched plaster, put in a laundry tub, hot water tank, and water coil in the furnace. We have painting, landscaping, construction on outbuildings and farming to do. How I envy people who sit around lonesome-like with nothing to do."[49]

Lowell also continued sharecropping and gardening. The 1943 harvest produced record quantities of fruit, berries, and vegetables. "We ate fruit galore, bottled 600 quarts, and cleared above expenses $200.00," he recorded with satisfaction. "At home we had corn, tomatoes, potatoes, cabbage, peaches, milk, eggs—a sow for winter plus chickens, two young goats, rabbits."[50]

The larger Bennion family also experienced adversities. Lowell's father had suffered from diabetes since age forty-five. In those pre-insulin days, his only treatment was diet, and Lowell clearly remembered the "tremendous willpower" he exerted in controlling his eating habits.[51] But circulation problems in his legs led to intense pain and eventually to gangrene. His left leg was amputated below the knee in 1939, when he was sixty-nine, along with some toes on his right foot. Quipping, "If I've got to die by inches, I'd rather die from the feet first than from the head," he learned to walk with a prosthesis.[52]

After Milton's retirement from the university in 1941 at age seventy-one, he immediately became general superintendent of the LDS Deseret Sunday School Union, then a salaried job that required considerable correspondence, counseling, and the editorship of *The Instructor,* a guide for church teachers. He maintained a full schedule from his desk at home by the telephone.

Deep sorrow visited the family when Wayne, Lowell's closest brother in age and affection, died in October 1942. A thirty-six year-old professor at USAC, he was unloading freight cars as a war volunteer at the Ogden Depot when a heavy box fell on him. He died of a ruptured kidney ten days later. Colleagues pooled gas rations to drive from Cedar City and Logan, where Wayne had taught, to attend the large funeral where he was eulogized by general authorities Antone Ivins and Stephen L Richards. Merle sobbed so steadily that her sister, Ethel, finally scolded, "You're crying more than Ione!"[53] Lowell paced the yard in solitary grief then found comfort in making himself useful. He rented a moving van and helped move Ione from Logan to her parents' home in Salt Lake City.[54]

Lowell's deferment was renewed, thanks in part to his growing family. In the spring of 1944 he was assigned to the Tooele copper smelter. During the next six months, except Saturdays and Sundays, Lowell "taught morning classes at the institute, milked the cow, went with my neighbor [student Reed Beckstead] out to Tooele, came home, milked the cow, and went to bed, got up the next morning, and went to the institute." He could have joined the army as a chaplain, but, he explained, "I had no desire to fight my German friends and I had my little kids and wife." This "war work" was "my contribution."[55]

Although Lowell worked willingly, his patriotism was not romanticized. To Bill Moran, then finishing a social work degree in Oakland, California, he wrote:

> Right now I am dumping ore out of cars. Other times I watch ore go by on a conveyor belt and pull wood, sacks, wire, metal, et al. out

> before it goes on up to the crusher. This is easy and monotonous like most smelter jobs.
>
> You are interested in the laborer's point of view? Here are a few observations. . . . There is no feeling of mutuality between management and labor. Neither one is seeking, that I can tell, to promote the interests of the other. For instance, there is not a decent place in which to eat, wash, or rest in the whole smelter—no lounge, reading or recreation rooms. No attempt is made to reward a fellow for his dependability, or creativity. You get hell now and then if you don't work, but you could work your head off without a word of commendation. After you work there for twenty years and operate a mill you earn the fabulous sum of $7.50 a day. I started out at $6.65 and will average about $8.00 or $9.00 if I stay on the dump regularly.
>
> As for the union. They have not asked me to join yet, but the fellows I work with are nearly all members, and their membership seems to mean about as much to them as does the priesthood to the adult Aaronics in the church. There seems to be a total lack, in this place, of any democratic process or effective activity in the labor union.[56]

In the same letter Lowell commented with irony that the Chamber of Commerce was asking the city commission to prohibit Japanese Americans from buying property: "So we, the great democracy of the earth fighting to preserve democracy, go about to prohibit American-born Japanese to own property in Salt Lake City." He added a revelation of how the experience had radicalized him: "When my smelter days are over, I believe I'll take up the fight somewhere, Bill. It will be all the more interesting to do so while still in my present position at the institute to see how the conservative element of LDS leadership will react."[57]

Then in May 1945 the war ended in Europe, with Hitler and Mussolini dead, and the Germany Lowell and Merle had known split between the Allies and the Soviets. On August 14, 1945, Japan's emperor Hirohito surrendered to General Douglas MacArthur, and the veterans returned. The news strengthened Merle's feeling of security during those months of another pregnancy. On December 13, 1945, the family welcomed the fourth son, Howard Wayne, a blond child who, at nine pounds, ten ounces, was their largest. A "happy, cheerful" baby, Merle noticed that he showed early signs of an artistic sense.

After his term at the smelter expired, Lowell took a second job as night watchman at Bennett Motor Company. Writing good-humoredly to a sister, he explained: "Merle thinks my motto should be: 'Never finish a job until you have taken on at least two more.' I teach Tues. and Thurs., three classes, at the institute. I spend five hours a night at Bennett Motor as night watchman, so I can study regularly and get some lessons written."[58]

On December 5, 1948, Lowell delivered the Joseph Smith Memorial Lecture at the Logan institute. This sixth annual lecture represented thirteen years of his creative, productive interaction with institute students and the immediately upcoming move of the program into a new building. He chose as his subject "Joseph Smith's Creative Role in Religion," describing how Mormonism's founding prophet "kept his eye on the unplowed field ahead. He turned over virgin soil. . . . Each day was a new day in the life of the prophet."

As Lowell captured his audience with a favorite theme, much of what he said reflected on his own life. He was in his prime and facing various "unplowed fields," eager to pursue his quest for the unified religious experience. "When man is creative," he said, "he emerges from the prison of his own mind. . . . The creative soul recreates life after the image he carries in his heart." Though religion is a conservative and saving force, "it must be more than that. It is also a dynamic force in life in harmony with man's urge to create."[59]

With the war's end, building restrictions were lifted, and Lowell and Ed were soon pressed for space. Frank West pointed out to church leaders that land purchased in 1941 at 274 University Street was still available for construction of a new institute building. Church president George Albert Smith said warmly, "Why, that building should have been constructed long ago. Go right ahead with it."[60] On November 1, 1947, ground was broken for the 35,000-square-foot structure. It cost approximately $375,000 with an additional $40,000 for furniture.[61] By 1948-49 a record 12,050 students, with 5,515 more in extension courses, were bulging classrooms.[62] About a thousand were enrolled at the institute, with Lowell and Ed still the only teachers.

They had asked Edward O. Anderson, church architect, to design a building "for the students, not the other way around."[63]

Their plans included two fireplaces that provided a cozy talking space. A circular room had three large storage closets and also opened into the lunchroom, "making a big place for parties and dancing and food." Upstairs the ballroom could be opened to create overflow seating for the chapel. Ed remembered with glee the "arguments about how much of a basement was needed. . . . Finally the architect and Lowell and I pulled a whizzer on [the Church Building Department], which they were glad we did later. . . . We wanted to know if the excavator could possibly make a 'mistake' and dig all the dirt out and haul it away and then get the footings in before anybody discovered it. They did. The room is the seminary teachers' training center and it served the Delta Phis [a fraternity for returned missionaries] until they bought their house."[64]

When the building needed an organ, Ed worked the proposal through the Church Building Department while simultaneously installing the cabinet. In the spring of 1950, determined that the landscaping would have one of the new-fashioned sprinkling systems, Ed and Lowell taught themselves how to cut and thread pipes, make nipples, and connect nozzles. "I grew up thinking they could do anything," recalled Ed's son, Ted. "They didn't wait for the contractor to do it. They just did this because it needed to be done."[65] With the students' help, they dug the pipe trenches and planted lawn, shrubs, and trees.[66]

On the morning of December 31, 1949, willing students hauled the office, lounge, and classroom furniture and equipment from the University Ward to the new institute. That afternoon they installed benches in the chapel, uncrated the furniture and placed it in various lounges and rooms, washed the windows, and scrubbed and polished the floor.

Shortly after midnight the rug was laid, and at 5:00 a.m. on New Year's Day, 1950, celebrants assembled for the dedication. Lowell officiated and welcomed the large audience. Frank West considered the building his finest monument and said so in his dedicatory address.[67] Church president George Albert Smith offered the dedicatory prayer and remarks. The *Deseret News* editorialized: "Perhaps never in the history of the Church have its youth been blessed with a more practical—or a more beautiful place to worship, study, and play."[68] A new decade and a new era had dawned.

NOTES

1. Lowell L. Bennion, Oral History, 103.

2. Ibid.

3. Peggy Fletcher, "A Saint for All Seasons: An Interview with Lowell L. Bennion," *Sunstone* 10 (Feb. 1985): 9.

4. T. Edgar Lyon, Oral History, 144, interviews conducted by Davis Bitton, 1975, James Moyle Oral History Program, archives, Historical Department, Church of Jesus Christ of Latter-day Saints, Salt Lake City, Utah. I used copies in possession of Lowell L. Bennion and Ted Lyon, son of T. Edgar Lyon.

5. Ibid., 145.

6. Merle C. Bennion, interviewed by Mary L. Bradford, 22 May 1987.

7. T. Edgar Lyon, Oral History, 143.

8. Ibid., 143.

9. Lowell L. Bennion, Oral History, 123-24.

10. Ibid., 87. *The Religion of the Latter-day Saints* (Salt Lake City: Church Education System, 1939) was revised with the assistance of Olive Belnap and reprinted in 1940, 1941, and 1965.

11. Franklin L. West, Audiotaped Reminiscences, n.d., Archives and Manuscripts Division, Harold B. Lee Library, Brigham Young University, Provo, Utah; transcript in Bradford's possession.

12. Lowell L. Bennion, Oral History, 94.

13. Ibid., 93.

14. Ibid.

15. Yvonne Welling Cassity to Mary L. Bradford, 11 Nov. 1989.

16. Lowell L. Bennion, Oral History, 163. Until the end of President David O. McKay's administration, an elder could perform civil marriages with special permission. Since that time only bishops and stake presidents can officiate at these non-temple LDS weddings.

17. Bill Moran, Diary, 12 Dec. 1939, quoted by permission of Olive Moran.

18. Lowell L. Bennion, Oral History, 114.

19. Ibid.

20. Ibid., 114.

21. Louise Livingston Erickson, interviewed by Mary L. Bradford, 23 Aug. 1988.

22. Lowell L. Bennion, Oral History, 93.

23. Lowell L. Bennion, *Today and Tomorrow,* MIA manual for fourteen- and fifteen-year-olds (Salt Lake City: Church Education Department of the LDS Church, 1942), 14.

24. Yvonne Welling Cassity, interviewed by Marie Jones, 16 Jan. 1990; tape and notes in Bradford's possession.

25. Edward L. Hart, interviewed by Mary L. Bradford, 6 July 1988.

26. Ibid. Lowell used the same comparison in "Seek Ye Wisdom," address to the priesthood session of general conference, *Report of the Semi-Annual Conference of the Church of Jesus Christ of Latter-day Saints,* 6 Apr. 1968 (Salt Lake City: Church of Jesus Christ of Latter-day Saints, 1968), 94-99.

27. Merle C. Bennion, Oral History, 43.

28. Lowell L. Bennion, "Today and Tomorrow," in *The Best of Lowell L. Bennion: Selected Writings 1928-1988,* ed. Eugene England (Salt Lake City, Deseret Book Co., 1988), 215-23.

29. Lowell L. Bennion, *Husband and Wife* (Salt Lake City: Deseret Book Co., 1976), 50.

30. Lowell L. Bennion, "My Memories of David O. McKay," *Dialogue: A Journal of Mormon Thought* 4 (Winter 1968): 47.

31. Class notes of Mary L. Bradford, "Courtship and Marriage," 13 Feb. 1952.

32. Louise Livingston Erickson, interviewed by Mary L. Bradford, 23 Aug. 1988.

33. All three are quoted in Lester Bush, "Birth Control among the Mormons: Introduction to a Persistent Question," *Dialogue: A Journal of Mormon Thought* 10 (Autumn 1976): 25.

34. Ibid., 155.

35. Ibid.

36. Fletcher, "A Saint for All Seasons," 11.

37. As quoted in W. E. Berrett, "The Church and the Negroid People," *Mormonism and the Negro* (Orem, UT: Bookmark, 1960), 22-23. Lowell gave a copy of the letter to Berrett but did not retain one for himself. The full letter is also cited in Lester E. Bush, Jr., "Compilation on the Negro in Mormonism," typescript, 1970, 251-52; photocopy in Bradford's possession.

38. Ibid.

39. Lowell L. Bennion, "Race," unpublished essay, typescript copy in

Bradford's possession.

40. Lowell L. Bennion, untitled speech to Medical Association, Salt Lake City, 31 Apr. 1989, photocopy of typescript in Bradford's possession.

41. Merle C. Bennion, Oral History, 47.

42. Ibid., 49.

43. Ibid.

44. Merle C. Bennion, Oral History, 52.

45. Ibid., 57.

46. Ibid., 55.

47. Lowell L. Bennion, Oral History, 121.

48. Merle C. Bennion, Oral History, 55.

49. Lowell L. Bennion to Frances B. Morgan, 14 Dec. 1943, photocopy in Bradford's possession.

50. Ibid.

51. Lowell L. Bennion, Oral History, 18.

52. Ibid.

53. Merle C. Bennion, interviewed by Mary L. Bradford, 2 Feb. 1988.

54. Ione and Wayne were childless. Wayne was buried near baby Laurel at Wasatch Lawn Cemetery. After a year of mourning, Ione returned to Logan, where a few years later she married Ted Daniels, a forestry professor at Utah State University.

55. Lowell L. Bennion and Merle C. Bennion, interviewed by Mary L. Bradford, 13 Feb. 1988, summary typescript, 4.

56. Lowell L. Bennion to Bill Moran, 4 Feb. 1944, photocopy in Bradford's possession. By "adult Aaronics," Lowell was referring to adult Mormon men who had not advanced to the Melchizedek priesthood to which most active Mormon men are ordained at about age eighteen or nineteen.

57. Ibid.

58. Lowell L. Bennion to Frances B. Morgan and Elmo Morgan, 9 July 1946, holograph copy in Bradford's possession.

59. "Joseph Smith: His Creative Role in Religion," Joseph Smith Memorial Lecture, 5 Dec. 1948, Utah State University, photocopy of typescript in Bradford's possession.

60. Franklin L. West, audiotaped reminiscences, n.d.

61. "Date for Dedication of Institute Building Set New Year's Day," *Deseret News*, 17 Dec. 1949, photocopy of unpaginated clipping in

Bradford's possession.

62. Ralph V. Chamberlin, *The University of Utah,* ed. Harold W. Bentley (Salt Lake City: University of Utah Press, 1960), 511.

63. T. Edgar Lyon, Oral History, 146.

64. Ibid., 146.

65. Ted L. Lyon, interviewed by Mary L. Bradford, 14 May 1988.

66. T. Edgar Lyon, "Historical Notes on the Salt Lake City Institute of Religion," typed notes in Bradford's possession.

67. Franklin B. West, audiotaped reminiscences, n.d.

68. "Date for Dedication of Institute Building." In 1953 the institute received a new pipe organ from the John and Edna Firmage family in memory of their deceased son. The dedicatory concert by Alexander Schreiner, attended by more than a thousand, inaugurated weekly "devotionals" with Robert Cundick performing on the organ. "Institute Dedicates New Organ," *Church News,* 3 Jan. 1953, 4.

CHAPTER 6

THE HEYDAY OF THE INSTITUTE (1950-60)

There is a quality of goodness and greatness and sacredness in every child of God. I will never write one off. He is my brother; she is my sister—flesh of my flesh, spirit of my spirit.
—LOWELL L. BENNION

The institute finally had a home of its own, a building to house its impressive growth. Lowell and Ed were at the peak of their powers, and their programs, honed over the years, reflected their maturity. The building presented a solid presence on the campus, in the church, and in the community during a decade remembered by students and staff as the heyday of the institute. Lowell said of this era, "The institute period is the time in my life when I had the closest, warmest, most comprehensive relationships with the most people. You know, I dined, danced, counseled, taught, prayed, and worshipped with these kids. I wept with them and laughed with them."[1]

As two Mormon historians observed: "The forties had been years of war and recovery . . . consolidation and renewal. The fifties would be years of transition and expansion."[2] Church membership reached one million in 1947 and 1.1 million in the 1950s, with almost half the membership under age twenty. Between 1949 and 1951 thirty-nine new seminaries were opened and five new institute buildings erected. In 1949 Ricks College became a four-year college and the First Presidency expanded the Church Board of Education to include the entire Council of the Twelve, giving the church's top leaders permanent and direct influence on educational policies.[3]

The year after the new institute building was dedicated,

George Albert Smith died and David O. McKay became the first Mormon president with a college degree. At seventy-eight, he was vigorous and charismatic, white-maned and handsome. A dedicated traveler, he visited the church's missions worldwide, spending time among the people and returning home to commit the church to serious development and building projects. His combination of gentle humor, zest for living, and expansive theology was especially appealing to Lowell, Ed, and their colleagues.

As always, Lowell preferred to spend his time not in administration but with students, so he arranged to hire Ethel Colton Smith, Merle's sister, as administrative secretary. She was a canny choice, warm and competent as she dealt with a fair share of student problems from her desk just inside the door of a generous reception area. Ed Lyon continued to relieve Lowell's mind by keeping the books. "I guess I steered the decision-making, policy making," Lowell admitted, "but I spent most of my time elsewhere. I taught a full load and did a lot of counseling, left the door open. I think of myself as a counselor and teacher, number one."[4]

During that first year in the new building, Lowell and Ed opened their circle to admit other colleagues. An attorney and popular seminary teacher, Marion D. Hanks, joined the staff part time. Hanks was called into the First Council of the Seventy (the church's third-ranking group of general authorities) in 1953 at the age of thirty-one but continued part time at the institute. Frank West, impressed by Hanks's seminary teaching at West High School in Salt Lake City, had asked him to go to southern California to open the early morning seminary program there. Hanks refused because, ironically, he "did not want to work for the church full time."[5] "Duff," as he was called by a generation of high school and college students, was a charismatic and vigorous addition to the institute staff and to the church hierarchy. Students especially enjoyed his classes on the Book of Mormon with their emphasis on the equality of humankind.

George T. Boyd was transferred to the Salt Lake institute from the University of California at Berkeley, where he had opened the LDS institute in 1946, also teaching at San Jose and Stanford. He had joined the Church Education System in 1945 in Tempe, Arizona, after teaching in Mesa's public schools and earning an M.A. from the University of Arizona. George, a native Arizonan a year younger than Lowell, had also worked as a CCC education advisor.[6]

Lowell, who was already acquainted with George, welcomed him as a "good thinker, . . . fine scholar and teacher, . . . and a good practicing Christian."[7] George gave no quarter to those who liked their philosophy diluted. His classes on comparative world religions challenged upper-division students, attracting a small but devoted cadre who took pride in keeping up on courses as difficult and stimulating as any "across the street." An avid ping-pong player, he also provided cutthroat competition in the institute's vigorous round-robins. One student recalled seeing Lowell standing patiently near the door holding George's hat and coat: "George, we'll be late for Hebrew," he called out. "Don't bother me," George shot back as he chased the ball once more around the table.

Decades later Marion D. Hanks reminisced about the faculty: "Ed Lyon was an iconoclast in a sense. He wanted to disrupt false notions of history, and he was great with facts and a great man in every way. George Boyd's emphasis was on ideas. . . . I hadn't met a mind quite like that before. . . . Lowell Bennion has influenced me from the beginning with a sense of balance that I admire greatly and which has been augmented through the years."[8]

Even though institute enrollment enlarged and grew more diverse, Lowell's and Ed's goal as directors remained the same: to interact personally with all the students, build safe bridges from the university to the church and from there to the larger world, and help students formulate a lasting philosophy of life. Lowell wanted to show students "the beauty and value of religion itself, trying to make the religious life meaningful and trying to convert them to Mormonism at its best . . . without being standoffish or without demeaning or diminishing other faiths."[9]

The physical facilities included a chapel, library, lounges, record-player, play rooms, lunch rooms, and snack-counter. Lowell saw in all of them an appropriate setting for both a laboratory and a "sanctuary" where young people could test themselves in a relatively "safe" place. He saw hundreds of students choose marriage partners and career paths within its walls and hoped to give them faith that the kingdom of God was within themselves, not in the institute.

Lowell articulated his underlying philosophy in a prepared speech for a humanities/social sciences seminar at the University of Utah that addressed the question: "How Shall We Judge One Religion as 'Better' Than Another?"[10] He declared that science, political science, anthropology, history, or economics is able to "tell us what the world is, where it is heading, where it has been, and where it may go," but not "where we ought to go—for what values we ought to live." The act of comparing religions must begin with religion's "functions in human life." He urged that religion ideally supports "faith, morality, and fellowship." Agreeing with Goethe, "Life divided by human reason leaves a remainder," he cited the human hunger for "some significant meaning or purpose to the whole of one's life." He dealt frankly with the claims of some religionists to be God's "chosen" people. Such a concept "must be made to square with the moral attributes of God, his impartiality and mercy." He also warned against allowing "theological beliefs, institutional interests, [or] aesthetic conviction" to "substitute for moral conviction and action." Lowell summarized: the "best" religion "keeps open the gates to heaven and the doors to human experience in other fields."

After this speech, University of Utah philosophy professor E. E. Ericksen wrote Lowell in glowing praise: "My first impression was to suggest that this paper should be given wide publicity throughout Zion. My second thought . . . Are our people mentally ready? . . . You have given some of us meat, wholesome food, that calls for digestion. Thanks to you; I have faith in you as a stalwart of Zion's youth."[11]

Institute curriculum was tested, revised, and improved as the years went by. Uniquely student-centered, it was geared to the least experienced, yet challenging enough for in-depth discussion. It offered courses in four departments: scriptures (classes in each of the LDS standard works); religious history (Jesus' teachings, world religions, Christian history, and Mormon history); doctrines and practices of the church (Mormon doctrine and philosophy, Restoration theology, Joseph Smith, church service and leadership training, and missionary training); and religion and life (courtship, marriage, and family life).[12] The modest charge of one dollar for institute classes and three dollars for Lambda Delta Sigma membership entitled students to a full program of worship services, dances, and activities. This included a forum for discussing "problems of religion and personal welfare" with the directors through "consultation and group discussions."[13]

The institute was a welcoming, nonjudgmental place for all persuasions, where all could ask provocative questions about faith in their daily lives. There were few tests and no grades. Students earned an hour of credit per semi-weekly course, with eighteen hours required for graduation from the institute program. Lowell or Ed approved—and sometimes suggested—a final project. An English major might be assigned to compile an anthology of poetry for use in worship services; a music major might select records for the worship services or the student lounge.

During the early 1950s the Korean War took some students, while many young men and a few young women served LDS missions. Young women continued to provide much of the institute's energy and creativity, and Lowell's classes on courtship and marriage gaining in popularity.

Nonstudents like Camilla Eyring Kimball and Lowell's aunt, Margaret Lindsay Summerhays, joined a cluster of matrons who became regular attendees. "Rather quiet in class, as they didn't want to interfere with the student process, but . . . refreshing because of their keen interest," recalled Lowell. A number of Mormon young people brought "boyfriends or girlfriends of another faith . . . to meet with us or to attend class." Both baptisms and marriages were common.[14] Ed Lyon took a special interest in ecumenical meetings with other campus religious groups. During the 1950s student Harlan Hammond represented Lambda Delta Sigma "in interfaith meetings with Catholic, Methodist and Baptist students once a month, where we tried to correlate our activities."[15]

Lowell and his colleagues aimed "to bring LDS kids together and get them acquainted on a broad basis, not just a romantic basis."[16] Student committees planned the many dances, parties, and service projects that led to increased interest in each other. In the small library with its fine collection of Mormon books, students studied for courses across the street. Others studied and napped in the lounges between classes while musicians practiced the piano and organ. They listened to records, ate lunch in the downstairs lounge and snack bar, and organized impromptu "cram" sessions for exams.

Lambda Delta Sigma was a mature, national organization which, at the Salt Lake institute, operated with six officers: a (usually male) president, a social vice president, a service vice president, a pledge/initiation vice president, a secretary, and a treasurer.[17] Lowell was their advisor.

Standing committees taught MIA youth and Sunday school classes in hospitals and conducted monthly worship services. Barbara Redford met her future husband, John Cook, at Lambda Delta Sigma where she served as an interchapter officer and as a member of the worship service committee. "So much of our time in the church we don't spend pondering and contemplating," she observed. "Brother Bennion loved music and knew you could say a lot and express religious feeling through good music. He didn't want us to multiply words. He wanted us to read some scriptures, hear some music and think about it. . . . I remember that he read the scriptures as if he loved them. It was the first time I had heard someone actually caress the words."[18] Social activities included non-date "matinee dances, carnivals, snow frolics and masquerades," while dinners and formals produced "fun with refinement, in a beautiful setting."[19]

Son Ben Bennion, a painfully shy student at Granite High School, blossomed when he began attending institute classes as a freshman in 1953. He found himself working on projects, planning social activities and worship services, and dating Sherilyn Cox, his future wife. By year's end he surprised himself by chairing a dance committee.[20]

Service projects were a core element of the institute experience. Rodney Brady, an undergraduate with a bright future as a college president and as CEO of Bonneville International, described a surprise house-painting party for an elderly woman that he coordinated under Lowell's direction.

> One evening approximately one hundred young people descended upon her home armed with all manner of tools, ladders, equipment, and supplies. Three hours later, her yard was totally cleaned and trimmed, her house was painted both inside and outside, her windows and dishes were sparkling clean, her carpets and rugs had been shampooed, and her roof, chimney, and door frames had been repaired and restored to first-class condition. . . . The woman . . . overwhelmed us with appreciation and thanks.

Lowell, who had talked with and reassured her through the entire evening, took her home to spend the night with his family to avoid the paint fumes.[21]

Douglas D. Alder, future president of Utah's Dixie College in the 1980s and 1990s, requested a service project more interesting than Sub-for-Santa. Lowell suggested that Alder's Lambda Delt chapter adopt a family for Christmas.

> That evening after a fine experience of taking gifts to a needy young family, we arrived at the Bennion residence in East Millcreek. Brother Bennion invited us to follow him in our cars. We drove a few blocks to the Ward. There behind the chapel was a small abode. We entered and found a lone elderly man awaiting us, the ward's former custodian. We performed our music as tears ran down his cheeks. Next we drove to a nearby gully, where a shack housed an infirm black couple. We could barely fit inside. We sang and played our Christmas repertoire. I noticed an arrangement of church books on the shelf. Brother Bennion explained that this man, who did not hold the priesthood, had often taught classes in their ward.[22]

Lowell considered Lambda Delta Sigma, with its four men's chapters and seven women's chapters, "our laboratory in which youth was trained in *leadership* and *service* and where fellows and girls associated in a variety of meaningful ways."[23] A former student wrote appreciatively: "It is amazing to me how you can take a person as a freshman or sophomore and in such a short time graduate them as chapter officers, interchapter officers, or trained members and send them out to fill positions in the church organizations."[24]

During this decade Lowell's teaching style emerged from his interpretation of Jesus as Master Teacher: "A good lesson is one idea, organized, illustrated, and applicable to those being taught." To keep hearers interested, Jesus used concrete language, evoked the five senses, and created proverbs and parables that stayed in the mind. Lowell believed that Jesus, the Master Teacher, concentrated not on rules but principles, using "teaching moments from life" focused on a single idea.[25] In courses on religion and faith, he suggested that if rote participation in ordinances had become deadening to one's spirit, "let [the sacrament] go by a couple of times, while you rethink your commitments and turn your heart toward quiet contemplation of Christ." He enlivened the concept of prayer by proposing that the worshipper "concentrate on one good thing that happened that day and be grateful instead of listing a long inventory of requests." In concentrating on one theme, one issue at a time, students were urged to focus on "the things that matter most," a balanced life in a holistic universe.

Lowell's presence in the classroom was low-key, almost casual. Eva Haglund, one of the older off-campus students, marveled at "Lowell's way" of quietly walking into class, as if "he was another student." He would ask, "'Let's see, can you play the piano? Would you conduct the singing?' Somehow the class would coalesce."[26]

Despite the low profile, Lowell's lessons were anything but haphazard. He wrote a syllabus for each course, with ideas outlined for discussion. He created a fertile discussion climate by encouraging questions and comments and tactfully discouraging nonpertinent or impertinent responses. He was always ready to summarize good thinking and to praise thoughtful answers. Well-planned questions formed the foundation of his lessons that built on the experiences and ideas of class members. Albert Payne, who joined the faculty in 1956, termed Lowell a "Socratic" questioner: "Lowell asked questions . . . as if he was really bothered by [the problem]. He had people sitting on the edge of their seats to try to help him get the answer. His genuine interest in the question and in the student and his deep humility must be factors in his success."[27]

Lowell was as willing to learn from students as he was to teach. They praised his "remarkable, supportive openness."[28] He relished a lesson from a medical student, married with children and a surgery residency in his future. "You have a long way to go before you start living, haven't you?" Lowell asked. "Hell, no," the young man replied. "I'm living now." Lowell made a mental note of this refreshing attitude for "older students who thought they were a little behind schedule."[29]

As a student, Eleanor Ricks described herself as a "highly idealistic person with a theology that consisted of repeating little vignettes I'd picked up in my Idaho Sunday school class." Lowell heard her respectfully but startled her by telling her when he disagreed. "If a view you were cherishing was based on a false premise, he minced no words about telling you. . . . It would shake you up but you wouldn't be offended."[30]

Eugene England writes,

> I remember a class at the institute in about 1953 on the nature of God. A student asked why, if God is no respecter of persons, as the scriptures and common sense clearly indicate, a difference existed in God's church between blacks and all others. I immediately answered, as I had been taught all my life, "Well, God is also a God of justice, and since blacks were not valiant in the preexistence, they are cursed with the just consequences." In the discussion following my remark, Brother Bennion . . . simply asked me how I knew blacks had not been valiant. When I had no answer but tradition, he gently suggested that the God revealed in Christ would surely let blacks know what they had done wrong and how they could repent, rather than merely punishing them—and since God had done no such thing, it seemed better to believe that blacks had been, and were, no different spiritually from the rest of us.

England did not feel "put down" by Lowell's response. Instead, "As I thought about this, . . . I came to realize . . . that many of my beliefs . . . were based on flimsy and unexamined evidence."[31]

Lowell often organized task groups, then had them report to the larger class. Although some of his courses had the same titles as those he taught in the 1940s, he had updated them to meet the individual needs of contemporary students. He often told them, "The purpose of life is self-realization and fulfillment for all people . . . to achieve quality living, to enlarge our souls, to meet our potential and to live and be what God made us. The purpose of life is within life, not outside it." Life and afterlife are all part of the same eternal life. The Mormon belief in a celestial kingdom is not a "reward" for "being good." We should not have to sacrifice this life for the next. "THIS life is purposeful, meaningful." If there were no life after this one, this life would still be worth living. Living the gospel and loving others are intrinsically worthwhile, not just stepping stones to a future life.

He took an expansive view of human nature. Intelligence was eternal and free. Co-eternal with God, people must accept responsibility for their own choices, neither blaming God nor the devil. God, in turn, "is good, impartial and NOT responsible for evil. . . . God may have to struggle with and work with nature, as a contractor has to use imperfect materials. . . . God's influence on me is all for good, but he has to work with me and He needs my cooperation."[32]

Elaine M. Castleton could recall Lowell's vivid teaching twenty-five years after her courses at the institute. "Using himself as an example," she recalled, "he said that if his wife had loved him only for his curly hair, 'where would we be now?'"[33] (Lowell was almost bald by 1940.) She remembered his telling how his son had picked a ripe-looking peach but threw it away after one bite because it was hard and bitter. Lowell compared the process of pruning, spraying, and fertilizing the tree to the slow maturation of friendship instead of the hasty demands of immature, romantic love.[34] Castleton added, "I used to puzzle in class about the *glow* emanating from his face, couldn't quite decide whether it was 'otherworldly' or the reflection of the lights on his head, but light there was and it filled me."[35]

Lowell's influence did not stop when students left the institute. Several missionaries reported that they were using Lowell's books along with the scriptures as missionary tools. W. Herbert Klopfer wrote from Lowell's mission field in Lucerne, "My training at the institute has done more for me in preparing me for my mission than any other place, including what my own ward has done."[36] A student wrote to say that she was teaching from his manual in her new ward. A former student serving in the Air Force "took your advice and tried to get some European culture, the Sadler Wells Ballet, the Opera, a visit to Hyde Park."[37] One couple, who had met at the institute, wrote from Japan asking for advice about helping a homeless family they had befriended.[38] Departed students wrote to announce engagements, sharing news about the births of children, or to ask for letters of recommendation. Parents begged him to check on student children; countless numbers wrote for clarification on doctrine.

Student response to Lowell's teaching and personality was, for the most part, profoundly positive. Friendships, marriages, and study groups were part of the long-term legacy of the close relationships that began at "the Toot" (institute). Some of these clubs and study groups were still meeting in the 1980s and 1990s. Elaine and Robert Castleton, their family raised, volunteered to teach in the Peace Corps in the Solomon Islands in 1989, a decision Elaine attributed in part to Lowell's influence a quarter of a century earlier.

Educational historian Fred Buchanan felt that Lowell had met him at the "roads diverging in the wood," when Buchanan was on the verge of jettisoning his Mormon values. Lowell discussed troublesome issues freely with the young man, made him "want to stay in the church," and "sent a flame to my conscience" by stressing the "moral dimension" of living religion. "Going to the institute was more than just getting my religious beliefs reinforced," he summarized. "It was an expansive and adventuresome experience."[39]

Garry Shirts, a freshman in 1952, thought Lowell Bennion could probably "walk on water" if he wanted to. Shirts's response was typical of the reaction of hundreds of Lowell's students, especially the young men and women who had either lost their fathers or whose fathers were inactive in the church. After a "moderately glamorous career at Box Elder High School," Shirts was disoriented at being just another freshman and, more seriously, seeing for the first time in his life "an alternative explanation of the way the universe worked." Lowell steadied him through this crisis of faith by providing him with an interpretation of Mormonism that made his religious faith more than a cultural system—one that was intellectually and spiritually stimulating. "It added zest and excitement to my life." As a result, Shirts said he

> came as close to worshiping him as any person could. I can still remember his distinctive gait, the way he stooped over when he walked, the look on his face when he sat on the back bench of the institute deep in thought and meditation. The look on his face during those times of worship seemed to be the personification of humility and piety. I took every class I could from him. . . . I engaged him in conversation whenever I had the opportunity. I talked about his ideas to my friends and relatives. I couldn't get enough of him.[40]

When Cozette Williams began dating Garry, she was somewhat put off by the fact that "he couldn't talk about anything but Brother Bennion" and was downright repelled by the ABC system of dating. This was Lowell's favorite dating system in which the young person would date two or more friends at the same time, dropping those where there was no progress in the relationship. "Garry and his friends would all compare notes," she complained.

"It was terribly demeaning. I told Garry I didn't want any part of Brother Bennion's ABC system. It felt like a system to help a group of young men pick out the best heifer." She also felt that Lowell regarded young women differently from young men.

> I came from the farm where the women were an integral part of the economic system. It took two people full time to make the farm work. My dad has great respect for my mother and considers her a full partner. Garry treated me that way, but Brother Bennion treated me as a person who had no stake in what was going on. It was not that he was openly hostile or said anything unkind, but there was clearly a place for me and it had pots and pans hanging on the walls.[41]

Lowell may have sensed distance from Cozette, but she never took his classes, and she chose not to share her views with him. Other women students believed the ABC method applied equally to them. Although men were nearly always the ones to do the inviting, Lowell encouraged young women to realize their right to say no and to choose their own company. Darline Anderson remembered that "Brother B. . . . organized both men and women with no discrimination at all, as it is taught and discussed today."[42]

In a leadership class Lowell asked students to write a constructive criticism for each member of the class, including himself. One student wrote, "Why don't you show the same interest in *all* of us that you do in *some* of us?" Lowell's belief in his own democracy was shaken, and he resolved to try harder to reach each individual.[43] He was sincere in his introduction to his popular manual, *The Religion of the Latter-day Saints,* "Any criticisms offered by teachers or students will be gratefully received."

Beyond the classroom, Lowell communicated steadfast interest and trust in his students as individuals. A troubled young man might be invited for Sunday dinner and the therapy of afternoon football on the back lawn with the young Bennion and Lyon boys.

As an example of the personal interest Lowell took in students, DuWayne Schmidt, a medical student, was injured so severely in an auto accident that he lost two years of schooling. "When I was suffering in the old county hospital with multiple fractures, Brother Bennion would appear several times a week. I'd ask, 'How did you get in?' And he said, 'I just told them I am Dr.

Bennion.' He would sneak in and hold my hand and visit and inspire me to struggle on."[44]

One young man, who had seen his father killed while crossing a highway, attended Lowell's classes for a year, then served a mission. Still troubled after his release, he was advised to see a psychiatrist. Lowell made the appointment with a competent man; but after a few sessions the young man came back. "I just want to talk with *you*," he said. Lowell listened to him, then asked him to serve on a committee "where he mingled with boys and girls, planned functions, and got into Lambda Delt." The combination of social activity and counseling "really pulled him out of it. He married and taught seminary and had a big family and got along fine."[45]

A young woman student, who credited her career as a clinical psychologist to Lowell's counseling techniques, praised his ability to

> take the whole cosmos and bring it down to where you could at least take a look at it and figure out what to do. Somehow he had the ability to bring everything into focus. . . . Wherever you went, he broadened the path a little bit, kicked a few leaves out of the path for you so it was a little clearer than it was before. I don't know anyone who came away from an encounter with him without feeling enhanced and empowered.[46]

One student asked him, "I have two proposals of marriage. Which one should I take?" Prepared to describe each young man and his characteristics, she stopped at Lowell's question: "What makes you think you should marry either one? You can choose not to choose, you know." Lowell's finely honed socratic method cut through a false dilemma. Lowell saved himself hours and hours of listening.

Lowell seldom overreached. When, in his regular counseling sessions with Lowell, Fred Buchanan began struggling with complex personal problems, Lowell promptly told him, "I can't help you there," and helped him find a professional counselor. Buchanan appreciated Lowell's willingness to withdraw from what was out of his range.[47]

The crowning recognition of Lowell's counseling and teaching techniques came in spring 1958 when President David O. McKay drove to the institute in his Cadillac and asked Lowell to speak in the priesthood session of the upcoming general conference. The topic: the dangers of going steady "too soon and too much." In a confidential tone the president declared, "They won't listen to us old fuddy-duddies, so I want you to talk at priesthood conference and tell them how to date." When Lowell offered to submit his speech ahead of time for approval, McKay gestured dismissively, "No, you know more about it than I do."[48] Lowell decided to define marriage as "more than romanticized recreation. Marriage is more than dates and affection. True, romantic love is part of marriage, a very beautiful part; but . . . marriage is also a business and financial partnership . . . an everyday and all day continuous companionship between husband and wife. This is one of the beautiful aspects of it. It is also the realistic part."[49]

In addition to his direct experience with students, Lowell's circle of influence expanded through his publications. In 1955 he published his most influential manual, *An Introduction to the Gospel.* This systematic description of basic doctrine and church practices was used in Sunday school classes throughout the church until the late 1960s. "You know, Jesus spoke profound thoughts in simple language," Lowell would later muse. Lowell's goal was that "an investigator or an old-time member could both look at my definition of humility and hopefully understand it."[50]

Lowell served on the church's M-Men/Gleaner Committee of the general board (1955-60), traveling to stake conferences throughout the church. His upbeat MIA manual *Goals for Living* (1952, reprinted in 1962), reached LDS youth until 1969 and asked such questions as, "How long has it been since I arose with a thrill to greet the dawn? When did I last kneel in prayer, overwhelmed with gratitude for the gift of life?" And "What are some of the things which cause people to lose faith in life?"[51] In 1959 the Church Education System published his *Introduction to the Book of Mormon and Its Teachings,* while in the same year church-owned Deseret Book Company brought out *Religion and the Pursuit of Truth,* an exposition of Lowell's belief that a harmonious philosophy of life can be composed from a balance of art, philosophy, science, religion, and daily experience. This was one of his most popular courses in book form. He also wrote scores of articles in church magazines, and his ideas on missionary work were published by the Church Education System.

Literary critic Eugene England appraises Lowell's writings as giving Mormon theology an "elegant intellectual shape . . . revealing its powerful moral implications." They "reflect [Lowell's] characteristic struggle against the tendency to 'pulverize' the gospel, to analyze and defend and explain it in small chunks that may have no logical connection and may, in fact, contradict each other." He declared that Lowell's books demonstrate "the coherent moral and spiritual force available in Mormon thought."[52] Edward L. Kimball, professor of law at BYU and son of Spencer W. Kimball, recalled from his student days that Lowell's approach as a writer was "just right for me. It was one that gave full credit to the intellect and yet had the interplay and overlay of faith."[53]

Lowell's books and articles grew naturally out of his class work and his speaking engagements, grounding his writing in a strong sense of audience. Son Steve called him an "itinerant preacher," much in demand at church and community meetings on a wide range of issues. He spoke at many high school and college graduations, at BYU gatherings, and at other institutes where he sometimes gave courses. He frequently addressed interdisciplinary or ecumenical groups on the University of Utah campus, trained other LDS teachers, and spoke to such community groups as PTAs, the Utah Association of School Counselors, and "Religion-in-Life" weeks at other universities. He spoke on the radio, moderated television programs, and delivered countless funeral sermons, his unsentimental yet comforting theology easing the pain of loss by giving hope to the living.

Meanwhile, on the home front Lowell's life continued hectic and happy as Merle competently mothered their four sons. Howard loved animals, especially the horse given him by his Uncle Len Folsom, which he rode almost daily. Ben, the designated irrigator, escaped the chore of daily milking that Doug, Steve, and Howard all assumed in turn, starting about age ten. Lowell worked with his sons nearly every Saturday, spring through autumn, sometimes unwinding with them on the weekends at a University of Utah football or basketball game. Ben, both uncomfortable and proud of being Lowell's son at the institute, greatly enjoyed their conversations while driving to and from the university—more father-and-son contact than Ben remembers except for "working in the yard." Lowell encouraged Ben to become a scientist but also cautioned him when he expressed an interest in teaching in the Church Education System. "Even then, in the 1950s, the institute teachers were under fire at times," Ben recalled. "I think he felt restricted."[54] It was a shadow on the horizon.

Lowell and Merle's last child, Ellen, born in the summer of 1952, came twenty years after Laurel's birth. Lowell wrote later in his "Memories":

> On the way to the hospital in our old red Chevy pickup, I stopped and said to Merle, "Get this into your head, my dear; this is going to be another boy."
>
> She said, "Okay, but get me to the hospital."[55]
>
> When I saw Merle after Ellen's birth, she was almost delirious with joy. She cried, "I did it, I did it, I did it!" Ellen's birth made history among our family, friends, and students. She came late, a gift of grace, and well-equipped with a quick mind and skillful hands."[56]

That same year, Cora Bennion, Lowell's mother, was named Utah Mother of the Year, honored by the governor and a trip to New York with Maurine for the national proceedings.[57] The next year Milton Bennion, Lowell's earliest and most enduring model, grew increasingly ill. In the summer of 1951 continued circulation problems caused by diabetes required the amputation of Milton's left leg above the knee. He was not strong enough to recuperate fully and steadily declined for two more years.

During the long hospitalization of his final illness, Milton received a priesthood blessing from Lowell and, with his family in constant attendance, enjoyed visits from numerous friends. As Milton's lethargy deepened, he still roused himself for President J. Reuben Clark's daily visits, shaking hands and responding in a strong voice, "I'm doing fine, thank you!"[58]

Milton and J. Reuben Clark, classmates at the University of Utah and members of the first fraternity in Utah (Delta Phi) in the 1880s and 1890s, often held opposing views on politics and religious education.[59] When Milton was Sunday school general superintendent, Clark blasted higher criticism as "calculated to destroy the simple faith of our people," stated that church schools should eliminate "all such teachings," and accused curriculum writers of "never really delv[ing] into our own church history or doctrines."[60] Milton, knowing both the knowledge-base and commitment of most church teachers and writers, could not agree.

Though mistrusting Milton's "progressivism," Clark respected his intellectual integrity and faith. Milton's last rally, then, was for a church leader who had become a compassionate friend. Milton died with a smile on his face on Easter Sunday, April 5, 1953, according to Lowell's brother Vaughn, who stood watch. At Milton's funeral at the Assembly Hall on Temple Square, David O. McKay, George R. Hill, Arthur Beeley, and E. E. Ericksen were the speakers. Friends and family immediately formed the Milton Bennion Memorial Foundation which funded an annual Rotary Club lecture and a distinguished education lecture at the University of Utah, then switched to sponsoring an annual scholarship in educational administration.

Lowell summed up his father's character: "Father combined in unusual fashion a profound understanding of the ethical life, based on his study of both religion and philosophy, and the ability to live in harmony with his learning and teaching. He was never known to act dishonestly or selfishly by his family or associates."[61] It was an ethical compass that Lowell had also internalized.

Lowell would greatly miss his running dialogue with his father on politics and ethics. Milton had scrupulously avoided volunteering personal advice, a rule he broke only once. During the 1940s both the philosophy and sociology departments at the University of Utah offered Lowell appointments. Milton, perhaps aware of intensifying opposition to his son's approach, advised Lowell to transfer. "I did not take his advice," commented Lowell simply. "I was having too good a time at the institute."[62]

Notes

1. Lowell L. Bennion, Oral History, 148.

2. James B. Allen and Glen M. Leonard, *The Story of the Latter-day Saints* (Salt Lake City: Desert Book Co., 1976), 541.

3. Ibid. Church growth exploded in the 1970s, 1980s, 1990s. Ricks College became a four-year college because of state laws requiring a four-year degree for teacher credentials. See *Church Almanac 1995-1996* (Salt Lake City: Deseret News, 1995), 420.

4. Lowell L. Bennion, Oral History, 122.

5. David B. Rimington, *Vista on Visions: A Golden Anniversary History of Church Education in Southern California* (Los Angeles: Department of Church Education of Southern California, May 1988), 22.

6. James B. Allen, Dale C. LeCheminant, and David J. Whittaker, comps. and eds., *Views on Man and Religion: Collected Essays of George T. Boyd* (Provo, UT: Friends of George T. Boyd, 1979), iii-iv.

7. Lowell L. Bennion, Oral History, 104.

8. Marion D. Hanks, "A Tribute to Lowell L. Bennion," in "The Triumph of Spirit: A Tribute to Lowell L. Bennion," B. H. Roberts Society, Salt Lake City, 9 Oct. 1986, audiotape in Bradford's possession.

9. Lowell L. Bennion, Oral History, 107.

10. Lowell L. Bennion, "How Shall We Judge One Religion As 'Better' Than Another?" Address to humanities-social sciences seminar, University of Utah, 7 Feb. 1956, 1, photocopy of typescript in Bradford's possession. Subsequent quotations from this speech are on pp. 3, 6, and 8.

11. E. E. Ericksen to Lowell Bennion, 4 Jan. 1958, photocopy in Bradford's possession.

12. Institute of Religion, "Announcement of Program," leaflets for school years, ca. 1950s, in Bradford's possession.

13. Ibid.

14. Lowell L. Bennion, Oral History, 107.

15. Harlan Y. Hammond, interviewed by Mary L. Bradford, 19 Feb. 1988.

16. Lowell L. Bennion, Oral History, 107.

17. Lowell L. Bennion to Donna Hunter, 25 Aug. 1954, photocopy in Bradford's possession.

18. Barbara Redford Cook, interviewed by Mary L. Bradford, 7 May 1988.

19. *Lambda Delta Sigma*, brochure (Salt Lake City: Institute of Religion, 1954), 1, photocopy in Bradford's possession.

20. Lowell Colton (Ben) Bennion, interviewed by Mary L. Bradford, 7 May 1988.

21. Rodney Brady, Diary, summer 1951, typescript, 100, photocopy in Bradford's possession.

22. Douglas D. Alder, "Lowell L. Bennion, The Things that Matter Most," *Teachers Who Touch Lives*, comp. Philip L. Barlow (Bountiful, UT: Horizon Publishers, 1988), 23-24.

23. Lowell L. Bennion, "Lambda Delta Sigma—to Mary," 19 Sept.

1988, handwritten notes in Bradford's possession.

24. Dorene Rushforth Jones to Lowell L. Bennion, "Thanksgiving Day," 1956, photocopy in Bradford's possession.

25. Lowell L. Bennion, comments on "My Art of Teaching," 4 Oct. 1987, handwritten notes in Bradford's possession. He compiled his ideas about teaching in a small book, *Jesus, the Master Teacher* (Salt Lake City: Deseret Book Co., 1980).

26. Eva Haglund, as quoted by her daughter, Elizabeth Haglund, interviewed by Mary L. Bradford, 3 Feb. 1990.

27. Albert Payne, interviewed by Mary L. Bradford, 7 Feb. 1988.

28. Eva Haglund, as quoted by Elizabeth Haglund, 3 Feb. 1990.

29. Lowell L. Bennion, *Jesus, the Master Teacher*, 116.

30. Eleanor Ricks Colton, interviewed by Mary L. Bradford, 24 Aug. 1989. She later married Merle's cousin, Sterling Colton, son of Hugh Colton.

31. Eugene England, "Introduction: The Achievement of Lowell L. Bennion," *The Best of Lowell L. Bennion* (Salt Lake City: Deseret Book Co., 1988), xiv.

32. "Lowell Bennion Class," notes kept by Louis and Mavonne Moench, in Bradford's possession.

33. Elaine M. Castleton to Mary L. Bradford, 10 June 1989.

34. Ibid. Lowell used the same comparison in "Seek Ye Wisdom," address to the priesthood session of general conference, *Report of the Semi-Annual Conference of The Church of Jesus Christ of Latter-day Saints*, 6 Apr. 1968 (Salt Lake City: Church of Jesus Christ of Latter-day Saints, 1968), 94-99.

35. Ibid., emphasis Castleton's.

36. W. Herbert Klopfer to Lowell L. Bennion, 17 Dec. 1956, photocopy in Bradford's possession.

37. Calvin Ashton to Lowell L. Bennion, photocopy in Bradford's possession.

38. Diane and Earl Benedict to Lowell L. Bennion, 14 July 1955.

39. Frederick S. Buchanan, interviewed by Mary L. Bradford, 9 Feb. 1988.

40. Garry and Cozette Shirts to Mary L. Bradford, 20 Feb. 1991.

41. Ibid.

42. Darline Anderson to Mary L. Bradford, 19 Feb. 1989.

43. Lowell L. Bennion, Oral History, 116; emphasis added.

44. DuWayne Schmidt, interviewed by Mary L. Bradford, 15 May 1988.

45. Lowell L. Bennion, Oral History, 148. In an interview with Mary L. Bradford on 13 February 1988, Lowell had this version: "I arranged for Dr. Moench to see him. He came in and said, 'I don't want to go to a psychiatrist. Could I come and talk with you?' So, I said, sure and he came and we visited. And then I put him on a committee. He mingled with fellows and girls on a social comm. and it was the combination and counseling and experience. I learned to combine them."

46. Carole Tuttle Lansdowne, interviewed by Mary L. Bradford, 30 May 1988.

47. Frederick Buchanan, interviewed by Mary L. Bradford, 18 Feb. 1988.

48. Lowell L. Bennion, Oral History, 126.

49. Lowell L. Bennion, "Toward a Happier Marriage," *The Instructor* 93 (June 1958): 166-69; *Conference Report,* 5 Apr. 1958, 83-87.

50. Lowell L. Bennion, Oral History, 141.

51. Lowell L. Bennion, *Goals for Living* (Salt Lake City: Church of Jesus Christ of Latter-day Saints, 1953), 14-15. The manual's success prompted the MIA to give him an honorary Master M-Man Award for 1952-53, usually earned by Mormon men before the age of thirty for service, gospel scholarship, and recreational activities. The nomination read, "No man can ever tell what tremendous force for good Elder Bennion has exerted in the lives of young men and women who have come to him in doubt and perplexity and left stronger in faith and determination to walk uprightly before their Lord." The citation also honored him for "anonymous acts of daily kindness" showing "how completely Lowell Bennion established his own true Latter-day Saint 'Goals for Living.'" Unidentified and undated newspaper clipping in possession of Merle C. Bennion.

52. Eugene England, "Introduction," *The Best of Lowell L. Bennion,* xxiii.

53. Edward L. Kimball, interviewed by Mary L. Bradford, 18 May 1988.

54. Lowell Colton (Ben) Bennion, interviewed by Mary L. Bradford, 7 May 1988.

55. Lowell L. Bennion, "Memories," 130, photocopy in Bradford's possession.

56. Lowell L. Bennion, Oral History, 121.

57. "Cora Bennion, Mother of the Year," *Salt Lake Tribune,* 13 Apr. 1952, B-12.

58. Vaughn Bennion, telephone interview by Mary L. Bradford, 4 Aug. 1990.

59. William G. Hartley, "The Delta Phi Debating and Literary Society and Utah's First Fraternity, 1869-1904," *Utah Historical Quarterly* 60 (Fall 1992): 364. Milton served as its president.

60. Quoted in D. Michael Quinn, *J. Reuben Clark: The Church Years* (Provo, UT: Brigham Young University Press, 1983), 176.

61. Lowell L. Bennion, "Foreword," in Milton Bennion, *Memoirs of Milton Bennion* (Salt Lake City: Milton Bennion Family, 1966), i.

62. Lowell L. Bennion, Oral History, 94. Waldemar Reed, chair of the Department of Philosophy, expressed regret at Lowell's refusal, adding: "I think you have done a great work where you are, . . . a work that not many others would see the need of doing." Waldemar Reed to Lowell L. Bennion, 7 Feb. 1946, typescript copy in Bradford's possession.

CHAPTER 7

The Unified Church Education System (1953-62)

At a conference of institute and BYU religious faculty, I . . . told the group . . . I thought we should not ask our students . . . to choose between their religion and their science.

—Lowell L. Bennion

Ernest L. Wilkinson became president of Brigham Young University in 1951, an event that institute teachers practically overlooked in their excitement about David O. McKay's calling as church president the same year. Wilkinson, a successful attorney in Washington, D.C., with no previous experience in school administration, was recommended by influential church leaders in Washington, D.C., whose number included Apostle Ezra Taft Benson, President Dwight D. Eisenhower's Secretary of Agriculture and future president of the LDS church.[1]

Wilkinson took hold of BYU immediately, formulating major plans for BYU's expansion based on projected burgeoning church population.[2] Even as new institutes and seminaries opened in places like Edmonton, Los Angeles, and Reno, Wilkinson was constructing a plan for new junior colleges that would replace most existing Church Education System programs in the American West. His plans for institutes would have far-reaching effects on Lowell, his family, and friends.[3]

In June 1953 the entire Church Education System was brought under Wilkinson as administrator (changed to "chancellor" in 1960).[4] Wilkinson's "unification" program led to Franklin West's retirement as Church Commissioner of Education in June 1953 at the age of sixty-eight. President McKay met with him and, according to West, in a brisk "minute and a half" informed him that his services "would soon be discontinued." West's only protest was the mild statement, "You know, I've run the department of education for eighteen years so smoothly that you didn't even know you had a department."[5] McKay acknowledged the point as he ushered West out, promising that West's retirement benefits would be upgraded (a compensation delayed until 1957).

When the *Church News* announced the change, it praised West's years of service that had produced sixty-two new seminaries and institutes in six states and Canada to serve 15,000 students.[6] Two days after the public announcement Wilkinson thanked West by letter for eighteen years of "successful piloting," assuring him that he, Wilkinson, "never expected" to be head of institutes and seminaries.[7] Publicly, he announced that the unified system would solve earlier problems of "trouble and discord."[8] West privately termed this reference as "just ridiculous."[9]

Still a vigorous athlete, West was not ready for retirement. As he sorted through his years as commissioner for reasons for his dismissal, he realized that some general authorities had resisted his successful efforts to negotiate retirement and social security benefits for church teachers in the late 1930s. He recalled that differences with President McKay were always on inconsequential matters, and he had never felt out of favor. Although J. Reuben Clark disapproved of much of his work, he had remained cordial. Certainly Adam S. Bennion and Harold B. Lee, both educators, had been supportive. Nearly everything he requested had been granted.[10] West believed that "there was a little feeling because I was a scientist, that I couldn't be an honest-to-goodness sound believer in the church's theology."[11] That Wilkinson doubted West's orthodoxy is shown in a diary entry two years later, when Wilkinson released the supervisor of all seminiaries. He noted that the "Executive Committee is suspicious of anyone associated with Dr. West."[12]

Wilkinson's authorized biography gives the impression that West retired of his own accord: "Because Dr. Franklin West retired from his position of Commissioner of Education at the same time Wilkinson was appointed, the transition to the new program was quite simple."[13] Wilkinson then appointed a man of administrative competence who was also a friend to Lowell and Ed Lyon—

William E. Berrett (also called Ed), already Wilkinson's vice president for religious instruction at BYU, a position he continued to hold as he became director of the seminary and institute system.[14] Berrett and Wilkinson then reappointed J. Karl Wood as institute supervisor with Joy F. Dunyon over seminaries, both "West men."

Two months after "unification" Wilkinson opened a week-long summer convention of Church Education System teachers and leaders with an aggressive defense of his program. He stated that BYU had previously been "pitted" against the institutes; that some institute instructors had advised students against attending BYU; and that some "wives have been more vocal . . . and more indiscreet" than the teachers themselves. This "unjustified feeling of rivalry between the church school and institutes," he explained, would be obliterated by the unification of the church system "so that each will better see the problems of the others."[15] Relentlessly he laid out his argument for "where Christianity in its most vital sense can be taught most effectively." Defining the institutes as "created to impart and preserve the faith of their fathers," Wilkinson lumped them with Sunday and auxiliary church programs as supplemental to the training of young LDS men and women. He conceded that they had "touched deeply the lives of many Latter-day Saint students" and cost only a fraction of a BYU student's education but accused them of failing "to reach the majority of young LDS men and women attending their affiliated universities."

In fact, the ideal was for Mormon students to attend "our church schools"—BYU and Ricks College in Rexburg, Idaho—"except when there are definite reasons for them attending other universities." The church schools would protect students from "mental conflicts" that might lead to apostasy, provide "a richer, more intensive offering" of courses, and guarantee social activities that would provide "much more opportunity for . . . proper mating."

He announced that LDS students should transfer to BYU if their classes allowed smoking in classrooms, if faculty members were hostile to Mormonism or were "jack-Mormon" (inactive), if marriage rates between Mormons and "outsiders" were high, and if the university were reluctant to grant credit for institute courses. These conditions could be translated as criticisms of the University of Utah on virtually every count. Not only would the church formally encourage students at such schools to transfer, he said, but instructors were expected to counsel prospective students according to "the policy I have here enunciated." He invited his audience to offer suggestions but with a caveat: "After those suggestions are made and decisions are finally resolved, we shall then ask you to be loyal in the performance of the determined policies."[16]

This was a dramatic shift away from Franklin West's freewheeling policies. It seemed clear to Lowell and Ed Lyon that Wilkinson was misinformed. Many instructors within CES had turned down more lucrative positions to remain at the institutes. BYU's activities were of little consequence to the Salt Lake institute except for jointly organized conferences and conventions—which had always been mutually productive and pleasant. Ed and Lowell could not validate the claim that students would be less troubled at church schools, receive richer course offerings, or engage in higher quality courting, but they felt confident about both the quality of their courses *and* their social activities.

A banquet to honor Frank West climaxed the week's activities. As one of the speakers, Lowell thanked West for the "free and open discussions in all of our meetings of religious and administrative problems." Ed Lyon, who had spearheaded a collection for a television set complete with a service policy, made the presentation speech and closed with one of West's sayings: "Give me a little more taffy when I am with you and a little less epitaffy after I am gone."[17]

West's response was warm, appreciative, and accepting of the status quo. A year later he wrote Lowell a nostalgic letter of regret: "I think I could have carried on easily for another ten years in the big work but others made that decision. I had my innings and time at the bat. Sooner or later someone else must carry the ball. I miss our faculty meetings. There was such freedom and [they] were so stimulating." Then he gave Lowell a word of encouragement and caution: "You must continue to be patient and carry on in the very wonderful way as in the past. The students will never forget the great help you are being to them in putting their faith on a firm basis."[18]

Clearly Wilkinson was pursuing a two-pronged strategy in dealing with the Salt Lake institute. He unfavorably compared it to others in terms of numbers of graduates, credit awarded, and the orthodoxy of its instructors. And he used transfers and leaves to isolate Lowell and Ed while he mustered support for his vision of church education.

Part of Wilkinson's vision was to replace the institutes, as far as practical, with LDS junior colleges as feeder schools for BYU. Wilkinson convinced general authorities in 1958 to buy a site in California; and in 1959 he announced, much to the consternation of University of Utah president A. Ray Olpin, that the church would build a new junior college in Salt Lake City.[19] He also alarmed educators at Ricks College in Idaho by reducing the school to a two-year college and proposing that it be moved from Rexburg to Idaho Falls. He lost headway, however, when church leaders later skeptically eyed the comparative price tags of junior colleges and institutes, first scaling back their plans, then abandoning them altogether. Wilkinson termed this failure his greatest disappointment next to losing a 1964 bid for the United States Senate.[20] At BYU he continually stressed the need for "loyal" instructors, keeping complaint files on "liberal" faculty members who lectured on such mild topics as unionism, and eventually planted student spies in the classes of some suspect professors.[21]

In 1954, as Wilkinson prepared for the CES summer school, he proposed to the Board of Education that "consideration be given to a number of the institute teachers, such as Lowell Bennion[,] . . . to be transferred to the religion faculty at the BYU."[22] The next month he reported to the executive committee that only twenty-nine students had graduated from the Salt Lake institute, while a hundred had graduated from Utah State University in Logan. The committee instructed Wilkinson to take up the problem "with Brother Bennion and with officials at the University."[23] Two weeks later Wilkinson suggested that all complaints to general authorities about the Church Education System be referred directly to him. The executive committee agreed, and Wilkinson went on to charge that the low numbers of graduates from the Salt Lake City institute reflected "the lack of administrative support from the University as compared with very strong support at Utah State."[24] During the summer, Wilkinson reported, 4,839 LDS students were attending the University of Utah but only 1,114 were enrolled at the institute. The executive committee authorized him to ask Salt Lake City stake presidents "whether certain teachers were responsible" for the lower numbers.[25]

One month later Wilkinson had gathered a "list of teachers who have critical attitudes," a list that included George Boyd, Bennion, and Lyon[26]; and in December he instructed Berrett to keep a file on "the right of individual members to not always agree as to doctrine." His personal position was that "there is a wide difference between the right of one to have different beliefs and the right to teach those beliefs in a church setting."[27]

When 200 Church Education System instructors and directors convened in the first session of their convention at the end of June 1954, the *Church News* billed the event as "graduate courses in religion . . . first-hand instruction from . . . General Authorities." Harold B. Lee, an apostle and member of the Board of Education executive committee, was in charge of three weeks on "Advanced Theology," with "personal lectures" by J. Reuben Clark, Jr., Joseph Fielding Smith, Adam S. Bennion, Marion G. Romney, and Henry D. Moyle—in short, the entire executive committee of the Church Board of Education. The second session, "Problems in Teaching Religion," was conducted by William E. Berrett and Joy F. Dunyon.[28]

Lowell had no idea that on August 2, before the opening of the second session, Wilkinson had sent Berrett a memo outlining his campaign against the Salt Lake institute: "In spite of a little impatience on the part of some members of my executive committee I was given permission NOT to disturb the status quo of teachers at the SLC institute this coming Fall. I promised, however, that both you and I would sit down with stake presidents and also with the teachers themselves and we would have very definite recommendations to make during the next year."[29]

Lowell, Ed, and George attended only the last week of the final session under Berrett, described by Wilkinson's diary as an "open session" on August 24. According to Wilkinson, Apostle Mark E. Petersen delivered a "very fine" discourse of two hours and twenty minutes on "revelation."[30] After this address, in response to a question Petersen defended the exclusion of black men from LDS priesthood ordination. He asked, "Is it not a reasonable belief that the Lord would select the choice spirits for the better grades of nations?" Asserting that he knew of "no scripture having to do with the removal of the curse from the Negro," he advised the instructors not to "speculate" about it, acknowledged that Negroes should have the "highest education" available and "drive a Cadillac if they can afford it." But "'what God hath joined together, let not man put asunder' can be reversed to read, 'what God hath separated, let not man bring together again.'"[31]

At this point Lowell rose and spoke from the floor: "This problem is about the most persistent that we have in our university." He confessed his difficulty in satisfying students' concerns, thanked Petersen for raising questions, and asked to raise several of his own. He then told of a student of mixed ancestry for whom David O. McKay had intervened to allow a temple marriage for his sister (see chap. 9). At this point Berrett tried to interrupt, but Lowell persisted: "I'm afraid I won't get my hand recognized again, Brother Berrett." He told of a second student who had posed a poignant question. "'If the Negroes sinned, what sin could they commit for which a merciful God'—as you speak of, Brother Petersen—'would not be willing to forgive, if they repented . . . with a contrite heart and a broken spirit?'" A third student had showed him a passage in the Doctrine and Covenants establishing that "all spirits are born in innocence." Was it fair, either from a human or a divine perspective, Lowell asked, to brand blacks as somehow deserving their exclusion because of undocumented choices in the preexistence?[32] (It is impossible to reconstruct the meeting from available sources after this point.)

The next morning, August 28, Joseph Fielding Smith spoke for two hours on his recently published book, *Man, His Origin and Destiny*,[33] repeating many of the points in previous classes at the summer session. He insisted on the view that the earth was only 6,000 years old and that no one and nothing had died before Adam and Eve's transgression. He concluded, "I hope you take what I'm saying [literally], because if you don't you have no business in the church school system."[34]

This issue represented an old struggle for Lowell and other institute teachers. Lowell always operated from the premise that forcing students "to choose between things that are on the periphery of religion and things at the heart of the gospel"—the ethical life and loving service—was a mistake, sometimes of tragic dimensions. Again he rose and spoke from the floor, "I'm interested not only in the questions discussed here, but in how to put them across to our students so that they may keep faith in the gospel. . . . I'd like to take just a minute or two to confess my faith in my method to see if it's sound in your opinion, President Smith."

Lowell said his original method as a young teacher had been "to pit religion against science and defend religion," but maturity had shown him that that "it wasn't very successful in terms of building faith and converting people." He added ruefully, "I didn't know enough, in the first place, about science to be authoritative." He had learned "another method," which he also described as "a confession of my faith." Lowell then bore witness to the existence of God, the divinity of Christ and his teachings, and the prophetic mission of Joseph Smith. He continued:

> Now I have been trying in recent years to concentrate on these convictions with my students. [If] there are things in science, . . . men's interpretation of evolution for example, that in any way contradict these basic gospel truths, I defend the faith against those ideas, against the notion that there is no God behind the creative process, or that Christ was not the son of God, or that man is not immortal and the son of God.
>
> But when it comes down to details like the exact process of how God created Adam on this earth and brought forth things on the earth, I say in the name of religion we don't know, and also that science has not come far enough along to be convinced either. . . . From either standpoint we don't have the final answer. However, I try not to get the student agitated against science, get him prejudiced against geology, and get him to feel that he has to choose between some science and the gospel of Jesus Christ. Rather I do everything in my power to help them believe in the gospel and respect the scientific method, but be critical of its findings.

Lowell pointed out that physicist Henry Eyring, geologist Fred J. Pack, and other Mormon scientists disagreed with Smith's view, tactfully leaving out general authorities like James Talmage, John Widtsoe, and even David O. McKay. In essence, he was arguing for diversity of thought and theory among the faithful.

"President Smith," he asked, "am I justified in teaching as fundamentals of the gospel of religion the laws of faith in Christ and the church, doing the best I can in these fields, and teaching my students to keep an open mind in those things that are not wholly unified or absolutely sure, [in order] to hold those young people (who may believe in the geological age of the earth) to the church?"

Apostle Smith responded at length. He was willing to "leave the age of earth alone." Then he focused on areas of "definite revelations," including teachers' "absolute duty" to teach that Adam was "not a descendant of a monkey." He then added flatly, "I just stated the facts as the Lord revealed them. There they are. And if I were a teacher, I wouldn't put any other kind of notion in the minds of the students."

George Boyd took the floor next.[35] "Brother Petersen, in our first meeting, you suggested a criterion by which we judge when a pronouncement is authoritative from officials of the church." He asked whether the frequent quotations from Brigham Young, Wilford Woodruff, Joseph Fielding Smith, and others should be "subjected to the same criteria," namely, "a unanimous decision" and a "pronouncement" of canonization by the church president. He summed up: "What is authoritative—coming from the past—in the nature of the criteria which has been set up for us in the present?" Boyd was continuing Lowell's argument by pointing out that opinions differed among church leaders past and present, not simply between church leaders and institute teachers.

Responding to Boyd's remarks, Smith stated that he accepted "anything the Prophet Joseph said . . . without reservation," then claimed that his own writings had been "sustained" and his interpretations of the Creation account in a Joseph Smith scripture, the Pearl of Great Price, had been "approved," though he did not say by whom. He then stated, contradictorily, "We do not have the privilege of private interpretation of it." One might believe the earth is a billion years old and remain in the church, "but if he goes around preaching that the authorities of the church are wrong, and the Lord has made a mistake in giving them revelation, then he has no business in the church."

In an earlier session J. Reuben Clark had delivered a sermon on this point that would be much read and reprinted over the next decades, "When Are Church Leaders' Words Entitled to the Claim of Scripture?"[36] Although he was strictly orthodox, he said, he was willing to keep an open mind on areas where revelation was not clear: "When any man, except the president of the church, undertakes to proclaim one unsettled doctrine, as among two or more doctrines, in dispute, as the settled doctrine of the church, we may know that he is not 'moved upon by the Holy Ghost,' unless he is acting under the direction and by authority of the president."

At the end of the conference Ed Lyon sat down at his typewriter and wrote a letter to the man he saw almost daily. "Dear Lowell," he began, "there are some things that I have to say and if I tried to say them, you would shut me off or make a joke of it. This is not a joking matter and I intend to be heard, so I am writing this little message." Ed lamented that the conference had continued with

> hardly a word being said about the student. . . . It wasn't until you raised your question on Thursday about the problem of a boy who needs to be treated as a Christian that anyone sounded a sweet note. . . . your words fell like manna from heaven on a starving people. . . . A Y man sitting back of me . . . said to me in a low voice as you finished, "What a thrill it must be to work with a man of love, vision, wisdom, and insight, as well as great faith. You are to be envied."

The letter continued: " You said everything that I had thought, but said it ten time[s] more pointedly and in a nicer spirit than I could have. . . . Others there felt the same way but none had courage to speak out as you did."[37]

Wilkinson's diary reported "a very profitable morning with real heavy information to follow."[38] Considering the events of the previous day, it is surprising that his diary noted approvingly of the institute teachers and their wives: "We have a very loyal group."[39]

Shortly afterward Lowell received a cordial note from Joseph Fielding Smith asking for a meeting with him and Ed. A few days later Lowell and Ed found Smith and Mark E. Petersen courteous yet unrelenting in defense of their interpretations. Smith hinted that his book was an important, even necessary adjunct to their institute texts. Lowell summarized dryly: "He called us in to . . . try to convince us that his position was right. He didn't succeed."[40]

Noted Mormon scientist Henry Eyring was in the anteroom when they left. That night Ed called Eyring to ask about his meeting with Smith and Petersen. Eyring said candidly, "I told Elder Smith that he was a good historian but a poor scientist."[41]

In this context, then, Wilkinson followed up on the topic of transferring Lowell that he himself had raised the previous spring. At the October joint meeting of the Board of Trustees and Board of Education, Wilkinson reported "the expressed desire on the part of members of the Executive Committee to have certain Salt Lake teachers transferred to other institutes as a possible means of increasing the effectiveness of the institute at the University of Utah." According to the minutes, "Adam S. Bennion expressed the opinion that the removal of an ineffective teacher from one place to another might not be a solution." President McKay then suggested that "the administration talk with each problem teacher individually." Wilkinson was assigned to conduct these discussions and make recommendations to the executive committee.[42]

At that same meeting Wilkinson also brought up two issues that bore directly on the Salt Lake institute: class credit and student wards. He received authorization to prepare a memo describing how credit was awarded for institute classes at other universities, and a committee was chosen to "wait on President Olpin at the U. of U. and discuss the matter more fully."[43] Unfortunately, the minutes do not relate if Wilkinson prepared the memo and, if he did, whether the meeting with Olpin ever took place.[44]

In November seminary supervisor Joy Dunyon offered to arrange a meeting for Lowell and Ed with President McKay to discuss Joseph Fielding Smith's views. This meeting preempted a proposal then taking shape among the institute faculty that "a committee of five or six men representing the institutes and BYU should seek an audience with President McKay." George Boyd, Lowell, and Ed went with Dunyon.[45] Lowell remembered their reception as cordial, with McKay "very understanding of President Smith. . . . [McKay] respected [Smith's] views, but stating that he himself felt that the earth is very old and that evolutionary ideas have much to commend them."[46] McKay "very emphatically" told them that Smith's book had not been "authorized or approved" and "did not represent the position of the church."

Feeling justified, the trio went back to work, learning soon afterwards that they had predictably aroused Wilkinson's ire in meeting with President McKay. It seems noteworthy that although Wilkinson had twice been assigned to visit with the "problem teachers," he had not yet met personally with Lowell or with the other Salt Lake institute teachers. Instead, he sent Berrett to question them. According to notes made by Boyd, Wilkinson wanted to know "who was responsible for arranging the interview? His purpose was apparently to scold us for going directly to President McKay instead of going through channels—himself and the executive committee."[47]

Lowell immediately wrote Berrett, assuring him that the three institute instructors had intended to see McKay even if Dunyon had not arranged it as a follow-up to their interview with apostles Smith and Petersen. Lowell assumed full responsibility for "initiating the [McKay] interview and for our conversation, which had to do entirely with the discussion of science and religion and President Smith's book." Lowell apologized for any "administrative problems" he may have created for Berrett and Wilkinson because of this interview and "my remarks at the convention." He added, "With a strong interest in the issues at stake and their effects in the lives of the youth of the church, one is a bit neglectful of administrative problems." In his twenty years at the institute, he reminded them, he had "never bypassed the commissioner of education" or taken relationship problems "to someone above him." He believed in negotiating "with the people concerned therewith." He had "always felt free—though I have done it rarely—to call on any of the brethren on some matter of doctrine or point of view."

In fact, Lowell asked, why *not* talk with general authorities who "have the time and interest to listen?" Then he spelled out the underlying question: "When one raises a point of view at variance with that held by the president of the Quorum of the Twelve, and finds the latter quite naturally unbending in his position and not inclined to give another point of view a fair hearing, to whom can one go to know if one's own position is in harmony with that of the church?" He recognized "the brethren are the general staff" but suggested, "We are on the 'firing line' every day." Why not have "more communication between us directly or through you brethren. We invite it."[48]

There is no record of Berrett's reply, but in December Wilkinson asked Berrett for a "better evaluation of teachers at the institute at the University of Utah after which we should converse with them and make recommendations if we are to make a determination."[49]

In July 1955 Dunyon was given a "leave of absence" and encouraged to seek advanced degrees at the BYU.[50] His replacement was thirty-year-old future apostle Boyd K. Packer, who had distinguished himself at the Indian seminaries in Brigham City and was completing a degree at BYU. Theodore (Ted) Tuttle, also a future general authority in the third-ranking Quorum of Seventies, became supervisor over the institutes.

Four months earlier, in March 1955, a direct blow had fallen on the University of Utah institute. Berrett told George Boyd to expect a transfer over the summer, probably to Reno, Nevada. Boyd vowed to refuse it. When the transfer came, however, it was to the University of Southern California in Los Angeles. George and Maurine Boyd unhappily gave in. Their family was comfortably settled in Salt Lake, with a newborn baby, and the compatibility of the teaching triumvirate of Salt Lake City was very satisfying. The Boyds had hoped to retire in Salt Lake City.[51]

Perhaps as an expression of affinity, University of Utah president Olpin asked Lowell to deliver the baccalaureate address at June 1956 commencement. His speech, "The Greatest of These," centered on Old Testament prophets who condemned the Israelites' formal worship because "the people, in daily life, practiced neither justice nor mercy." The corrective to formalism was love—"doing, giving, helping, serving."[52] Wilkinson sent Lowell his congratulations on "a very convincing statement of the indispensable need of love in all our human relations."[53]

A few days later President McKay summoned Wilkinson and Berrett to discuss Dunyon's firing and rumors about a rift between President McKay and Joseph Fielding Smith. Lowell's name was not spoken, but Wilkinson noted that Lowell was the most likely candidate as the origin of the rumors. Lowell, of course, knew nothing of this. Wilkinson said he had fired Dunyon for "disloyalty" in going over Berrett's head in setting up the meeting between the Salt Lake institute instructors and President McKay.

"I should add here," Wilkinson continued, "that the executive committee had felt that Dunyon was not loyal to Brother Berrett or myself, or to them, and that he was continually having third parties make representations to President McKay. . . . It would be best to have completely loyal men in this position." He pointed out that Dunyon's work had also been criticized for following "the extremely liberal views of Dr. West on interpretation of Old Testament miracles." McKay promised not to interfere with administrative decisions but "asked both of us to be tolerant, understanding, and kind with members of the system who for a temporary time depart from church doctrine because, he said, they often after further education and learning generally become devout members."[54] Wilkinson candidly recorded McKay's "deep concern lest we drive some of the deep-thinkers of the Church out of the Church. He was very desirous that in our Church School System we should help young people make an adjustment between the teachings they might receive in college and the doctrines of the church."

The church president's clear exposition of Lowell's own philosophy may have impressed Wilkinson enough to stay his hand for a few more years. As the minutes of board meetings suggest, President McKay and Adam Bennion usually failed to issue direct orders to Wilkinson on any of the projects he cherished. Instead, they raised questions, discussed related issues, and called for further study, while most of the executive committee and additional members of the Board of Education were gradually coming to Wilkinson's position.[55]

Lowell felt clouds gathering over the institute, but he resolutely immersed himself in the things that "mattered most" to him: walking with individual students along their paths of faith and learning, showing them opportunities for service, and exploring dimensions of religion. It is possible to argue that mounting a truly effective defense might have assured him another decade at the institute, but he chose not to. Although he missed George Boyd, his relationship with Ed Lyon deepened. New instructors were sent to the institute without consultation with him, but most were congenial colleagues who bore their share of the load. Albert Payne, from the seminary at Spanish Fork, Utah, was hired full time along with part-timers Alfred C. Neilsen and Wendell Rich, also veterans of the CES. Payne would describe his five years as a "glorious time." He immediately noticed that Lowell and Ed had bulging classrooms, with "kids sitting in the hall trying to get a look" while his own mustered barely twenty-five. "I knew I was with two giants."[56] Lowell thought Albert and Alfred "fit very well into the spirit of the program. Albert was a good teacher and a good thinker."[57]

While complaints of low enrollment continued, new faculty increased. During the late 1950s "we had two or three other teachers come in that were sent to us. We didn't have any choice."[58] Seminary supervisor Boyd Packer was apparently interested in giving promising seminary teachers experience at the institute level. Albert Payne had proved so adept at his job that other seminary instructors were added. Some were simultaneously working on degrees at BYU.

Meanwhile, Wilkinson met with Ray Olpin in early 1959 and asked him why "we did not give credit for non-sectarian courses." Olpin, who recorded the meeting in his diary, replied, "I didn't know that the hierarchy was . . . interested in this," explaining, "The institute would stand to lose if we were to move in and try to tell them what to teach or how many hours a student should take and supervise the selection of faculty . . . and other things that the Church might not like."[59]

Olpin, no doubt sensing that Lowell's danger was the university's opportunity, began courting him for an administrative position in the spring of 1961. After Olpin's dean of students, Willard Blaesser, announced plans to leave in the spring of 1962, Olpin, who had long felt the university needed a Mormon counselor, tested the reactions of his colleagues to the possibility of hiring Lowell, praising his "stature and background." Academic Vice President Daniel Dykstra enthusiastically concurred: "Certainly no one who knows Dr. Bennion would complain at his appointment. It would be a master stroke if we could get him."[60]

In June Olpin told Lowell that "what we needed was someone who understood the mores of the area, and who had experience in the church, for I felt that no one would really have an understanding of the way of life which Mormonism represents unless they had participated in it." Lowell seemed impressed, so Olpin described a plan for centralizing student activity and counseling.

Its director needed to be "a man with reputation, with stature, who was well known to the Mormon community here, yet who was not in any way, shape, or form prejudiced in his views, to take over that kind of work for us." He knew of Lowell's "fine work across the road," and he knew Lowell "could stand up and represent people of all faiths, denominations—people who were students as well as faculty members and townspeople."[61]

Although gratified by Olpin's high opinion of him, Lowell still felt firmly committed to the institute. He was part of it—it was part of him. Olpin reported to his diary that Lowell offered two reasons for delaying—he was a poor administrator and he wanted "to write and do creative thinking." Olpin promptly countered that he would not burden Lowell with administrative details. On the contrary, "we wanted [Lowell] to be sort of a free-lancer, someone to have an open door for anyone who wanted to come for a word of encouragement and guidance." Lowell said only that he would think about it. Olpin was frustrated at what he called the "the seemingly utter disregard on the part of the dean of students office for the interests of the people who are indigenous to this area—people of pioneer descent."[62]

When Olpin brought up Lowell's name at a board of regents meeting five months later where, some officials balked at Lowell's church counseling background. Olpin retorted, "If they wanted someone to perpetuate the status quo . . . that would be difficult for a man like Lowell Bennion, but if he were to be given a free hand, he might make a very definite contribution."[63]

When Olpin pressed Lowell for an answer early the next year, offering him the dean of men and part-time professor positions, Lowell "expressed a considerable amount of interest in this possibility but said he would like to think about it for a week or two."[64] Dean Blaesser, sent to confer with Lowell, reported "an even greater respect [for Lowell] than he had before" but noted that Lowell wished to stay at the institute because "he was enjoying better relations with the church officials now than he ever had—that they had given them free rein to do anything he wishes there, and he had a feeling that he could do more good for the students if he didn't try to shift positions at this time."[65]

Lowell was even more sought-after as a church speaker around the state and at BYU. As Olpin recorded in his diary,

"Things have brightened for Lowell Bennion, for he is a favorite of both President [David O.] McKay and Elder [Hugh B.] Brown. As a matter of fact, I was told that Elder Brown has him in mind as his first choice for an apostleship when a vacancy occurs."[66] At the death of Apostle Henry D. Moyle, Apostle Brown had been elevated to first counselor in the First Presidency. Though Olpin failed to record his source, he echoed rumors rife at the institute ever since McKay's ascendancy. Students whispered that Lowell was being considered for an apostleship—especially at the time Adam Bennion was called and again at his death.

Lowell had little reason to worry about his relationship with general authorities. Even Joseph Fielding Smith had agreed with Lowell on the dubious missionary practice of "kiddie-dipping" during the Moyle Baseball missionary years of the late 1950s and early 1960s. A returned sister missionary had remorsefully confessed that she and her companions had been under such extreme pressure to meet baptismal quotas that "we bought candy bars and gave them to little children to bribe them" on months when baptisms were low.[67] When Lowell protested to Apostle Smith in early 1961, Smith had responded candidly and supportively:

> I am satisfied completely that the Spirit of the Lord is not in it. . . . I have learned from direct and accurate authority that in this great drive they have been baptizing children who are not old enough to comprehend and frequently without the consent of their parents. . . . How long we will permit this thing to go on, I am not prepared to say, but the idea of baptizing and converting afterwards has never been successful and in my judgment never will [be].[68]

It is not clear why Lowell voiced his protest to Smith instead of to Henry D. Moyle himself. In fact, Moyle presented himself as a hearty ally of Olpin's recruiting efforts. Olpin told his diary that Moyle had promised to persuade McKay to encourage Lowell to accept his proposal: "We'll tell [Lowell] to do it!" Olpin also talked with Richard L. Evans, apostle and member of the University of Utah's board of trustees. He also spoke with McKay's son, Llewellyn, a professor of German at the university.[69]

Neither Olpin nor Lowell knew that three months earlier Wilkinson, with Berrett's concurrence, had changed his tack slightly and had urged Moyle to call Lowell as a mission president.[70] Although Lowell was "probably the greatest institute teacher in the Church . . . he does not do a good organizational job of getting as large an attendance of University of Utah students as we would like." A "change in leadership" would, Wilkinson argued, would bring more students to the Salt Lake institute. Besides, Lowell "needs" this experience to "become wholeheartedly devoted to the missionary program. When he returned he would be very valuable to us as an institute teacher." Lowell and Merle certainly would have accepted such a calling.[71] There is no record that Moyle ever responded.

On February 13, 1962, Lowell finally declined the offer "to become associate dean of students." A disappointed Olpin asked if Lowell had heard from the First Presidency. Lowell explained that Hugh B. Brown had telephoned to say that "Henry D. Moyle had brought up the subject [of the appointment] at the Monday meeting of the first presidency, and the first presidency had considered inviting him to meet with them about it." Instead, Brown had telephoned Lowell and, as Olpin interpreted it, "held out to him possibilities and opportunities that lie ahead in the church."[72] Olpin may have interpreted Lowell's statement to mean a future apostleship, but to Lowell it almost certainly meant his continued position at the beloved institute.[73] Olpin did not give up, however, and offered Lowell a year's appointment if he could take a leave of absence from the institute.[74] He offered to clear the idea with Wilkinson, and Lowell agreed.

Wilkinson and Olpin had been friendly enemies since their college days. On the issue of Lowell Bennion, however, their interests met, though for different reasons. When Olpin telephoned Wilkinson in late February about the leave for Lowell, "Ernest was most cooperative, . . . thought he could have an answer by tomorrow," and agreed with Olpin on Lowell's counseling skills although he warned Olpin that Lowell was "a poor administrator." Olpin's rejoinder was low-key: "I informed Ernest that I didn't want to do anything that would jeopardize the standing of Lowell Bennion in the work he is doing. I just felt that since he is working with the same students and is familiar with the U. or U., it would be easier for him to join ranks with us for a year than for someone who comes from afar."[75]

Olpin grumbled privately, "We get criticisms from church people about not having good LDS counselors . . . but when we try to get them, we get opposition from the church."[76] Next day he attended a luncheon where Hugh B. Brown and Richard L. Evans were also guests. That night he summarized the unsatisfactory and confusing information they gave him:

> Apparently the church higher-ups have been discussing this case repeatedly since it has become known that we would like to have Lowell Bennion become associate dean of students. . . . Someone on the executive committee of the BYU board of trustees has been raising questions about the possible transfer of Lowell Bennion from the institute to the U. faculty. After talking to President Brown and Richard Evans, it was not clear to me who was standing in the way of whom. We don't know exactly how Lowell Bennion feels, but he has indicated that he would do whatever the church president felt it best for him to do. President Brown said there are two or three major activities, which would involve Lowell Bennion, that are under discussion at the present time, and he thought I should talk to President McKay today if I can . . . for just this morning they were talking about this problem which Dr. Lowell Bennion faces.

Evans, Olpin noted, "seemed more concerned about the fate of Lowell Bennion if he were to transfer to the university. He said, 'I think he would want to know what the future has in store for him.' Both of the men seemed to feel better when I told them we would like to have Lowell Bennion come to the university for a permanent appointment, but it was only at his [Lowell's] request that we had withdrawn our offer . . . and sought to get him to fill in."[77]

Olpin returned to his office and called Claire Middlemiss, McKay's personal secretary, requesting an appointment. Middlemiss phoned a few hours later and said that McKay could be found inspecting the university's Pioneer Theatre, then under construction. Olpin searched for him without success. When Blaesser innocently dropped by late in the afternoon to ask about Lowell, the frustrated Olpin "hit the ceiling."[78]

The next day Llewellyn McKay arranged for Olpin to join his father in a tour of the new theater. Olpin then climbed into McKay's back seat and explained his hopes to acquire Lowell's services. McKay agreed "one hundred percent," expressed a preference for a permanent appointment rather than a one-year leave, but said that "it would depend on what Dr. Lowell Bennion wants," because they would not want to call him and tell him what to do. McKay closed the interview by assuring Olpin that if Lowell would "call and communicate with them and express his desires, they would certainly concur and go along with our wishes."[79]

It must have seemed to Olpin that his strenuous efforts would pay off. But there is no record of Olpin's reporting this conversation to Lowell, and Lowell, interviewed during the 1990s,[80] had no memory of such a conversation. Not surprisingly, the plan stalled. Did Lowell again put Olpin off by promising to "think about it," or did Olpin, for some reason, fail to tell him to call McKay? On April 11 Brown and Olpin met on a downtown street, with Brown assuring Olpin that the First Presidency was "thoroughly agreeable to Dr. Bennion coming to the university." Olpin recorded his resolve to "get Dr. Bennion in my office and have a showdown talk with him."[81]

If Olpin had such a "talk," he failed to record it and Lowell failed to remember it.[82] Yet by May 19, 1962, when Olpin again encountered Brown, nothing had happened except that Blaesser had resigned. Brown told Olpin that the First Presidency had felt "a little reluctance . . . to urge Bennion to accept the position under the present organization and personnel in the dean of students office, but if it were the dean's position, it might be a different story."[83]

Olpin was back where he started, with Lowell again recommended for the dean's spot.[84]

NOTES

1. See Woodruff J. Deem and Glenn V. Bird, *Ernest L. Wilkinson: Indian Advocate and University President* (Provo, UT: privately published, 1978), 281-82.

2. Wilkinson to William E. Berrett, 31 Aug. 1953, Wilkinson Collection, Presidential Papers, University Archives, Harold B. Lee Library, Brigham Young University, Provo, Utah. Unless otherwise noted, all quotations from Wilkinson's papers are from this collection.

3. At that time the entire First Presidency and Quorum of the Twelve sat as both Board of Education for the Church Education System and as Board of Trustees for Brigham Young University. These boards met together usually in June at the end of the school year and again in September or October at the beginning of a school year. The CES board usually met in the morning and reconvened as the Board of Trustees in the afternoon. Each September they elected an executive committee to handle business for both bodies with Wilkinson sitting on both boards. During the decade 1952-62 Joseph Fielding Smith, president of the Quorum of the Twelve, chaired the Board of Education executive committee. Its members were Harold B. Lee, Marion G. Romney, Henry D. Moyle, and Adam S. Bennion. Bennion, Lowell's cousin, a university-trained scholar, and former commissioner of LDS church education, was sympathetic to institute programs but was junior to the other apostles.

4. Ernest L. Wilkinson, Diary, 28 Apr. 1960, records that David O. McKay changed the title because "where one is head of several universities he usually has the title of chancellor, as in the case of various educational setups throughout the United States."

5. Franklin L. West, Audiotaped Reminiscences, n.d., Archives and Manuscripts Division, Lee Library, transcript in Bradford's possession.

6. "Church School System Unified," *Church News,* 11 July 1953, 2.

7. Wilkinson to Franklin L. West, 13 July 1953.

8. Ernest L. Wilkinson, "The Place of the Institute in the Church School System: Address to Institute and Seminary Teachers at [a] Convention Held on Brigham Young University Campus, 20 August 1953," unpaginated typescript, photocopy in Bradford's possession.

9. West, audiotaped reminiscences, n.d.

10. West successfully defended his programs and his teachers to earlier presidents Grant and George Albert Smith. He records that when "some general authorities were knocking down Lowell Bennion" he had defended him and felt secure in his own ability to negotiate "the work of the Department" (ibid.).

11. Ibid.

12. Wilkinson, Diary, 10 June 1955. West was responsible for publication of Heber Snell's scholarly work on the old Testament, *Ancient Israel: Its Story and Meaning.* Wilkinson joined Joseph Fielding Smith in repudiating it, and West, who had intended to use it as a text, had to be

satisfied in placing it in institute and seminary libraries. See chap. 4 for additional background. In fact, nearly all the textbooks West commissioned met a similar fate. Under his sponsorship, several educators authored texts on scriptural scholarship. These included Russel B. Swensen, Sidney B. Sperry, and Daryl Chase. See also Gary James Bergera and Ron Priddis, *Brigham Young University: A House of Faith* (Salt Lake City: Signature Books, 1984), 44 n.

13. Deem and Bird, *Ernest L. Wilkinson,* 491.

14. Berrett was an attorney who had distinguished himself as special prosecutor for the U.S. Office of Price Administration during World War II and as assistant U.S. attorney in Alaska. His career in CES began in 1925 when he served as principal of Roosevelt Junior High seminary. He was an editor for the church when West recruited him to assist in manual publication.

15. Wilkinson, "The Place of the Institute in the Church School System," n.p.

16. Ibid.

17. T. Edgar Lyon, "Tribute to Franklin L. West: Retirement Dinner at BYU," 22 Aug. 1953, T. Edgar Lyon and Hermana Forsberg Lyon Collections, archives, Historical Department, Church of Jesus Christ of Latter-day Saints, Salt Lake City, Utah.

18. Franklin L. West to Lowell L. Bennion, 10 July 1954, photocopy of typescript in Bradford's possession. West died 21 October 1966 at eighty-one; Hugh B. Brown, then first counselor in the First Presidency, was principal speaker at the funeral. "Dr. Franklin L. West, Former USU Dean, Dies," *Salt Lake Tribune,* 22 Oct. 1966, 5.

19. Olpin recorded in his diary his shock at reading a *Deseret News* announcement of plans for an LDS junior college in Salt Lake City for its estimated population of 4,500 college-age Mormons. He denounced it "one of the biggest mistakes my church had ever made . . . a decisive factor in separating the people of two religious groups" and recalled that McKay himself had once told him it was wrong to call BYU "the church school" and the University of Utah "the gentile school." For the press, however, Olpin issued a calm statement: "The news . . . comes as a complete surprise. We hope that a development of such importance will be coordinated with the existing higher education program of the area and will not be competitive with it." A. Ray Olpin, Diary, 6-7 Jan. 1959, Olpin Collection, Presidential Papers, University Archives, University of

Utah, Salt Lake City.

20. Deem and Bird, *Ernest L. Wilkinson,* 631; Ernest L. Wilkinson and Leonard J. Arrington, *Brigham Young University: The First One Hundred Years* (Provo, UT: Brigham Young University Press, 1978), 3:428-37.

21. Bergera and Priddis (in *Brigham Young University: A House of Faith,* 202) observe: "In his attempts to secure an ideologically pure faculty, Wilkinson adopted a number of measures which, in retrospect, proved to be both ill-conceived and counter-productive."

22. Board of Education Executive Committee Minutes, 20 May 1954, 3, University Archives, Lee Library. This activity took place without Lowell's knowledge. But Lowell's name continued to appear in Board of Education minutes and Wilkinson's papers, evidence that Wilkinson may have considered him an obstacle to his plan. His diary fails to mention Lowell after 1962.

23. Executive Committee, Minutes, 3 June 1954; present were Joseph Fielding Smith, Harold B. Lee, Marion G. Romney, Adam S. Bennion, and Wilkinson.

24. Ibid., 17 June 1953.

25. Ibid., 15 July 1953.

26. Wilkinson, untitled memo, 16 Aug. 1954.

27. Wilkinson to William E. Berrett, 21 Dec. 1954.

28. "Elder Lee Conducts Course for Teachers," *Church News,* 24 June 1954, 4.

29. Wilkinson to William E. Berrett, 2 Aug. 1954.

30. Wilkinson, Diary, 24 Aug. 1954.

31. Mark E. Petersen, "Race Problems—As They Affect the Church," address given 27 Aug. 1954, in Lester Bush, comp., "Compilation on the Negro in Mormonism," bound typescript, 1970, Appendix VII, 377, copy in Bradford's possession.

32. From questions and answers following Petersen's speech, photocopy of partial typescript in Lowell L. Bennion's and Bradford's possession. This typescript is also the source of Lowell's comments, which follow.

33. Published April 1954 by Deseret Book Company, it includes a foreword by Mark E. Petersen stating that its purpose is to "help LDS students of science preserve their faith." Quoted in the *Church News,* 3 Apr. 1954, 3.

34. Joseph Fielding Smith, "The Origin of Man," 28 Aug. 1954, with questions and answers; name of note-taker and transcriber unknown; photocopy of typescript in Bradford's possession. For a summary, see *Church News* for 31 July and 21 August.

35. Ibid.

36. J. Reuben Clark, Jr., "When Are Church Leaders' Words Entitled to the Claim of Scripture?" *Church News,* 28 Aug. 1954; reprinted in *Dialogue: A Journal of Mormon Thought* 12 (Summer 1979): 68-81.

37. T. Edgar Lyon to Lowell L. Bennion, 28 Aug. 1954, photocopy in Bradford's possession.

38. Ernest L. Wilkinson, Diary, 28 Aug. 1954.

39. Ibid., 27 Aug. 1954.

40. Lowell L. Bennion, Oral History, 95.

41. As quoted by Joseph Lynn Lyon, interviewed by Mary L. Bradford, 26 Sept. 1990.

42. Board of Education and Board of Trustees, Minutes of a joint meeting, 8 Oct. 1954. Nine of the fifteen apostles and First Presidency attended: David O. McKay, Joseph Fielding Smith, Spencer W. Kimball, Henry D. Moyle, Marion D. Romney, Adam S. Bennion, Richard L. Evans, George Q. Morris, and Mark E. Petersen. The board routinely reelected the executive committee already serving: Smith, Lee, Moyle, Romney, and Bennion.

43. Ibid.

44. Another change that affected the institutes was the formation of independent student wards. The executive committee deactivated the student wards and reassigned all students to local stake presidents.

45. George T. Boyd, "Notes from an Interview with President David O. McKay," (meeting in Nov. 1954), record dated Mar. 1955, 4 pp., photocopy of typescript in Bradford's possession.

46. Lowell L. Bennion, Oral History, 96.

47. Ibid.

48. Lowell L. Bennion to William E. Berrett, 23 Nov. 1954, carbon copy in Bradford's possession.

49. Wilkinson to William E. Berrett, 7 Dec. 1954.

50. Instead he organized his own financial consulting business in 1958, settled in East Millcreek near Lowell and Ed, and was called as first counselor to a stake president in 1962. See *Church News* articles: "Joy Dunyon Given Leave of Absence as Seminary Supervisor," 16 July 1955, 4; "Boyd K. Packer to Succeed J. F. Dunyon," 33 July 1955, 4; "East Millcreek Installs Counselors," 7 July 1962, 3.

51. George T. Boyd, interviewed by Mary L. Bradford, 4 Feb. 1982. Boyd became director of the institute at the University of Southern California on 23 May 1964.

52. Lowell L. Bennion, "But the Greatest of These . . . ," baccalaureate address at the University of Utah, 3 June 1956, reprinted in Eugene England, comp., *The Best of Lowell L. Bennion* (Salt Lake City: Deseret Book Co., 1988), 231-34.

53. Wilkinson to Lowell L. Bennion, 6 June 1956, photocopy in Bradford's possession.

54. Wilkinson, Diary, 10 June 1955.

55. Wilkinson was counting on his junior colleges to replace the institutes in the western states. In October 1957 he presented to the Church Board of Education the "anticipated number of college age Latter-day Saints" "that could not possibly be accommodated in Provo." He then argued for a ring of junior colleges in the western states. Smith, Richards, and Clark supported the proposal, and in December 1955 the board voted to limit BYU to 12,000-15,000 students. Wilkinson was given permission to buy land in Salt Lake City, Los Angeles, and to investigate possibilities in Phoenix, San Francisco, Portland, Oregon, Spokane, and Boise-Caldwell. By summer 1960 the church had purchased about 1,650 acres in five states at more than $8 million, with the possibility of additional land in the eastern U.S., the South, New Mexico, even Europe. Land was purchased in Idaho Falls for the transfer of Ricks College. After considerable opposition from church and local leaders in Rexburg that decision was rescinded and Ricks remained in Rexburg. In the fall of 1955 a new junior college opened in Hawaii. But opposition to Wilkinson's plans was building. George Romney, president of the Detroit

stake, wrote to President McKay arguing for institutes and seminaries as excellent missionary tools, and a study led by Roy West for the church showed that institute graduates were as likely to marry in the temple as BYU graduates. Such arguments as these combined with the church's growing financial burdens motivated the First Presidency to cut the CES budget by 40 percent in 1960. Then with the help of Boyd K. Packer, elevated to assistant to the Council of the Twelve and a member of the Board of Education who argued that the money could be better spent on illiterate new members in Mexico and elsewhere, the church voted to cancel the junior college plan. See Wilkinson and Arrington, *Brigham Young University*, 3:149-62.

56. Albert Payne, interviewed by Mary L. Bradford, 14 May 1987.

57. Lowell L. Bennion, Oral History, 104.

58. Ibid.

59. Olpin, Diary, 17 Jan. 1959.

60. Ibid., 29 June 1961.

61. Ibid.

62. Ibid., 30 June 1961.

63. Ibid., 28 Nov. 1961.

64. Ibid., 3 Jan. 1962.

65. Ibid., 18 Jan. 1962.

66. Ibid.

67. Lowell L. Bennion, Oral History, 147.

68. Joseph Fielding Smith to Lowell L. Bennion, 13 Mar. 1961, photocopy in Bradford's possession.

69. Olpin, Diary, 18 Jan. 1962.

70. Wilkinson to Henry D. Moyle, 15 Dec. 1961, photocopy in Bradford's possession.

71. Lowell L. Bennion and Merle C. Bennion, interviewed by Mary L. Bradford, 22 Sept. 1990.

72. Olpin, Diary, 13 Feb. 1962. Minutes of the First Presidency meetings that would confirm this are unavailable for research.

73. As Ed Lyon wrote his family, "Lowell had been offered Blazer's [sic] place at the U, and when he turned it down Olpin went to the First Presidency to get them to persuade Lowell to accept it, and Pres. Moyle said he thought it would be a good thing. Pres. Brown called Lowell down and told him about it, and said he could do as he pleased." T. Edgar Lyon to "Donna and Laurie," 17 June 1862, typescript copy in Bradford's possession.

74. Olpin, Diary, 13 Feb. 1962.

75. Olpin, Diary, 27 Feb. 1962. The minutes for the Executive Committee meeting of March 1 show that Lowell's leave of absence was brought up but tabled until Harold B. Lee could "have the opportunity to discuss the matter with Richard L. Evans, apostle and member of the University's board of regents." (Lee, George Q. Morris, Marion G. Romney, and Howard W. Hunter attended that meeting.) Despite Wilkinson's promise, Olpin heard nothing by mid-March when he asked Richard L. Evans, "What was holding up the decision?" Evans evasively replied that "they were having a little trouble" about Lowell's leave of absence but "thought it might work out all right." He, too, promised to call Olpin.

76. Ibid., 22 Mar. 1962.

77. Ibid., 23 Mar. 1962.

78. Ibid.

79. Ibid., 24 Mar. 1962.

80. Lowell L. Bennion, interviewed by Mary L. Bradford, 2 Jan. 1990.

81. Olpin, Diary, 11 Apr. 1962.

82. Lowell L. Bennion, interviewed by Mary L. Bradford, 2 Jan. 1990.

83. Olpin, Diary, 11 Apr. 1962.

84. Since other records are unavailable, it is tempting to read between the lines of those that are. Lowell's supporters on the Board of Education were apparently loathe to encourage him to leave for anything less than the dean's job. When Henry Moyle lobbied the First Presidency, President McKay balked at exerting his influence. Wilkinson hoped that McKay would provide a painless way to remove Lowell. In his diary he laments that the general authorities could not reach a conclusion about

Lowell. Olpin unwittingly played into Wilkinson's hands. When Wilkinson asked the Board of Education to vote on Lowell's leave of absence to serve in the University of Utah's Counseling Service, it was "tabled until Richard L. Evans could discuss the subject with Apostle Lee" (Board of Education Minutes, 1 Mar. 1962).

CHAPTER 8

LEAVING THE INSTITUTE (1962)

I don't believe in being defeated twice,
once by circumstance and
once by myself.

—LOWELL L. BENNION

On May 29, 1962, as Ed Lyon sat in his office preparing for a meeting with Lowell and William E. Berrett, Berrett appeared at his door fifteen minutes early. "Now that you have your doctor's degree cinched, have you and Lowell thought about teaching at the 'Y' instead of here?" Berrett asked.

Surprised and suddenly chilled, Lyon replied, "I can't speak for Lowell, but I have no desire to go. I hoped I could finish out my remaining six years here before retirement." Lyon reminded Berrett that feelers in the past had always found him cool to the idea. Nothing had changed.

Berrett pointed out that something had: the political climate surrounding the institute's work. "Brother [Harold B.] Lee and some of the brethren have said that neither Lowell nor you are making the greatest contribution to the church that you could in this place." He added somewhat awkwardly, "At the 'Y' your interest would be much greater, and you would have time to write books for the institute course of study."

Lyon might have reminded Berrett that student interest in his courses had always been high and so had his and Lowell's curriculum production, but he grasped the point. Berrett tried to appeal to Ed Lyon's scholarly sense by describing a possible appointment to BYU's church history department: "If you could go down there, you could give the school a decent course in the history of Christianity and one in the history of American Christianity." Summarizing the situation in a letter to his children, Ed wrote: "I told him I was not interested in moving, but if they forced me to, I'd probably have to accept it."[1]

Lyon and Berrett then joined Dale Tingey (who had replaced Boyd Packer as institute supervisor after Packer was made a general authority), Lowell, and a young faculty member. Wilkinson and Berrett had hired the latter, a BYU graduate and former seminary teacher, to teach at the institute. According to Lowell, this "young upstart, without saying a word to us, went down to the church historian's office [headed by Joseph Fielding Smith] and said that Ed and I were teaching false doctrine." A friend in the historian's office had informed Ed, and Lowell asked for the meeting with "our colleague-critic . . . in a nice way," then had Berrett come up for a more formal settlement. "We asked our accuser to say what he thought was false doctrine, Lowell recalled. Then we explained our idea of revelation, and of God, and we were cleared by Ed Berrett."[2]

With no chance to brief Lowell on his own meeting with Berrett before leaving for a one-day Memorial Day vacation, Ed returned to find Lowell waiting for him.

"Did you get an ultimatum from Ed [Berrett]?" Lowell asked.

Lyon faced up to the unpleasant fact that Berrett had not just been on a fishing expedition. He recounted his visit with Berrett and his desire to stay where he was.

"Well, he gave me two choices," Lowell said. "No, three choices. Teach half time next year at the institute and spend the other half writing a course of study; . . . take a leave of absence at full pay and spend all my time writing; or go to the 'Y' to teach, either full-time or part time." Lowell faced the situation squarely: "At any rate, I am through here as director, and am being replaced by Joe J. Christensen."[3]

Both men knew and liked Christensen.[4] A Ph.D. from Washington State, he was currently director of the institute at Moscow, Idaho, and a former religion teacher at BYU. They knew he was scheduled to begin teaching at the Salt Lake City institute—but as a replacement, they thought, for an ailing instructor.

On April 1, just six days after University of Utah president A. Ray Olpin's meeting in President David O. McKay's car, the church

Board of Education had heard a report from Ernest Wilkinson that because the Moscow institute had recorded a "greater number of baptisms . . . under Christensen" than in all its history, Wilkinson was proposing that Christensen be transferred to Salt Lake. The minutes do not specify his position. Perhaps Wilkinson did not mention it; for when Counselor Henry Moyle "questioned the wisdom of transferring Christensen until the other two brethren had been transferred elsewhere," the board referred the matter to the executive committee "for further study."[5] On May 31, two weeks after another informal chat between Olpin and Counselor Hugh B. Brown and two days *after* Berrett's announcement to Ed Lyon, the Executive Committee of the Board of Education voted to transfer Christensen to Salt Lake City. The committee voted furthermore to encourage Lowell "to accept the position offered him at the U. of U." Berrett reported on his meeting two days earlier that alleged doctrinal heresy at the Salt Lake institute "had been based upon misunderstandings and exaggerations." This meeting was chaired by Joseph Fielding Smith and attended only by Harold B. Lee, Gordon B. Hinckley, and Ernest L. Wilkinson.[6]

Obviously in a hurry to implement the changes, Berrett and Wilkinson had spoken to Ed Lyon two days before the executive committee meeting and to Lowell the next day. When Lowell asked for Berrett's reasons, Berrett offered "hazy" criticisms that the brethren were dissatisfied with institute enrollment and that Lowell had criticized Moyle's missionary plan. It is fair to say they probably had a point. Enrollment in 1960 was 1,002 at a time when 6,172 LDS students were enrolled among the University of Utah's total student body of 9,058. Even though this figure was up from 1955 enrollment, it was probably not considered progress. But Lowell thought his second reason sounded more convincing.[7]

Lowell and Ed struggled to process this news. With characteristic selflessness, Ed put his friend first, describing Lowell's "real shock" in the letter to his children: "He has devoted the greatest part of his constructive life to the cause, unselfishly giving of himself because he loved the youth, and had assumed that as he was drawing big crowds to his classes, [and] was recently called to the new Church Coordinating committee as one of two planners in the youth-age group, that he was in good standing."[8]

Ed's supportiveness went further. After his conversation with

Lowell, he went to his office and telephoned the news of Lowell's "release" to Ray Olpin.

President Olpin asked, "Is Lowell there now?"

Ed answered, "Yes."

"Tell him not to leave," Olpin ordered. He was at the institute in fifteen minutes, offering Lowell, according to Lyon's desk diary, a position as dean of men (or students) at a salary $3,000 a year higher than his current one.[9] Olpin's quick response must have been warming, and Lowell, after postponing decisions for a year, could have taken decisive action. But he needed to ponder, to pray, to meditate about his future, and to talk with Merle. Once again Olpin left empty-handed.

In fact, a decision was being made about the institute that very week. Apparently acting on instructions from Wilkinson, Berrett prepared a contract for Lowell with a $300 raise and the notation, "On leave of absence to do research."[10] It was the same method they had used to remove Joy Dunyon in 1955. And, strangely enough, Lowell received it on June 6—the very day that Wilkinson participated in the semi-annual joint meeting of the First Presidency and Twelve acting in their dual capacity as BYU's Board of Trustees and as the Church Education System's Board of Education. The agenda was complicated, with "Lowell Bennion" as the last item.[11] David O. McKay presided at the meeting, with apostles Joseph Fielding Smith, Henry D. Moyle, Harold B. Lee, Marion G. Romney, Spencer W. Kimball, Mark E. Petersen, LeGrand Richards, Howard W. Hunter, and Gordon B. Hinckley in attendance. Excused were Hugh B. Brown, Richard L. Evans, Ezra Taft Benson, and Delbert L. Stapley. Brown's and Evans's absences were critical because of their repeated conversations with Olpin about Lowell's possible appointment.

Those present formally approved Christensen's appointment as director of the Salt Lake institute, then had "a full discussion of certain problems relative to the services of both" Lowell and Ed. They tabled the "decision"—without specifying what it was—until "the chancellor discussed with Elder Richard L. Evans the present status of negotiations for the appointment of a new dean of students at the University of Utah."[12] In other words, they failed to authorize a transfer or change for Lowell or Ed Lyon.

Wilkinson's diary records additional details on this "rough session."[13] He clarifies that the "long" discussion concerned whether Lowell should be transferred to the BYU or merely allowed to remain as a staff member. "There were all kinds of opinions expressed, which prompted me to comment that where there was this diversity of opinion among the authorities, it was impossible for me, as an administrator, to act. After which, President Moyle told me that I had had instructions the previous month to terminate his [Bennion's] services. The minutes, however, show that President Moyle was wrong in his memory."

That same day Lowell received his contract. Unaware of the meeting, he telephoned Ed Berrett, asking why a decision had been made for him. Berrett did not answer the question directly, only telling Lowell that he was to "take the year off and finish the Book of Mormon course he is now writing, then do a Courtship and Marriage class text. . . . Joe Christensen was to be director, and that Lowell would not be returning to the institute."[14] It is not clear where Berrett obtained the right to offer Lowell the chance to stay with the system as a writer, or "editor," or a possible professorship at BYU. The Board of Trustees minutes do not mention this either, so Wilkinson must have proposed the option, possibly to placate Berrett, who was fond of Lowell and Ed Lyon.[15]

That afternoon Olpin told his diary that Lowell's "position at the institute has changed. . . . He and Dr. Lyon will not be kept at the institute next year. [In this statement he misread Ed's concern for Lowell's situation as a description of Ed's own.] They are supposed to report to BYU as members of the teaching staff there. Dr. Bennion may be asked to spend one year writing for the church and then engage in teaching." Lowell assured him that he did not want to teach at BYU but might want to write while seeking other employment. They discussed the on-going reorganization in the student affairs office. Olpin's attempts to find a new Dean of Students had failed. Lowell, whether through reticence or genuine reluctance, refrained from expressing a clear desire for the job, and Olpin ended the interview ambiguously. "I told him I would talk with some of the other [candidates] . . . and get in touch with him soon again."[16] Although Olpin expressed no doubts to his diary about Lowell's ability, he was hesitant to press his suit since Lowell still seemed reluctant.

Lowell left his office for home on June 6 resigned about his removal but hoping for a hearing with the Board of Education. Two days later on June 8 Ed Lyon's contract arrived—he was still listed as associate director with the usual $300 raise.

Again, the two friends compared perceptions. With Lowell leaving, the seasoned and committed Ed Lyon was the obvious choice for the new director. Lowell had "heard that I was not made director, or acting director," reported Ed, "because some of the brethren had been angered by my review of the [Richard] Vetterli book [*Mormonism, Americanism, and Politics,* 1961]. . . . No one . . . has let me know how they felt, although I am close as a phone—so don't know what the score is on that account."[17] Both of them interpreted it, as Ed said, as a trend to "put younger men in and get rid of the older ones by getting them to the 'Y.'"[18] Berrett had hinted that "younger blood would have a greater appeal to the students,"[19] a specious reason since students typically overflowed their classrooms and stood in the hall waiting for seats. In 1962 Lowell was almost fifty-four and Ed five years older, with both men healthy and feeling in their prime. Wilkinson was nine years Lowell's senior.

Ed's ambiguous position, though less threatening, was perplexing. He wrote his children, asking them to fast with him and Hermana "to help us make the decision. . . . I don't know whether to . . . stay on without Lowell." Hermana felt as if she had "rocks in my stomach. . . . We'd talk until late and then waken and talk in the middle of the night and then sleep briefly and waken early and talk again."[20]

Ed Lyon was awarded the Ph.D. in history from the University of Utah at June commencement. With a flicker of triumph, Hermana reported "the spontaneous applause that came from so many when [Ed] walked down the ramp. I'm glad Pres. Wilkinson was there to hear it." Proudly, she added that the television news reported that "by all odds the most popular graduate was T. Edgar Lyon."[21]

Merle felt that "unjust forces" were at work, but the stoic Lowell kept many of his thoughts and feelings to himself, trying to carry on as normally as possible. On June 8, only two days after Lowell received his contract and the same day Ed Lyon received his, Wilkinson called Olpin and "said he had heard from President Moyle that we might be interested in having Lowell Bennion for dean of students." When Olpin told him no firm decision had yet been made, "Ernest went out of his way to say he would do everything possible to encourage him to come if we wanted him." Wilkinson then undercut this endorsement by letting Olpin know that he "was not as enthusiastic about Dr. Bennion as are many of the more liberal officials of the LDS Church."[22] When Richard L. Evans openly asked Olpin at a June 12 meeting of the university's Board of Regents what position he would offer Lowell, Olpin responded noncommittally: "We are not ready to make any direct offers."[23] (Wilkinson's papers say nothing of this meeting.)

On June 15 Wilkinson wrote Berrett that he had "discussed with President Moyle *your* recommendation that we have Lowell Bennion do some editing (writing of books) next year instead of teaching classes. I thought it would get immediate approval, but it did not. Apparently this situation is more deepset than any of us realize." Wilkinson asked Berrett to draft a letter, detailing the books Lowell should write. "I think it would be well for you to check this not only with your present associates," Wilkinson admonished, "but also with Boyd Packer because I know that President McKay has the greatest confidence in him, and if I could say that Brother Packer approves, it would go a long way in helping us."[24] Elder Packer, mentored by Harold B. Lee, had risen to the rank of general authority in September 1961 as assistant to the Quorum of the Twelve and would join the Board of Education's Executive Committee in fall of 1962.

Apparently Berrett wanted to ask Lowell to remain on the CES staff as a writer, while Moyle and Wilkinson, and perhaps Smith and Lee, had already decided that Lowell should leave the system. Unlike Berrett, Wilkinson had no personal affection for Lowell and was only impatient for action. Keeping Lowell in the system was acceptable as long as Lowell gave up the Salt Lake institute.

Berrett himself, interviewed in 1987, said that terminating Lowell was "the hardest task I ever had as an administrator" and explained, "Everybody who works for the church knows that he has many bosses. And he doesn't always have the liberty of those who work under him. I don't suppose anybody could teach as freely as Lowell taught without having some opposition."[25]

Berrett also expressed his admiration for Lowell: "Lowell devoted his life to people, especially to teenage youngsters. He kept himself in poor financial condition because he gave all he had. He spent his money as well as his time and intelligence on this. . . . I admire what he has done." As a teacher, Berrett said, "Lowell expressed great balance and judgment." There was "nothing fanatical about his teachings or his writings. The fanatics in the church are hard to live with."[26] It was without personal animosity, then, even with personal respect that Berrett reluctantly delivered the death blow to Lowell's institute career.

When other candidates refused him, Ray Olpin, instead of pressing Lowell further, asked Daniel Dykstra, academic vice president, what he would say to the appointment of Olpin's executive assistant, Neal A. Maxwell, as dean of students. "Tremendous!" Dykstra replied. "He would command the respect of the students, the faculty, and everyone who works with him."[27]

On June 20 Olpin offered Maxwell the deanship, suggesting that Maxwell approach Lowell about an assistant deanship. Meanwhile, on June 16 Berrett had met again with Ed Lyon, asking him directly to "please stay at the institute."[28] With his Ph.D. completed, Ed was now getting feelers from the university's history department to teach part time with a view to a full-time appointment.

On June 21 the Church Board of Education appointed Joe J. Christensen director of the Salt Lake institute, although the announcement was not made public until early August. On June 29 Wilkinson asked Berrett for a copy of a letter to the First Presidency that would "authorize me as of June 20 to have Brother Bennion work as editor for next year."[29] Wilkinson's memo does not clarify whether such a letter would make Lowell's intended position retroactive or if Wilkinson was requesting a copy of an existing document. Lowell, stoically carrying on and speaking candidly only to Ed and to Merle, knew nothing of these maneuverings. Berrett promised Lowell a meeting with the Board of Education in early September.

By June 25 Lowell and Ed, who had not yet signed any contracts, again discussed their futures. As Ed described it, "Lowell thinks I should stay at the institute another year (or more, perhaps), but turn all the Lambda Delt accounts and affairs over to the younger men. Then I should teach, and spend the time that I have formerly spent in Lambda Delt affairs, visiting with students, etc., and start a definite study program to prepare myself to write a history of Christianity for the Church institutes—make it a worthwhile project."

Lowell's possible solution for himself: "to take a year off and write a book on courtship and marriage, and try to get it published by a national publisher." But Ed, as he wrote his family, urged Lowell to "take the dean of students job . . . then let his assistants do most of the detail work and use his time to develop a worthwhile program for students on the campus as he did with Lambda Delta Sigma for the institute. I think he could do a great work there." Lowell promised to think about it, adding that if he were to accept a university offer, he wanted Ed as his assistant.[30]

Three days later, on Thursday, June 28, Ed Lyon telephoned Hugh B. Brown to complain of the "disreputable deal given Lowell L. Bennion." Brown, who had not been present at the June 6 Board of Education meeting, "said he did not know of it and wanted to see Lowell. I gave him Lowell's phone number, and on Friday afternoon he spent a half hour with him. He felt it had been unfair to Lowell but did not seem to know what could be done." Brown was leaving on a trip that same afternoon, not to return until July 9, but "he made an appointment with Pres. McKay for Lowell and Pres. Brown to see Pres. McKay when he returns." Ed summarized pessimistically: "I don't know what good it can do. The damage has been done. It was announced at the 'Y' on Friday last [during the week-long seminar for CES personnel] that Lowell would be writing text books for the institutes next year—the Executive Committee (Joseph Fielding Smith, *et al.*, had just approved this leave the previous day). Lowell just smiled. He doubts it, and thinks he'll just quit the system and do something else—perhaps go to teach at the U. of U."[31]

On July 2 Hermana wrote to her children, giving them the latest developments. Berrett had telephoned Lowell, asking an incredible question: "From what I hear, you are hurt over this change!!" (Exclamation points Hermana's.)

"After a man has spent his life building something & then it is snatched out of his hands for no good reason, I think he has a right to be hurt," Lowell responded pointedly, challenging Berrett's justification of slipping enrollment. He pointed out that his and Ed's classes had increased in both number and size over the years and insisted he "had a right to know who it is that has ordered this and why."

Berrett scolded Lowell for his "attitude." It was having a deleterious effect on "the morale" of other CES teachers.

"Have you thought what it does to my morale?" Lowell asked. He then related his conversation with Brown, reporting that neither he nor the First Presidency knew about the change. Berrett said that "he thought the first Presidency had given their consent."[32] Hermana added, "Br. B. has aged 5 years in the last few weeks."[33]

That afternoon Olpin met with both Bennion and Neal Maxwell, asking Lowell if he would be willing to "join us as an assistant dean or a counselor of students with some instructional rank."[34] The University of Utah Board of Regents appointed Maxwell dean of students on July 9; and Maxwell reported the next day to Olpin that "Lowell Bennion is almost ready to come work for us, and the newly announced program on juvenile delinquency, under Dr. [Ray] Canning, could use part of Dr. Bennion's time, and he is very anxious to participate in this. He also wants to do some writing." Olpin told Maxwell that he had arranged a meeting with McKay to "tell him of our desire to get Dr. Bennion and have the president encourage him to come here."[35]

Lowell's refusal to make a commitment at this late stage looks like indecisiveness, but he was still waiting for a meeting with President McKay. When President Brown returned on July 9, he telephoned Lowell that the church president had instructed Brown to tell Lowell that he could be "of greater service at the University than doing what the [Church] Department of Education wanted done."[36] Lowell would come to feel that President McKay, by refusing to intervene or influence his decision, was protecting Lowell's "free agency." During the remainder of his life he expressed only feelings of love, respect, and appreciation for presidents McKay and Brown.[37]

On July 3 Wilkinson asked Ed Berrett for a list of complaints against Lowell, obviously preparing for a meeting at Lowell's request a few days later.[38] Wilkinson summarized this two-hour meeting, held July 11, in a lengthy letter dated July 13 to McKay.[39] He explained that his reason for writing was the calls he had received about the reassignment of Lowell Bennion. He identified five "complaints" as reasons for this and summarized Lowell's response to each accusation. The first was Lowell's consistent failure to "actively recruit students."[40]

Lowell and Ed had always found comparisons to Utah State and other largely Mormon colleges unfair. Other campuses had not suffered from the religious schism that plagued Salt Lake City, nor were other campuses as commuter-oriented as the University of Utah. Lowell answered that both he and Brother Lyon have always attracted large classes, as compared to other teachers, and that he "thought students ought to take institute courses of their own free will without . . . social pressure."

Wilkinson conceded that there was "some merit" to Lowell's opinion that the Utah institute should have the "strongest teachers . . . men as strong as he is" but concluded that "on balance we have had to use some of our strongest men as directors at some of the other institutes."

Wilkinson's second "complaint" was that Lowell had been "quite lax" in insisting on scholastic requirements, giving only pass/fail grades, with no outside assignments or papers. He reported Lowell as saying that these requirements conflict with religious motivation.

Wilkinson then brought up the old accusation that Lowell had not "fought for recognition of the institute as a certified school whose credits could be transferred to the U. of U. for graduation purposes."[41] "We have urged him to upgrade scholarship requirements and avoid 'snap' courses, bringing them up to the quality of BYU," Wilkinson summarized. "He admits he has not done this." The legal term, "admits," automatically slants the report, making what could have been a clarification into a concession. Elders Packer and Theodore Tuttle—former seminary and institute supervisors who had become general authorities in 1961 and 1958 respectively—had reported that despite "many conferences" with Lowell, he refused to pursue university credit for such courses as the Bible, marriage relations, and comparative religion. These two men agreed that "as long as Brother Bennion was director, little improvement would be made in this respect."

Lowell had never made a secret of his lack of support for credit courses nor the politically difficult obstacle such a proposal would encounter at the University of Utah. Six years earlier Berrett and Wilkinson had pushed Lowell to seek credit, and Olpin had advised against it. After Wilkinson's 1959 meeting with Olpin, he did not pursue the matter further.[42]

Wilkinson's fourth reason was Lowell's unorthodox position on the "Negro question" and the missionary program. As always, Lowell saw the ban regarding blacks and the priesthood in terms of its impact on individual lives. One of his most powerful experiences was one that President McKay would remember. About 1956 or 1957 a blond male freshman, fighting back tears, told Lowell after a Sunday school class, "They asked me to pass the sacrament today, but I couldn't because it's believed in my town that my grandmother in South Carolina had Negro blood." He and his brothers and male cousins had been denied ordination to the priesthood but had remained active in the church "because my mother asked me to and I love her." Not long after, however, he dropped out of school and Lowell lost contact with him.

Then one morning he appeared in Lowell's office to report that his sister was planning to marry in the temple. Mark E. Petersen and Joseph Fielding Smith, both apostles, had promised to consult with the Twelve.

"Keep me posted," Lowell told him.

A few days later the young man called to report the marriage had been scheduled for the following Friday, but the young couple would not be married in the temple.

"Let me see what I can do," Lowell said.

He went to Hugh B. Brown, then assistant to the Quorum of the Twelve, who listened thoughtfully and made an appointment for Lowell with President McKay the next morning.

McKay greeted Lowell cordially, then asked, "What's on your mind?"

Lowell explained the situation involving the marriage and the wider ramifications to the family then summarized: "President McKay, in my experience, the gospel builds life. Here I see it tearing it down."

McKay confided that in 1954 he had discontinued the practice in South Africa of tracing a convert's genealogy to certify its "purity." Then he mused, "When problems like this come to me, I say to myself, 'Sometime I shall meet my Father in Heaven, and what will he say?'"

Lowell responded quickly, "He'll forgive you if you err on the side of mercy."

McKay smiled, "But don't you think it's a little too late to do something about it?"

Lowell responded simply, "No, sir."

McKay paused then said, "Leave it to me."

Within a day or so Lowell heard from the young man that his sister would be married in the temple. Lowell recalled that McKay had said, "Now if we let the girl go, it means we should let the boy go too, doesn't it?" Lowell had replied, "Yes, if he's worthy." Two months later the young man asked Lowell to ordain him an elder preparatory to a mission call.[43]

Doug Alder, one of Lowell's students during the early 1950s, was troubled about the issue and noticed that Lowell "dealt with the dilemma mainly by loving black people and keeping up a dialogue with black leaders." Rather than making the "matter one of public confrontation," he "took the high road of patient emphasis on New Testament morality."[44]

Now Wilkinson reported to President McKay:

> He has been quoted many times as saying that he cannot give a satisfactory explanation for the failure of the Church to allow the negro [sic] to receive the priesthood. He does not deny having made this statement many times, although he says of late he has not made it publicly but only to students who have inquired of him about it. It has been reported that he has taught that the time would soon come when the Church would give the priesthood to the negro and that the policy of denying them the priesthood was unfair and not in accordance with the justice of god [sic]. In my conference with him I told him that he ought to be able to justify the failure to give the priesthood to the negro by taking into account the conduct of the negroes in the pre-existence, but it was apparent to me that he does not quite accept this explanation.[45]

This was not Lowell's and Wilkinson's first exchange on this topic. Eight years earlier Wilkinson had responded to a letter from Lowell who told him the story of the blond student banned from passing the sacrament. Wilkinson had replied with apparent sympathy: "Your stories on the Negro question are heartrending to say the least. I will follow [the] counsel of the brethren on these matters, but I intend a long conference with them on the matter."[46]

In fact, he had asked Berrett to research the issue of the blacks and the priesthood. Berrett's resulting essay, "The Church and the Negroid People," was published in John J. Stewart's 1960 *Mormonism and the Negro.*[47] After a brief history of the policy toward blacks in the church, Berrett reaffirmed the ban and offered as a possible reason "the conduct of spirits in the pre-existence."[48] He concluded his arguments by quoting the letter McKay had written Lowell in 1947 admitting that he knows of "no scriptural basis for denying the Priesthood to Negroes. . . . I believe the real reason dates back to our pre-existant [sic] life."[49] Lowell was still unable to agree with the pre-existence theory.

The fifth and last "complaint" was Lowell's "criticism of the pressures put on missionaries to hurriedly baptize people into the Church." In fairness, Wilkinson added that "some of the General Authorities" had agreed with Lowell. He does not summarize Lowell's defense on this point but simply records that Lowell "is still of the same opinion."

Wilkinson then evaluated Lowell as "by far a great teacher, as competent as any in the system . . . in spite of certain reservations on doctrinal points. . . . He has had a great influence for good on the lives of thousands of students." He also quoted Lowell's view that courses in the institute should be "determined by the teachers who are on the firing line [rather] than by the Board of Education."

Wilkinson explained that he told Lowell "that we would be most happy to have him on our College of Religious Instruction faculty at the BYU." Lowell had no problem responding to this: "He says he had three objections to coming to the BYU: (1) He did not agree with our practice at the BYU of requiring students to take courses in religion and insisting on the same scholastic standards as in other courses; he thought students ought to take courses in religion on a voluntary basis, (2) He thought there was not enough intellectual freedom for teachers at the BYU, (3) He felt that certain teachers at the BYU in their theological teaching were too dogmatic." Lowell added that he had never felt right about being compensated for teaching religion and "perhaps it is time for a change" in his career.

Wilkinson, who may not have known that McKay had already

declined to meet with Lowell, asked McKay to "remember that he has unbounded love and respect for you. . . . I have asked Bro. Bennion to see me again and to make a decision in 24 hours." Wilkinson may have felt that Lowell was still considering his revised position within CES; but that very day, without referring to the Wilkinson meeting, Lowell wrote an understated letter to his son Steve, then serving a mission:

> It might interest you to know that I will not be at the institute next year. Some of the board are a bit critical of my administration and views and felt that a change might be good. I quite agree with the "change might be good," but think that our philosophy of what is important in institute work is sound. . . . So I have accepted two half-time jobs at the U. (1) a sort of associate dean of students and (2) assistant director of a study on how to prevent juvenile delinquency. The latter is government sponsored and ties with my interest in youth and my church assignment. While I leave the institute with some regret, the new tasks are most challenging.[50]

When Olpin informed McKay of Maxwell's appointment, the church president commented, "I thought you were considering Dr. Bennion." Olpin answered simply that he hoped Lowell would accept the position of associate dean of students. President McKay dropped the subject, only "agree[ing] that in Maxwell, whom he didn't know except by reputation, and in Lowell Bennion, we would have a strong dean of students office."[51]

Lowell did not report to Wilkinson within twenty-four hours as ordered. Instead, two weeks later Lowell wrote a gracious letter to Wilkinson thanking him for the meeting and announcing that he had decided to accept an appointment at the university. Expressing thanks for "the richness of my life as an institute teacher, the past twenty-seven years," he admitted he was leaving "reluctantly," adding, "I am not sure that I will ever find another work which will give me as much satisfaction." He also assured Wilkinson that he was leaving "without bitterness or ill-will toward anyone." Claiming that Wilkinson had always been "fair and gracious," he thanked him for "support in the past" and anticipated a "continuing friendship between us."[52]

Since this was one of the few—if not the only—private meeting Lowell would ever have with Wilkinson, it may well be that both were impressed with each other. Wilkinson may have decided, especially in the light of so much outcry, that Lowell was worth keeping. At any rate, Lowell came away with the uneasy feeling that he had not yet heard the real reasons for his dismissal.

By July 30, however, Wilkinson was lecturing Berrett:

> This year I want a procedure whereby I will know more of what is going on in the institutes and seminaries. . . . I was chagrined that not until the crisis arose regarding Lowell Bennion and T. Edgar Lyon, did I know that Bennion had practically refused to keep rolls and had practically no methods of grading his students. Had I known that, I am sure I would have resolved the matter much earlier. We should ask for monthly reports, citing progress and irregularities, so we can get the whole picture.[53]

This memo demonstrates yet another procedure by which Wilkinson planned to manage daily activities at institutes. It also makes it clear that Lowell's independence was intolerable to him. Perhaps a fuller history of Wilkinson's role in church education will show that it was through such technical matters as record keeping that Wilkinson exercised control over staffing rather than persuading the Board of Education and Board of Trustees of perceived heresies or "disloyalty."

On July 18, 1962, Lowell received a letter from his friend, Leonard Arrington, economics professor at Utah State University: "I cannot imagine the institute without you and Ed, nor is it possible to comprehend the loss to the church educational system resulting from your transfer. In almost every age group you have made solid and lasting contributions in manuals and textbooks."[54] Arrington's letter represents hundreds of letters of protest sent to Lowell, Ed, Wilkinson, and Hugh B. Brown. In spite of Lowell's objections, students launched a letter-writing campaign to Brown and Wilkinson.

Word of Lowell's termination spread quickly. Hermana and Ed Lyon reported dozens of calls coming daily from around the country. "People are really stirred up," Hermana wrote to her sons in mid-July.[55] A typical outraged reaction was that of Fred Buchanan, then finishing his education degree at the University of Utah. He wrote in his diary, "This is really a shock to me—it bodes ill for the future of the church, I'm afraid. . . . Too many want blind, unquestioning faith. Thank God for men like Brothers Bennion and Lyon. They *think and have faith* in some power beyond men." To the claim that they were "too old to teach," he scoffed, "What a joke!" He pinpointed CES's methods as the chief outrage: "What a travesty of justice—twenty-eight years in the system and then to be 'promoted' without consultation." Buchanan was among the former students who launched the letter-writing campaign, enthusiastically quoting Joseph Smith: "It feels so good not to be trammeled."[56]

DuWayne Schmidt recalled, "Many of us were so upset at his being squeezed out of . . . the institute that many of us were on the forefront in making a protest. . . . We sent a letter to Joseph Fielding Smith, . . . [who] typed out a sweet letter to Alice [Schmidt, Smith's cousin], saying 'This is a good brother. He's done nothing wrong. We needed him somewhere else.'"[57] In a letter to colleague George Boyd on September 19, Ed Lyon commented that "doctors, lawyers, teachers, and housewives" had written letters of protest to the First Presidency, Wilkinson, and Berrett. "Unfortunately they did not get the facts straight," he admitted. "[They thought] that Lowell had been thrown out with no offer of any kind, and that I had also been moved out, which, of course, was not true, as I did receive the usual contract." Ed described letters coming "from all over the world and many from missionaries in the field."

> Of course they go unheeded, and no one is willing to make acknowledgement that a serious blunder was made. Several of the General Authorities have told Lowell, or others, that they were amazed that Lowell left. They had been given the impression this was something that Lowell wanted and were amazed that he was hurt by it.
>
> One of the wheels in the department admitted to me that they cannot let Lowell know who is responsible for this, and also that [the young instructor's] report to the brethren was a determining factor in his removal. He also admitted . . . that [this instructor] had been sent to us with certain instructions, but denied they were sent to spy on us.[58]

Ed explained that in response to these protests Wilkinson issued a form letter stating that they were relying on rumors, that Lyon had not been moved out and would still be there, that Lowell had been offered a promotion but had chosen the work at the U. He sent Lowell a copy, and Lowell wrote him a letter asking that Wilkinson tell the truth about his dismissal.[59]

Wilkinson's secretary responded to Lowell's letter saying that Wilkinson was out of town and would reply when he returned. Ed was skeptical: "He has been back several weeks."[60] In fact, Wilkinson failed to answer Lowell's letter and instead took the public position "that it was a promotion for Bro. Bennion and he can't help it if Bro. Bennion took it in the wrong way."[61] Lowell, unable to explain the situation to his puzzled and angry students, had nothing to reproach himself for.

Merle's sister Ethel, administrative secretary at the institute, expressed her own feelings in a letter to Steve Bennion in mid-August: "I guess by this time you know how we have been stirred up around here. . . . We don't get time to do much besides answer the telephone, letters, and personal calls about your Dad's leaving. . . . To me the institute is your Dad and Ed, and when they leave I am not sure I will want to stay." She was sorry about teachers who had to cope with the onslaught of complaints and questions but "not sorry enough that if your Dad can use me in his new office, I wouldn't go on a moment's notice."[62]

Merle had written an equally candid letter to Steve in mid-July. "Ben's reaction, as he so aptly put it, was that he was sad and mad." Hundreds of protests, both verbal and written, had come from former and present students and friends. She described herself as "sad that your Dad's whole-souled devotion to his work and the fact that he is a wonderful teacher have been completely overlooked by the brethren. . . . The whole affair has been handled poorly. It's been hard on Dad, but he is not bitter and will never lose his faith." She urged Steve not to let it disturb his faith.[63] Doug was succinct: "I think Dad got a rotten deal, but he is really looking forward to his work at the U."[64]

On July 26 the church-owned *Deseret News* announced Lowell's appointments at the University of Utah as assistant dean of students and director of community services of the Utah Center for the Prevention and Control of Juvenile Delinquency. Lowell's second appointment, with Dr. Ray Canning in the sociology department, would be funded by a large federal grant—$150,000—and the university would be one of only two universities west of the Mississippi conducting such a study.[65] Both appointments were effective September 1. The university's graduate dean, Henry Eyring, promptly declared Olpin's appointments of Maxwell and Lowell "a stroke of genius."[66]

Lowell was still clinging to his hope for a meeting with the church Board of Education or its executive committee. He waited out July, and when the meeting Ed Berrett had promised failed to materialize he wrote a gracious letter to Berrett, apologizing for any "distress and concern . . . that may have affected adversely on the morale of your faculty," bade farewell to a "professional position in which a person can build such a fine relationship with so many young people," and added, "I shall also have the pleasure of serving the cause we love (voluntarily and freely)."[67] Minutes of the Board of Education show that Berrett and Wilkinson did ask for a meeting with Lowell in late September, but the board voted to "table" it.[68]

Salt Lake City newspapers published Wilkinson's announcement on August 5 in the *Deseret News* and August 11 in the *Church News* that the "institute directorship was left vacant when Dr. Bennion resigned to accept a position as assistant dean of students at the university." In announcing Joe Christensen's appointment—which had actually been made in May—Wilkinson added, "Dr. Bennion has been a great force for good at the Salt Lake institute. . . . He has restored faith in the hearts of hundreds of young men and women and guided their lives into productive paths. He has been one of the outstanding teachers and writers of the church." Expressing regret that "Dr. Bennion had decided not to accept an assignment to continue with the unified church school system by writing several planned courses of study," Wilkinson claimed that "the challenge of the community service position . . . appealed very much to him and he accepted it with our knowledge and understanding."[69]

Lowell was exasperated by the announcement but especially by Wilkinson's request, transmitted two weeks later, that Lowell "stop all the rumors." On August 20, from the ranch, Lowell wrote to Wilkinson:

> Rest assured that I have done nothing to encourage rumors or discussions about my leaving the institute. I would be happy if people would let the matter drop. This morning I refused a request on the part of

> some former students to hold a testimonial in my behalf. . . . Your statements to the press and others were, I suppose, as well done as could be expected . . . though they do convey inaccurate impressions. . . . Nothing was said to me about writing for *two years,* but only for one. And the implication of your statements is that I left the institute to do a job that was more appealing to me. This, of course, is certainly not true. I should have preferred to remain at the institute where I feel I might have served God and man best. I chose to go to the U. only after it was made plain to me that I was no longer welcome at the institute.[70]

Lowell described to Wilkinson his difficulty in explaining "to my students, to their parents, and to other friends why I am leaving." He continued,

> To some . . . it appears either that I am walking out on them, or that the church is letting me down. My approach has been to brush the whole thing off by saying that a change will likely be good for everyone concerned, and that it is not good for an institution to be too closely identified with an individual or two. . . . Would you care to tell me more specifically why I was released . . . and by whom . . . in order to pass on the truth to those who inquire.[71]

There is no record that Wilkinson ever replied. But in a letter to Ezra Taft Benson two-and-a-half years later, he explained why he felt he had lost his 1964 senatorial campaign by a humiliating margin:

> By direction of the Board of Education, I removed Lowell Bennion as Director of the institute at the University of Utah. He had flatly refused to do any proselyting for L.D.S. students with the result that we had a smaller percentage of L.D.S. students in the Salt Lake institute than any other institute in the Church. Although I informed Bennion he could remain as a teacher, he chose to go as Associate Dean of Students to the University of Utah. Many rumors erupted in Salt Lake County as to the reason for his dismissal and this hurt me in that county.[72]

Wilkinson's version obscures his part in convincing the board of his views and contains at least one statement that can be misunderstood: He had only hinted at an offer of a teaching position at BYU and definitely not offered Lowell the option of "remaining" as a teacher at the institute. This letter reveals, however, that

Wilkinson was not prepared for the public anger generated by his treatment of Lowell.

Many felt that the whole episode may have been unnecessary. Hermana Lyon wrote her sons in late August that "a man in the history department at the Y . . . said he had talked to Ed Berrett a few days ago and he said Wilkinson would like to undo the whole mess if he could now, and Ed [Berrett] had said that if they had only listened to him and had Lowell in to talk with him, it would never have happened."[73]

Although Lowell understood Wilkinson's role as administrator and harbored no personal animosity, he had been uncomfortable with Wilkinson's style, goals, and insistence on being the only spokesman to the general authorities. Interviewed in 1990, Lowell still felt that a face-to-face meeting with the executive committee of the Board of Education would have allayed his anxieties.[74] Yet asked what might have happened if President McKay had intervened and kept him on, Lowell answered, "I would have had to leave anyway. The way [CES] was being [managed] I couldn't have stayed on."[75]

In April 1968 President McKay asked Lowell to address the general priesthood session of the worldwide general conference on education. His sermon, "Seek Ye Wisdom," was well received and published in the June 1968 *Improvement Era* as well as in the official conference reports. He prefaced the speech with a note of gratitude to President McKay: "I am thankful for his trust and faith in me. I am also grateful for the example which he has set for us in the field of education. President McKay loves the Lord with all his mind, as well as with his heart and soul. I know this from personal experience."[76]

Although Wilkinson's willingness to take direct action makes it easy to cast him as the villain, the reality was more complex. If more information were available, the picture might be even more complicated, with many personal agendas coming together.[77]

Obert Tanner, Lowell's friend and neighbor, saw Lowell's dismissal in strongly ethical terms:

> The church had a very great and a very good man, and the church should have been more careful. If you were to ask why Christianity lived, it's because mankind took a good man and nailed him to the

> cross, put a spear wound in his side, and a crown of thorns on his head—and mankind can't forget it. All over the world you have that portrayal of what happened to a good man. . . . I'm not criticizing the church. They did what they thought was right. I just think they did wrong.[78]

The psychological stress of the summer of 1962 almost exhausted Lowell and Merle, but an unusual spiritual experience gave Lowell peace. One night Lowell had a powerful dream. "I looked to the foot of the bed—and there was Jesus Christ, looking at me and smiling. He held out his arms in blessing, and I felt peace and comfort."[79] That vision sustained Lowell for the rest of his life.

NOTES

1. T. Edgar Lyon to Donna and Laurie (Lyon), 17 June 1962, photocopy in Bradford's possession. Additional background comes from Ted Lyon, interviewed by Mary L. Bradford, 6 May 1988. Ted returned from a mission that year and his father described this occasion to him.

2. In Peggy Fletcher, "A Saint for All Seasons," *Sunstone* 10 (Feb. 1985): 10.

3. T. Edgar Lyon to Donna and Laurie (Lyon), 17 June 1963.

4. Lowell L. Bennion, Oral History, 162.

5. Board of Education, Minutes, 25 Apr. 1962, Ernest L. Wilkinson Collection, Presidential Papers, University Archives, Harold B. Lee Library, Brigham Young University, Provo, Utah. Members attending included David O. McKay, presiding, Henry D. Moyle, Hugh B. Brown, Joseph Fielding Smith, Harold B. Lee, Spencer W. Kimball, Ezra Taft Benson, Mark E. Petersen, Marion G. Romney, LeGrand Richards, Richard L. Evans, Howard W. Hunter, and Lowell's neighbor, Gordon B. Hinckley.

6. Executive Committee, Minutes, 31 May 1962.

7. T. Edgar Lyon to Donna and Laurie (Lyon), 17 June 1963.

8. Ibid.

9. T. Edgar Lyon, Desk Diary, 31 May 1993, in possession of Lyon family and used by their courtesy. Olpin's diary for this date does not men-

tion this meeting.

10. T. Edgar Lyon to Donna and Laurie (Lyon), 17 June 1963.

11. Board of Education, Minutes, 6 June 1962.

12. Minutes of the Board of Education Executive Committee, 31 May 1962.

13. Wilkinson, Diary, 6 June 1962. The full minutes of those meetings and the journals of general authorities involved might present some of Wilkinson's descriptions and conclusions in a different light, were they available.

14. T. Edgar Lyon to Donna and Laurie (Lyon), 17 June 1963.

15. Although Berrett was interviewed on other aspects of Lowell's work, he refused to comment, describe, or provide any information on the events of Lowell's leaving the institute in 1962.

16. Olpin, Diary, 6 June 1962, Olpin Collection, Presidential Papers, University Archives, University of Utah, Salt Lake City.

17. T. Edgar Lyon to Donna and Laurie (Lyon), 17 June 1963. In his 1974 oral history he speculated on the reason he was not given the director's position. In addition to his obvious sympathy for and identification with Lowell, he had panned Vetterli's anti-communist book in the *Utah Alumnus* and Wilkinson was "quite chagrined that I should not support [the author's] interpretation." As his papers show, Wilkinson endorsed Vetterli's writings. (See T. Edgar Lyon, "Politics and the Mormons," *Utah Alumnus,* Feb. 1962, 7-9.)

18. Ibid.

19. Ibid.

20. Ibid.

21. Ibid.

22. Olpin, Diary, 8 June 1962.

23. Ibid.

24. Wilkinson to William E. Berrett, 15 June 1962; emphasis added.

25. William E. Berrett, interviewed by Mary L. Bradford, 5 May 1987.

26. Ibid.

27. Olpin, Diary, 19 June 1962.

28. T. Edgar Lyon, Desk Diary, 16 June 1962.

29. Wilkinson to William E. Berrett, 29 June 1962.

30. T. Edgar Lyon to "Hi, You All" (children), 25 June 1962, photocopy in Bradford's possession.

31. T. Edgar Lyon to "Dear Laurie/Dear Family-members," 1 July 1962, photocopy in Bradford's possession.

32. Hermana Lyon to Jamie and Laurie (Lyon), 2 July 1962, photocopy in Bradford's possession.

33. Ibid.

34. Olpin, Diary, 2 July 1962.

35. Ibid., 10 July 1962.

36. T. Edgar Lyon to James F. and A. Laurence Lyon, 22 July 1962.

37. Lowell L. Bennion, "Memories," 73 (photocopy in Bradford's possession), called Brown "a confidential friend until his death" in 1975 but never discussed the circumstances of his termination with Brown. Lowell Bennion, interviewed by Mary L. Bradford, 17 May 1989.

38. Wilkinson to William E. Berrett, 3 July 1962.

39. Wilkinson to David O. McKay, 13 July 1962.

40. The Salt Lake institute's enrollment for the previous five years ranged from 24.2 to 30.6 percent of total university enrollment—lower than any other institute. Utah State had enrolled 50.1 percent, while only eighty students graduated from the Salt Lake institute in 1961.

41. Wilkinson to David O. McKay, 13 July 1962.

42. Wilkinson explained to President McKay that Elder Packer had faulted the reputation of the institute at the University of Utah, claiming that it attracted only inferior students and no student leaders. Lowell found this accusation unfounded. It was true that the institute had not recruited for popularity and glamour, often reaching the lonely, the handicapped, and others who often turned out to be academically superior. As for leadership, the institute routinely entered candidates in student government races and social contests. Its members served on yearbook and newspaper staffs and on homecoming and songfest committees.

43. Lowell L. Bennion, "Memories," 63-64; Lowell L. Bennion, Oral History, 127-28.

44. Douglas D. Alder, "Lowell L. Bennion: The Things That Matter Most," in *Teachers Who Touch Lives: Methods of the Masters,* comp. Philip L. Barlow (Bountiful, UT: Horizon Publishers, 1988), 26.

45. Wilkinson to David O. McKay, 13 July 1962.

46. Wilkinson to Lowell L. Bennion, 17 Sept. 1954.

47. John J. Stewart, *Mormonism and the Negro* (Orem, UT: Bookmark Division of Community Press, 1960), 1-24. Board of Education, Minutes, 3 May 1961, a meeting that included McKay, Moyle, and Smith. Wilkinson gave each general authority a copy and announced he would be distributing it to all seminary teachers.

48. Ibid., 16.

49. Ibid., 19.

50. Lowell L. Bennion to Steven D. Bennion, 13 July 1962, photocopy in Bradford's possession.

51. Olpin, Diary, 14 July 1962.

52. Lowell L. Bennion to Wilkinson, 30 July 1962, copy in Bradford's possession.

53. Wilkinson to William E. Berrett, 30 July 1962.

54. Leonard J. Arrington to Lowell L. Bennion, 18 July 1962, photocopy in Bradford's possession.

55. Hermana Lyon to "Dear Sons" (Jamie and Laurie Lyon), 16 July 1962; Lowell L. Bennion, conversation with Mary L. Bradford, 17 May 1990.

56. Frederick Buchanan, Diary, 28 Aug. 1962, private possession.

57. DuWayne Schmidt, interviewed by Mary L. Bradford, 14 Feb. 1988.

58. T. Edgar Lyon to George Boyd, 19 Sept. 1962, photocopy in Bradford's possession.

59. Ibid.

60. Ibid.

61. Hermana Lyon to "Dearest Donna and Laurie and Blair (Lyon)," 3 Aug. 1962, photocopy in Bradford's possession.

62. Ethel Colton Bennion to Steven Don Bennion, 8 Aug. 1962, pho-

tocopy in Bradford's possession.

63. Merle C. Bennion to Steven Don Bennion, 19 July 1962, photocopy in Bradford's possession.

64. Douglas C. Bennion to Steven D. Bennion, 19 Aug. 1962, photocopy in Bradford's possession.

65. "U. of U. Taps Aide for Dean Duties," *Deseret News and Salt Lake Telegram,* 16 July 1962, B-1.

66. Olpin, Diary, 26 July 1962.

67. Lowell L. Bennion to William E. Berrett, 30 July 1962, copy in Bradford's possession.

68. Board of Education, Minutes, 17 Sept. 1962. LeGrand Richards and Boyd K. Packer were welcomed as new members at this time.

69. "Dr. J. J. Christensen Gets U. Institute Post," *Deseret News,* 5 Aug. 1962, B-1; "New Director Named for U. of U. Institute of Religion," *Church News,* 11 Aug. 1962, 4. There is no indication that Lowell was asked for a comment or that he volunteered a statement.

70. Lowell L. Bennion to Wilkinson, 20 Aug. 1962, photocopy in Bradford's possession.

71. Ibid.

72. Wilkinson to Ezra Taft Benson, 2 Feb. 1965, 2, photocopy in Bradford's possession.

73. Hermana Lyon to her sons, 22 Aug. 1962, photocopy in Bradford's possession.

74. Lowell L. Bennion, interviewed by Mary L. Bradford, 19 May 1990.

75. Ibid.

76. Lowell L. Bennion, "Seek Ye Wisdom," in Eugene England, ed., *The Best of Lowell L. Bennion: Selected Writings, 1928-1988* (Salt Lake City: Deseert Book Co., 1988), 191.

77. George Boyd traced the situation to Joseph Fielding Smith's views on science and blacks and the priesthood. Boyd recalled that Smith had once reviewed a manual of Lowell's with the words, "There is no religion in it." According to Boyd, Adam S. Bennion had confided to him in 1954 that "Brother Smith was behind the movement to break up the faculty at

the University of Utah institute" (George T. Boyd, interviewed by Mary L. Bradford, 4 May 1987). Lowell wrote in his "Memories" that he had found Smith "kindly and honest . . . We knew where he stood, and I respected him even when I disagreed with him" ("Memories," 73).

78. Obert C. Tanner, interviewed by Mary L. Bradford, 10 May 1988.

79. Lowell L. Bennion, conversation with Mary L. Bradford, 19 Sept. 1988.

CHAPTER 9

RECOVERY AND RENEWAL

(1963-70)

I've been grateful for my institute experience because of my preoccupation with religion on a thoughtful level and the thousands of students I've known warmly and closely and exchanged ideas, feelings, and aspirations with. I don't know anybody who's had a richer relationship with students. . . . I say that modestly, but with appreciation.

—*LOWELL L. BENNION*

When Marion D. Hanks, British Mission president, heard the rumors of Lowell's dismissal, he wrote him a short note: "I want to know the reasons. I'm over here trying to preach righteousness and truth, and I've heard rumors and want to know." He later remembered,

> Lowell wrote me a magnificent letter with some reasons—enrollment and [so on]—but calming me down, even at that point. Christian in every way, too big for the people that were chewing at his hamstrings. It had to hurt him and badly, but this man was not just a philosopher, he was a saint. He handled that. He didn't obscure it, but he didn't point out the negatives, either. He said, "I managed not to please somebody, so we go on to other things." He took it better than his defenders and protagonists who wanted to cause a stir. He put that down. The kingdom exists for the people, and he didn't want to hurt them.[1]

From that basis and with that example, Hanks then wrote candidly and comfortingly to Lowell's son, Steve, still serving a mission in Scotland,

> I believe that maybe this [termination] is what should have happened . . . My own life and the lives of countless others have been materially and richly affected by his marvelous teaching and more importantly by his great soul. It has been a sad thing so far as I am concerned, but again, I think and hope that perhaps the future will not only set things in order, but demonstrate that this is the best thing for your dad.[2]

Lowell's pioneer stoicism helped him put the incident behind him. "[Lowell's] never been vindictive," Merle recalled. "I've never heard him say anything bad about any of these people." She added frankly, "I've said plenty, but not Lowell." For himself, Lowell replied simply, "Well, don't you know what the Savior said?"[3] He bore no ill will for those who were messengers, like William E. Berrett. Lowell had always enjoyed Berrett's company and understood that Berrett disliked his role in Lowell's release.

Family members and friends of the Bennions and Lyons agreed with James F. Lyon, Ed and Hermana's son, then a student at Harvard, who commented: "I would have to say the two men who came out of that [departure] with greater Christian charity and forgiveness and understanding than anyone else were Dad and Lowell Bennion. They managed to put aside all ill will and acrimony . . . and simply refused to talk negatively about it."[4]

The main reason for Lowell's attitude was his love for the church. "Next to my family, it has done the most to shape my life and give me life's values," he later wrote in his memoirs, "but I distinguish between gospel and church. The church is the instrument, the vehicle, to inculcate the gospel into the lives of men and women. It was established by Christ . . . 'to perfect the Saints'. . . . The church is both divine and human."[5] He realized that he could be loyal to imperfect men and imperfect institutions. "I love my country but not everything it does. I love my wife and family but I don't agree with all their values and choices. I think the Church can be the church of God and still be imperfect because it consists of men—good men—but of men, including leaders, who are human as well as inspired."[6]

It was no doubt great therapy for Lowell to spend most of the summer in the Teton Valley where he was building his boys' ranch. It embodied many of the institute's values and helped him remain involved with teenagers (see chap. 10). He had a strong ability to focus on the present and avoid worrying. Gardening was restorative; and he sincerely believed that he should concentrate on the richness and goodness of life. After the session ended at the ranch in late August, Lowell took Merle, Howard, and Ellen on a rare, week-long vacation to Idaho, Canada, and Montana.

Returning to Salt Lake City a day or two before school started, he faced the disheartening task of cleaning out his office in the building he had planned, helped build, and administered. Merle recalled that "the day Lowell moved out [of his office], I just thought, 'How can he ever take this?' But oh, I admired him so much." Poignantly but without self-pity, Lowell wrote to Steve: "I just finished packing the last book out of my office. I feel about as empty as the office looks, but I am sure my new assignments will challenge me. If not, I'll quit and be Obert [C. Tanner]'s gardener and write books." There was no resentment in his closing paragraph: "I am glad to be home again to get things done. I am a poor spectator of life. My satisfactions lie in *creation, service,* and trying to keep my *integrity.*"[7] His son Steve would later report, "He drank of the bitter cup and didn't become bitter."

On September 1 Lowell moved into his office in the Park Building at the University of Utah just "across the street." He was philosophical about the change, explaining years later: "Life certainly turns on decisions. When I decided to go to the institute instead of going to Snow College to teach academic subjects, it changed my whole life's activity. I've often wondered what would have happened to me . . . had I stayed in the secular field."[8] (See chap. 11.)

There were still difficult moments to handle at the institute. On September 20 a Lambda Delta Sigma convention welcomed delegates from thirty chapters at Western universities. Ed Lyon found the meetings "flat without Bro. Bennion's guiding hand," and demoralized students concluded the meetings "weren't up to par."[9] At the concluding banquet Alma Burton, administrator of CES seminaries, gave Lowell and Ed a "combined eulogy." Hermana Lyon wrote to her sons:

> Bro. Bennion's reply tore your heart. His voice broke and he couldn't go on twice. He spoke of feeling like a duck out of water in his new office and he referred to his funeral [moving out of the institute] which had taken place a few weeks ago. He said several times, "Now I'm not going to get sentimental." Then he would, because this Lambda Delt has meant so much to him, but most of his time (and it was only a brief talk) he talked about the purpose of Lambda Delt existing to help people. A student had referred to him as "liberal," and Lowell accepted it as a term of honor, if he could define it as caring more about people than anything else. He said people are the most important thing in the world and the Church exists only to serve people.

The farewell gifts were ironic: To Lowell, whose time at the institute had run out, CES gave a self-winding wristwatch, and to Ed, uncertain about his place for the next year, "a Samsonite 3-suiter."[10]

On September 21 Merle wrote a hurried letter to Steve from the neighborhood laundromat. She described the testimonial banquet at Lambda Delta as "wonderful, albeit a trifle sad" and Lowell as "becoming more and more immersed in his new jobs. . . . It is a terrific adjustment to make after nearly twenty-eight years in the same job." She added realistically, "He is not embittered, but I can tell it has taken its toll."[11]

Ed Lyon had moved from his assistant director's office into a small cubicle with a desk, locker, and filing cabinet. "It is also the room where the sacrament is prepared," he wrote his children, "but I'm not around on Sunday, so it doesn't conflict. I don't expect to spend much time there anyway."[12]

Many people who respected Lowell's silence called the Lyons. On August 8 Hermana had written to the children: "We are getting many phone calls and visits and letters . . . which make it difficult to put back of us and get on with our lives."[13]

Ed's status had remained in doubt during most of the summer. When Berrett asked him to stay at the institute on June 16, Ed agreed; but on July 16 Hermana wrote the children that Ed's first choice would be "something . . . from the U," and his second choice would be a year's leave to write manuals and "look for something else more to his liking."[14] The next day Berrett offered Ed a year's leave of absence at full pay to write the manual for the institute's History of Christianity classes. Ed accepted. "This is better than going back to the institute," he said resignedly. Then, two days later, Berrett also asked him to write a teacher's outline for the institute's LDS Church History course.[15]

This was followed by an offer from the University of Utah to teach a single course in American history and an offer from Murdock Travel Agency to lead a tour of the Holy Land. He accepted both. Then Berrett blandly asked him to teach winter quarter at the institute since the teacher they hoped to hire had rejected their offer.[16] In a letter to a former student he explained: "Enrollment dropped, so they asked me to teach 1/3 winter and spring quarters. I had over 400 in my classes, and this made the statistics, the only part that matters anymore, look good."[17]

In December 1962 Lowell penned a Christmas message to Ed: "I am torn between an utter sense of inadequacy on the one hand and lack of necessity on the other. It is almost like praising myself to praise you—you have become so much a part of my life and thought. . . . You are the best scholar and teacher of history in the church and I hope somehow that you will spend the next 20 years leaving a legacy to the generation to come both in their hearts and in print."[18]

That first school year was hard, but new doors opened for the Lyons. Ed conducted additional tours to eastern and southern Europe throughout the 1960s and 1970s. Hermana accompanied him on his trips abroad, and Merle eagerly awaited the Lyons' reports to study groups and Relief Societies, for the two couples remained close. In the autumn of 1963 the church's Nauvoo Restoration, Inc., hired Ed as its research historian. "This has been like a new life," he said happily. "One of my greatest joys has been to walk the streets of Nauvoo in the evening and imagine what Joseph Smith felt like when he was walking those same streets."[19] By 1964 he was working three days a week "to assure that Nauvoo, once auspicious center of Mormondom in Illinois, be authentically restored."[20] In the early 1970s Leonard J. Arrington, the first professionally trained official church historian, asked him to author a history of Nauvoo for a planned sixteen-volume sesquicentennial series.[21]

Even apart from his friendship with Ed, Lowell had no trouble maintaining a gentle bridge to the institute, creating an exemplary relationship of continuing commitment without claiming special authority. Joe Christensen's administration was "none of my business." But he spoke to a group of medical students each year and to Lambda Delta Sigma groups and to devotionals" nearly every year."[22] Dale LeCheminant, an instructor who began teaching at the institute in 1962, wrote to George Boyd that he had seen Lowell after a spring address in 1963 "putting his arm around Joe Christensen as if to say, 'No hard feelings.'"[23]

Christensen, who was called as general authority (First Quorum of the Seventy) while president of Ricks College in 1989, was a successful director. Neal Maxwell felt Christensen was the perfect replacement for Lowell. "Joe was mindful of how hard it is to follow Lowell Bennion. And you can't take anybody's place like that, but Joe settled in nicely, I think . . . and had a lot of Lowell's same qualities."[24]

In January 1964 Ernest Wilkinson took a leave of absence to run for the U.S. Senate, and the Board of Trustees split his two positions as chancellor of church education and president of BYU. When the voters of Utah rejected Wilkinson, he resumed control of Brigham Young University. The acting chancellor, Harvey L. Taylor, continued to administer the church school system, including institutes and seminaries. In 1970 Neal A. Maxwell left his position at the University of Utah to become Commissioner of Church Education. Berrett was reassigned from his position as vice president and administrator of seminaries and institutes to writer and editor of the history of church education.

In his centennial history of BYU, coauthored with Leonard Arrington, Wilkinson explained that the presidency "was a big enough job for any one man."[25] In his biography he admitted that after McKay's death in January 1970 he "sensed that the new Church administration might have a different perspective on the place and role of BYU"[26] and resigned in June. Dallin H. Oaks, later a chief justice of Utah's Supreme Court and later still an apostle, was appointed president of BYU. Ernest L. Wilkinson died in 1978.

Big changes were also in store for Lambda Delta Sigma. In April 1964 thirty-nine-year-old Paul H. Dunn, a popular seminary and institute teacher in California and a colleague of George Boyd, was called to the First Council of the Seventy. Harold B. Lee, then spearheading the correlation movement to bring all church administrative entities into a priesthood line, streamlining church organization and creating a centrally planned teaching curriculum, asked his advice: "You have come from college and university campuses. What do we need to do to help these kids?" Dunn proposed a new organization, the Latter-day Saint Students Association (LDSSA), which, along with campus and singles wards, would operate under priesthood direction. According to Dunn, the Church Education System was being run by "paid clergy" and not by "the priesthood."[27] ("Paid clergy," long a negative buzzword, was usually applied derisively to other religions by loyal Mormons who overlooked the facts that the male instructors and directors in CES were also priesthood holders and that general authorities were paid.)

Dunn felt that Lambda Delta Sigma was a "Mickey Mouse" organization everywhere but inside Utah because of its co-ed structure. He proposed making it into a women's sorority and creating a separate men's fraternity. Dunn, who had just been elected national president of Delta Phi, the returned LDS missionary fraternity, proposed that it open its doors to nonmissionaries.

Dunn then asked for Lowell's response. As he recalls, Lowell "had no objection," and said, "'Times change, Paul, and I understand that.'"[28] Lowell, however, said later that he was so surprised that he had "to take a breath." He recalled his acquiescence not as approval, but as yielding to the inevitable.[29] Merle was shocked when Lambda Delta Sigma was assigned to the Relief Society. How could the Relief Society administer a campus organization?[30]

Since Lambda Delt was one of Lowell's most beloved creations, it pained him to see its aims misunderstood. To assume that priesthood was not operating because a general authority was not in the direct chain of command seemed unnecessarily legalistic. The general authorities had approved Lowell's design from the beginning. Though women and men socialized and worked together, they could and did separate into their own chapters for many of the group's activities.

Wilkinson had launched an investigation of Lamba Delta Sigma in the spring of 1962, unbeknownst to Lowell. On Wilkinson's instructions, Berrett prepared a six-page defense, diplomatically giving credit to John A. Widtsoe for its founding. He stressed its public relations function on campus, acknowledged that the Salt Lake chapter with 700 members "serves the greatest need," and urged that it "be continued" where it succeeded "in holding young people in the Church."[31] Interviewed in 1988, Berrett declared, "It . . . was never successful except in a large institute like U. of U. . . . It failed in the small ones."[32] Lowell's records contradict this assertion, but he did nothing to stop the changes.

Instead, like Ed, Lowell reached out to embrace the opportunities of a new life. The 1960s were turbulent years for any American college campus, and the University of Utah was no exception (see chap. 11). He continued an intensive schedule of speaking engagements at church and community groups around the state. Merle was grateful that they also could find time and incentive to travel. Her appetite for travel never abated. In 1959 the Bennions' former boarder, Paul Jones, an investment banker, and his wife, Mildred, invited Merle and Lowell to go to Europe as their "guides," all expenses paid. Lowell, who hated being on the receiving end of such largesse, was about to refuse when he saw the light in Merle's face and realized she was ripe for a bargain. "Merle was and is wild about travel," he said later, "but I was more interested in getting a boys' ranch." He finally told her, "We'll do it if you'll agree to buy a ranch."[33] The deal was struck. From then on both travel and ranch life figured in their plans.

Ben was working on his degree at the University of Utah that summer, and his new wife, Sherilyn Cox Bennion, was employed in public relations, having graduated in 1957. Doug was serving a mission in Australia, while seventeen-year-old Steve worked a road repair job and milked cows at his Salt Lake home. Garry and Cozette Shirts, friends and former students, agreed to stay in the Bennion home and care for six-year-old Ellen. These arrangements were satisfactory for everyone but thirteen-year-old Howard, who spent a reluctant summer at Mark Wilson's Wyoming ranch. "I felt left out," he recalled. "Why couldn't I go to Europe?" It was a relevant question since Lowell insisted that Paul and Mildred take their own three children and Mildred's mother.[34] But Lowell was unwilling to incur further costs on behalf of his own family.

The ranch schedule proved grueling for Howard—up at 5:00 each morning and working until 9:30 every evening. When his parents came for him at summer's end, Howard ran to the car with arms outstretched and tears streaming down his face.[35] Merle felt guilty for leaving him, but the trip was the chance of a lifetime.

She enjoyed her first plane ride to New York City and a delightful production of *My Fair Lady,* after which the party went by steamship to Bremerhaven, Germany. There the two men took the wheels of two Mercedes Benz diesel cars, purchased in New York by the Joneses. They traveled in style, four to a car, following an itinerary that included Lowell's missionary and student haunts in Germany, Switzerland, Austria, and France. Then on to Denmark, Holland, Italy, Scotland, England, and Wales.

It was typical of Lowell that he squeezed in some church work en route. Responding to a request by Joseph T. Bentley, president of the General Board of the Young Men's Mutual Improvement Association, Lowell checked on the progress of MIA programs in Europe.

In Bavaria, the Bennions looked up Milton's friend, Max Haenle, who thanked them for the care packages the Bennions had sent after the war by giving them a delightful, five-day tour of his beautiful hometown, Tübingen, which, according to Haenle, was the "seat of democracy" in Bavaria.

It was a glorious trip for Merle, awakening longings for more travel. Because they had kept up their German, she and Lowell made good guides. As she experienced the glory of the great Renaissance artists, she felt her mind and spirit stirring with a desire for additional education. The trip proved a rich seeding-in for the many summers ahead when she would be expected to keep up her end of the ranch bargain. She fleetingly hoped for a move back to their old neighborhood within walking distances of the university's treasure house of classes, lectures, and performances, but the children knew that Lowell would never agree. Howard remembers his father gazing up at Mt. Olympus from their yard and musing, "I could never move from here. I want to be able to look at this mountain every day. If I go blind, I'll still have it in my head."[36]

Still, Lowell's position at the university and the greater freedom offered as the children grew up and left home encouraged Merle to take more classes. She added to her earlier credits by taking "Great Books" from Charles Monson, philosophy from Lewis Rogers, and enough credits in German for a major.

They maintained an active social life among Lowell's colleagues at the university, participated in cultural events, and assuaged their homesickness for the institute by keeping up with their study groups. The reading group, organized when Lowell came to the university in 1935, lasted until the early 1980s.[37]

Ed Lyon often conducted discussions at institute firesides and arranged with Lowell to "teach" a series of lessons on faith to his extended family. He also retained the kindly habit of dropping by to repair broken pipes and to help with Lowell's remodeling tasks. Once when Ed's neighbor, Bill Mulder, discarded an attic staircase, Ed retrieved it for use in the Bennion basement.

From March to September 1970 Lowell supervised fifteen or twenty students on the University of Utah's fourth study-abroad program. The program was headquartered at Christian-Albrechts University, a distinguished institution in Kiel on the Baltic that was three hundred years old and boasted 8,000 students. The Utah students lived in campus dormitories or private homes and took classes taught in German, where they grappled with political science, history, literature, and philosophy. Merle "boned up" on German grammar before departing. She and Ellen "took classes along with the students, and I was free to browse in the library," Lowell recalled. Merle proudly earned eighteen credit hours in German while Ellen earned ten. On weekends the students and the Bennions took side trips within Germany and to Holland and Denmark.[38] Although Lowell enjoyed the relaxed pace, he complained of feeling "lazy and parasitical," lacking "church work and contacts with people which are part of my bread and butter."[39]

Four months later the students went home, leaving Merle and Ellen anticipating two months of travel alone with Lowell. Characteristically he invited along a young man he had been counseling. Merle and Ellen wedged the youth and his luggage into a newly purchased Volvo and enjoyed the Leningrad Ballet in London, their first visit to Scandinavia, and two weeks in Great Britain and Holland—including visits to Bennion ancestral sites in Wales.[40]

In March 1977 another pleasurable travel opportunity opened up. Their friend, Pat Jarvis, who had formed her own travel business, invited Lowell to be the guide on a trip to Israel. This trip attracted former students and friends of the Bennions, including

Emma Lou and Mel Thayne and their five daughters, enchanted with the idea of hearing about Jesus in the Holy Land from one of the best Christians they knew. "People came to hear you," Jarvis told Lowell. In return Lowell "paid attention to everybody in the group." He took the occasional crabbiness of his tired charges philosophically ("hardship reveals character") and, when a woman introduced herself as "married to so-and-so," would respond, "There is more to you than that."[41]

Emma Lou Thayne, who published *Once in Israel,* a collection of poems and diary entries based on their experiences, captured a vignette of Lowell in action:

> At noon on this Saturday turned Sabbath, our guide from home, Lowell Bennion, is the speaker at church in the King David Hotel. His topic is grace. He talks of gratuitous light, warmth, nourishment, beauty—from whom? From where? He is all face, clear as a candle. Handsomely gnomelike, ruddy, beamingly bald, he smiles as if we shared some cosmic secret, bright in his believing, believable.
>
> When he is finished we sing, "I Know That My Redeemer Lives." His face is shining. Next to me on both sides I know my daughters' faces are silver. We cannot look at each other as we sing.[42]

This was the first of three trips to Israel and Greece and another to Egypt for Pat's tours between 1977 and 1980. "On the second trip, a couple of people said one of the most wonderful moments of their whole lives was when Lowell talked about the Sermon on the Mount at the Sea of Galilee," Pat recalled.[43]

Pat Jarvis hired Lowell to accompany a group of forty-nine through southern Germany, Austria, and Switzerland in the fall of 1977. Coincidentally, the group arrived on the eve of his and Merle's forty-ninth wedding anniversary. Lowell was impressed with the lack of "urban sprawl so common to Utah from Brigham City to Springville," rejoiced at the beautifully kept fields and forests, freshly washed by rain, and marveled at the "little churches with onion-copper domes" and the "dark Guernsey-like cows with white spots." Vienna seemed dirtier than they'd remembered, but it was worth the trip "to see that . . . beautiful red glass window in St. Stephen's church.[44]

Once again Lowell proved that he was not really a tourist. As they moved through Switzerland, he imagined an ideal trip that concentrated more on villages and less on cities. Where and what he ate was of little importance. He was disgusted when the group voted to bypass Tübingen in favor of shopping for cuckoo clocks and was surprised when few rated opera and organ recitals high on their lists. En route to Strasbourg he reread Albert Schweitzer's *Out of My Life and Thought,* impressed anew by the philosopher-physician's emphasis on doing. "He is one of my heroes!" he noted, adding a line from Goethe: "In the beginning was the deed."[45] This was consistent with his favorite proverb paraphrased from the *Bhagavad-Gita:* "To action alone thou hast a right, not to its fruits." It was a call to ethical action, regardless of the consequences—which, after all, are beyond control.

Lowell felt relieved when the trip ended and he could return to "constructive tasks," as he put it, but Merle exulted in the experience. "Travel opens up the world," she declared. They even discussed spending a few months after retirement in Vienna or London.[46]

Though travel was refreshing, Lowell found deep renewal in the daily exercise of working in the garden. Since moving to East Millcreek in the 1940s, he had planted the acres behind their house in vegetables, later working the shrinking yard with neighbors and ward members. Anyone who wanted to work could share in the harvest.

Lowell had the patience to wait until the peaches on his tree were absolutely ripe before he picked them, even if it meant that some would fall. Not for him the usual system of picking green and waiting for ripening. "Some of the most delicious peaches I've ever eaten came off his trees," Louis Moench recalled nostalgically. He also attributed the greenness of his own lawn to a Good Samaritan load of fertilizer delivered by Lowell.[47]

The garden was organized so that different crops would mature throughout the summer, "two or three hundred tomato plants, . . . lots of cabbage, broccoli, beans— . . . about half of the garden is potatoes." Lowell would mulch and cover his carrots in the fall, then dig up part of a row when he wanted tender, juicy carrots to eat or give away.[48]

Not only did Lowell grow vegetables, but he baked his own bread, slowly savoring pieces hot from the oven, dripping with butter and honey. He preferred fruit and nuts to fancy confections.

In the only poem of his career he summed up his personal philosophy and summarized his personal healing:

Learn to like what doesn't cost much.
Learn to like reading, conversation, music.
Learn to like plain food, plain service, plain cooking.
Learn to like fields, trees, brooks, hiking, rowing, climbing hills.
Learn to like people, even though some of them may be . . . different from you.
Learn to like to work and enjoy the satisfaction of doing your job as well as it can be done.
Learn to like the songs of birds, the companionship of dogs.
Learn to like gardening, puttering around the house, and fixing things.
Learn to like the sunrise and sunset, the beating of rain on the roof and windows, and the gentle fall of snow on a winter day.
Learn to keep your wants simple and refuse to be controlled by the likes and dislikes of others.[49]

NOTES

1. Marion D. Hanks, interviewed by Mary L. Bradford, 22 Mar. 1989.

2. Marion D. Hanks to Steven D. Bennion, 22 Sept. 1962, photocopy in Bradford's possession.

3. Lowell L. Bennion and Merle C. Bennion, interviewed by Mary L. Bradford, 26 Jan. 1990; Merle C. Bennion, Oral History, 76.

4. James Lyon, reminiscences taped in response to a list of questions from Mary L. Bradford, 10 Mar. 1989.

5. Lowell L. Bennion, "Memories," 64, photocopy in Bradford's possession.

6. Ibid., 64.

7. Merle Bennion, interviewed by Mary L. Bradford, 19 May 1990; Lowell L. Bennion to Steven D. Bennion, 30 Aug. 1962, copy in Bradford's possession. Obert C. Tanner, long a member of the philosophy department at the University of Utah, was a successful jeweler and philanthropist. His landscaped grounds were the showplace of East Millcreek and his numerous donated fountains brightened cityscapes across the country. He and Lowell had been friends since Lowell's return from Europe in 1934.

8. Lowell L. Bennion, Oral History, 151.

9. Hermana Lyon to "Dearest Jamie and Donna and Laurie [Lyon],"

11 Sept. 1962, photocopy in Bradford's possession.

10. Ibid.

11. Merle C. Bennion to Steven D. Bennion, 21 Sept. 1962, photocopy in Bradford's possession.

12. T. Edgar Lyon to Jamie, Laurie and Donna (Lyon), 17 Sept. 1962, photocopy in Bradford's possession.

13. Hermana Lyon to "Dearest Donna and Laurie and Blair" (Lyon), 8 Aug. 1962, photocopy in Bradford's possession.

14. Hermana Lyon to "Dearest Sons" (Jamie and Laurie Lyon), 16 July 1962, photocopy in Bradford's possession.

15. T. Edgar and Hermana Lyon to their sons, begun 16 July, concluded 22 July 1962, photocopy in Bradford's possession.

16. T. Edgar Lyon, Oral History, interviews conducted by Davis Bitton, 1975, typescript, 184, James Moyle Oral History Program, archives, Historical Department, Church of Jesus Christ of Latter-day Saints, Salt Lake City, Utah. I used copies in possession of Lowell L. Bennion and Ted Lyon, son of T. Edgar Lyon.

17. T. Edgar Lyon to George Littke, 4 Nov. 1963, photocopy in Bradford's possession; used by permission of Lael Littke.

18. Lowell L. Bennion to T. Edgar Lyon, 22 Dec. 1962, T. Edgar Lyon Papers, LDS archives; typed copy in Bradford's possession.

19. T. Edgar Lyon, "Teaching Religion with Joy and Love," *Church News,* 2 Aug. 1975, 14.

20. Dale C. LeCheminant, "T. Edgar Lyon: Scholar and Man of Faith," *Daily Utah Chronicle,* 25 Oct. 1978, unpaginated clipping in Bradford's possession.

21. Ed immersed himself in this project until just before his death in 1978 when he turned over four chapters and his materials to Glenn M. Leonard, who continues to work on this project in addition to his duties as director of the LDS Museum of Church History and Art in Salt Lake City.

22. Lowell L. Bennion, Oral History, 162.

23. Dale LeCheminant to George Boyd, Apr. 1963, photocopy in Bradford's possession.

24. Neal A. Maxwell, interviewed by Mary L. Bradford, 26 Sept. 1988.

25. Ernest L. Wilkinson and Leonard J. Arrington, *Brigham Young University: The First Hundred Years* (Provo, UT: Brigham Young University

Press), 3:197.

26. Woodruff J. Deem and Glenn V. Bird, *Ernest L. Wilkinson: Indian Advocate and University President* (Provo, UT: privately published, 1978), 502.

27. Paul H. Dunn, interviewed by Mary L. Bradford, 22 Feb. 1987.

28. Ibid.

29. Lowell L. Bennion, interviewed by Mary L. Bradford, 24 Feb. 1989; Lowell L. and Merle C. Bennion, interviewed by Mary L. Bradford, 17 May 1991.

30. Lowell L. and Merle C. Bennion, interviewed by Mary L. Bradford, 17 May 1991. The First Presidency and the Twelve established LDSSA in 1967 and appointed Dunn its first director, succeeded later by Marion D. Hanks. When Hanks was called as mission president in Hong Kong in 1980, the organization had no "general priesthood direction" until Rex W. Williams was called as director in 1989. The last national convention was held in Provo in May 1989. Today the local stake president is automatically "campus priesthood leader" and "chairman of the LDSSA executive committee." R. Scott Lloyd, "A Priesthood 'Umbrella' for LDS Students," *Church News*, 24 Nov. 1990, 9.

31. William E. Berrett to Ernest L. Wilkinson, 10 May 1962, Wilkinson Collection, Presidential Papers, University Archives, Harold B. Lee Library, Brigham Young University, Provo, Utah; photocopy in Bradford's possession.

32. William E. Berrett, interviewed by Mary L. Bradford, 5 May 1988.

33. Lowell L. Bennion, "Memories," 87.

34. Merle Colton Bennion, Oral History, 73. Despite this rocky beginning, Howard succumbed to the spell of the Teton country. "I thought I'd never go back," he confessed, but he worked on Mark Wilson's ranch every summer until he was twenty and "then lived with them two solid years." Howard W. Bennion, interviewed by Mary L. Bradford, 15 Feb. 1989.

35. Ibid.

36. Howard W. Bennion, interviewed by Mary L. Bradford, 15 Feb. 1989.

37. Merle Colton Bennion, Oral History, 73. The reading group included a mix of institute and university couples and relatives, like Maurine and Len Folsom and Paul and Oa Cannon, with old friends, Bill and Olive Moran, Clarence and Lydia Romrell, Roy and Nell Groberg, Roy and Jessie Buckmiller, and the Lyons. Merle and Hermana exchanged ideas

from Merle's calling in the ward Relief Society and Hermana's as a member of the General Board of the Relief Society.

38. Lowell L. Bennion, Oral History, 164.

39. Lowell L. Bennion to Laurie Newman DiPadova, 5 June 1970, copy in Bradford's possession.

40. Lowell L. Bennion, "Memories," 93.

41. Pat Jarvis, interviewed by Mary L. Bradford, 15 July 1988.

42. Emma Lou Thayne, *Once in Israel* (Provo, UT: Brigham Young University Press, 1980), 29.

43. Pat Jarvis, interviewed by Mary L. Bradford, 15 July 1988.

44. Lowell L. Bennion, Diary, 17, 23 Sept. 1977, photocopy of holograph in Bradford's possession.

45. Ibid., 29 Sept. 1977.

46. Ibid., 29 Sept. 1979; Merle C. Bennion, interviewed by Mary L. Bradford, 14 May 1987.

47. Louis Moench and Mavonne Moench, interviewed by Mary L. Bradford, 13 Feb. 1988.

48. Doug Bills, interviewed by Lisa Stringham, 23 Mar. 1988, notes in Bradford's possession.

49. Lowell L. Bennion, untitled poem, in Eugene England, ed., *The Best of Lowell L. Bennion: Selected Writings, 1928-1988* (Salt Lake City: Deseret Book Co., 1988), xxiii.

Milton and Cora Lindsay Bennion family portrait, ca. 1910. Back left: Cora, Milton, and Clair; front left: Wayne ("Pat"), Lowell, Milton ("Lynn"), and Maurine. Children born after this photograph were Ruth (who died in infancy), Grant, Frances, Margaret (who also died in infancy), and Vaughn.

left: *Milton Bennion (left), en route home from his mission in New Zealand, stopped in Rotterdam to visit his missionary brother, Edwin ("Teddy") Bennion, on April 24, 1893.*

below: *In 1925 Lowell Bennion (right of trophy) played on Forest Dale Ward's Young Men's Mutual Improvement Association basketball team when it won the all-church tournament. The champions are (back left): Wayne Bennion, Richard Hansen, Coach John Buehner, George Cameron, and Jack Freeze; front left: Paul Olsen, Vern Anderson, Lowell Bennion, and Richard Bird.*

Forest Dale Hoop Team Wins M. I. A. Interstake Meet

The 1925 inter-stake M. I. A. basketball tournament came to a close last evening when the Forest Dale ward team, representing Granite stake, defeated the Twenty-eighth ward team of Salt Lake stake in the titular contest. The winning team will receive a silver loving cup emblematic of the tourney championship. The champions shown in the picture, left to right are: Standing—Wayne Bennion, Richard Hansen, John Buehner, (Coach) George Cameron, Jack Freeze, captain. Kneeling—Paul Ol-

Merle Colton Bennion's parents—Sterling LeRoy Colton and Lula Camp Colton—at the time of their wedding in 1897.

Teenage Merle Colton as a student at LDS High School.

left: *Courtship days of Merle and Lowell.*

below:. *A Colton family swim in the Great Salt Lake with everyone wearing rented Saltair swimming suits. Lowell's broad grin and curly hair mark him out about fourth from the left toward the back row. Merle, wearing a two-color swimming cap, is in front of him.*

FAREWELL TESTIMONIAL

IN HONOR OF

Elder Lowell L. Bennion

PRIOR TO HIS DEPARTURE FOR THE
SWISS-GERMAN MISSION

TO BE GIVEN IN THE

FOREST DALE WARD CHAPEL

ASHTON AVENUE & 7TH EAST

THURSDAY EVE., OCTOBER 11th, 1928

PROGRAM 8:15 O'CLOCK VOLUNTARY CONTRIBUTIONS

MAGAZINE PRINTING CO.

Lowell's missionary portrait and the program announcing his departure on October 22, 1928.

Lowell and missionary companions don local peasant women's costumes and pose for the camera in Minden, Germany, June 1930. From left: Lowell Bennion, Billy Morrell, and Floyd Cannon.

Merle about 1929. Lowell carried this photograph with him on his mission.

Newly united in Paris, Lowell and Merle pose before Notre Dame Cathedral in June 1931.

Merle and baby Laurel ("Laurie"), a plump, good-natured girl born on November 14, 1932, died six months later on May 17, 1933.

Milton and Cora Bennion family portrait, ca. 1934.
Left to right: Grant, Milton, Marjorie, Vaughn, Pat, Merle, Lynn, unidentified, Katherine, Ione, Elmo, Cora, Lowell, and Frances.

above: *Merle, Lowell, and baby Lowell C. ("Ben") Bennion, born on May 7, 1935. The car is an Oldsmobile Lowell later sold to Sterling McMurrin.*

right: *Lowell on the lawn of the Tucson, Arizona, LDS institute of religion building with sons Ben and Douglas, born July 4, 1938.*

Lowell's and Merle's first purchased home, thanks to a loan from Milton Bennion, at 352 University Avenue.

Lowell and Merle "roughing it" on a rare vacation.

Cora Bennion, Utah's 1952 Mother of the Year.

Milton Bennion, after resisting diabetes for nearly forty years, died in 1953 at the age of eighty-two.

T. Edgar Lyon, Lowell's close friend and colleague.

above: *LDS institute of religion graduation, June 1957. From left: Marion D. Hanks, Lowell L. Bennion, and LDS church president David O. McKay.*

left: *Lowell at his Teton Boys Ranch.*

Lowell and Merle Bennion family portrait, ca. 1989. Back left: Ellen, Ben, Doug, Steve, and Howard; front left: Merle and Lowell.

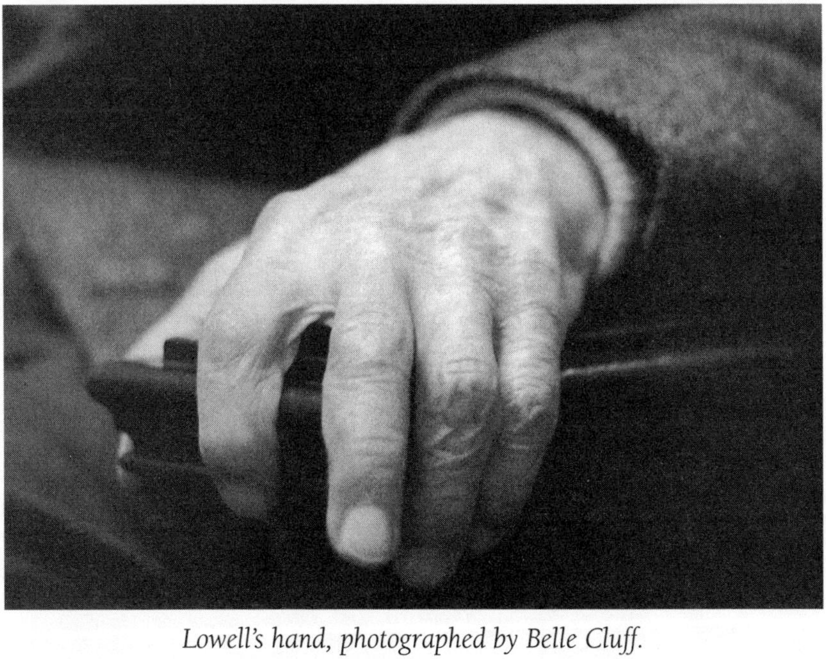

Lowell's hand, photographed by Belle Cluff.

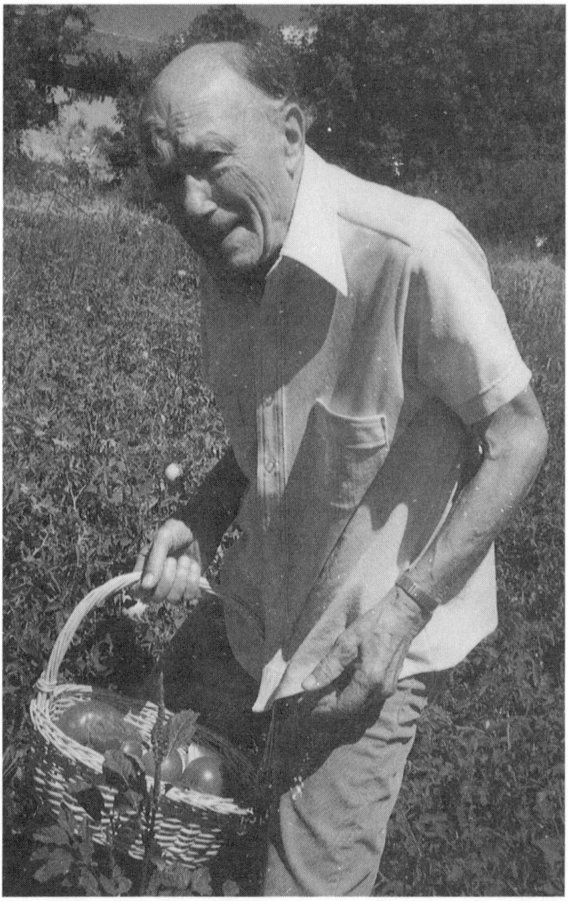

left: *Lowell's fondness for gardening never left him. Here, in spite of Parkinson's disease and other health problems, he gathers vegetables to share with others.*

below: *Lowell responding to a resolution passed by the Utah legislature in February 1992 honoring him for his years of selfless service to the state's needy. (Photograph by Belle Cluff)*

CHAPTER 10

THE TETON VALLEY BOYS RANCH (1961-85)

We had eleven and twelve year old boys standing . . .
and defending their beliefs and ideas.
It was really something.

—LOWELL L. BENNION

Sitting in a circle, occasionally gazing at the soaring Tetons outside the A-frame lodge's big windows, sixteen boys between the ages of eleven and seventeen discussed personal values with Lowell at his "dream ranch" in the Idaho mountains. "Nothing we said went unnoticed nor unchallenged if he found it lacking," Steven Huefner remembered from his three summers (1975-78) as a counselor. "Lowell always managed to nurture when he challenged," he said. The talk was punctuated by Lowell's laugh, "not loud or deep but hearty and full, a spontaneous and unselfconscious laugh filled with enough warmth to be embracing."[1]

Another setting for spiritual and social self-discovery was the "chapel in the pines." John Durham Peters, who spent the summer of 1973 on the ranch, described this "secluded thicket surrounded by good, stiff, straight, and tall pines with logs for benches." Lowell used the integrity of the pines—"unchangeable, constant, true to their place in the world"—to illustrate "how much he had yet to learn about being true to himself and his ideals." Peters was "amazed that such a man should worry about integrity. . . . My amazement gradually became epiphany" as he realized that "goodness comes from the recognition of one's own shortcomings, not from a one-time hurdler's leap over them." Peters also absorbed Lowell's broad view of Mormonism as a world religion. "The genius of Mormonism is not its uniqueness but its kinship to all true religions in its ethical core." Not just a "Wasatch phenomenon," Mormonism, in the view Lowell shared with these boys, was "capable of filling and blessing the whole earth with service and love."[2]

Lowell had dreamed into reality a "Utopian ranch, serenely situated with water, isolated, and available for a song," a non-profit enterprise for the purpose of "building boys into self-respecting and self-reliant men."[3] In the twenty-four years from 1961 to 1985 more than 2,000 boys, attracted mainly by word-of-mouth, came to the Teton Valley Boys Ranch.

The roots of the dream formed in Lowell's teenage summers on Uncle Teddy's land. These roots deepened at the institute where he taught young people the principles of hard work, unselfish service, and clear thought. After moving Merle and the boys to the four-acre "farm" in East Millcreek in 1943, Lowell continued to search, and his sons grew up with his dream. As Steve recalled, "We'd be sitting in the front room, getting ready for Sunday dinner, and Dad would read the want-ads: 'How does this one sound? —a hundred and eighty acres of mountains and cultivated land, forty acres forested, there's great water near the mountains.' . . . We'd say, 'Yeah, Dad, that's great.' But he never gave up."[4]

Part of Lowell's motivation was concern for his sons. Ben, a superb irrigator for the Bennion garden, learned much about farming that gave him an appreciation for the country.[5] His hobbies, music and mountain climbing, "pleased his father," according to Steve, "but the next two sons were not as studious and were more social in their interests. It was then that Lowell began looking for a ranch."[6]

When he taught summer courses at Ricks College in 1954, Lowell visited the ranch owned by Grant Wilson and Sharol Duffin Wilson, both former students, just west of the Tetons in Alta, Wyoming. He asked them "if there were any farmer in the area who could use a husky lad of nearly thirteen who knew how to milk a cow." The "husky lad" was Steve, who spent the summer of 1954 working on Grant and Sharol's ranch. The next summer both Steve and Doug, who had spent the previous summer on Branson Neff's (an East Millcreek neighbor) farm near Manila, Utah, worked on the ranch of Grant's brother, Mark Wilson. All told, Steve spent five summers at Grant's ranch.[7] Ranch work involved moving long lines of sprinkler pipes on alfalfa fields, weeding, cultivating peas, grain, and potatoes, and hauling hay. They fed chickens, gathered and candled eggs, milked cows, and rode horses. The magic worked for them as it had for Lowell and Wayne a generation earlier.

But Lowell longed for the chance to touch boys beyond his own sons—a working ranch where boys could test their muscles against man-sized tasks and where they could puzzle through the process of organizing a job efficiently. Sharing the dream were former students and colleagues, like Jack Adamson, who sent ideas back from his observations of summer camps in the East,[8] Garry Shirts, and Fred Buchanan.

Merle was supportive but not enthusiastic. For twenty years she had fed, clothed, and educated five children on an institute teacher's salary, squeezing out extra funds for dinners and refreshments for students, feeding and housing frequent guests. Lowell's willingness to borrow on their life insurance made her wonder if he had inherited not only Uncle Teddy's ranch fever but his "plunging Bennion blood." (Some of Ted's investments had sent him into long-term debt that Milton had patiently helped pay off.)[9]

In the spring of 1960 Lowell met with Dr. LeGrand Larson, who owned Moose Creek Lodge and a motel not far from Mark and Grant Wilson's ranches. Larson agreed to rent the motel as housing for the summers of 1960 and 1961 in exchange for help on his ranch. The boys would paint rooms, do small repair jobs, and fix fences around the ski lodge, which would also serve as dining hall and meeting place.

With only a few weeks to prepare, the experiment began in early June 1960 and was organized into two sessions of four weeks each, with a week between sessions. Garry and Cozette Shirts, who had two young children, were the camp managers that first session for "thirteen to twenty boys ranging in age from eleven to seventeen." Merle acted as occasional cook and laundress, while also caring for a neighbor's baby. "I went up that first year," she recalled, "and oh, we worked hard!—relieving the others."[10]

Garry's memories of the rented setting at Moose Creek Lodge remained vivid:

> The Tetons soared behind, and the trees, grass and blue sky combined to make it an overwhelmingly beautiful setting. The area had only a two-month growing season, but what a glorious two months. [The ranch] had a main dining hall and four or five cabins. It was bordered on one side by a road and on the other by Moose Creek. It had a wooden fence around the perimeter. Horses were corralled in one end of the ranch. We also had a volleyball net and trampoline. Baby deer would feed with the horses. One fawn adopted us as family and participated in most of our activities.[11]

The schedule called for a morning of work and an afternoon of play. According to Richard Nelson, physician, ranch investor, and friend, "Lowell worked the boys eight hours a day at first . . . but it didn't take him long to figure out that four hours of work and four of play would be better."[12]

Cozette and Garry Shirts received a salary of $1,000 and generally found the experience both challenging and rewarding. "We learned a great deal about ourselves," commented Garry, "and . . . began to view Brother Bennion as a person and not a saint."[13]

One of those humanizing moments occurred on a particularly trying Sunday when Cozette tried to roast a turkey for Lowell's visit. As the hungry campers gathered around the table, she discovered that the turkey was still almost raw. Embarrassed, she announced a delay. "Brother Bennion was clearly irritated," Garry recalled. They later learned that the leaky oven could not hold heat. Cozette finally cut the bird up and fried it. "The boys took it in stride, but Lowell didn't," recalled Garry. The young couple began to think "that perhaps Brother Bennion thought of us as hired help rather than as partners."[14]

Other problems emerged in the Edenic setting. Garry was puzzled about why some of the boys wanted to stop at Victor's little drugstore after a morning's work when they seldom bought anything. He was horrified to learn that several were stealing candy bars and toys. "That was discouraging. Here we were trying to impart some important values to these young boys, and we discovered we were serving as their chauffeur while they robbed a small town merchant."[15]

The first summer was hard because it was the "shake-down" cruise; the second summer was hard because of the emotional turmoil of Lowell's termination from the institute. Burt and Joy

Chamberlain managed the ranch that summer with the help of an excellent cook, Veda Thompson, a local woman in her forties. She and her daughter, Noleen, cooked lunch and dinner six days a week at the ranch each summer until her death two decades later.

Burt Chamberlain, a full-time social worker in the Salt Lake City schools, was persuaded to manage the ranch by Lowell's moving description of his dream. But actually handling the logistical, practical, and emotional responsibility of dozens of boys seven days a week was drastically different. He and his wife Joy often felt stranded by Lowell's frequent absences. Lack of tools and real structure were frustrating. Only years later did it occur to Chamberlain that work crews of boys could have relieved him and his wife of much of the stress. Though exhausted, they had learned so much by summer's end, they still evaluated their experience as "good" with "no unhappy campers."[16]

Lowell's colleagues, Ed Lyon, George Boyd, and Albert Payne, offered encouragement but did not invest in the project or become involved except to visit and to send their sons. "Dad was always fixing things for Lowell," Lynn Lyon recalled, "but didn't do much with the ranch. It was one of Lowell's dreams and interesting, but Dad left it to Lowell."[17]

For the boys it was designed to benefit, the rough edges of those shake-down years were not very important. Lowell's friend and colleague, Edith F. Shepherd, sent her only son, Bob, for the first two years, and she reported the ranch as "a good social and work experience . . . a wonderful program" and invaluable maturation experience for an only child.[18]

Richard Nelson sent eleven-year-old Eric to an early camp. Eric later became a counselor and horse handler until his mission at nineteen and then for one summer afterwards. When Eric tried to break a "spoiled horse" of bad habits, Lowell asked him what he'd named the horse. "I'm going to call him 'Dammit,'" said the exasperated Eric, "because that's what I say every time I'm on him." From then on even Lowell called the horse "Dammit."

Eric and his father kept a list of the evening programs Lowell convened in those first years: how to use and carry tools; first aid; capital punishment; the usefulness of college; outdoor survival; and self-esteem. There were talent nights and guest speakers. On Sundays the boys met in the Chapel in the Pines where each who wished could share ideas on an announced topic like "Why I Am Proud to Be an American."[19]

Moose Creek Lodge was a stop-gap. In June 1960 Lowell opened successful negotiations for property owned by Francis Weeks, three-and-a-half miles west of Victor, on the opposite side of the Tetons from Jackson, Wyoming. Its "seclusion and rugged splendor" reminded Lowell of his beloved Switzerland. To his sister Frances, Lowell described the site as "80 acres of farm land and 80 of forest country in the Teton Valley that is out of this world for beauty for the reasonable price of $18,000."[20] Emma Mosher, Lowell's and Merle's friend who had accompanied Merle to Europe in their youth and who derived her meager income from sewing temple clothes, contributed $2,000. Lowell raised the rest by borrowing on his life insurance and selling two acres of his East Millcreek farm to his neighbor, O. C. Tanner.

In the summer of 1962, the year Lowell left the institute, they opened shop at the Victor property. Fred Buchanan, Lowell's loyal student and friend, volunteered to be one of the counselors and camp manager. In his diary he described the Victor ranch as a "delightful spot surrounded by pine-clad hill and near a rushing mountain creek." Although some of the campers were "terribly spoiled and some very inept," Fred rejoiced in the physical exertion. He found his religious skepticism waning as he prayed nightly with the boys. He became attached to the youngsters who in turn tolerated his bagpipe reveilles.[21]

Buchanan, like Garry and Cozette Shirts, outgrew some of his classroom adulation of Lowell. In a ranch discussion group, when each boy was asked to say one negative and two positive things about another member of the group, Buchanan complimented Lowell on his vision but critiqued his lack of organization, scheduling, and "sense of time."[22]

In 1964 the adjacent 160-acre ranch, Teton Peaks Ranch, was offered for sale. Fearing that someone might turn it into a dude ranch, thereby cutting off access to the mountains and the rolling Forest Service land on either side, Lowell bid on the land. He had no idea where the asking price of $25,000 could be found. Once again his students came to rescue. John and Barbara Redford Cook had been active members of Lambda Delta Sigma.

John, now a physician, had worked with DuWayne and Alice Schmidt at the institute and had fond memories of Lowell's medical seminar. When Cook told Schmidt, newly returned to Utah from his medical residency, about Lowell's dream, they collaborated in forming an investment group to buy the property. Schmidt saw it as an opportunity to "repay Lowell" for his influence on himself and his wife and to expose their children to Lowell's brand of Christianity. As Barbara Cook would later describe it, the two men were attracted to Lowell's dream of "contrasting roughness with fineness, primitive nature with refining discussion of the gospel."[23] Schmidt appreciated a plan "that allowed boys to clear land like the pioneers and to develop muscles and feel manly."[24]

Other doctors and their wives were easily recruited.[25] Robert A. Parry and Richard Stucki, also former institute students, volunteered as well, and Parry became the group's accountant. Feeling that "there is no way we can pay him back for his impact on us, for his philosophy of freedom and trust," they nevertheless decided to try.[26] Some borrowed money to raise the necessary $25,000. Schmidt's shocked father scolded, "You can't buy your own house, but you can go in on a ranch!" But after a visit to the "garden of Eden" in the Tetons, "he understood."[27] Ironically, Richard Nelson had been bidding on that same ranch, but when the investment group approached him, he willingly "became part owner instead of *the* owner."[28]

One of Lowell's conditions was that anyone who needed to withdraw his funds could do so at any time. Nelson took part of his interest in the land and built a small house that enabled him to spend enough time there to keep the group posted on developments in the region. Stucki withdrew his money and moved to Moab, but the others felt with Schmidt that "it was the best investment we ever made." As the Schmidt sons grew old enough to become part of the ranch and their daughters took turns as cooks and laundresses, the ranch became woven into their family life, a project that spanned a generation.

When the group met, they "would plan things to improve: fix up the bunkhouse or the wash house, put in a new water system or put new power in. We would all meet together and decide how much we each needed to kick in to make improvements." From the accountant's perspective, Lowell "never worried about the money. It would come in from some place, and he and the boys and the leaders would build what was necessary and buy what was necessary with the money."[29]

Lowell's attitudes toward money were simple: "I haven't cared much about money in my day. I have read the 'Sermon on the Mount' too many times."[30] He had learned from his father's sad experience not to borrow money for speculative purposes and not to invest in things that he could not understand or control. He felt that his East Millcreek farm and Teton ranch were "profitable economic moves" because they gave him "much pleasure and ego satisfaction," and had increased in value.[31]

The ranch always remained a nonprofit venture. "We had to put in a little extra to keep it going," Parry recalled, "but that was part of it. I guess anyone around Lowell tended to accept the idea of doing a little extra for others."[32]

But the geographical base was firm. Buying the extra acreage doubled the boys' territory, and the connection with the national forest gave them "a whole mountain to roam."[33] Much of the ranch's success depended on Dale Marcum, a Teton Valley neighbor, farmer, schoolteacher, bishop, and member of the core staff. He aided in almost every aspect of ranch development, from building to planting, to working with the boys. Art Kearsley, a horse wrangler, famous for his long-winded, comical, and salty stories, was the expert on ranch life. "Art could talk your head off, was quick to make up his mind, and wanted things up front," recalled Rodney Schmidt. "Lowell would put things off and would be vague about physical arrangements. . . . More than once Art would stomp out of Lowell's shack, gather up his horses, and vow he wouldn't be back." But he always came back because "they shared a strong love of working with boys."[34] Once Art tracked two runaway boys on horseback and brought them back. He rode herd on them for the rest of the summer, with the result that "they were among the proudest when they finished."[35]

In addition to this more or less permanent staff, six or eight older boys worked as counselors. Often a camper's parents helped in return for reduced tuition or no tuition.

One year in the 1970s one of the senior counselors bought beer and cigarettes for the boys. The other counselors found the contraband in the library, confiscated it, and telephoned Lowell, fully expecting him to fire the offender. "Let me come up and see if I can talk to him," Lowell said. He worked with the young man the rest of the summer with no further difficulty.[36]

Lowell seldom gave direct instructions, instead expecting counselors to use a combination of creativity and common sense. "He would ask for opinions, and he fostered freedom and liberty," recalled the youngest Schmidt, Brian, a counselor during the late 1970s. "He let us be creative." This laid-back style was a shock to one counselor. Experienced with delinquent boys, tight controls, and strict schedules, he was horrified to find boys "running around" and doubly horrified when the other counselors told him, "That's the way it's supposed to be."[37]

Discipline was a minor though persistent problem. Sid Frazier, a counselor during the 1970s, seized control of an out-of-hand boy by dunking him in the horse trough. "Horsetroughing" became the accepted punishment for swearing, with the result that swearing virtually disappeared.[38]

Jeffrey Schmidt, the eldest Schmidt child, was head counselor in 1976 at age twenty-two. He looked back in amazement on his experience from his perspective as a pediatrician and father. People entrusted their sons to Lowell and his young assistants "almost blindly," he marveled. He shook his head over the legal liability no one ever worried about. The ranch had fire insurance; but there was no health, accident, medical, or liability insurance on the ranch, the staff, or the campers that there is today. "I don't know if it was faith or ignorance," he commented, but there was never a problem. Jeffrey recalls seeing Dale Marcum "on top of the A-frame putting shingles on, no ropes or anything. We boys climbed up and cleaned the big windows." There were accidents, including broken bones, but nothing permanently disabling and no fatalities. Jeffrey concluded that in spite of risks, he wanted his own children and his young patients to have the same chance to "get away from Mom and learn to figure out who they are on their own—working, playing, thinking—to build their self-esteem."[39]

The newly purchased ranch already had a few buildings, and a never-ending series of building and remodeling projects filled the air with hammering for the next twenty years. A broken-backed barn became a "little exercise place" after investors secured cables to the roof and straightened it out. "We didn't want to tear it down," said Parry, "because that was the flavor of the place."[40] An old ranch house was dubbed the White House and set aside as an impromptu residence for investors, their families, and neighbors. The children called it "bugs house," because of the winter's accumulation of dead insects along the windows. There was also a run-down bunkhouse and wash house.

Allen Price, an architect and former student of Lowell's, submitted designs for a lodge to Lowell—designs simple enough that the boys themselves could contribute part of the labor. The lumber would be cut from the surrounding forest. Lowell also consulted his nephew, Kent Morgan, an architectural student at the University of Utah. Morgan drafted up Price's plans for Lowell's conception of an A-frame lodge that served for meetings and dining, and recalled that Lowell had thought through the need for a bunkhouse, library, tackhouse, bathhouse, log house for guests, and swimming pool.

Fifty-three-years-old when the ranch began, Lowell quickly took on the look of rancher. The ruddy Bennion complexion tanned under a battered cowboy hat. His razor-blue eyes focused on the sky but were quick to attend to the expressions of others. Grandson Lindsay Bennion, Doug's eldest, fondly recalled his grandfather's "rancher alter-ego in old coveralls and a beaten up cowboy hat, standing on the deck of the A-fame making work assignments."[41]

Heidi Schmidt's favorite memory was seeing Lowell drive a team of "big work horses" hauling a load of manure for the garden. "He'd ride like a twenty-year-old. It was as though he had lost his age and was full of energy and spunk."[42]

Steve Bennion summed up the ranch:

> This is neither a dude ranch nor a profit-making venture; nor is it a rehabilitation program equipped to help boys with serious behavioral problems.[43] Our whole purpose is to build good boys into self-respecting and more self-reliant young men. . . . The ranch's goals are to help the participants (1) learn to work and enjoy working, (2) increase self-confidence, (3) increase health and physical stamina, (4) improve ability to get along with others, (5) learn specific work and outdoor skills, and (6) appreciate nature.[44]

While this formula was being refined, Merle provided stability at home. The youngsters would "come to our home the night before their first day of camp. We bedded them down on the back lawn," she recalled.[45] Those who lived nearby would drive to the Bennion home the next morning to eat breakfast before departing on "The Magic Bus," an old school bus that became legendary for its regular breakdowns and its artistic graffiti.

Lowell's commitment to his dream came at personal and family cost. In 1990 Merle recalled her own part: "I did a lot down here that he doesn't appreciate. Put them up, placated the mothers, fed them—I spent hours." She was proud of the ranch's achievement, but the memory of loneliness still stung. Turning to Lowell during the interview, she asked, "Why didn't we run it together, Lowell?"[46] He had no answer.

Robert Parry also noticed. "His wife, his kids, his associates, kind of bent to his drive. . . . I think that Merle, that little angel, has through the years subordinated her interests to support him . . . but she rarely let on."[47]

Strange as it may seem to the present generation, the question of a parallel experience for girls and young women never came up. Two or three teenage girls, usually the daughters or sisters of ranch investors or counselors, worked in the kitchen and laundry. They were welcome to join in the social and recreational activities, and at least one girl, Susan Lindsay, recalls her experience there as "the summer I grew up."[48]

Daughter Ellen Bennion spent eight summers between the ages of twelve to twenty serving as breakfast cook, laundress, and assisting Veda Thompson in the kitchen.

Katherine England, a cook one summer in the 1970s and a "sophisticated seventeen-year-old," reinforced Lowell's discussion of the A-B-C dating method by giving the girl's version of "how to behave on dates, and how to ask a girl out." Recalled Stephen Bradford, then sixteen, "We got information that we were too cool or too embarrassed to ask about."[49]

By the late 1960s and early 1970s the ranch had a smooth routine. It still ran in two sessions of four weeks each, but now with thirty to forty boys, ages twelve to fifteen, per session. A day at the ranch meant arising at 6:00 a.m., making beds and sweeping bunkhouses. After breakfast Lowell or his substitute organized the boys into work groups, describing how each job was to be done under the supervision of the counselors. Sometimes the whole group tackled a large project—like digging the swimming pool—but usually several projects were in the works—building, cleaning, maintenance, fence-making, and clearing land.

Lowell taught "respect for every type of job," recalled George Handley, a counselor from Connecticut.

> He would take time to explain how to use the tools, how to get them ready, how to put them away. It seemed just as important to him as anything else. This reverence for manual labor inspired many of us. He spoke of the three characteristics of a job well done: (1) Be functional; i.e., a post hole should withstand the winter; (2) Be sound; and, (3) Be aesthetically pleasing (a fence post should be well placed.)[50]

The boys also worked for neighboring ranchers, sometimes for pay to be reinvested in the ranch, more often as service. Like the Lambda Delts, they spread into nearby communities to paint a house, help in the fields, or clean the sidewalks. Lowell's approach to this service was low-key and matter-of-fact. Handley observed, "It was never said that we were there to learn to serve. Discussing it, as is often done in church, makes you too much aware that you are serving. Lowell never liked that. . . . No patting ourselves on the back."[51]

Part of Lowell's program for teaching the boys responsibility was paying them for their work—$50 per session. Jeffrey Schmidt recalled those one-at-a-time interviews and accountings at camp's end. "That was big time—for twelve-year-olds to get a check for their work on the ranch!"[52]

Stephen Bradford, a "city kid" from the East, internalized Lowell's idea of hard work. "My idea of working outdoors was cutting lawns," he confessed. "At the ranch, we went out into the woods and chopped trees, carved lumber, split the lumber, built fences, built a barn, saw the whole process of how things were made. We would . . . harvest things from nature to use in building projects. It gave me an appreciation for what the earth can provide."[53]

Lowell nearly always worked with the boys in the mornings while writing lessons and counseling with boys in the afternoons.

He often returned to his garden for individual time with a boy who needed a little therapy and low-key discipline. When a boy became so obstreperous that the counselors voted to send him home, Lowell said, "I'd rather err on the side of mercy. I'll take him to work in the garden." The results were predictable: "The little devil would calm right down."[54]

The afternoons devoted to play were as valuable, in Lowell's opinion, as the work. Boys were free to swim in the pool, raft or tube on the river, hike, ride horses, organize softball, basketball, and volleyball games, play the piano in the lodge, or curl up under a tree with a book. Sometimes they went into Victor to shop or see the "mellerdrama" at the lone theater. Only a few options were out: no television, radios, knives, or guns. But boys who had worked together all morning, using their minds to solve problems and their muscles to achieve solutions, found it easy to play together.

Brian Schmidt recalled a catalogue of homemade fun:

> Once, after a hike, we found an old car, rusty and awful. We started playing on it and posing. It got funnier and funnier, so we divided into groups to take pictures. . . . We used to have tumbling contests, and we'd made signs with numbers like the Olympics. . . . Some would write things on the bus with magic markers . . . It was creative work. Pat King designed the Pat King Memorial Toilet. He put designs around the toilet with magic markers. Then in the afternoon, he'd play the saxophone on the roof of the bunkhouse.[55]

Lowell, or "Doc," as they called him, joined regularly in the afternoon games. One boy remembered playing volleyball with Doc. "He would compliment people and make you feel good—'It's a rally, boys!' He would clap and get excited. His team would win not so much because they played better but because they played together."[56]

Another part of the fun was participation in Victor's 4th and 24th of July parades. In 1980 the boys chose the theme "Use Your Freedom to Vote" and created a float for both presidential candidates—Ronald Reagan and Jimmy Carter. Another year Lowell quipped, "I've had an idea in mind for years and have never used it: . . . 'Give me your tired, your poor, your huddled masses'—and just use boys as they are." The float was a fabulous success. The boys, deliberately ungroomed, huddled together on the wagon, holding their sign.[57]

The evenings were memorable parts of the ranch experience. After hearty suppers, in good weather the boys met outdoors at the chapel for discussions; in bad weather they formed a circle in the A-frame. Steve Bennion felt that these evening sessions met Lowell's need for intense interactions with young minds, assuaging the loss of his beloved institute.[58] The discussions revolved around timeless topics: the nature of God, current affairs, nuclear disarmament, civil rights, the Vietnam conflict. Boys lined up on either side of an argument. With Lowell as referee, "no matter the age, the kids knew they all had important things to say that would be respected by others."[59]

Lowell arranged parallel experiences for the staff. Boyer Jarvis, an associate of Lowell at the University of Utah, brought his wife Pat and their two sons to the ranch in 1967. Pat acted as assistant cook and Boyer did carpentry work. "Some of the evenings," recalled Boyer, "when the kids [were] doing things that didn't require close supervision, Lowell would gather his staff people—about half a dozen—and we talked about things." There Boyer first began thinking analytically about Vietnam. Lowell "was not satisfied just to let people ruminate but was always challenging people not to just use their minds but to prick their consciences as well."[60]

Although approximately 90 percent of the boys were Mormons, Lowell wanted members of other faiths or of no faith to feel welcome. Parents who expected Lowell to insist on Sunday church attendance in Victor were sometimes disappointed, for Lowell refused to "push and shove people into activity."[61] It was easy for the boys to attend church if they chose. Someone always provided transportation, and no other activities were scheduled. Lowell himself attended Sunday meetings and sometimes taught Sunday school classes in Victor. But anyone could drift into Sunday evening gatherings in the pines and feel at home. It "was never a testimony meeting, though it had the same atmosphere," recalled Brian Schmidt. "Doc would offer a subject, and whoever felt like expressing themselves could get up. We talked about such subjects as where we expect to be in ten years. Less churchy people were impressed. We would burst into tears sometimes."[62]

Those who were not Mormon added a cosmopolitan flavor to the mix—a Jewish boy from New York, a Russian *émigré,* a young Frenchman. Recruiting boys was not difficult. Since some boys could not afford the $300 tuition, Lowell found ways to support them. "Lowell was the finest Christian gentleman I've ever known," said Albert Payne. "If a widow came along with a boy, the boy went."[63]

Ed Lyon's grandsons came to the ranch in the 1970s. James Lyon observed that his two sons learned to work and that both now "speak in reverent tones of Lowell." The second son was "a little close-minded" as an adolescent, but "ever since Lowell Bennion he sees the gospel with the same broad view Lowell has."[64] Bennion relatives also made up a share of the attendees. Vaughn's son Ricky called his session at Moose Lodge "slave labor,"[65] but cousin Richard Lindsay reported that "the discussions and the informal classes had a lasting effect on [his three children's] search for knowledge and their value systems."[66]

Merle's cousins, Sterling and Eleanor Colton, sent all three of their sons. "We loved [Lowell] and admired him so much that we wanted our children to have some exposure to him," explained Eleanor. "He didn't run such a tight ship that they couldn't have fun," but the boys learned the "joy of honest labor."[67]

The ranch let Lowell achieve, for at least a short period, his dream of simple living and high thinking. His quarters, despite the ironic title, "Doc's Mansion," were minimal—-just a small shed "right in the middle of the action . . . between the trampoline and the bathhouse, beside the A-frame."[68] In twenty-four years Lowell never occupied more luxurious quarters. The "mansion" housed a double bunk under a sloping tin roof. Lowell slept on the bottom bunk on a foam pad and sleeping bag, while the top stored "junk" used for repair work. A sheet of plywood served as a desk beneath a small window with yellowed curtains. An inverted drum was his seat, and a piece of pipe served as a closet for his clothes. The boys often noticed that the naked bulb behind Doc's curtains outlasted "the rest of us into the night, and it was almost impossible to be up before Doc in the morning."[69]

Esprit de corps was usually high. The ranch rapidly developed its own legends, folkways, practical jokes, and elaborate hoaxes. As a university student in the late 1980s, Brian Schmidt collected some of these for a senior honors thesis that described how the ranch became a rite of passage, one that created its own social matrix.

As the youngest in his family, Brian had been acculturated in ranch lore long before he was old enough to attend. He recalled,

> My brothers returning each summer with the stories and pictures of what went on at camp. . . . My family would set up the slide projector and I would see and hear the adventures my brothers had been involved in. . . . I loved to hear their stories. . . . I would hang around as they bragged to their city-dweller friends about the fish they caught or the bear they saw . . . how my brother broke his arm in the pickup truck, the boy who hitched from New York, and the pranks they played.[70]

Lowell created a memorable ghost story—"The Piano Wire Murders"—that became part of legend. Newcomers would run to ask him if it was true. "In part," he would answer, and add yet another detail. According to Brian's version, rowdy trappers rendezvousing in the valley raped and murdered some Indian women. "The next year one of the trappers . . . was found hanged by a piano wire in a tree where the women had camped," a scene that was repeated each year for the next ten years until finally the rendezvous was abandoned. The killings were mysteriously linked to Old Joe, a solitary Indian "who sold Doc the ranch." When Lowell took possession, he found in the little log cabin "a piano with eleven strings missing." And "some say" Old Joe still returns to the ranch. The boys shrugged off the stories, said Brian, "but when they were on camp-outs they would often be scared to leave the group."[71]

Lowell saw the core of the ranch as building self-esteem, forging character in physical achievement, exploring principles, and learning about unselfish service. He downplayed his own influence, but boys who struggled to capture the essence of their experience at the ranch located its impact in Lowell's personality and example. "You were away from your family with a big group of boys, and you thought you would be indistinguishable," recalled Stephen Bradford. "But when he'd look you straight in the eye, you knew he cared about you as an individual. He differentiated among boys. You'd carry back increased self-confidence."[72]

Jeffrey Schmidt remembered a quiet moment with Lowell when he was sixteen and he confessed to Lowell his fear of the devil. "Jeff, are you serious?" Lowell said, surprised. "Listen, you tell the devil to go to hell!" It was a one-sentence summation of Lowell's philosophy that, instead of worrying about the evil "out there," each person should accept responsibility for his or her own thoughts, beliefs, and actions.

The ranch became a living network that constantly replenished itself, but the strength that Lowell drew from it could not renew his health indefinitely. By the early 1980s it was clear that Lowell could no longer spend all his summers there, tracking all of the details necessary to keep it running. A painful memory for Ellen and Steve was the day they gently pointed out the obstacles caused by his failing health and asked him to consider giving up the ranch. Lowell finally conceded the point and retired in 1985, but he refused to sell. For three years it stood vacant.

Once again Lowell's students found the solution. Richard (Dick) and Susan Jacobsen bought the ranch from Lowell and Merle in late 1988. At that time Dick turned to his brother Ted Jacobsen and to Steve Bennion and said, "Let's get the Boys Ranch running again." With Lowell, Lorin Pugh, Jeff Schmidt, and Richard Nelson, Ted and Steve formed a non-profit board to run the Bennion Teton Boys Ranch.

To gear up for operations, the board met twice a month for six months to organize, publicize, and hire a staff. The old A-frame lodge, judged "structurally deficient," was burned down and replaced with a new lodge, designed and built by Ted Jacobsen and the Jacobsen Construction Company in time for the summer session of 1990.

In late 1989 Steve Bennion, now president of Ricks College, gratefully accepted the invitation of Dick and Susan Jacobsen to have Ricks use the ranch during the academic year "if Ricks could come up with a proposal that both the Jacobsens and Ricks felt good about." A proposal to use the ranch as a "training location to build self-esteem, service, work ethic, and leadership," called the Teton Mountain Leadership Institute, was organized by Mack Shirley and Jerry Price of the student life office. Lynn Smith of the sociology department became its first director. The parallel purpose of both the boys ranch and the Teton Mountain Leadership Institute was pleasing to Lowell, the Jacobsens, and Ricks College. The director since 1993 was Brian C. Schmidt, who described his position as an "ideal" combination of "teaching college students on the rustic ranch property and serving the community below the Teton Mountains."[73]

Steve Bennion described the training program, which welcomes women, as a boon to a number of Ricks's students—as many as 2,000 in a year. It also touches students who are not otherwise involved in leadership development and provides selected retreats for college employees.[74] Rather than restricted to student body officers or other formal leaders, the classes are open to anyone who wishes to learn more about leadership, time management, personal values, stress management, and the building of relationships. This arrangement allowed for year-round use of the ranch but did not replace the summer sessions for boys.

In June 1989 seventy-two boys pioneered the reopening, with two counselors living in each of the three bunkhouses and supervising the activities. For three summers Steve Peterson served as camp director, and Kathy Peterson, his wife and an artist, coordinated the arts and crafts program. In 1992 and 1993 Gordon and Kathleen Lindsay, Lowell's cousins, directed the summer session. Lowell still made occasional appearances, led discussion groups, and worked in the garden when his health permitted.

Lowell accepted with equanimity criticisms of his administrative skills. The ranch, he said, is "where I learned how poor I am as a detail man." Like most creative people, he had a high tolerance for ambiguity and disorder, but he delegated easily and seldom failed to encourage his staff to dream their own dreams. Boldly he attempted new plans, abandoning failures quickly and without regret. His ability to draw out the best in others overcame administrative deficiencies. It seems safe to say, "He was not a manager. He was a leader."

Lowell also supported a similar venture in Utah. In 1963 he described his ranch to Bill Hutchinson, personnel director of the Granite School District in Salt Lake City, who told Lowell, "We really need a ranch like yours in the Salt Lake Valley. There are at least one hundred kids a year in the district alone who need a place to live because they can't get along at home."[75] He and Lowell met with schoolteacher Normand Gibbons, state legislator

Dix McMullin, and attorney Gordon Madsen. Gibbons located a fifteen-acre property in Kearns that could be purchased for $1,500 an acre. After protracted negotiations, they established the Utah Boys Ranch. "We did it on nerve because we had no funds whatsoever," Lowell recalled.

Since most of the boys were Mormon, Lowell appealed to the LDS church for funding. His first contact, the Presiding Bishop's office, with responsibility for youth and physical properties, told him, "You are in for a lot of work and trouble," and refused assistance. The men bought the first five acres for $11,000 and began to build a house "on faith and credit." Halfway through the plan, creditors threatened suit, so Lowell wrote to the First Presidency, asking for $10,000. Again the answer was no, and the answer from various acquaintances was silence.

A few days later Lowell was startled to receive a message from President David O. McKay's secretary: "President McKay is mailing you a check for $10,000," a gift from the president's emergency fund. The gift "saved our necks and our credit rating," Lowell recalled. Gibbons pronounced it the "boost we needed."[76] It was also personally heartening to Lowell, a gracious gesture relatively soon after his departure from the institute. David O. McKay's support of the Utah Boys Ranch communicated continuing respect.

With donated furniture and food, the Utah Boys Ranch established three homes dedicated to reclaiming teenage boys from the ravages of society. By 1994 the ranch had expanded to a campus of seventy-seven acres in West Jordan, Utah, that offered "early intervention" for troubled boys, many without families or guardians. It boasted a home atmosphere, education, clinical therapy, moral and spiritual values, and was operated entirely as a nongovernment charity.[77] Another dream realized.

NOTES

1. Steven Huefner to "Mom and Dad" (Robert and Dixie Huefner), 10 Nov. 1988, photocopy of typescript in Bradford's possession.

2. John Durham Peters, "Memories of the Ranch," unpaginated, 10 June 1988, typescript in Bradford's possession.

3. Huefner to "Dear Mom and Dad," 10 Nov. 1988.

4. Steven D. Bennion, interviewed by Mary L. Bradford, 26 Sept. 1990.

5. Lowell Colton (Ben) Bennion, interviewed by Mary L. Bradford, 7 May 1988.

6. Steven D. Bennion, "Summary History of the Bennion Teton Boys Ranch," 14 Feb. 1992; typescript, 1, photocopy in Bradford's possession; hereafter "Ranch History."

7. Ibid., 2.

8. Jack Adamson to Lowell L. Bennion, 27 Dec. 1954, photocopy in Bradford's possession. Adamson became a respected member of the English faculty and vice president of the University of Utah in the 1960s.

9. Merle C. Bennion and Lowell L. Bennion, interviewed by Mary L. Bradford, 26 Jan. 1990.

10. Ibid.

11. Garry Shirts, interviewed by mail by Mary L. Bradford, 20 Feb. 1991.

12. Richard J. Nelson, interviewed by Lisa Stringham, 21 Mar. 1989, audiotape in Bradford's possession.

13. Garry Shirts, interviewed by Mary L. Bradford, 20 Feb. 1991.

14. Ibid.

15. Ibid.

16. Burt Chamberlain, interviewed by mail by Mary L. Bradford, 1 Apr. 1991.

17. Joseph Lynn Lyon, interviewed by Mary L. Bradford, 26 Sept. 1990.

18. Edith F. Shepherd, interviewed by Mary L. Bradford, 17 Feb. 1988.

19. Richard Nelson and Eric Nelson, interviewed by Lisa N. Stringham, 21 Mar. 1989, tape and transcription in Bradford's possession.

20. Lowell L. Bennion to Elmo and Frances B. Morgan, 20 June 1961, photocopy in Bradford's possession.

21. Frederick S. Buchanan, Diary, 14 June 1962, photocopy in Bradford's possession.

22. Ibid.

23. Barbara Redford Cook, interviewed by Mary L. Bradford, 7 May 1987.

24. DuWayne Schmidt, Alice Cannon Schmidt, and their children (Tracy, Jeffrey, Rodney, Heather, Heidi, and Brian), interviewed by Mary L. Bradford, 22 July 1988; hereafter cited as DuWayne and Alice Schmidt Family.

25. These physicians were Richard Nelson, Chase N. Peterson, Madison H. Thomas, William S. Jordan, Alan P. Thomas, and Gilbert Tobler.

26. Robert A. Parry, interviewed by Lisa Stringham, 21 Mar. 1989, tape and transcription in Bradford's possession.

27. DuWayne and Alice Schmidt Family, interviewed by Mary L. Bradford, 14 Feb. 1988.

28. Richard J. Nelson, interviewed by Lisa Stringham, 21 Mar. 1989.

29. Robert A. Parry, interviewed by Lisa Stringham, 21 Mar. 1989, tape and transcription in Bradford's possession.

30. Lowell L. Bennion, "Memories," 87, photocopy in Bradford's possession.

31. Ibid., 85-86.

32. Robert A. Parry, interviewed by Lisa Stringham, 21 Mar. 1989, tape and transcript in Bradford's possession.

33. Ibid.

34. Rodney Schmidt, interviewed by Mary L. Bradford, 21 Mar. 1989.

35. Brian C. Schmidt, interviewed by Mary L. Bradford, 13 Feb. 1988.

36. Ibid.

37. Ibid.

38. Ibid.

39. Jeffrey, DuWayne, and Alice Schmidt, interviewed by Mary L. Bradford, 14 Feb. 1988.

40. Robert A. Parry, interviewed by Lisa Stringham, 21 Mar. 1989.

41. Richard Lindsay Bennion, interviewed by Lisa Stringham, 14 Mar. 1990.

42. Heidi Schmidt Shipp, with the DuWayne and Alice Schmidt Family, interviewed by Mary L. Bradford, 14 Feb. 1988.

43. After the second year, when a severely troubled boy burned down

a bunkhouse, Lowell concluded that his ranch was not really organized for the reformation of juvenile delinquents but rather for "boys who were a little shy or who were having a hard time developing self-esteem." Quoted by Richard Nelson, interviewed by Lisa Stringham, 2 Mar. 1989, tape in Bradford's possession.

44. "Ranch History," 3.

45. Merle C. Bennion, interviewed by Mary L. Bradford, 17 May 1987.

46. Lowell L. Bennion and Merle C. Bennion, interviewed by Mary L. Bradford, 16 Jan. 1990.

47. Robert A. Parry, interviewed by Lisa Stringham, 21 Mar. 1989.

48. Susan Lindsay Gong, conversation with Mary L. Bradford, 3 Mar. 1990.

49. Stephen L. Bradford, interviewed by Mary L. Bradford, 15 May 1989.

50. George Handley, audiotaped reminiscences, 17 July 1989, in Bradford's possession.

51. Ibid.

52. Jeffrey Schmidt with DuWayne and Alice Schmidt Family, interviewed by Mary L. Bradford, 14 Feb. 1988.

53. Stephen L. Bradford, interviewed by Mary L. Bradford, 15 May 1988.

54. George Handley, audiotaped reminiscences.

55. Brian C. Schmidt, interviewed by Mary L. Bradford, 13 Feb. 1988.

56. Ibid.

57. Ibid.

58. Ibid.

59. Ibid.

60. Boyer and Pat Jarvis, interviewed by Mary L. Bradford, 15 May 1989.

61. Elizabeth Strobel Card to Mary L. Bradford, 4 July 1988.

62. Brian C. Schmidt, interviewed by Mary L. Bradford, 12 Feb. 1988.

63. Albert Payne, interviewed by Mary L. Bradford and Eugene England, 5 May 1987.

64. James F. Lyon, audiotaped reminiscences, ca. 10 Mar. 1989.

65. Vaughn L. Bennion, interviewed by Mary L. Bradford, 9 Feb. 1988.

66. Richard Powell Lindsay, interviewed by Mary L. Bradford, 28 Oct. 1989. Gordon and Kathleen Lindsay became directors of the ranch in 1992.

67. Eleanor Ricks Colton, interviewed by Mary L. Bradford, 10 Aug. 1988.

68. Steve Huefner to "Mom and Dad," 10 Nov. 1988.

69. George Handley, audiotaped reminiscences.

70. Brian C. Schmidt, "Teton Valley Boys Ranch: Individual Identity and Group Cohesion through Folklore," Senior Honors Project, University of Utah, Aug. 1990, 4, photocopy in Bradford's possession.

71. Ibid., 10.

72. Stephen L. Bradford, interviewed by Mary L. Bradford, 15 May 1989.

73. Brian C. Schmidt to Mary L. Bradford, 23 Feb. 1993.

74. "Ranch History," 5.

75. Lowell L. Bennion, "Memories," 86. The quotations from Lowell that follow are from this source.

76. Normand Gibbons, interviewed by Mary L. Bradford, 19 July 1988.

77. *Utah Boys Ranch, Today a Boy's Success, Tomorrow a Nation's Destiny,* 5500 West Bagley Park Road, West Jordan, UT, 84088, copy in Bradford's possession.

PART THREE

HALLS OF IVY

In 1982 the University of Utah awarded Lowell an honorary Doctor of Humane Letters degree. Here he receives his hood from longtime friend J. Boyer Jarvis (left) and University of Utah president David P. Gardner.

CHAPTER 11

CALM CENTER IN A STORM (1962-74)

I made up my mind to enjoy life, come hell or high water.

—LOWELL L. BENNION

In September 1962, as Lowell moved across the street from the institute to the University of Utah, he was fifty-four and at the peak of his intellectual and physical powers. Leaving regret and nostalgia behind, he turned to his tasks as assistant dean of students and director of Community Services at the Utah Center for the Prevention and Control of Juvenile Delinquency under the sociology department. The university, plagued by a long history of tension between Mormons and non-Mormons, welcomed administrators who were skilled in building bridges. At the back of Lowell's mind lay the feeling that his father would have approved of. A *Deseret News* editorial also approved: Lowell's "essential counselor's skill—the ability to get the student thinking introspectively and analytically about his own problems" would help to "rebuild confidence in man's two greatest sources of strength—God and himself."[1]

As Lowell settled into his office in the northwest corner of the Park Building at the university, he found a ready welcome from colleagues. Neal Maxwell, the personable and articulate dean of students and another devout Mormon, was his friend. So was Jack Adamson, academic vice president. A third friend, Boyer Jarvis, had recently returned from Washington, D.C., where he had assisted Sterling McMurrin, U.S. Commissioner of Education, and was now executive assistant to President A. Ray Olpin.[2] Jarvis applauded Lowell's appointment, saying it gave Lowell "access to the entire student body in ways that he never had before."[3] McMurrin, who returned to his post as professor of philosophy in 1963, was pleased at the arrival of another "Dean Bennion."[4]

Down the hall from Lowell was Elizabeth Haglund, assistant director of university relations, a cousin to Hermana Lyon, and loyal friend to the Bennions. Lowell was already acquainted with Virginia Frobes, an Episcopalian dean of women, associate dean of students, a trained psychologist, and a woman whose energy impressed her colleagues. Frobes was convinced that LDS students needed someone who could discuss problems of belief and experience. By November, Neal Maxwell told Olpin that "everything was going fine in his end of the hall, and that Dr. Lowell Bennion was very valuable and was ingratiating himself with everyone concerned with student counseling."[5]

Lowell's duties at the university provided plenty of variety from the start. For two years he had "direct administrative responsibility" for the Marriage and Family Counseling Bureau, the Counseling Center, the Student Military Adviser, was liaison to psychiatric services, and worked on these committees: Artists and Speakers, Foreign Student Advisory Council, Orientation of New Students, Student Affairs Committee, Student Welfare Fund Board—"everything but finances," he quipped to Bill Moran.[6] On such committees Lowell consistently negotiated with competing factions, suggested simplified goals, outlined practical action, and concentrated on individual outcomes.

He reestablished his institute open-door policy for personal counseling and met with all students appearing before the Student Behavior Committee—a judicial group composed of six faculty and six students who passed judgement on student misbehavior. The common offense was vandalism. One group of students painted BYU's large block "Y" on the mountain above campus a lurid red—the U's color—before a game.[7] When the university president handed "the whole counseling chore" of some misbehaving athletes to Lowell, Maxwell praised him for doing "a wonderful job, . . . loving and yet tough."[8]

"I enjoyed it," he said of his counseling responsibilities. "I won't say I was thrilled with it, but it was a very meaningful task. I wasn't there to defend the students regardless of circumstance, but to see that justice seasoned with mercy was executed."[9] "He . . . never gave up on a student," Frobes recalled. Even when she threw up her hands, "in his mind the student would yet improve and the victory was still in the future—thus he never saw failure."[10] When a student cheated on an examination, Lowell expressed faith in him "to the point where Virginia thought I had gone out on a limb," he recalled, but the student steadied himself, "earned a master's degree in business administration," and gratefully presented Lowell with a copy of his thesis.[11]

His philosophy of discipline combined love and firmness. Love enabled them to feel accepted and firmness built their self-respect. He explained, "It gives them a chance to be what they ought to be, and they know that. In human relations people have to first feel accepted in order to feel comfortable and to function. Then, . . . to establish their own self-esteem . . . they need to come through and measure up. Maybe I'm a little weak on firmness at times, I grant you, but I *try* to combine those two things in my human relationships."[12]

Not surprisingly, disaffected and disillusioned Mormon students found their way through his door. During the turbulent 1960s when student activism swept a generation, Olpin's successor, James C. Fletcher, remembered that Lowell was especially helpful in talking to "the LDS contingent," including some returned missionaries who "had joined the radicals."[13]

Much of Lowell's effectiveness came from his bone-deep respect for each human being and the sanctity of human agency. When Lowell reviewed a policy document on campus security, he noted, "We need a paragraph reminding officers that college students are not youngsters to be disciplined, but adults. All members of the campus community—faculty, students, and staff—should be treated as adults, as self-directing agents."[14]

As director of Community Services of the Utah Center for the Prevention and Control of Juvenile Delinquency (a federally-funded agency set up by Ray Canning,[15] acting dean of the College of Letters and Sciences), Lowell enjoyed working with Canning and paid high tribute to the business and civic communities for finding solutions to delinquency. "I could pick up the phone and call the superintendent of public instruction or the head of AFL or the CIO and Chamber of Commerce," he recalled, "and every one of them would say yes, they would meet and brainstorm."[16]

Canning's motto, "Let's not spend money on old ideas," appealed to Lowell. He found community leaders "discussing all kinds of possibilities and showing willingness to make financial sacrifices in terms of their own products." It was "very exciting."[17] Canning cheerfully acknowledged, "Lowell could do this better than I. It was a question of networking, and it worked fine" during Lowell's two years with it.[18] After seven years Canning's Delinquency Center "fizzled . . . and was forgotten."[19]

This networking took Lowell before many influential groups, including the PTA Congress and the Utah Peace Officers Association. "The causes of juvenile delinquency are varied and complex," he told them, "but one of them seems to be that the American culture creates many desires without providing the means of satisfying them."[20]

Lowell's popularity as a speaker and his socratic way with questions led him to moderate a weekly *Great Issues* series on the campus KUED television station beginning in January 1963. He called on friends with expertise. Ray Canning discussed conformity. Attorney Richard Bird, a childhood friend, joined with Professor Joseph Catmull of the speech and drama departments to discuss "The Good Life." David Bennett, a former institute student now teaching in the philosophy department, appeared on the "Faith and Reason" session. The program that roused the most interest was a discussion on liberalism versus conservatism, featuring Fred Buchanan, John Bennion, and Jack Adamson, who declared himself a "tired liberal." Peacemaker Lowell summarized by suggesting that "one ought to be liberal when needed and conservative whenever that position was needed."[21]

In 1964 Olpin retired after eighteen years of service, to be replaced by Dr. James C. Fletcher. Fletcher, scion of a famous Mormon family of teachers and scientists from New York and California, a physicist who would leave the university to become twice director of NASA. Energetic and charismatic, he stepped into the cauldron of the 1960s with enthusiasm and helped the university take significant steps toward maturation. Under him the faculty grew to 1,000 and the physical plant added the medical school, Marriott Library, Special Events Center—now the Jon Huntsman Center—and Research Park complex. For the latter he negotiated the purchase of 320 acres from Fort Douglas above the university, a hopeful partnership between the university's researchers and technicians and the community's business entrepreneurs.

Interviewed in 1991, twenty years after his departure from the University of Utah, Fletcher vigorously praised his associates in the dean of students' office as "super people," who cared about students. He had immediately tapped Maxwell as vice president and Frobes as dean of students, the first woman to hold the job. Lowell became associate dean and Elizabeth Haglund director of university relations. Fletcher commented that "Lowell was very helpful because he had a good relationship with the LDS students, especially the ones that had turned sour."[22] Frobes added that Lowell also bridged the metaphorical gap between the campus and the powers downtown. "Lowell became an important interpreter of what we were trying to do. The conservatives in the community—LDS or not—were so frightened by what was happening throughout the nation in higher education—-student unrest, drugs, rebellion against authority, sexual permissiveness—that even though we didn't seem to be having problems, they were sure we were."[23]

In fall 1963 Henry Frost, head of the sociology department, opened a new door for Lowell by asking him to teach a two-hour graduate seminar on Max Weber.[24] In autumn 1967 Thomas O'Dea, a Catholic sociologist at the University of Utah, left to chair the Department of Religious Studies at the University of California at Santa Barbara. Mormon scholars had received his work on Mormons with excitement,[25] and the sociology department asked Lowell to teach O'Dea's sociology of religion and sociology of knowledge classes. From then until his retirement in 1972 Lowell taught each class once a year. He commented modestly, "I came to enjoy and do a fair job in the sociology of religion, [but] . . . the sociology of knowledge class required more background than I had."[26] One of O'Dea's students recalled that the sociologist once digressed in a lecture to comment that "if Lowell had really concentrated on Weber when he got back from Europe, he would have preceded [Talcott] Parsons. . . . That would have put him in a position to be the main expert in America."[27]

It was one of history's small ironies that Lowell wrote his dissertation on Weber, who was virtually unknown to Americans in

1933 but had come to be regarded as the leading social theorist of modern times. Now after years of braiding Weber's philosophy through his institute lectures, Lowell relished the opportunity to dive deeper, applying Weber's concept of priestly versus prophetic leadership to the role, function, and expression of religion in society. He enjoyed explaining Weber's process of rationalization as the key to understanding Western culture and the rise of bureaucratic organization as an expression of that rationalization. Exploring the bureaucratic dynamics of large ecclesiastical institutions provided stimulation with insight for Lowell's students.

Lowell had a strong intellectual affinity with Max Weber. His background, training, and teaching experience converged to support Weber's choice of the individual, rather than institutional structures, as the basic unit of analysis in discussing social reality. To young sociology and philosophy students struggling to find the balance point between experimental individualism and social responsibility, this approach was helpful. He also taught students to construct descriptions of such institutions as a bureaucracy, marriage, church from observation, then to analyze those descriptions theoretically. This exercise helped students separate personal value judgments from "reality." In looking at the concept of "prophet," Buddha was an "exemplar" prophet (who led by personal example) while Isaiah was an "emissary" prophet (who transmitted a message from God). Lowell added his own assessment—that Jesus was a combination of both.[28]

In his courses Lowell, always the synthesizer, blended Weber with other intellectual heroes, particularly Kant and Goethe. Kant, who figured prominently in Weber's thought, believed that reality "must be organized and receive meaning" through the mind. Kant distinguished between the world of nature and the world of morality—what *is* and what *ought to be.* Nature could be known empirically, but God, immortality, and freedom could not.[29] Weber developed a separate ethic of responsibility that related means to ends.

Goethe, both Lowell's and Weber's literary hero, was "the greatest thinker in the universal sense that Germany had produced."[30] His *Faust* could be read as biography. Lowell enticed students to enter spiritual realms through the door of their intellectual insights.

"Teaching in addition to a full time job was strenuous, and I never felt I did it full justice," Lowell lamented.[31] His students, however, welcomed the clarity of thought that Max Weber and Lowell seemed to share. Two students who were profoundly influenced by Lowell's sociology of religion class were undergraduate twins, Gary and Gordon Shepherd. They had returned from a stint in the military and LDS missions in Mexico "without a clear sense of direction or plausible career path to follow." Lowell's class crystallized their emerging interest in social science and set them on the road to doctorate degrees in sociology and a jointly authored book, *A Kingdom Transformed: Themes in the Development of Mormonism* (Salt Lake City: University of Utah Press, 1984), which they dedicated to Lowell. To Gordon, Lowell became a "spiritual hero. . . . I had never previously encountered such a powerfully compelling, symmetrical blend of intellectual and moral integrity in a single individual."[32] In the classroom Lowell acknowledged students' comments, "adroitly weaving them into the framework of his lecture with gentle self-deprecating humor." Gary concluded that "beyond his intellect and verbal powers of persuasion, these . . . small acts . . . constantly impressed me with the honesty and humility of Lowell Bennion."[33]

Students found his classes "low-key, low pressure, and conversational. . . . The thing that impressed me," Dennis Lythgoe recalled, "was that he was never a glad-hander, always unassuming. Some may have thought he was not terribly friendly because he didn't go out of his way to impress, but he was a genuine person. His classes were interesting because it was one-on-one without being threatening. He would put a flash of personality into it—like his laugh. . . . You'd be talking about something very seriously, and then suddenly he'd give that big belly laugh!" Never dependant on notes, he would walk back and forth and stop at a student's seat to talk with him "up close. He'd write things on the board, but most of it was in his head. You had a feeling things would come out differently depending on how the class reacted."[34]

Lowell befriended some students who became lifelong friends. One was Annie Laurie Newman (DiPadova), a Mormon convert from Williamsburg, Virginia, who transferred to the University of Utah in the fall of 1967. Her parents had been dismayed by her conversion to the new "sect," and her former university had relieved her of a student government position. A graduate student in sociology with a philosophical bent, she took classes from Lowell and Sterling McMurrin, both of whom invited her home to dinner.

Natalie McMurrin and Merle Bennion both took to this bright, likable young woman with the Southern accent and went out of their way to include her in family activities. "It wasn't someone in my bishopric or anyone else" who reached out so promptly and effectively, she recalled. In fact, she found Salt Lake City "a cold place" apart from her friendship with the Bennions and McMurrins. Lowell guided her master's research and chaired her thesis committee. In winter quarter 1969 Newman became Lowell's teaching assistant. He offered, "I'll make a deal with you. I'll teach you how to teach if you will teach me the new material in sociology." She soon realized that he "had forgotten more than I would ever learn, but it made me feel I could contribute something."[35]

Lowell's skills as teacher and counselor made him a pivotal figure in an interesting, though short-lived, university experiment with social relevance. In May 1968 the administration gave a hearing to representatives of the Christian Action Ministry Academy (CAM) from the "heart of the Chicago ghetto." CAM placed "drop-outs, lockouts, and fallouts" in academic settings where they could "develop the necessary skills and self confidence to succeed in regular university work." It was "a second chance for a college education." It caught the administration's imagination, and they agreed to participate. Under the university's "2 percent exemption" rule, which allowed the admittance of a limited number of students who otherwise lacked academic credentials, six African American CAM students entered the University of Utah for fall semester 1968. Their way was paid from CAM, with additional funding from the university's Associated Students, federal Equal Education Opportunity grants, and individual contributions from faculty members, and students living in the residence halls.[36] Each of the six received tutoring from volunteer students, and Lowell conducted a tailor-made sociology seminar on "urban problems" for the six, augmented by three Job Corps blacks and a small group of interested white students in winter quarter of 1969. Eight students completed the course.[37]

Lowell ran the seminar in his most relaxed style. The group met in a conference room, gathered in a circle with no tables. Newman was "rather annoyed" because she felt the students were disrespectful, calling Lowell by his first name, and were less interested in learning than in delivering meandering speeches on their political perceptions. Lowell "seemed too accepting, too passive, too kind," Laurie commented. "I kept wanting to tell them to shape up. 'Do you know who this man is?'"[38] For Lowell's part, he asked two students to work with him in the dean of students' office, accepting their informality without turning a hair and listening to their problems because he felt they needed "to vent."[39]

President Fletcher termed the experiment only a partial success. Set up in his absence, when he learned of it, he pointed out the absence of a significant black community in Salt Lake City and protested, "We shouldn't be bringing Chicago ghetto students in; we should be bringing Chicanos here because Chicanos are right here in Utah."[40] Apparently only two finished their schooling at the University of Utah.

Without requesting the promotion, Lowell was made a full professor of sociology in the spring of 1969. In recommending his promotion, Virginia Frobes said, "It is difficult to appraise the total contribution of Dean Bennion . . . academic, administrative and also deeply personal. I believe he represents a significant model for students in objectivity, gentleness, wisdom and integrity." Among his achievements, she listed "revising and formalizing a new student disciplinary system for the university," bringing together religious leaders, and providing students with meaningful religious experience. She called him "creative and willing to take the initiative in exploring new directions, both in educational and administrative areas."[41] Three years after becoming a full professor, he was awarded tenure, an irregularity that his dean termed "an unusual advancement—from untenured Lecturer to a tenure-producing position as Professor."[42]

Although Lowell appreciated both decisions as a mark of his colleagues' esteem, he eschewed political games at the university as he did at the institute. In fact, despite his decidedly liberal philosophies, he took little part in local politics during his entire life except for civic appointments, which he almost invariably accepted, and two brief flashes of activity as a candidate. The first came in February 1964, when J. D. Williams, a liberal Mormon professor of political science at the University of Utah and director of its Hinckley Institute of Politics, wrote a letter to the *Salt Lake Tribune* naming his three most viable Democratic candidates for governor: attorney John Boyden, Sterling McMurrin, and Lowell Bennion.[43] Ed Lyon, who reported this development to George Boyd, added that Lowell "is a bit interested."

Williams, who described himself as a "disciple of Lowell," invited a "couple of Democratic chieftains" and Lowell to lunch. They "regarded [Lowell] with such enormous affection" and respected "his commitment to the public welfare and the public interest." At the same time Williams noted that "I was not at all sure that the soft virtues, if I may use that phrase, . . . would have fitted him for political office and the tough decision-making that would be involved."[44]

It is difficult to know how seriously Lowell considered the proposal or how forcefully the chieftains argued their case; but when the time came for a decision, Lowell thanked his backers and announced: "It is not the time for me to run for governor. . . . I have decided against this measure because of personal and practical reasons."[45]

Lowell was proud of the fact that during the late 1960s and early 1970s the University of Utah never developed the ugly violence and mistrust that tortured and shut down other campuses during anti-Vietnam demonstrations. Virginia Frobes was an eager advocate of student rights, and her open-door policy kept the frustration threshold lower than it might otherwise have been. Fletcher was also accessible and proactive. When Jerry Rubin's free speech movement, which started at Berkeley, reached the University of Utah, Fletcher called in all the "student radicals except two who wouldn't come" and had a series of meetings to air their problems. "We said we'd work on them as best we could, and this kind of settled things down," he recalled.[46]

It was not as easy as he made it sound. Robert Welch, head of the John Birch Society, outraged liberals with an inflammatory Communist-conspiracy speech on campus in January 1970, followed by Jerry Rubin in February. Rubin, one of the infamous "Chicago Seven," had earlier been fined $5,000 and given five years for inciting to riot. His speech to the university community, sponsored by four student committees, was so filled with epithets and calls to violence that it was not published.[47] Fletcher called it "a symbolic, theatrical event rather than a scholarly presentation."[48]

Two weeks later Lowell participated in a panel discussing policies on student violence and, according to Gene England, "gave a persuasive plea, based on long personal experience with universities, . . . for maximum freedom for all on campus, even for peaceful civil disobedience—but only in order to pursue true and rational persuasion, not revolution through violent coercion, which destroys the rule of law and the very nature of universities."[49] Lowell was "opposed to student violence because it will be met with counter-violence and, instead of effecting desired change, will likely polarize an opposition stance of law and order." Lowell proposed such alternatives as nonviolent protest that does not interfere with the rights of others, responsible student government, reasonable procedures, and shared governance.[50]

When Lowell left in March for Kiel, Germany, with the university's international study program (see chap. 9), he missed the ugliest threats of the spring of 1970. After a former official of Students for a Democratic Society (SDS) called for a "cultural revolution" in an April speech on campus, the university's Institutional Council asked for a legal opinion from the state's attorney general about the speaker's right to incite a possible riot.[51] With tensions at an all-time high for conservative Utah, "Neighborhood Emergency Teams," consisting of armed neighborhood vigilantes, organized in the Salt Lake City area to "defend" against students and blacks who might attack. Fletcher remained calm. "There was some noise and a lot of marching around the campus, but school was not suspended and the National Guard was never called in."[52] By the time Lowell returned in the fall, things had quieted down.

Had he been around, however, he almost certainly would have pursued the same course as before. He avoided affiliation with groups or movements, listening instead to anyone who needed to talk. Elizabeth Haglund remembered a telling image from this period: "The students who wanted change would meet out by the flagpole and join hands and sing 'We Shall Overcome,' and [Virginia] Frobes would be out there singing with them, and

Lowell would be standing in the background, smiling at all the students that came by, but not participating."[53] As the university's public relations director, Elizabeth Haglund called Lowell "a pivotal man" whose influence came from a "strongly held, quietly expressed moral view about student roles and behavior." She praised "the steadiness of his views and his personality, and his ability to deal without rancor with everybody."[54]

Next to Fletcher, Virginia Frobes was probably in the most difficult position, and Lowell credits her with much of the university's relatively peaceful passage through the anti-war demonstrations. "She is very bright, flexible, and democratic," he said. He praised her ability to build an informal team among colleagues and her ease with all students. "She really liked students with different backgrounds, different temperaments, different philosophical positions," mused Lowell. "She liked Mormon kids, although she disliked some of our ideas." He reported her quip, "'Eternal marriage is too long.'"[55] Ramona Adams, associate dean of Student Affairs and Services, praised Frobes's courage and creativity. While other colleges outlawed SDS, turning them into underground groups, Virginia "just made them register. We knew exactly who they were, and we dealt with them and talked to them."[56]

Lowell's assignment on this trouble-shooting team was to head the committee that drafted a thirty-five-page student code, adopted in September 1971. The project, "a comprehensive guide of student freedoms and responsibilities,"[57] had actually begun in 1963 when Lowell worked with an ad hoc committee on a two-year study of the university's disciplinary system.[58] He pronounced this experience an "education in due process,"[59] and the final document included a student bill of rights, modeled after the United States Bill of Rights, specifying forbidden conduct, procedures, protections, and sanctions. The Student Behavior Committee, composed of five faculty members and five students, had "jurisdiction to hear all charges of misconduct against individual students" as long as they had not broken state or federal law. The right to demonstrate, for instance, was protected as a "legitimate means of expression" as long as demonstrations did not "unduly disrupt the functioning of the university or interfere with the rights of other members of the university community." The code protected free discussion in the classroom "relevant to the subject matter" but stated that "students have no right to impinge on the freedom of instructors to teach or students to learn."[60]

Lowell welcomed the opportunity to work with attorneys on specific issues of procedural fairness, but Fletcher felt that Lowell and Neal Maxwell helped "make sure that the lawyers didn't . . . get too legalistic" and produce merely a list of prohibitions. "Lowell and Neal and Virginia . . . emphasized what students could do and their right to appeal."[61] It was a "pioneering effort," according to Ramona Adams. "Schools all over the country . . . asked for copies."[62]

Even as the code did its good work, the team was unraveling. Neal A. Maxwell became LDS Church Commissioner of Education in June 1970; in March 1971 Fletcher became administrator of the National Aeronautics and Space Agency in Washington, D.C., and was replaced by Provost Alfred C. Emery. He appointed Virginia Frobes his special assistant and vice president for student affairs. She was surprised when he failed to appoint Lowell dean of students, choosing instead Michael J. Patton, a psychology professor. Frobes conceded, however, that Lowell would have disliked the "highly political" nature of the deanship, even though he merited the promotion.[63]

She was right. Lowell had no desire for the job nor would he have welcomed the administrative burdens, but he missed the camaraderie and vigorous exchanges of views with Frobes and other officials in the dean's office. The change "took away a good deal of creativity for me," he acknowledged, and increasing specialization meant that "we didn't know the policies of the university like we had done."[64] The reorganization meant "one too many layers of administration," and he found himself carrying out decisions that he "had no part in [making] and with which [he] disagreed."[65]

When he took a call in June 1972 from attorney J. Thomas Greene, he was ripe for a new opportunity. Greene was chair of a committee seeking a new director for the Community Service Council in downtown Salt Lake City. This group, organized in 1904, had evolved into a private, nonprofit umbrella agency, sponsored by United Way, that facilitated the work of an increasing number of government and private service agencies that supplied direct services.

Lowell listened sympathetically as Greene described the unsuccessful search. Since 1966 Lowell had served on its board, even as its president, and was harmonious with Eva Hancock, who had ably headed the council for fourteen years. Even earlier they had served together on the citizens' advisory council of the Salt Lake Hospital.[66] He had chaired one committee "in the sensitive field of adoptions," according to Eva, that "not only evaluated needs and services but set forth a new concept of budgeting," and he had chaired a second committee that developed a youth services program for "pre-delinquent youth in conjunction with the juvenile courts, the schools and other community agencies."[67]

Greene then asked Lowell to consider taking the job. Greene complained that the candidates they approached had refused the job. Then Greene called him again and at the Idaho ranch a few days later announced, "I have had a revelation. I believe you are the next director."[68] "Methinks your inspiration lurketh from beneath," Lowell quipped even as he was tempted by the opportunity to leave "the halls of ivy for the real world," as he put it.[69] Greene recalled, "We really had to talk him into it,"[70] but the council's need coincided with Lowell's growing desire, as he neared retirement, to put into practice some of his ideas for serving the needy.

When he discussed it with Merle, she was less than enthusiastic, having grown to love her proximity to university life. But she could tell that it was something he thought he should do and did not complain. When he discussed it with Virginia Frobes in July 1972, she pronounced the loss of Lowell "a very serious blow for the university" and negotiated an arrangement with Emery that Lowell could retain a "20% teaching appointment" in the sociology department for 1972-73, an arrangement that, in effect, let him continue as a university employee with full benefits. Frobes hoped that after Lowell tried the new position for a few months he "might want to return to a different kind of job" at the university.[71] Emery concurred and generously urged Lowell to regard his new appointment as no more than "a temporary diversion from the university."[72]

Lowell's friends at the university were pleased at the contributions they knew he would make but regretted the lost association. The chair of the Student Behavior Committee, in making its annual report, praised Lowell's contributions "as committee clerk, student counselor, and as Solomon. He has performed all of those tasks efficiently and with a fine human touch. It is rare to find one who is so compassionate and understanding of human frailties and who is neither supercilious nor mawkish."[73] (See chap. 13 for Lowell's work at CSC.)

Simultaneously that summer Williams asked Lowell to run on the Democratic ticket for the state legislature in the traditionally Republican House District 17. This time Lowell said yes. Familiar with the legislature's work from university-related testimony, lobbying, and committees, he hoped to introduce much-needed bills to benefit the delinquent, the homeless, the elderly. Merle ironically quoted the family motto: "Never finish a job before taking on two more."

With the help of J. D. Williams, Lowell began a district campaign consisting of low-key meetings and a single flyer. The *Deseret News* quoted his promise to "scrutinize every proposal including my own to see whom it will benefit, whom it will injure, and is it worth the cost?" His chief interests were "the fields of education and social services—the two most costly functions of government."[74]

Lowell ran an old-fashioned gentleman's campaign. When one local leader asked him what he was willing to do for his vote, Lowell replied, "I don't need your vote."[75] He lost, but the 54.4 to 45.6 margin was the closest a Democrat had ever come to winning that seat and in 1994 this record still stood. Williams concluded that Lowell's "extraordinary appeal across the whole spectrum almost gave him the victory" and speculated that Lowell could have won had he possessed the necessary "fire in the belly."[76]

In January 1974, after splitting his time between CSC and the university for a little more than a year, Lowell resigned his appointment in the sociology department. He gave three reasons for his decision: "I turned sixty-five in late July and have no right to teach next year except by invitation. And I have never appreciated teachers who have held on as long as they possibly could. . . . I am not carrying my share of the faculty work load" by being headquartered off-campus, he said. And third, he found directing the CSC "very demanding, so I am not able to devote the time to research in sociology per se as one who teaches should."[77] He taught his last class in the spring of 1974. David P. Gardner, the new president, praised his "unusual empathy for students and their concerns" and called him "one of Utah's most valuable citizens."[78]

Elizabeth Haglund, appraising Lowell's decade at the University of Utah, voiced a private tribute:

> Lowell affected the whole university without ever being in a prominent position—he has never sought prominence. People would come to him and would go away and then things would begin to happen. Lowell's name was never attached to it. . . . The psychology of that is very intriguing to me. What kind of person can care so little about his own needs and care so greatly and understand so deeply about how to provide help for others' needs? Lowell is a man of mystery in many ways.[79]

NOTES

1. "A New Dean for the University," *Deseret News*, 9 Aug. 1962, 3.

2. Lowell performed Pat and Boyer Jarvis's marriage when he was still at the institute.

3. Boyer and Pat Jarvis, interviewed by Mary L. Bradford, 15 July 1987.

4. Sterling M. McMurrin, interviewed by Mary L. Bradford, 9 Feb. 1988.

5. Olpin, Diary, 23 Nov. 1962, Olpin Collection, Presidential Papers, University Archives, University of Utah. Apparently unaware of Olpin's efforts to recruit Lowell, Maxwell later said that he and his carpool companion, Ray Canning, had schemed to bring Lowell to the university under the dual contract with both their offices that Lowell, in fact, finally accepted. Neal A. Maxwell, interviewed by Mary L. Bradford, 26 Sept. 1987.

6. Lowell L. Bennion to Bill Moran, 14 Mar. 1963, photocopy in Bradford's possession.

7. Lowell L. Bennion, Oral History, 157.

8. Neal A. Maxwell, interviewed by Mary L. Bradford, 26 Sept. 1989.

9. Lowell L. Bennion, Oral History, 157-58.

10. Virginia P. Frobes, interviewed by Linda Sillitoe, 1 Sept. 1989,

notes in Bradford's possession.

11. Lowell L. Bennion, Oral History, 159.

12. Ibid., 159-60.

13. James C. Fletcher, interviewed by Mary L. Bradford, 15 Mar. 1991.

14. Lowell L. Bennion to Campus Security, 20 Jan. 1965, photocopy in Bradford's possession.

15. A Mormon, Canning had left BYU after Franklin West and Wyley Sessions were "retired, fired, or moved on." He noticed that even though Lowell had suffered similar treatment, "his response remained Christ-like. He exuded *religion* in the best meaning of the term" (Ray Canning to Mary L. Bradford, 16 May 1990).

16. Lowell L. Bennion, Oral History, 159.

17. Ibid.

18. Ray Canning, interviewed by Mary L. Bradford, 19 July 1988.

19. Canning to Bradford.

20. As quoted in "Teach Child Values, PTA Speaker Asks: Meet Favors Continued Federal Aid," *Salt Lake Tribune,* 12 Oct. 1962, B-22.

21. Buchanan, Diary, 10 Apr. 1963, copy in Bradford's possession; "Watch Channel 7," *Deseret News,* 17 Apr. 1963.

22. James C. Fletcher, interviewed by Mary L. Bradford, 15 Mar. 1991.

23. Virginia Frobes, interviewed by Linda Sillitoe, 17 Sept. 1988, notes in Bradford's possession.

24. Henry H. Frost to Ray R. Canning, 20 Aug. 1963, photocopy in Bradford's possession.

25. See Robert S. Michaelson, "Thomas F. O'Dea on the Mormons: Retrospect and Assessment," *Dialogue: A Journal of Mormon Thought* 12 (Spring 1978): 44. A Weberian scholar, O'Dea wrote *The Mormons* (Chicago: University of Chicago Press, 1957); he died in 1974.

26. Lowell L. Bennion, "Memories," 78, photocopy in Bradford's possession.

27. Owen Kendall White, phone interview by Mary L. Bradford, 22 Mar. 1991.

28. Lowell L. Bennion, *Max Weber's Methodology* (Paris: Les Presses Modernes, 1933), 44-45.

29. Lowell L. Bennion, interviewed by Mary L. Bradford, 17 Sept. 1990.

30. Ibid.

31. Lowell L. Bennion, "Memories," 77.

32. Gordon Shepherd to Mary L. Bradford, 16 June 1988.

33. Gary Shepherd to Mary L. Bradford, 30 Jan. 1990.

34. Dennis L. Lythgoe, interviewed by Mary L. Bradford, 9 Nov. 1987.

35. Laurie Newman DiPadova, interviewed by Mary L. Bradford, 26 Nov. 1991.

36. "President's Report" to the Board of Regents, Oct. 1968, University Archives, University of Utah; photocopy in Bradford's possession. Provost Alfred C. Emery sent the faculty a letter on 26 July 1968, appealing to them for contributions "to support these six students, who are trying to escape the ghetto, during the first year they are studying at the university." Because of their academic deficiencies, the administration discouraged part-time employment during their first year. Emery estimated the expenses for tuition, dormitory board and room, books, and supplies at about $12,000 for all six; student government had contributed $1,000 and dormitory students had contributed an additional $500.

37. Lowell L. Bennion, Faculty Vita: Classroom Instruction, 12, photocopy in Bradford's possession.

38. Laurie Newman DiPadova, interviewed by Mary L. Bradford, 2 Dec. 1988.

39. Lowell L. Bennion, conversation with Mary L. Bradford, 28 July 1990.

40. James C. Fletcher, interviewed by Mary L. Bradford, 15 Mar. 1991. Under Fletcher's guidance, the university ran a successful program for Hispanic students that began with a summer's tutoring in "how to write and speak English and how to study." He added, "This may be the thing I'm most proud of at the university."

41. Virginia P. Frobes to Ted C. Smith, chair of the sociology department, 16 Jan. 1969, copy in Bradford's possession.

42. William F. Prokasy, dean of the College of Letters and Sciences, to Thomas C. King, academic vice president, 5 Feb. 1969, University Archives, University of Utah; photocopy in Bradford's possession.

43. As reported in T. Edgar Lyon to George T. Boyd, 6 Nov. 1963, photocopy in Bradford's possession.

44. J. D. Williams, interviewed by Mary L. Bradford, 10 Feb. 1988.

45. "Bennion Says No to Backers on Governor Race," *Utah Daily Chronicle*, 6 Feb. 1964, 1.

46. Fletcher, interviewed by Mary L. Bradford, 15 Mar. 1991.

47. "No Campus Speaker Above the Law," *Deseret News*, 18 Mar. 1970, described Rubin's speech as "littered" with obscene words, gestures, "mockeries of justice, advocacies of such crimes as burning down the University and child molestations." Unpaginated clipping in Bradford's possession.

48. James C. Fletcher, quoted in "'U' Speaker Policy Aired," *Deseret News*, 21 Feb. 1970, unpaginated clipping in Bradford's possession.

49. Gene England, introduction, "What Should Be the University Policy with Respect to Student Violence?" typescript of Great Issues Forum, University of Utah, 25 Feb. 1970, photocopy in Bradford's possession.

50. Ibid.; "Violence: No Place At 'U,' Aide Says," *Deseret News*, 26 Feb. 1970, A-1.

51. LaVar K. Chaffin, "U. Council Requests Opinion on Obscenity," *Deseret News*, 14 Apr. 1970, unpaginated clipping in Bradford's possession.

52. Fletcher, interviewed by Mary L. Bradford, 15 Mar. 1991. The most dramatic confrontation came on 8 May after the Kent State massacre, when about 2,000 activists rallied in front of the Park Building for a sit-in. About 900 of them entered the administration building and presented Fletcher with a list of demands. He listened to them, fielded questions, then suggested they leave before the police arrived. There were a few arrests but no disruption of classes.

53. Elizabeth Haglund, interviewed by Mary L. Bradford, 3 Feb. 1990.

54. Ibid.

55. Lowell L. Bennion, Oral History, 155.

56. Ramona B. Adams, interviewed by Mary L. Bradford, 12 Feb. 1988.

57. Lowell L. Bennion, "Memories," 78.

58. Report of the Ad Hoc Committee Appointed to Study the Disciplinary System of the University of Utah, 28 Aug. 1963, typescript copy in Bradford's possession.

59. Ibid.

60. Ibid.

61. Fletcher, interviewed by Mary L. Bradford, 15 Mar. 1991.

62. Ramona B. Adams, interviewed by Mary L. Bradford, 12 Feb. 1988.

63. Virginia F. Frobes, interviewed by Linda Sillitoe, 1 Sept. 1989, notes in Bradford's possession.

64. Lowell L. Bennion, "Memories," 79.

65. Ibid.

66. Mission statement from CSC brochure, 212 West 1300 South, Salt Lake City, Utah.

67. Eva V. Hancock to Ted Smith, 17 Jan. 1969, typescript copy in Bradford's possession.

68. Lowell L. Bennion, Oral History, 183.

69. Ibid., 183.

70. J. Thomas Greene to Mary L. Bradford, 13 Jan. 1988.

71. Virginia Frobes to Alfred Emery, 12 July 1972, University Archives, University of Utah; photocopy in Bradford's possession.

72. Alfred Emery to Lowell L. Bennion, 15 July 1972.

73. Owen Olpin to President Emery, Annual Report of the Student Behavior Committee, 3 Aug. 1972, photocopy in Bradford's possession.

74. "House Districts 17, Lowell L. Bennion, Democrat," *Deseret News*, 24 Oct. 1972.

75. Reported by Renee P. Carlson, present at a fundraiser in Salt Lake City.

76. J. D. Williams, interviewed by Mary L. Bradford, 18 Feb. 1988.

77. Lowell L. Bennion to Alfred Emery, 5 Jan. 1974, photocopy in Bradford's possession.

78. David P. Gardner to Lowell L. Bennion, 1 Aug. 1973, photocopy in Bradford's possession.

79. Elizabeth Haglund, interviewed by Mary L. Bradford, 3 Feb. 1989.

CHAPTER 12

Personal Convictions, Public Issues (1962-78)

What a reflection on a "Christian" nation that civil rights must be debated and legislated!

—Lowell L. Bennion

Led by an unfaltering sense of what was right, Lowell was at the vortex of major issues during the 1960s. Many of these involved the LDS church. After five generations of public persecution and prosecution, post-war Mormonism was a force to be reckoned with. (In 1950 only 7.7 percent of members lived outside North America; by 1960 the percentage had grown to 10.4, as missions opened in Asia, the Pacific, Australia, and Latin America.[1]) Parochialism was a luxury this expansive, multinational church could no longer afford, even though the transition was painfully swift for some, too-long delayed for others.

In a 1965 article in an LDS church periodical Lowell declared that the problem of civil rights was "even greater than communism."[2] It was a bold statement during an era that still remembered Senator Joe McCarthy's witch hunts. The church's international growth probably acted as a corrective against a fortress mentality.

Growth issues led to the second great challenge for the church—the creation of "correlation." A favorite project of Apostle Harold B. Lee, it gained momentum with his gradual seniority during the late 1960s, moved into higher gear during his eighteen-month tenure as church president in the early 1970s, and sustained its momentum throughout the rest of the 1970s, 1980s, and into the 1990s. It was a doctrinal streamlining under priesthood authority which led to greater efficiency and greater cost savings. In retrospect, it looks very much like the corporate models of the late 1950s and early 1960s with elaborate pyramids of hierarchy, tight chains of command, strict reporting systems, and rigid delegation of authority.

Whatever its efficiency in providing leadership, correlation had some unintended negative consequences, some of which still burden the church today. All auxiliaries, including the Sunday school, the youth organizations, and the women's Relief Society had operated with a fair amount of autonomy and fiscal independence. Under correlation, they lost both. They also lost their publications. The *Relief Society Magazine, The Instructor* (Sunday school), the *Improvement Era* (youth organizations and general adult reading), and mission magazines, including the British Mission's *Millennial Star,* the oldest continuous publication in the church, were collapsed into *The Ensign* in January 1971. It was designed to serve the needs of all adult members with separate magazines for children and teens. Each organization had produced its own yearly manuals based on the perceived needs of its members. Now a central committee determined needs, selected writers, and wrote the lessons for each organization. A committee saw that lessons were "correlated" with the Book of Mormon, Doctrine and Covenants, Old Testament, and New Testament in a repetitive four-year cycle.

Called to the Youth Correlation Committee in January 1962, Lowell enjoyed the association with good friends like Rosebud Jacobsen and Edith F. Shepherd but wearied under the tedium that correlation spawned. (Apostle Richard L. Evans chaired the committee with Lowell, Edith Shepherd, and Daniel Ludlow as personnel. The *Church News* for January 17, 1962, announced that the committee would organize planning groups, and "as work progresses, more will be added.") "We tend to repeat ourselves in priesthood and Sunday School and Relief Society and the Young Women and Young Men programs," Lowell observed. "I'd like to see a manual written around . . . the spiritual needs, the human needs of an individual . . . drawing from all sources, instead of trying to cover so many sections of the Doctrine and Covenants or the Book of Mormon."[3] During this service, from 1962-72, he wrote a single Sunday school manual, *The Scriptures of the Church of Jesus Christ of Latter-day Saints,* declaring, "I've never worked as hard in a job in the Church and achieved so little as I felt I did during those ten years on Correlation."[4]

Lowell believed that these manuals, committee-revised and edited and published anonymously, dampened creativity and discussion. If a manual carried an author's name, class members would feel less intimidated about disagreeing—but manuals produced by committees and published by the church took on a scripture-like aura. Too much reverence for manuals and too little accountability created a recipe for ennui. These correlated manuals often lacked "development, depth, and unity."[5]

After ten years Lowell requested a release and gladly returned to East Millcreek Twelfth Ward where he became a Sunday school teacher, high priests group leader, and teacher development teacher. He maintained an intensive speaking schedule, addressing sacrament meetings or firesides and speaking frequently at the funerals of former students and colleagues. Being back in the ward gave him free rein for "the relational aspects" of church work that he loved: "teaching, 'visiting the sick and afflicted,' and planning and participating in service projects." He confessed, "The institutional aspects of religion—checking on people's attendance at meetings, getting people to the temple or to the church farm—some of it essential—drives me up a wall."[6]

The issue of civil rights was probably the most agonizing question of the mid-twentieth century for a liberal and believing Mormon. The church had instituted the policy of denying priesthood to black men as early as the 1850s. As a university administrator, Lowell stepped out of the public silence imposed upon him earlier by his church employment to become, in his own quiet way, a spokesman for civil rights.

In Utah blacks numbered only about 5,000, residing mainly along the Wasatch Front. Naturally, in a state more than 70 percent Mormon equality issues were linked with the LDS priesthood ban. Racial tensions flared not only between blacks and whites but between Mormons and non-Mormons and, within the church, between liberals and conservatives.

Until 1960 the national media paid little attention to the Mormon priesthood ban. But when prominent Mormon businessman George Romney became governor of Michigan, the media's eyes turned toward the Mormon church. During the ensuing decade public criticism of the LDS policy toward blacks spread throughout the nation and even internationally. Missionary work in Nigeria was strangled when a Nigerian student reported to his government on the church's "racist" policy in 1963.[7] When Lowell read the Nigerian newspaper account—which described the explanations for the policy this student had been given at a California institute—he "blush[ed] in shame and anger to read it. We have sown the wind and are reaping the whirlwind."[8]

"Shame" and "anger" were uncommon words for Lowell. A few days later Lowell accepted an invitation to debate religion professor Chauncey Riddle at BYU. Armed with a doctorate in the philosophy of science from Columbia, Riddle was regarded at BYU as a leading intellectual. The topic was billed as "liberalism versus conservatism," but the "Negro question" inevitably became the crux of the discussion. Lowell's abrupt departure from the Salt Lake institute was well known. Most people, not understanding BYU president Ernest L. Wilkinson's role, believed that his attitude toward the priesthood ban had caused his change of career. Students and members of the community jammed the Joseph Smith Building auditorium, standing along the sides, filling doorways, and spilling into the hall.

Lowell, as first speaker, began by quipping, "I come from an alien institution which is seventy percent Mormon." In his inclusive way he tackled definitions. "A society without a good conservative element is not a well-balanced society. The color-giving, life-giving element in our society is the liberal element."[9] And liberals could be orthodox or unorthodox. While definitions shift, he asserted, "the Mormon religion contains both elements. . . . The standard works are conservative as is the authoritative, bureaucratic structure of our church."

The liberal mind is unafraid to focus on anything, including religion. "Thou shalt love the Lord thy God with all thy heart and with all thy mind and with all thy strength," he quoted from the New Testament. Religion may transcend reason, he suggested, yet "a liberal person would call into question anything that contradicted his basic experience in life and the logic of his experience and thought."

Reason, experience, revelation, and intuition are ways of

knowing, he maintained, that comprise a system of checks and balances. Revelation and intuition should be checked by reason and experience, reason and experience by revelation and intuition.

Once in a class of seminary teachers one had asked another, "Would you kill Brother Bennion if [a high church authority] asked you to?" The other replied, "I surely would." This understandably alarmed Lowell: "I have met people in the church who thought they would do anything that anybody in authority told them to do and then it would be that authority's responsibility if they did wrong." He declared that "a liberal respects authority but believes that it should be exercised in humility," with "no respect for authoritarianism."

Riddle did not challenge Lowell's definitions. Instead he created his own framework based on his view of the "strait and narrow," challenging both "right" and "left." "Persons on the right tend to glory in past revelations, in past prophets" taking scriptures as "extremely authoritative, not to be challenged, and they do not live by their own revelation but by the revelation of others." On the other hand, he said, the people on the left reject revelation, depending instead on reason or science "as Brother Bennion has said."

Choosing a Bible story Lowell had often discussed in class, Riddle asked, "Was it reasonable to take Isaac out and slay him? No, it was not reasonable . . . [but] Abraham trusted the Lord, and if He tells us to do something . . . this should be sufficient."

In summary, he defined the "strait and narrow" as conservative, or "hanging on to that thing that is most precious . . . the Lord, Jesus Christ." He closed with a fervent wish that he and "Brother Bennion will see eye-to-eye" because "if ye are not one, ye are not the Lord's."

Lowell said with gentle humor. "I don't trust reason ultimately any more than Brother Riddle . . . but I think there are also difficulties in trusting one's private inspiration. How do you know whether or not your inspiration is the Lord's, particularly if your inspiration seems to differ from that of a colleague in the same department . . . or your bishop or your stake president or a general authority?"

Riddle was happy to answer this "most fundamental question:

"I have never in my life seen an occasion when my own personal revelation disagreed with anything my stake president or my bishop has told me to do." The second difficulty was to ask if it is consistent with the scriptures and prayer. "It should be reasonable, but remember that our reason is not God's reason. . . . Somehow I think we had better trust in him and be, in a sense, blind in obedience to him if necessary. But let's make sure it is to him that we have our blind obedience." He paraphrased Lowell's original framework for checks and balances—authority, revelation, reason, and experience.

When Lowell asked, "What if two revered authorities disagree?" Riddle's answer was, "Ask the Lord." When Lowell retorted, "Then you and the Lord and one of the authorities are right," Riddle responded: "The General Authorities are acting from unity and unanimity of opinion and we can abide by what they say."

Riddle then asked Lowell for his "premises." Lowell replied, "I think the premises for religion are in revelation. You see, I agree with you."

Then suddenly Riddle shifted the ground of the argument from the philosophical to the ethical: "Is it moral to deny the Negro the priesthood?" he challenged Lowell.

Lowell responded with another question: "What would you do if a practice you taught were, from a rational point of view, contrary to basic principles of the gospel of Christ and inspiration, after thoughtful, persistent prayer?"

Riddle replied, "Maybe I would decide I couldn't belong to such an organization, I don't know, . . . [or] maybe I would decide that I had better go back and put this on the shelf a little bit." What people often think of as moral is often just prejudice, he said. "How do we know the mind of God? . . . If I disagree with President McKay, I realize that I'm out of line. . . . If we challenge revelation on the basis of whether it is moral or not we are on shaky ground."

Lowell responded gently, "I'm willing to walk by faith in darkness. . . . [but] the problem [comes]. . . when I'm called upon to do something that goes against . . . the spirit that I am accustomed to hearkening unto, when it's also against what I think is the very heart and soul of the gospel of Jesus Christ and of theology . . . I can't just be happy in the present practice of the church to deny the Negro the priesthood."

Dale LeCheminant reported that the audience burst into applause.[10] Lowell remained focused on Riddle. "Brother Riddle," he continued, "you say our wisdom is not God's wisdom . . . but . . . do we abdicate and say, 'We can't act on our best knowledge and inspiration at the moment?' I am not fighting the church on it. I follow President David O. McKay. I love him, and I have told him exactly how I feel about this Negro problem . . . and he let me teach at the institute of religion for over two decades."

Riddle admitted, "This problem also bothers me." Lowell replied, "I hope it bothers every Latter-day Saint."

Riddle continued, "The prophets have said there is a reason, but they haven't told us what the reason is." Comforted by the statement of Brigham Young that the time will come "when these people will have every opportunity that anyone else has," he made the familiar argument that only a small portion of the world's people bear the priesthood anyway, so the Negroes should be happy for church membership itself.

Lowell moved from the theoretical to the immediate: "If it were your child that was turned away from the ward at the age of twelve because of the color of his skin, how would you feel?" He then turned his plea toward the large audience:

> I have a feeling that God's revelations to us individually and to the church as a whole depend upon our minds, our eagerness, upon our search, upon our questions, upon our moral disturbances, if you will, upon our needs. It might be that you and I, and all of us in the church, because of our sins, or because of our lack of thinking upon the great fundamentals that Christ taught, because of not having the Spirit of Christ, may sometimes be at fault for our limitations. It may be that the Lord can't get through to us sometimes on things. Therefore we ought to be thinking and searching and praying even over this Negro problem.

The audience was divided over the outcome of the debate. One listener said he thought Riddle won the first round and Lowell the second. Some thought Riddle had meant to embarrass Lowell by bringing up the Negro issue. Later that week a letter appeared in the BYU student newspaper "strongly urging the [BYU] president to extend an apology to Lowell for this underhanded tactic."[11]

Lowell confessed himself disappointed at the direction the evening had taken. He had expected a classical debate structure. When Riddle shifted the ground to his own framework, the academic nature of the exercise slid away. But Lowell also felt satisfied that he had been free to express himself on the priesthood ban in a large public meeting. He was convinced that a change was in the wind. The papers were full of speculation, and everywhere people discussed the possibilities.

In fact, Lowell had received a phone call from Hugh B. Brown shortly before general conference in April 1962, assuring him that change was imminent.[12] In June 1962 Wallace Turner quoted Hugh B. Brown in the *New York Times:* "We are in the middle of a survey looking toward the possibility of admitting Negroes . . . The whole problem . . . is being considered by the leaders of the church in the light of racial relationships everywhere."[13] Almost immediately the church-owned KSL-TV reported that "Brown said he was misquoted" and Joseph Fielding Smith stated: "Church doctrine does not provide for admission of Negroes to the priesthood in mortality."[14]

Leaders of the NAACP announced plans to picket Temple Square at the October 1963 general conference unless the church made a statement on the civil rights legislation pending in the state legislature. Brown read a carefully phrased First Presidency statement: "There is in the church no doctrine, belief, or practice that is intended to deny the enjoyment of full civil rights by any person regardless of race, color, or creed. . . . We call upon all men, everywhere, both within and outside the church, to commit themselves to the establishment of full civil equality for all of God's creatures."[15] There was no picketing, but Lowell privately predicted continuing difficulties: "Our discrimination in regard to the priesthood cuts too deeply into self respect to be accepted by the Negroes here or nationally."[16]

The ban remained in place for more than a decade while the sweeping Civil Rights Act of 1964 was passed, while students from various colleges and universities protested at BYU basketball games, while awareness and discomfort rose among church leaders and members.

Lowell's sympathies lay with the black people of his acquaintance in Salt Lake City. These included Monroe and Frances

Fleming who lived in East Millcreek, and the Len Hope family that had converted in Cincinnati and migrated to Utah. As a missionary, Marion D. Hanks had befriended the Hopes in Cincinnati and had initiated meetings in their home when the Hopes were unwelcome in the branch. When the Hopes visited Utah, they stayed with the Hankses, and Hanks tried to dissuade them from moving to Utah. "I didn't think we were ready for them," he recalled. "I tried to tell them to be happy in Cincinnati where they had become fully accepted."[17]

Acting on his principles, Lowell readily took opportunities to work for social justice. He was appointed to a committee sponsored by the City and County Commissions to establish a Salt Lake Commission on Civil Rights in January 1965. He admired Calvin L. Rampton, a Democrat elected governor in November 1964, who eloquently called for civil rights legislation: "The government of this state owes a solemn, abiding moral obligation to effectively guarantee these rights to all its citizens."[18] Rampton eliminated discrimination in public accommodations and employment, but the legislature failed to pass a housing bill and to establish a Utah Civil Rights Commission. He countered with an executive order creating "essentially the same organization," the Utah Executive Commission on Civil Rights.[19] This commission sponsored an ad hoc "conciliation committee" which Lowell chaired during the summer of 1965. Chair of the state commission was attorney Adam M. Duncan, "a veteran champion of civil rights and former chairman of the Utah State Advisory Committee to the U.S. Commission on Civil Rights."[20] Lowell's committee consisted of J. D. Williams, Bob Mukai, and two officers of the Utah chapter of NAACP—Johnie Driver and Charles Nabors.[21] Although the commission's studies of discrimination in real estate transactions, housing, and employment of women did not lead to fair housing laws, such an organization, pointed out sociologist David Brewer, "provides the channels through which norms are made real to individuals in the community, and individual complaints are communicated for further . . . adjustments."[22] Adam Duncan and Lowell both felt that the LDS priesthood ban was the real, though invisible, stumbling block to fair housing legislation.[23]

By late September 1965 the U. of U. *Chronicle* recorded that a "surprising number of supposedly intelligent residents of Salt

Lake City" believed that a "Watts-like riot will take place . . . when the Mormon Church gathers for general conference" in Salt Lake City.[24] The riots never came although some downtown businesses remodeled to eliminate street-level windows and the police department readied its canine patrol. "The significant event was the rumor itself," reported David Brewer.[25]

Coinciding with general conference was the publication of the October 1965 *Instructor,* the magazine for the church's Sunday school officers and teachers. It contained an article by Lowell in his usually temperate tone, expressing "an unusually strong position for a Mormon publication"[26]:

> The biggest problem in the world today . . . even greater than communism, is the need of men of all races, cultures, and societies to feel their own worth and dignity as human beings. Man has a long and shameful history of subjugating and humiliating his fellowman for economic, political, religious, racial, or other reasons.
>
> In the name of religion and humanity this practice must come to an end. We may have superior talents, more possessions, and other advantages over each other, but . . . It is my belief that white men are not superior to men of other races . . . .
>
> What a reflection on a "Christian" nation that civil rights must be debated and legislated! If we had faith in Christ, we would be anxiously and voluntarily engaged in seeing that Hawaiians, Indians, Negroes, Orientals, and every other ethnic group of people in our midst had equal opportunity for education, culture, employment, and housing as we who are Caucasian. If we believed in the ethical monotheism of the prophets and the fatherhood of God and in the teachings of Jesus, legislation in this area would be as superfluous as painting the lily white.[27]

In 1968 Lowell reviewed an essay by David Brewer in which Lowell called the church's black exclusion policy "the most critical social issue facing the Mormon Church today." He charged that the priesthood ban has "increased racial prejudice among Mormons." Lowell praised presidential hopeful George Romney as an individual Mormon who had "worked hard and effectively to promote civil rights despite the lethargy of the people as a whole," and he declared that "basic Mormon theology and the Mormon ethic give no justification whatever for racial discrimination." Though such an assertion might surprise both Mormons and others, he insisted, "withholding the priesthood from the Negro is not a doctrine of the church; it is church *practice*, which needs to be justified by church doctrine." He pointed out that "no new revelation is needed to change doctrine; there need only be a change of practice," and most Mormons would welcome a change and adjust quickly.[28] But signs of institutional change were disappointingly few for the remainder of the 1960s and the early 1970s.

Dialogue: A Journal of Mormon Thought, an independent quarterly, was founded at Stanford University in 1966 by two graduate students, Wesley Johnson and Eugene England, one of Lowell's former students. Lowell became a member of the board of advisors, predicting accurately, "I knew it would be a mixed blessing, that it would bring problems and misunderstandings from headquarters. . . . But . . . it's creative, intellectual, and I've never been afraid of exposing the gospel to thinking."[29] From the beginning, it took a liberal stance toward the priesthood ban. U.S. Secretary of the Interior Stewart Udall (also a former student of Lowell's) wrote a letter that inspired dozens more on the subject of racial prejudice. Karl Keller, who had been both a Lambda Delta Sigma and University of Utah campus leader, wrote a moving account of his freedom ride in the South. Some of Lowell's past and present colleagues—Heber Snell, Sydney Sperry, Sterling McMurrin, and Lowry Nelson—published articles, and *Dialogue* offered a forum for the fledgling Mormon History Association, also founded in 1966.[30] In 1973 it published Lester E. Bush Jr.'s seminal essay, "Mormonism's Negro Doctrine: An Historical Overview," the single most influential article on the subject.[31] Pronounced controversial by some, *Dialogue* was received as a breath of fresh air by many Mormon students, scholars, and artists.

Lowell's first written contribution appeared in *Dialogue's* fourth issue: "For by Grace Are Ye Saved." At the time Lowell believed he was the only church writer discussing the subject of grace. He concluded with the plea: God "is asking us to believe in grace, to learn in our dealings with fellowmen to rid ourselves of prejudice, intolerance, covetousness, and hate, and even to rise above justice and to live life on the plane of grace."[32] Lowell also coedited, with Diane Monson, a theme issue on family life in 1967.

Leonard J. Arrington was sustained in the 1972 general conference as official church historian, the first with professional training and the first who was not a general authority. Arrington had discovered Lowell Bennion in 1935 when he found Lowell's first manual, *Why Religion?*, just what he needed as a high school senior. He avidly read Lowell's later writings. As a graduate student, he sent his articles to Lowell as "the leader of LDS intellectuals," who encouraged his "attempt to write something that would help Mormons and non-Mormons think about our culture in a positive way."[33]

In October 1971 Lowell rejoiced to learn that apostles Gordon B. Hinckley, Thomas S. Monson, and Boyd K. Packer had set apart three black men, Ruffin Bridgeforth, Darius Gray, and Eugene Orr, as the presidency of the Genesis Group—the first organized LDS group for and led by African Americans. Lowell had met Bridgeforth through Monroe Fleming, hosted a joint Genesis Group/high priest dinner in his ward ("It was the first time many of my group had ever eaten or visited with blacks"[34]). He asked Bridgeforth to speak in his ward. Bridgeforth was greatly heartened by Lowell's willingness to say forthrightly that he didn't understand the priesthood ban. For him, Lowell's steadfast hope that "the policy would change . . . influenced others, and . . . gradually whites came to have a feeling that things *could* change."[35]

In 1970 Laurie Newman, then teaching sociology at the church-owned Ricks College in Rexburg, Idaho, wrote for advice. Exercised about the priesthood ban, she wondered whether she should request an appointment with President Hugh B. Brown, counselor to McKay.

Lowell pointed out: "Brother Brown is not in a position to move the church at the moment or he would have done so." He advised against agitating for change but suggested she answer questions from students by admitting that she did not understand why a Negro cannot hold the priesthood. She could express sympathy for the black students' feelings and look forward to change. She could say, "I hope when that day comes, I will have overcome my own prejudice so I will be able to accept him in full fellowship."[36] Laurie took his advice.

Others could not emulate Lowell's patient though unyielding approach, and an uncomfortable test of his moderation came in a friend's crisis. John W. Fitzgerald, a former seminary teacher and an elementary school principal in the Granite District, was excommunicated in December 1972 after making public his disagreement with the priesthood ban by writing letters to and publishing articles in the *Salt Lake Tribune* and making speeches at local non-Mormon churches. Six months earlier he had asked Lowell to review an article arguing that the reasons for the priesthood ban ought to be discussed openly in public forums.[37]

Lowell first complimented Fitzgerald on a position "well taken and well stated," offering a characteristic suggestion: "It is my notion that an article, speech, lesson ought to have a single idea to carry maximum punch, and I like your main idea of *why not* look at the issue in the open very much and believe it deserves a single emphasis. . . . Oh yes . . . I prefer to call the denial of the priesthood a practice or a policy rather than a *doctrine* or a *theology*."[38]

Fitzgerald's stake president tried him for his membership on December 13, 1972, charging him with "failure to sustain the authorities of the church, conduct unbecoming a member by holding the church to ridicule and criticism through his teachings and publications, and advocating false doctrine."[39] Fitzgerald asked Lowell to testify at his church court. Since Lowell knew the stake president, he telephoned him to express his hope that mercy would prevail. Meanwhile Fitzgerald submitted long affidavits that declared his support of church authorities and his belief in the prophet and in continuous revelation. Lowell appeared as a witness before the court of fifteen men (three members of the stake presidency and a high council of twelve). As he recalled his testimony in later years, he told them that "I actually agreed with John but not with his methods. He had been indiscreet and had embarrassed the church by speaking about the priesthood problem at other churches."[40] Other witnesses included Ray Canning, Brigham Madsen, and Sterling McMurrin, who sent a letter stating that Fitzgerald was neither heretic nor apostate but "a man who deeply loves the church and places the highest value on his church membership."[41] The trial's verdict was disfellowshipment with the stipulation that Fitzgerald promise to refrain from writing on the subject of racism. When he refused, a second trial resulted in his excommunication.

Fitzgerald was offended by Lowell's testimony. He wrote Lowell: "Your comment that I had been 'indiscreet' had nothing, really, to do with the issue. Indiscreet by whose standards? If being indiscreet was and is a crime, then Socrates, Jesus, Savaronola, Luther, Calvin, Joseph Smith and others, though proved right by history, were all guilty." He accused Lowell of protecting himself, "but you didn't help me, not that I could see." Whereas the other witnesses "really put their reputations if not their church membership on the line, you did not." He challenged the sincerity of Lowell's usual approach of saying he didn't know why the priesthood was withheld from black men. "I submit that you do know or you have a very good idea why."[42]

Interviewed years later, Fitzgerald summarized: "Lowell sold himself and not me" at the trial. "He . . . has tried for nearly thirty years, working from within the church, to persuade the brethren to abandon the discrimination, but without results, which he admits."[43]

The philosophy that had comforted Bridgeforth and others over the years only angered Fitzgerald, and Lowell's efforts to persuade the stake president bore little weight with his pained friend.

In writing to the stake president before the trial, Fitzgerald noted that many others had disagreed with authorities, "including Dr. McMurrin who has published his thoughts, and Dr. Lowell Bennion, who agrees with me, but who has not published on the subject, yet neither is threatened in any way. Where is the consistency in such action?"[44]

Three years later, when Fitzgerald's wrath had diminished, he asked Lowell to review his account of the trial and other papers he would present to the University of Utah library. Lowell responded, "I have read your material with interest and sympathetic understanding. . . . I have made it abundantly clear to the brethren and many others that I share with you the pain of what the LDS Negro policy has done to both blacks and whites. . . . My main concern is *how* to bring about change. On this, you and I may differ . . . For the time being, I am keeping several options open."[45]

Lowell was stubborn in his belief that change was better effected from within. "You can't do much if you take yourself out." He recalled the example of a young man who had decided to give most of his belongings to the poor and to live frugally. He had come to Lowell wanting to write to the general authorities and accuse them of apostasy because they were not doing the same. Lowell convinced him that describing his life and his motivations and asking for support "in a positive way" would be more productive.[46]

Fitzgerald, for his part, remained friendly and in later years said, "I have often wondered why the general authorities of the LDS church have not called Lowell Bennion to be one of the Twelve Apostles. . . . Lowell is a kind, gentle, humble man, just the kind we need where his influence could have been felt all through the church."[47]

On January 18, 1970, after a lengthy illness which had left him basically dysfunctional during the last years of his life, David O. McKay died without rescinding the ban. Lowell wrote a tribute for *Dialogue,* which included an account of their conversations about the priesthood ban.

Eight years later, on June 7, 1978, Lowell was in his office when friend and neighbor, Stuart Poelman, telephoned about a report that had just come over the radio. The First Presidency[48] and Quorum of the Twelve had announced the lifting of the ban for worthy black males.

The announcement read:

> Aware of the promises made by the prophets and presidents of the Church who have preceded us that at some time, in God's eternal plan, all of our brethren who are worthy may receive the priesthood, and witnessing the faithfulness of those from whom the priesthood has been withheld, we have pleaded long and earnestly in behalf of these, our faithful brethren, spending many hours in the Upper Room of the Temple supplicating the Lord for divine guidance.
>
> He has heard our prayers, and by revelation has confirmed that the long-promised day has come when every faithful, worthy man in the Church may receive the holy priesthood, with power to exercise its divine authority, and enjoy with his loved ones every blessing that flows therefrom, including the blessings of the temple.
>
> Accordingly, all worthy male members of the Church may be ordained to the priesthood without regard for race or color (D&C: Official Declaration 2:9-11) .

During the next several days dozens of calls poured in from friends, colleagues, and former students. When *Dialogue* editors asked Lowell to record his feelings, he declined. "Let's just be happy and go on." But Stuart Poelman remembered Lowell's undisguised exuberance.[49] Son Doug recalled: "Oh, he was thrilled about the black revelation. Dad was not an emotional man, but that was [one] time there was emotion in his voice."[50]

Lowell could have submitted to *Dialogue* an article on "Prejudice" that he was drafting. He had written it after meeting some young black investigators considering baptism. He had told them,

> Revelation was a two-way communication process—that it wasn't just lightning from heaven . . . that man had to be hungry for it and be ready for it and be receptive to it before God spoke to them. . . . In my judgment, we had inherited a lot of prejudice against the blacks from our American background of slavery and so on, and weren't ready for it. We had to wait for a prophet who was sufficiently humble and faithful and disturbed over the issue and seeking.[51]

The investigators had accepted this explanation and asked him to perform the confirmations at their baptisms. He gladly accepted the invitation. Their embrace after the ordinance left him feeling justified in "being honest with people, acknowledging our limitations as well as our strengths."[52]

Lowell's article concluded: "I began this article with a confession and wish to close it with a prayer. Lord, forgive me my pride, my prejudice, my self-righteousness; open Thou my eyes, my ears, my mind, and my heart to the needs and pleadings of thy children and my brothers. Help me to never again judge a man's worth by the color of his skin. Help me, Lord, that I may not close my eyes to the suffering of those near and dear to Thee."[53]

NOTES

1. See James B. Allen and Glen M. Leonard, *The Story of the Latter-day Saints* (Salt Lake City: Deseret Book Co., 1976), 563-64.

2. Lowell L. Bennion, "Religion and Social Responsibility," *The Instructor,* Oct. 1965, 391.

3. Lowell L. Bennion, Oral History, 138.

4. Ibid. The period that Lowell recalled as arid, Emma Lou Thayne

remembered as one of her most satisfying church callings. She was asked to work with Lowell and Edith Shepherd on lesson manuals for LDS young women (YWMIA). In an echo of Lowell's freewheeling style, she was trusted to select other writers with whom she worked and whose lessons she edited.

5. Ibid.

6. Lowell L. Bennion, "Memories," 56-57, photocopy in Bradford's possession.

7. Lester E. Bush, "Mormonism's Negro Doctrine," *Dialogue: A Journal of Mormon Thought* 8 (Spring 1973): 67; James B. Allen, "Would-Be Saints: West Africa before the 1978 Priesthood Revelation," *Journal of Mormon History* 17 (1991): 230.

8. Lowell L. Bennion to George Boyd, 21 Oct. 1963, copy in Bradford's possession.

9. "The Liberal and Conservative View in Mormonism, Dr. Lowell L. Bennion and Dr. Chauncy Riddle," 28 Mar. 1963, typescript in possession of Lowell L. Bennion. Additional quotations of their speeches are, unless otherwise noted, from the same source.

10. Dale LeCheminant to George T. Boyd, 30 Apr. 1963, photocopy in Bradford's possession.

11. Ibid.

12. Lowell L. Bennion, interviewed by Mary L. Bradford, 12 Sept. 1990.

13. Wallace Turner, "Mormons Weigh Stand on Negro," *New York Times*, 7 June 1963, unpaginated clipping in Bradford's possession.

14. Bush, "Negro in Mormonism," 176, photocopy in Bradford's possession.

15. "Position of Church on Civil Rights Affirmed," *Deseret News*, 6 Oct. 1963, A-l.

16. Lowell L. Bennion to George Boyd, no date, photocopy in Bradford's possession.

17. Marion D. Hanks, interviewed by Mary L. Bradford, 22 Mar. 1989.

18. Quoted in David L. Brewer, "Utah Elites and Utah Racial Norms," Ph.D. diss., University of Utah, 1966, 137.

19. Calvin L. Rampton, *As I Recall*, ed. Floyd A. O'Neiland Gregory C. Thompson (Salt Lake City: University of Utah Press, 1989), 145.

20. Ibid.

21. "Rights Body Views Two Utah Studies," *Salt Lake Tribune,* 1 Aug. 1965, unpaginated clipping in Bradford's possession.

22. Adam M. Duncan, memo, "To the Members of the Governor's Executive Commission on Civil Rights," 4 Mar. 1966, photocopy in Bradford's possession; Brewer, "Utah Elites and Utah Racial Norms," 141.

23. Adam M. Duncan to Mary L. Bradford, 10 Mar. 1991.

24. *Utah Chronicle,* 29 Sept. 1965, 1.

25. Brewer, "Utah Elites and Utah Racial Norms," 138.

26. Bush, "Negro in Mormonism," 176.

27. Lowell L. Bennion, "Religion and Social Responsibility," *The Instructor,* Oct. 1965, 391.

28. Lowell L. Bennion, "Commentary [on David L. Brewer]," "The Mormons," in *The Religious Situation: 1968,* ed. Donald R. Cutler (Boston: Beacon Press, 1968), 549.

29. Lowell L. Bennion, Oral History, 141.

30. *Dialogue: A Journal of Mormon Thought*: Karl Keller, "Every Soul Has Its South," 1 (Summer 1966): 72-79. The autumn 1966 issue introduced the Mormon History Association with articles by Leonard Arrington, Richard L. Bushman, James B. Allen, Klaus Hansen, Robert Flanders, Thomas Alexander, Davis Bitton, and P. A. M. Taylor.

31. Bush, "Mormonism's Negro Doctrine," 11-68.

32. Lowell L. Bennion, "For by Grace Are Ye Saved," *Dialogue: A Journal of Mormon Thought* 1 (Autumn 1966): 104.

33. Leonard J. Arrington, interviewed by Mary L. Bradford, 23 May 1982. In 1970 Arrington identified Sterling McMurrin, Lowell, and BYU professor Hugh Nibley as "still in the mid-course of their contributions to Utah and Mormon intellectuality." He summarized with a useful simplification: "McMurrin is concerned with ideas, Bennion with people, and Nibley with the faith." He lauded Lowell's *Religion and the Pursuit of Truth* as "marked by a warm humanity and humble absence of provinciality." Leonard J. Arrington, "The Intellectual Tradition of the Latter-day Saints," *Dialogue: A Journal of Mormon Thought* 4 (Spring 1969): 13.

34. Lowell L. Bennion to Laurie Newman DiPadova, 12 Mar. 1970, photocopy in Bradford's possession.

35. Ruffin Bridgeforth, interviewed by Linda Sillitoe, 4 Mar. 1991, notes in Bradford's possession.

36. Lowell L. Bennion to Laurie Newman DiPadova, 18 Feb. 1972, photocopy in Bradford's possession.

37. John W. Fitzgerald, "Why Not!" draft of manuscript, John W. Fitzgerald Papers, Special Collections, Marriott Library.

38. Lowell L. Bennion to John W. Fitzgerald, 12 May 1972, Fitzgerald Papers; photocopy in Bradford's possession.

39. Jay J. Campbell to John W. Fitzgerald, 11 Dec. 1972, Fitzgerald Papers; photocopy in Bradford's possession.

40. Lowell L. Bennion, conversation with Mary L. Bradford, 30 Jan. 1990.

41. Sterling McMurrin to Jay J. Campbell, 11 Dec. 1972, Fitzgerald Papers; photocopy in Bradford's possession.

42. John Fitzgerald to Lowell L. Bennion, 16 June 1974, Fitzgerald Papers; photocopy in Bradford's possession.

43. John Fitzgerald, interviewed by Mary L. Bradford, 19 Jan. 1990.

44. John W. Fitzgerald, "Addendum and Questions to President Campbell (with comments)," undated, Fitzgerald Papers.

45. Lowell L. Bennion to John W. Fitzgerald, 24 July 1975. On 4 April 1978 Lowell wrote to thank Fitzgerald for a monetary contribution to a community anti-poverty program: "I appreciate your values and share many of them. . . . Our methods differ presently, but I shall continue to preach and write on behalf of Amos, et al." Photocopy in Bradford's possession.

46. Lowell L. Bennion, interviewed by Mary L. Bradford, 10 Dec. 1989.

47. John W. Fitzgerald to Mary L. Bradford, 17 Nov. 1989.

48. Spencer W. Kimball was then president of the church. Joseph Fielding Smith had briefly succeeded David O. McKay, followed, even more briefly, by Harold B. Lee.

49. Stuart Poelman, comment at a study group, 27 Aug. 1989, at the Bennion home.

50. Douglas C. Bennion, interviewed by Mary L. Bradford, 19 May 1987.

51. Lowell L. Bennion, Oral History, 204.

52. Ibid., 204.

53. Lowell L. Bennion, "Prejudice," typescript, 2.

PART FOUR

THE "REAL" WORLD

CHAPTER 13

THE COMMUNITY SERVICES COUNCIL (1972-88)

I used to teach religion; now I practice it.

—LOWELL L. BENNION

When Lowell moved from the university to the Community Services Council in downtown Salt Lake City, he was in a sense embarking on the final lap of his journey. To many he represented the sage and philosopher who had earned the right to retire to his books and garden. But driving him was an ideal captured by his motto from the *Bhagavad-Gita*—"To action alone thou hast a right, not to its fruits." His declining years became his harvesting years, drawing on his skills as entrepreneur, networker, and humanitarian.

As in every other career change in Lowell's life, his challenges at the Community Services Council came as an invitation and an opportunity. He had not applied for the job, rather he answered a call. Lowell's annual salary, which began at $18,000, although modest when compared to similar positions in other cities, "was fairly good from a Salt Lake City standpoint."[1]

Founded in 1904 as the "Community Welfare Council," the CSC had evolved into an umbrella agency facilitating the work of more than one hundred service agencies, mainly through planning and research. "Community Services Council seeks to ensure that community resources are utilized efficiently and effectively." It was a private, non-profit organization, sponsored by Community Chest, then by its successor, United Way.[2]

Eva Hancock, a professional social worker who had received the governor's award for "dedicated and exemplary community service," led the agency for seventeen years. Under her was a staff of social workers to run "an agency's agency."[3] As a clearing house, CSC identified needs and planned the best way to distribute funds to the appropriate agencies. When Lowell took the directorship, the Community Services Council facilitated a spectrum of 140 government and private agencies that provided direct services to citizens who required social, health, and recreational assistance. Its "Volunteer Center" published a directory listing all service agencies that required volunteers.[4] Roland V. Wise, another member of the search committee, past president of CSC, and Salt Lake's regional director for the Internal Revenue Service, pointed out the challenge facing the new director: he or she had "to be acceptable to hundreds of organizations."[5] Wise knew that "Lowell had a strong feeling about direct aid for the homeless and hungry that wasn't being covered very effectively. Lowell, with his stature in the community and his knowledge and his desire and interest, was just a natural" for the job.

Lowell had served a long apprenticeship in community service on a variety of social agencies, like the Salt Lake County Hospital Board, the Utah Association of Mental Health, the board of the Crossroads Urban Center (a nondenominational outreach program for the needy), and Utahns Against Hunger. He helped found the Salt Lake County Commission on Youth, dedicated to anti-child abuse and anti-drug legislation. In March 1979 Utah governor Scott Matheson appointed him to the Utah State Board of Family Services. In 1983 a group of agencies made him "chairman and peacemaker among them for the first year"[6] of the first homeless committee.

At CSC, rather than centralization and consolidation, he encouraged the growth of new agencies. "I think we can tolerate a number of agencies doing the same thing but for different people," he recalled when interviewed later about this period.[7] He noticed that a large segment of the population was not being served, such as the elderly who required dental work, the homeless, the disabled, the poor. He acknowledged that "institutions are better at providing health care or paying bills or providing food," but "I don't find institutions—the government, for example—really meeting human needs," he said. "People need to feel their own worth, and they need to be creative and productive in life."[8]

Eva Hancock's strength had been in coordinating the funding of social agencies statewide and handling procedures, policies, and paperwork. Lowell's focus was on direct services, in some ways reducing the scope of CSC's influence while deepening it. He had noticed that people in dire straits had "plenty of advocates in the community, but we need people who can deliver a service."[9] As J. Thomas Greene, put it, Lowell wanted to turn words into action. "He saw all the needs assessment stuff as a lot of paperwork and busywork. He already knew the needs, could easily see more, saw little reason for the institutionalization of it."[10] The change in directors thus signalled a change in direction for the organization. Lowell's goal was simple: "I went in there with the idea that we could figure out what the problems of the community were and do something about them."[11]

Lowell had two great strengths as a leader: he was collaborative, a team-builder; he led by example. His team-building skills drew and held together an eclectic range of community leaders as members of the board. Greene was president and another basketball friend from Forest Dale, attorney Richard L. Bird, was vice president when Lowell took over. On the board were Alberta Hill Henry, a dynamic community relations coordinator for the Salt Lake School District,[12] Father Lawrence P. Sweeney of St. Patrick's Church (Catholic), Robert L. Simpson, counselor in the LDS church's Presiding Bishopric and managing director of LDS Social Services, and Mike Romero, director of the Guadalupe Center, which served Salt Lake City's Hispanics. The thirty-member board was supported by a six-member ex officio board that included Salt Lake County commissioner Conrad B. Harrison and other business and political leaders. Attorneys, bankers, insurance executives, university professors, and women from the Junior League, League of Women Voters, and other women's organizations also found their niche. A later board member, Richard Haglund, a consultant to small businesses, was impressed at how well these people worked together. "Lowell was a wonderful leader in small group networking."[13]

Community activist Robert (Archie) Archuleta, who worked with Lowell at the Crossroads Urban Center, called him "a pioneer who would go where the Saints fear to tread."[14] Esther Landa, former president of the National Council of Jewish Women (1974-

79), agreed: "He was always concerned with the entire community, not just with the LDS community."[15]

Alberta Henry recalls the same strength from Lowell. She was a vocal and often dissatisfied member, "complaining exactly as I had done on every committee before that—'When it comes to problems, who's got more problems than minorities?' Lowell said, 'Then we ought to do something about it.'" He asked Henry to form and chair the minorities committee and recruit people from each community ethnic group.[16] In some organizations this would have been an isolating mechanism. In Lowell's organization it was a networking maneuver. Henry recalled sitting spellbound during a brown-bag planning lunch as Japanese members of her subcommittee told of their World War II interment at Topaz, a tar-paper shack encampment in Utah's west desert. Henry realized that "before, all those groups had kind of been a clump in my mind; but, you see, they're all different. Sometimes I didn't want [those meetings] to ever stop."[17]

In a decade when leadership meant time management, goal setting, delegation, productivity, and accountability, Lowell's low-key, collaborative approach, with emphasis on quality and teamsmanship, was ahead of its time. Thus it was an unexpected honor when he received an award from the American Society of Public Administration in 1983. Roland Wise, a past winner, nominated Lowell after the organization widened the award to include community leaders. "I observed him as president and as executive director and as board member," Wise said. "They are all different requirements for management and administration, and he did every one of those beautifully!"

He pointed out that to be an effective board member, "You have to be a good communicator and listener and be able to reflect to the executive what the needs are, and support and work with other agencies." A director has to be strong in coordination, training, and communication. "Not many can come close to Lowell." Wise lauded Lowell's skills in recruiting the right people and then trusting them to perform. He also respected Lowell's persistence. "He is not easily dissuaded. He doesn't hit you over the head with it, but he sees that it is done—he just works quietly at it."[18]

Lowell provided direct services, not because he wanted to inspire his colleagues, but because feeding the hungry, clothing the naked, and visiting the lonely were intensely satisfying to him. His full-time assistant, Elaine Smart, another award-winning community worker who had managed CSC's volunteer activities since 1969, developed a fierce loyalty to him as she noticed "he does not ask anyone to do anything he wouldn't do himself. That changes it from being a nice idea for someone else to an invitation to come in and be a part of it."[19]

Theodore E. (Ted) Keefer, hired to help coordinate programs for the elderly, was a man about Lowell's age who had worked in hotel management. He became Lowell's boon companion and cited Lowell's battered pick-up as evidence that Lowell had no false pride. "Lowell hauled everything in that pick-up—furniture to help someone move between apartments, paint cans and brushes, boxes of food, and suitcases of clothes." Ted admitted: "He did not have a reputation as a great driver." The truck had "backed into everything," and the staff wondered if an "angel on his shoulder" kept him from being "plowed up at the side of the freeway all the time."[20]

Charles Johnson, an ordained Church of Christ minister who became director of United Way in 1978, called Lowell "a combination of an Old Testament prophet who wants to give you his vision of what should be and a New Testament good Samaritan, who doesn't stand back and talk, but steps in to do the good work himself."[21] Johnson likened Lowell's ideals to Gandhi's motto, "We should live a simple life that others may simply live," and commented, "That is Lowell's motivation. He keeps himself simple. If he moves beyond that, seeking recognition—that is using energy that could be serving someone else."

Lowell's emphasis on direct services coincided with a national trend away from planning agencies, partly because federal regulations required every agency to "have its own master plan."[22] United Way was "pushing and shoving" in the early 1970s to take over CSC's coordinating, research, and budget functions, according to Roland Wise. Lowell had no intention of fighting turf battles over administrative tasks he had no interest in performing and "never lost his temper" but would "just weave and bob with it." Without being confrontational, Lowell had the ability to take a "very strong position and enunciate direct statements about what must happen, and the goals and objectives."[23] As the council relinquished its research and evaluation to United Way, it continued publishing its directory and expanded its coordination of volunteer work that brought agencies together. Dealing with United Way on a program-by-program basis was often a hassle—a lot of "jumping through hoops," according to Wise.[24]

From 1972-82 Lowell and a core "not highly paid" staff of eighteen—some part time—developed or revised nine main programs that had taken the following shape by the late 1980s: (1) "Food for the Hungry"—The Salt Lake Food Bank; (2) "Community Links"—The Information and Referral Center; (3) "Hands and Hearts That Help"—The Volunteer Center; (4) "Community Helping Community"—The Ouelessebougou-Utah Alliance; (5) "Success Through Independence"—The Independent Living Center and the Elderly and Handicapped Services.[25] The Voluntary Action Center (later the Volunteer Center) recruited about 2,000 volunteers—encouraging whole families to donate time—for 133 agencies, publicizing the work through newspapers and conducting necessary training.

CSC managed the Independent Living Center (now the Transitional Living Center) with backing from the Utah State Rehabilitation Office and a staff of health care professionals from the University of Utah's Rehabilitation Center. It is a six-plex apartment building in which five quadriplegics receive practical, vocational, and educational training for a year so they can live outside nursing homes and families. They attend the Trade Technical College or the University of Utah and may go on to jobs from there, their places taken by another five a year or so later. One 1977 graduate, Debbie Mair, earned an M.A. in social work and now heads the Utah Independent Living Center, a private, non-profit agency. Richard K.Winters calls her a "shining example" of a handicapped person acquiring independence.[26]

Lowell also formed "Functional Fashions," run by a volunteer with muscular sclerosis who designed clothes for the handicapped. Volunteer seamstresses custom-designed clothes for handicapped clients with velcro fastenings and zippers instead of buttons, slip-ons rather than fasten-ins, and easy front or side fastenings for hands with limited mobility. Some clients, for the first time, experienced the solid boost in self-esteem of dressing themselves and attending to their own bathroom routine. More than seventy-five volunteers gave 2,500 hours to this program in the first three years of its existence, but it died in the 1980s when United Way could no longer fund it.

Lowell concentrated many programs on the elderly "because they need services and they appreciate them and are not begging for them."[27] He hired Florence Leonard, a former school teacher about his own age who had received training as a medical gerontologist at the University of Toledo. He asked her to be the council's contact with elderly women in the Salt Lake area who were "all sole alone" and to also help supervise the work of the "Befrienders"—single volunteers, couples, or even whole families who "adopted" a woman who might require medical care, chores, or food but who always yearns for attention and friendship. In 1989 she was working with a list of one thousand names.

Leonard was professionally qualified to assess medical as well as emotional necessities. "For instance, a lady needs to go to the hospital and calls me. I take her to the hospital and see her through the surgery, whatever. I take care of her."[28] She made appointments for health care for those afraid to do it for themselves. She arranged for clothing, often shopping for it herself, and could order food through the Food Bank at any time.

A satisfying part of the job for Leonard was seeing the volunteer spirit lead to greater independence. She told about a retired doctor who volunteered to help a woman with a broken back. "After he treated her back, he put in a garden for her and she was able to can enough vegetables to see her through the winter on her social security."[29]

Lowell often subsidized Leonard's work. She remembered that he "took the money out of his pocket and handed it to me" when an elderly woman lacked some necessary furniture. "Another time he gave me $100 for some help with horrendous utility bills for a client."[30]

The Salt Lake Food Bank, later the Utah Food Bank which sometimes edged into neighboring states, was a resounding success. It cooperated with other agencies in collecting food through special drives, donations, and wholesale purchases and then distributing to ten food pantries in the valley, which in turn delivered it to families in emergency situations. Closely kept records helped avoid abuse. The Boy Scouts became the Food Bank's largest gatherer with additional help from Utah Power and Light. Lowell saw to it that some of the more poverty-stricken recipients were given maintenance aid beyond emergency assistance.

To Lowell all direct services were satisfying, but feeding the hungry was one of his favorites. With Ted Keefer, Lowell turned into a food gatherer himself, making weekly rounds of the local Albertson's supermarkets and, with the stores' permission, retrieving the bent cans and ripped flour sacks that had been withdrawn from sale. There they were, as Keefer put it, "two old guys climbing around in a dumpster." When Albertson's informed Lowell that another organization had contracted with them to salvage damaged goods, Lowell simply called the other organization and signed it up, too.[31]

During the winter of 1977 Lowell decided to appeal to schoolchildren for Thanksgiving and Christmas drives. The Boy Scouts agreed to take over the collection component during a national Care and Share Week in a house-to-house drive through Salt Lake City's neighborhoods. Utah Power and Light Company contributed collection bags to make it easier. Soon wholesale grocers were donating by the truckload. Smith's Food King, a locally owned company, and Farmer Jack, briefly a successor to Safeway, each developed surplus food plans, sometimes donating groceries valued in the hundreds of thousands of dollars.

The food bank, with help from the LDS church, expanded from one room into a warehouse. There volunteers sorted the food before transporting it to designated "food pantries" each week. These pantries had specific geographical boundaries and rules. Some were large permanent soup-kitchen projects like those run by St. Vincent De Paul and the Salvation Army. Some were small, like Jeanne Dudley, who began feeding the homeless one Sunday morning with a loaf of bread and the contents of the family coffeepot at the south end of Pioneer Park, under the viaduct. By 1988 the Food Bank supplied about fifteen pantries.[32]

A more personal approach was the program developed by Persis Meheles, hired in 1982 as food warehouse manager. Her first impression of Lowell was of "a funny little man in a brown serge suit coat and unmatched trousers."[33] Meheles helped him develop a program in which volunteers would take food to the elderly then stay and visit. They instructed the volunteers to give their charges a hug before leaving. Meheles recalled that after discussing this with Lowell, he "twinkled, 'Yeah, and sometimes you even get a peck on the cheek.'"[34]

Meheles's temperamentally short fuse sputtered against Lowell's laid-back philosophy. During one upsetting meeting, Meheles demanded, "Don't you ever get mad? You should be mad right now!" Later when all was calm again and Lowell was leaving, Meheles said, he turned, looked at her, and said meaningfully, "I *can* get mad."[35]

When Lowell insisted that Meheles attend a certain meeting with him, she retorted, "My salary doesn't indicate that I ought to attend meetings." When he persisted, she said, "You know that if I go, I'll lose my temper and just get up and spout off." "That's why I'm taking you," he deadpanned.[36]

Meheles summed up her feelings about her boss: "Lowell Bennion is a Christian. He just happens to be a Mormon, and, as far as I'm concerned, that's beside the point." They shared a common interest in Eastern philosophy. From such ancient sources, she felt, he drew the strength to "see what he could do, do it, and shut out the rest."[37]

CSC's Information and Referral Center, continued from Eva Hancock's administration, published a Directory of Human Services—information on the services, fees, and functions of over 300 public and private nonprofit agencies and organizations. Its staff was trained in crisis intervention, aiding callers by reviewing problems and suggesting solutions. If necessary, they made arrangements for advocacy and follow up. It advertised itself as "the place to call when you don't know where to call."[38] The council also "created and operated programs linking the efforts of other agencies concerned with a given problem so that duplication and overlap are avoided."[39] Director Rita Inoway and her staff answered about 20,000 telephone calls a year. She identified a consistent element in Lowell's approach: "Dr. Bennion impresses the staff to take time, to listen to people. There's not enough money to meet all the needs, but the human need of having another person to talk to *can* be met."[40]

Everyone involved with CSC had a favorite program—the one he or she worked with most closely—but some stand out in an appraisal of the 1970s and 1980s. Alberta Henry's minorities committee explored ways to introduce a larger audience to Utah's rich ethnic history. CSC received a grant from the Utah Endowment for the Humanities in 1975-76 that funded ten two-hour seminars, each one devoted to one of Utah's ethnic groups: Afro-American, Native American, Chinese, Japanese, Polynesian, Jewish, Greek, Italian, Slavic, and Hispanic. For ten Wednesday evenings people from Salt Lake City and surrounding communities gathered to hear a scholar's lecture, followed by a panel consisting of members of that ethnic group interacting with each other and the audience. The program was repeated in part for the women's facility at the Utah State Prison.

In the final report to the Utah Endowment for the Humanities, Lowell wrote: "Concentrating a full evening on each group with major input from the group itself gave those present an opportunity to sense the feelings and concerns and [they] left with a good deal more than a superficial brush." His appraisal was that the strongest programs were those dealing with Greek, Japanese, Native American, and Jewish Utahns.[41]

One of the members of the minorities committee, Helen Z. Papanikolas, an historian specializing in studies of the Greek population in Utah, embarked on a larger study. The result was *The Peoples of Utah*, a path-breaking collection of essays by historians "especially qualified by blood ties and training" and representing more than a dozen of Utah's distinctive cultural groups.[42]

Lowell's interest in minorities did not stop with community education. Darius Gray, an acquaintance of Lowell from the LDS Genesis Branch and a member of the CSC Board, praised CSC: "The minority communities on the west side received not just tacit support but active support. I was surprised at the degree to which the CSC programs were targeted to those communities and their willingness to work with other agencies."[43]

Lowell was acutely aware that decent people, who had been steady wage-earners, often slipped helplessly into poverty and became unable to repair their homes as age made hands unsteady and sight uncertain. He arranged for plumbing and carpentry repairs to be handled under a contract with the Salt Lake County Division of Aging. His group did chores for about 600 elderly individuals, mostly widows. For six years the program thrived. For example, 1,999 volunteer hours were donated to this service in

1982 alone. Volunteers shoveled snow, did lawn and yard work, housekeeping, home repairs, and painting. They were able to help some older workers and some handicapped persons find employment. Unfortunately, the contract was not renewed in 1988.

Volunteers were also available with strong backs and arms when someone "has to be moved and is without a dime." Lowell and his pick-up frequently headed such expeditions. He also coordinated chores with his religious assignments. During his service on the stake high council and as a ward bishop, he arranged many service projects, always with a personal touch. John Fitzgerald, Lowell's excommunicated friend, sent in a cash contribution and received a personal letter describing how his money had helped an elderly woman pay for a screen door for "her two-room shack." The installation had been done by members of Lowell's high priests' group while they listened to LDS general conference on the radio.[44]

Lowell had little sympathy with socialism, having observed the bureaucracy it produced in Europe. "Free enterprise is the best system in the world for 85 percent of [the people in] this country and the other advanced countries," he asserted. "But there are about 15 to 20 percent who can't compete, physically or mentally." They are disabled or entirely unmotivated. Private charity is usually inadequate to meet such long-term demands, and he saw as valid "compassionate social justice" from the government. He dreamed of a system "where everybody can work who is able, and where the work is adapted to their capacity instead of making the people adapt their limited capacities to the profit motive of somebody else." He lamented gently, "I wish I were smart enough to figure out a system for the lost 15 to 20 percent." He wished for a contemporary counterpart of the Civilian Conservation Corps, which he had experienced first-hand in 1934.[45]

What about the possibility of welfare fraud? "It's hard to know whether the people who ask for food are the ones who need it the most," he acknowledged. "Some may take advantage of a free gift." In that case, however, Lowell always gave them "the benefit of the doubt." But when people asked for money, Lowell insisted on seeing them personally and discussing each situation. Lowell usually tried "to meet the immediate need" but coupled it with longer-term solutions: helping recipients apply for food stamps, get a job, and "figure out other ways to maintain themselves in the long pull."[46]

Charles Johnson used to debate social justice with Lowell: "My feeling is that if you can change an institution, you can change an individual. . . . Lowell's point was always, 'Well, you're right, but—if you can change the individual, it'll spread through the group.' We were working with the very same goals in a different way," Johnson concluded. "It takes both."[47]

Lowell's strengths as a leader could also be weaknesses. His hands-on style meant that he would rather visit a poor widow than do a "power lunch" with a CEO or patiently write grant proposals and deal with committees, bureaus, and funding agencies. As a result, CSC was always short of money. In 1976 Lowell wrote cheerfully to his sister Frances: "I am busy running a food bank for the hungry, chore services for the elderly who are poor and sans family to help, and developing a housing unit and health facilities for the motor handicapped. . . . All I need is $3,000.00 for the three projects, so if you have any philanthropic friends, let me know."[48]

Archie Archuleta noticed that Lowell preferred to dig into his own pocket rather than ask others to contribute money. But once he learned he *had* to ask for food, Archuleta said, Lowell became one of the better "food gatherers."[49] Elizabeth Haglund, who joined the board in 1972, saw Lowell's "powerful personal influence" as a logical way to increase the Community Services Council's limited funding. But Lowell was sometimes the greatest obstacle. He was "so busy dealing up close" that he had little interest in making a network of influential contacts and then milking it. "Lowell didn't care who liked him or who didn't like him," commented this public relations expert, "and that was a handicap in some ways."[50]

Richard Winters agreed that Lowell was unwilling to lend his name to fund-raising efforts. "I have tried to find somebody that Lowell has asked for money—I don't think there is a single soul that he has really asked for money," mused Winters. "He has told thousands about what he is doing and they make contributions because of it, but I can't find anybody he actually put the arm on and said, 'I want you to make a contribution to this.'"[51]

One employee suggested to Lowell that he take the financial

pressure off all of them by walking across the street from his home and asking an affluent friend for a hefty donation. "He dead-eyed me and said, 'I will never ask my friends for money.'"[52]

In 1988, when Winters replaced Lowell as director, the bookkeeper assured him that in eleven years they had never missed a payroll, "but there were times when Doc didn't take his check." In thin times Lowell paid the salary of some workers. "So what he got paid here just went through him and back into the program." When Winters incredulously asked him, "How can you run this place?" Lowell answered, "It always seems to come out all right."[53]

Lowell liked the flexibility and independence of CSC. "We sense a need and we design a program to meet it," he commented with relish. "We don't wait for the legislature. We just go ahead and do it."[54]

Winters echoed what others had noticed. "Lowell just hated numbers. Even on the United Way forms, some of the information was just guestimates. To keep track of what you were doing did violence to Lowell's belief that you don't let your left hand know what your right hand is doing. You don't count your volunteers, but sources want to know."[55]

In 1984 Keith Whisenant, by then chairman of CSC, became aware of drought and starvation in Africa. He noted that the commodities did not always reach those most deserving, so he approached the board. At first several board members expressed reluctance because "we have enough to do right here in Utah." Norma Matheson, Don Pugh, and Lowell himself felt this way at first, but when Whisenant and other members of the board organized meetings for community leaders to discuss African problems, they decided to identify a community of villages that Salt Lake City, the Wasatch Front, and Utah could help "in a way and in a place where results could be certain" and somehow personalized.[56]

On recommendation from Care International, Whisenant and six others travelled at their own expense to Mali and, after a second expedition led by Don Pugh, decided on the Ouelessebougou region as their choice. Their first project, jointly carried out with Africare, was "to dig some very expensive wells."[57] Dissatisfied with the collaboration, they then became a private volunteer organization, and Salt Lake City became sister city to the Ouelessebougou region in southern Mali with seventy-two villages of about 35,000 people. Though other communities have exchanged financial, economic, and cultural aid as part of sister city programs throughout the USA, this one was "developmentally driven," the first project of this magnitude operated community-to-community by volunteers.[58] With the CSC as the umbrella organization, Whisenant formed the Ouelessebougou Alliance. Don Pugh became its first formal chair. In 1993 Marion D. Hanks, on emeritus status from the LDS church, served as alliance chair, making two trips to Mali to perform hands-on service for these people.[59]

In the fall of 1985 the LDS church called a fast on behalf of starving Ethiopians, which generated $6 million in aid, greatly increasing interest in and awareness of Africa's problems. According to Whisenant,

> Lowell was interested in the Alliance because he could sense the broad community interest and frustration of not knowing what to do about this tragedy . . . in drought-stricken Africa. Although reluctant at first because of his traditional focus on local needs, he quickly committed his heart and resources to helping the Alliance. . . . He liked the interest of the many school children who began school projects to dig a well or build a garden fence . . . in a Malian village.[60]

After Lowell's retirement, one of the Mali volunteers, medical student Madelyn Silver, sent the Bennions a Christmas card reporting her experiences in accompanying two optometrists on a two-week medical expedition to Mali during the summer of 1990. It forever changed her perspective on life and her "values, motives, and what I want to accomplish in the field of family medicine and family practice. . . . I catch an inkling of the depth of caring Jesus Christ must have felt for the people of this world—all equal, all important, all brothers and sisters inside." She included a poem that moved Lowell and Merle, describing the terrible physical needs in Africa and her hope of "white hands reaching to lift black hands higher," only to learn humbly through her service that "it was black hands that lifted white hands higher."[61]

When Lowell began thinking about retirement in 1987, his colleagues at the Community Service Council agreed that the burden was too heavy for the aging Lowell, but, in the words of chairman Whisenant, "It would be great if we could clone Lowell to keep the program going in ways that would be consistent with his values and dreams."[62]

Lowell participated in the search for his replacement. Among the several candidates, his choice was the fifty-seven-year-old Winters, a businessman who had worked at Western Steel, at Bennett Paint, and finally in his own consulting firm. Lowell trusted him. Lowell had recruited Winters to the board six years before, and he had since served in both the vice president and president positions. His wife, Mary Nebeker Winters, shared his background and interest in volunteerism. Approvingly, staff member Florence Leonard recalled that as "befrienders" the Winterses had bathed and cared for a lonely woman and then had purchased a plane ticket so she could join her family.

Though a search committee was formed, the board quickly approved Winters. He, however, had misgivings: "I didn't think I could do it. How do you follow Lowell Bennion? . . . The first time someone said, 'Oh, you're the new Lowell Bennion,' I had an anxiety attack."[63] So did some of the clients. Winters picked up the phone to hear a woman asking for Lowell. "He's retired," Winters explained. "Oh, what will I do?" the woman wailed. Winters finally persuaded her to tell him that her refrigerator "had pooped out." Since she had just paid her taxes, there was no repair money. Through "a little network" at CSC, Winters arranged to repair her refrigerator at a cost of twenty dollars.[64]

Lowell's formal retirement came in the fall of 1988 when he was eighty. He retained the title of executive director emeritus with office space available whenever he wished. Just before his retirement, Lowell was given the Richard D. Bass Achievement Award, an unrestricted $5,000 grant established by Utah governor Norm Bangerter to recognize the accomplishments of Bass, the first Utahn to climb the highest peak on each of the world's seven continents.[65] Lowell immediately gave the money away to undisclosed recipients.

The next summer Winters tried to convince Lowell to lend his name to a gala fund-raiser, tapping the dozens of people who would "give thousands of dollars" if Lowell asked directly. But Winters bumped into a familiar wall and replaced the gala with a down-home picnic where friends could "come and have a hot dog" in honor of the Bennions at Wheeler Historic Farm in Salt

Lake Valley. About 400 attended the event on June 16, 1989, and made donations amounting to about $20,000. Winters presented Lowell with his portrait by Keith Eddington and paid tribute to him as a "gentle, unassuming, unique man who has powerfully helped us—as individuals and as a community, to know the satisfactions of loving our neighbors and doing good to those around us."[66]

Lowell worked at CSC a few hours a week where he continued to network. As director, Winters could report, "We are having lots of fun." He saw himself as following in Lowell's footsteps but seeking to consolidate and expand programs with ever-changing priorities. Whereas the food bank, started by Lowell in 1977, consisted of Lowell and friends in his pickup, by 1990 the council had gathered and distributed over $3.5 million in food to every part of the state. It had also reached into Wyoming, southern Idaho, and Nevada. Winters found that mapping food distribution was satisfying and creative.[67] In the early 1990s Winters saw the LDS church's broadening outreach to the needy both in Utah and internationally as a response to Lowell's brand of Christianity. "'We Take Care of Our Own' is being left behind," he said. "Lowell is an effective conscience of the church. By hanging on, with no bitterness and no recriminations," he had lived to see his values adopted.[68] Not only was the church supporting the Utah Food Bank in major ways, but it donated food and clothing to struggling eastern European countries and sent experts abroad to help evaluate needs.[69] Starting in December 1991, fast offerings could now be designated for "humanitarian aid."[70]

At Lowell's retirement, Whisenant had also spelled out what he saw as CSC's chief challenges:

> 1. People want to help people who help themselves. However, those who are most deserving are also among the most independent. We often don't reach them.
>
> 2. Providers are often cyclical in their giving and service, depending on time, money, and competing demands.
>
> 3. Intimate involvement is what people really want. That takes time, resources, and a quality project with scope. Too many weak projects compete successfully with good projects for scarce resources.[71]

In the early 1990s Winters spearheaded the Merle and Lowell

Bennion Fund to raise money for a new building and better equipment. The Utah legislature agreed to match funds. On January 24, 1995, "a table of dignitaries christened the expansive new home for Utah's Food Bank and five other agencies that comprise Salt Lake's Community Services Council . . . It was in the name of Lowell L. Bennion and his late wife Merle, that the renovated building at 1025 South 700 West was dedicated."[72] Winters was especially proud of the addition of Merle's name: "Everyone knows Lowell couldn't have done what he did without her," he pointed out. Utah governor Mike Leavitt and first lady Jackie Leavitt compared Lowell to Moses and declared, "I know of no other person whose goodness exemplifies that we need in the community." When Leavitt turned to Lowell with the words, "May God bless you, keep you happy, and keep you working for the community," a "spontaneous shout of 'We love you' from someone in the audience echoed off the high ceiling and concrete walls of the food bank warehouse where a couple of hundred people had gathered." [73]

After his retirement, Lowell was still much in demand. He was immediately asked to serve on the LDS church's Committee on Aging under Keith McMullin and Lyle Cooper at the church's Welfare Services. Lowell promptly suggested expanding successful CSC programs like chore service, telephone reassurance, and "befriending." In addition to better relationships with home teachers and visiting teachers (regular visits from representatives of the local ward bishop and Relief Society president), he suggested that the church "pick a ward where there are a hundred widows and assign a well-off ward to take care of them. . . . We could stimulate every stake to look into the needs of the elderly, to be creative, to take initiative." He had a "dream" that the church could plan fifty apartments on five acres, where the elderly could take care of their own land and each other, with a common dining hall and recreation. Moving beyond aging, he also recommended that LDS meetinghouses should be used for daycare and preschool services. "It's a waste to leave them empty so much of the time."[74]

Thus, even at age eighty-four and no longer actively involved in managing direct services, Lowell's influence continued to spread. And in an unexpected way the establishment of the Bennion Center at the University of Utah helped a new generation learn his values (see chap. 15).

NOTES

1. Roland V. Wise, interviewed by Mary L. Bradford, 21 Mar. 1990.

2. Mission statement, CSC brochure, 212 West 1300 South, Salt Lake City, Utah, no date.

3. Eva Hancock, interviewed by Linda Sillitoe, 13 Oct. 1990, notes in Bradford's possession.

4. For instance, under "Children and Youth" were listed boys and girls clubs, child care organizations, the Family Support Center, the "Make a Wish Foundation," the Neighborhood House, Odyssey House, Utah Youth Village, and other county programs. Under "Education and Tutoring," a volunteer could choose among various school districts, the Guadalupe Schools, the Literary Action Center, and Head Start. Under "Elderly," the Salt Lake County Aging Services—Meals on Wheels and senior daycare services. Under "Health," foundations like the Diabetes Foundation and other associations such as Muscular Dystrophy and Multiple Sclerosis and various hospitals. Crossroad, St. Vincent De Paul, Travelers Aid, the New Hope Refugee Center, Ronald McDonald House, Salt Lake Rape Crisis Center were also included. Unfortunately, few records from Hancock's tenure were preserved.

5. Roland V. Wise, interviewed by Mary L. Bradford, 21 Mar. 1990.

6. Lowell L. Bennion, Oral History, 7.

7. Ibid.

8. Ibid., 8.

9. Ibid., 4.

10. J. Thomas Greene, interviewed by phone by Mary L. Bradford, 13 Dec. 1993.

11. Lowell L. Bennion, Oral History, 8.

12. In 1971 Henry received the Civil Rights Worker Award from the Utah National Association for the Advancement of Colored People (NAACP). In the 1980s she would be elected president of the Utah chapter of the NAACP.

13. Richard Haglund to Mary L. Bradford, 28 June 1991.

14. Robert (Archie) Archuleta, interviewed by Linda Sillitoe, 21 Oct. 1988, notes in Bradford's possession.

15. Esther Landa, interviewed by Linda Sillitoe, 22 Oct. 1988, notes in Bradford's possession.

16. Alberta Henry, interviewed by Linda Sillitoe, 6 Sept. 1988, notes

in Bradford's possession.

17. Ibid.

18. Roland V. Wise, interviewed by Mary L. Bradford, 21 Mar. 1989.

19. Elaine Smart, interviewed by Mary L. Bradford, 23 and 29 Mar. 1989.

20. Theodore Keefer, interviewed by Linda Sillitoe, 22 Aug. 1988, notes in Bradford's possession.

21. As quoted by Sillitoe, "Lowell Bennion: A Worker for Practical Religion," *Deseret News Today Section,* 4, undated clipping in Bradford's possession.

22. Charles Johnson, interviewed by Mary L. Bradford, 24 Sept. 1990.

23. Roland V. Wise, interviewed by Mary L. Bradford, 21 Mar. 1990.

24. Ibid. Unfortunately, neither CSC nor United Way retained minutes or records from this period nor do individual directors have personal records.

25. Community Services Council brochure, 212 West 1300 South, Salt Lake City, Utah, "Service Through Sharing—since 1902," no date.

26. Richard K. Winters, interviewed by Mary L. Bradford, 22 Mar. 1989.

27. Lowell L. Bennion, Oral History, 2.

28. Florence Leonard, interviewed by Mary L. Bradford, 8 Oct. 1989.

29. Ibid.

30. Florence Leonard, interviewed by Linda Sillitoe, 20 Dec. 1988, notes in Bradford's possession.

31. Theodore (Ted) Keefer, interviewed by Linda Sillitoe, 22 Aug. 1988, notes in Bradford's possession.

32. Richard K. Winters, interviewed by Mary L. Bradford, 22 Mar. 1989 and 11 Aug. 1993.

33. Persis Meheles, interviewed by Linda Sillitoe, 16, 19 Sept. 1988.

34. Ibid.

35. Ibid.

36. Ibid.

37. Ibid.

38. "77 Years of Personalized Response to People in Need," Salt Lake Area Community Services Council brochure, 2900 South Main Street, Salt

Lake City, Utah, 1982, copy in Bradford's possession.

39. Ibid.

40. As quoted in Sillitoe, "Lowell Bennion: A Worker for Practical Religion," 4.

41. UEH [Utah Endowment for the Humanities] *Five-Year Report 1975-80, Period I, 1975-76: Utah's Ethnic Minorities*, Booklet. The Utah Endowment for the Humanities contributed $2,060.46; CSC's local match was $3,118. The program at the women's facility, "Ethnic Minorities in American Society," had proportional matches: an award of $300 with a local match of $648.50.

42. Helen Z. Papanikolas, "Introduction," *The Peoples of Utah* (Salt Lake City: Utah Historical Society, 1976), 9.

43. Darius Gray, interviewed by Linda Sillitoe, 1 Feb. 1991, notes in Bradford's possession.

44. Lowell L. Bennion to John W. Fitzgerald, 21 Apr. 1978, photocopy in Bradford's possession.

45. Lowell L. Bennion, Oral History, 2-3, 145.

46. Ibid., 185.

47. Charles Johnson, interviewed by Mary L. Bradford, 24 Sept. 1990.

48. Lowell L. Bennion to Frances B. Morgan, 29 Dec. 1976, photocopy in Bradford's possession.

49. Robert (Archie) Archuleta, interviewed by Linda Sillitoe, 22 Aug. 1988, notes in Bradford's possession.

50. Elizabeth Haglund, interviewed by Mary L. Bradford, 20 Sept. 1990.

51. Richard K. Winters, interviewed by Mary L. Bradford, 11 Aug. 1993.

52. Ibid.

53. Ibid.

54. Lowell L. Bennion, interviewed by Mary L. Bradford, 9 Aug. 1988.

55. Richard K. Winters, interviewed by Mary L. Bradford, 11 Aug. 1993.

56. D. Keith Whisenant to Mary L. Bradford, 10 Feb. 1994.

57. Ibid.

58. Ibid.

59. Jan Thompson, "Like a Rope Lowered from Heaven," *This People,* Summer 1994, 15.

60. Keith Whisenant to Mary L. Bradford, 10 Feb. 1994.

61. Madelyn Silver to Lowell and Merle Bennion, 22 Dec. 1990, photocopy in Bradford's possession.

62. Keith Whisenant to Mary L. Bradford, 3 Feb. 1994.

63. Richard K. Winters, interviewed by Mary L. Bradford, 11 Aug. 1993.

64. Ibid.

65. "Lowell Bennion to Receive Bass Achievement Award at a Snowbird Reception," *Deseret News,* 29 Apr. 1988, B-1.

66. *Salt Lake Tribune,* 16 June 1989, E-1.

67. Richard K. Winters, interviewed by Mary L. Bradford, 11 Aug. 1994.

68. Ibid.

69. After the success of the first Ethiopian fast in January 1985, a second fast in November 1985 raised an additional $3.8 million for general humanitarian assistance. In October 1991 the church reported that fast donations from 1985 were still being used to relieve suffering in Nigeria, Ghana, Zimbabwe, and Kenya and that members had continued to make unsolicited donations. Garth Mangum and Bruce Blumell, *The Mormons' War on Poverty: A History of LDS Welfare, 1830-1990* (Salt Lake City: University of Utah Press, 1993), 248-49.

70. Ibid.

71. Keith Whisenant to Mary L. Bradford, 2 Dec. 1987.

72. Nancy Hobbs, "Groups Christen New Food Bank, Honor Volunteer," *Salt Lake Tribune,* 25 Jan. 1995, 1.

73. Ibid.

74. Lowell L. Bennion, interviewed by Mary L. Bradford, 18 Sept. 1990.

CHAPTER 14

PRIVATE LIVES (1962-88)

Don't get married and use your husband or wife as a crutch. . . .
Whether you are single or married, you have to get
most of your satisfaction out of your own life,
out of your own self, your
thinking and doing.

—*LOWELL L. BENNION*

As Lowell took straightforward steps into the world of the University of Utah and the broader public service arena, the Bennion children grew up, and Merle, less involved in Lowell's professional life than at the institute, explored new paths and cherished connections. Although she was active in the church as Relief Society president and teacher, her desire for further education flamed. "I didn't want to be one of those grandmothers who sits and rocks and feels sorry for herself," she decided. "I didn't want to be an adjunct wife. . . . I had to have a life beyond that of husband and children."[1]

Words continued to be a passion with Merle, and she had fallen permanently in love with Germany. In 1971 she had registered for eight hours of German at the University of Utah. A *Deseret News* profile on "space-age grandmas" attending college featured Merle: "Everything about the German language and culture fascinated me," Merle said, "and even though I often feel tired, I feel the mental stimulation is good for me. . . . It keeps me from getting bored and boring others with my aches and pains." A photograph showed her in the library taking notes. "I wanted to learn more, much more," said the knowledge-hungry Merle.

She also found time to pursue her passion for music with

discipline and commitment. She had taken fifteen piano lessons as a girl of twelve or thirteen; then in her fifties she took weekly piano lessons from Bonnie Lauper Winterton, well-known in the Salt Lake Valley for her expertise in piano, organ, and choral conducting, who some years before had moved into the Bennions' ward. "She made me really work," Merle recalled happily, "and I did."[2] Winterton's teaching gave Merle a fine touch and sharpened her ear. Winterton also taught daughter Ellen, who showed early aptitude.

After Merle had studied for two years, Winterton found three students for her to teach, thus launching a late career. Her upright piano bequeathed by her grandfather gave way to a Steinway grand, purchased from Bonnie Bennett, a violinist with the Utah Symphony. Merle opened her first bank account. Though she never charged more than a few dollars per lesson, numbers of students swelled over the years to a maximum of thirty-seven, and she liked the feeling of independence her own money gave her. As she entered her eighties, she was still teaching about thirty students. "She charges a bare minimum," Lowell commented proudly in 1975, "so that no one is barred for lack of funds; [she also] gives free lessons when a missionary is in the family. She not only teaches piano but builds confidence and social poise in her students. Many parents sing her praises."[3]

After Winterton, Merle and Ellen studied with two other excellent teachers, Noreen Emerson and Carol Lee Gale Erickson, a "real musicologist." Winterton also encouraged them to begin the organ, so Merle and Ellen took lessons from Tabernacle organist Roy Darley. During the 1960s, with Merle also in her sixties, she rose early, fixed breakfast and cleaned house, then went to the ward meetinghouse to practice the organ for two hours. She usually spent two more hours on the meetinghouse piano to avoid the interruptions of home.[4]

The first time she was asked to play for the Relief Society, she forgot a passage but recovered when Winterton called out, "You can do it, Merle!" Marjorie Hinckley, who was present in the meeting, corroborated that all of the women were "just praying for you."[5] "Sure enough, I did it!" Merle recalled. "I became the Relief Society organist, and then director of the Singing Mothers . . . and I was still practicing every day, rain or shine." She was "learning what I had missed . . . and hadn't had the opportunity for before."

Because of a pregnancy, Bonnie arranged to transfer Merle to another teacher, where she worked steadily away until conflicts in schedules meant she had to take lessons at 9:00 p.m. "I was just too tired," she confessed.[6] Her health suffered with the onset of arthritis and a spill she took at church during the 1960s in a highly waxed hallway, breaking her pelvis and sending her to bed. The accident exacerbated her arthritis and led to knee replacement surgery in 1977.[7]

Merle passed on her love of music to her children with varying degrees of success. Until he was sixteen, Ben refused lessons but then practiced diligently until his mission call. Steve, Doug, and Howard also studied piano but were often "lazy" about practicing, although Steve surprised Merle one summer by returning from the Wilson ranch with a difficult Rachmaninoff prelude completely memorized. Doug, who since childhood had impressed the family with his singing voice, continued to love music and lead choirs. Ellen became an accomplished pianist and organist.

Merle shared a love of sports with her husband and sons, watching basketball, football, and baseball. Her great love, however, was art, and she visited museums whenever possible, filling in with television specials, magazine articles, and books. She adopted photography as a hobby. Long active in PTA, she was secretary for the high school PTA the year Steve was student body president. And she renewed an old interest in family genealogy, recalling how often she had accompanied her grandmother Colton to the temple to do work for her relatives. She researched the Coltons and helped her sister and cousins compile a family history.

An important part of Merle's and Lowell's intellectual life was membership in study groups. In addition to participation in their first reading group, which lasted from the mid-1930s until the early 1980s, Lowell formed a second study group during his decade at the University of Utah. He dubbed it the University Sunday Night Group and included many university friends.[8] Merle enjoyed the breadth of subjects and the stimulating books they read. Lowell enjoyed the philosophical turn of many subjects, especially as they related to human values, Max Weber, and his own thinking.[9] "His mind is always churning," Merle commented.

In the early 1970s Emma Lou Thayne and Ramona Adams formed a monthly Lowell Bennion Study Group.[10] Each member took turns recounting his or her "spiritual journey." Ramona Adams recalled, "This group didn't mind asking hard questions, and they don't always come up with the right answer."[11] The program was often shaped by Lowell, who prepared provocative discussion questions.

Merle was especially fond of this study group—which still meets monthly in members' homes—because women spoke as often as the men. Historian Maureen Beecher taped Merle's spiritual journey and used it as a beginning for oral history interviews she conducted with Merle and Lowell for the LDS church archives.

The Bennions also belonged to the Cannon-Hinckley dinner group that meets and eats at the Lion House monthly to hear important speakers. Founded by church president Gordon B. Hinckley's father, it attracts local and visiting general authorities, community leaders, and scholars. The Bennions also belonged to the Aztec Club, a dinner-speech group of University of Utah professors.

Merle enjoyed her association with the Literary Arts Guild founded in 1962 by her ward Relief Society. When asked to join, she responded, "Oh, I'm too old for your age group!" But she changed her mind when she was assured, "Anyone who loves literature the way you do, we want in this group." One book review became a musical production when she invited Bonnie Winterton to assist in presenting Goethe and his life and songs. "I read the lyrics of some of his songs and showed slides." Members were encouraged to share their original poetry or prose, and Merle found herself amassing quite a collection of her own poems on a variety of subjects. When she read Scholem Asch's *Mary*, she composed a poem as part of her review. "So many of the artists [in the slides] I've learned don't worship her, but they revere her." Her program included some of the great paintings of Mary she had seen in Europe and Barbra Streisand's version of "Ave Maria." She also composed a poem for a book review of *Madame Bovary*. For an evening of light entertainment, she wrote a poem to Lowell.[12]

In the late 1950s Merle served as Relief Society president in the East Millcreek Second Ward with Marjorie Hinckley and

Libbie Lambert as her counselors. Asked to speak to the congregation when her new calling was announced, and introduced by the bishop as the "strongest woman in the ward," Merle stood and, because her leg had "gone to sleep," fell on her way to the pulpit. As her counselors burst into tears, Merle righted herself and said, only half in jest, "I have never been so upset by a calling!" Whatever the task, Merle approached it serenely and with humor. "She is . . . the most disciplined woman I've ever known," Marjorie Pay Hinckley recalled. Nothing was ever allowed to reach crisis stage. When the Relief Society was assigned to furnish two rooms in the new ward building, Merle and her counselors organized quilting bees, catering projects, bake sales, and a bazaar that achieved the goal within a year. Marjorie added:

> She was really a *relief* society president. . . . She cared a lot more about going into a home where there was some need than planning a fancy social or luncheon. . . . Her priorities were always right. And she was such an inspiration to all of us because she was . . . a very educated woman. I don't know that she had any degrees . . . but education with her was a personal thing that was ongoing and still is. When she got up to give a lesson it was just pure joy because she was so knowledgeable. She was an avid reader. . . . She read always with a purpose. [In the case of] an author that she was exploring . . . she would read everything by him. . . . When she started a project she never let go.[13]

In recognizing Merle's achievements, Lowell wrote in his memoirs:

> I commented earlier on Merle's beauty and our courtship and marriage. At high risk, I shall further remark on [Merle's] character, achievements, and values.
>
> I must hand it to her for courage. When she was married, [a doctor] told her if she became pregnant she might lie on her back for nine months and risk her life in childbirth. With a weak heart she gave birth to two girls and four husky boys, all super well and strong. And she took marvelous care of them; kept them clean, nourished them, and loved them dearly. I thought she looked like the Madonna, herself, as she held our first baby.
>
> If she had any fault as a mother it was in being too permissive. Her children, to this day, can do no wrong! (Slightly exaggerated, but not much.) She has been fiercely loyal in defense of her young, and worried

> herself into grayness over their problems. As the kids have married, she has been a perfect mother-in-law, interfering not one whit, and being most supportive and generous to in-laws and grandchildren.[14]

The four boys grew up and left home before or during Lowell's decade at the University of Utah, leaving Ellen as the cherished last child, her teenage interests overlapping with Merle's broadening activities. Ben was an ardent hiker who "knew every inch from Millcreek to Big Cottonwood. He and his friends would actually run up Beehive Mountain [their name for Grandeur Peak]," younger brother Doug said admiringly.[15] Ben served a mission in West Germany, while his wife-to-be, Sherilyn (Sherry) Cox, graduated from the University of Utah and was awarded a Fulbright Fellowship for study in Munich for 1957-58. In a happy repetition of Merle's and Lowell's European idyll, Sherry met Ben after his mission ended, and they were married in the LDS Swiss temple in January 1958. They studied in Munich and toured Europe until August 1958 then returned to Utah. Ben finished courses at the University of Utah, after which both entered graduate school at Syracuse University in New York. In 1964-65 they returned to Germany with a grant for Ben's research in cultural geography. Their first child, Wayne, was born in Hamburg in 1964. They both received their doctorates at Syracuse, Ben in geography, Sherry in journalism. They accepted appointments at Indiana University where their daughter, Lorilynn, was born in September 1965. In 1970 they settled at Humboldt State University, Arcata, California, as professors of geography and journalism, respectively.

Both Ben and Sherry subsequently published articles and books. With photographer Gary B. Peterson as coauthor, Ben published *Sanpete Scenes*,[16] an interesting history of Sanpete County's small towns and rural landscapes with over 400 illustrations and maps. His younger brother Steve, as president of Snow College in Ephraim, helped "sponsor" this prize-winning book.[17]

Sherry published the culmination of many years of research in rare historic newspapers: *Equal to the Occasion: Women Editors of the Nineteenth-Century West*.[18] Ben's sense of time and place inspired Merle to accompany him and Sherry on two of the Mormon History Association's annual meetings to the British Isles in 1987 and to Hawaii in 1990.

Second son, Douglas Colton, served his mission in Australia, a continent so vast that his train ride to his first assignment was 1,600 miles long. He was taken aback to discover on his first Sunday there that the course of instruction was Lowell's *Introduction to the Gospel.* The elders quorum president introduced him as the author's son and advised the class briskly, "'So if you have any questions about the gospel, just ask Elder Bennion.' Yes," Doug acknowledged, "there was pressure in being his son."[19]

After his mission he returned to the University of Utah where he married Sandra Peterson on August 1961. Lowell, in announcing this engagement to his sister Frances, described Sandra as a "fine girl—talented, bright, and of unusually pleasant disposition."[20] Doug graduated with a degree in secondary education and took a job at Westlake Junior High in the Granite School district, where he and Sandy became parents of Richard Lindsay and Lona in 1962 and 1965. During the 1970s two more sons were born: Christian Douglas in 1970 and David Sterling in 1971.

When the marriage ended in divorce in 1974, Lowell and Merle saw no reason for blame or accusation. Merle steadfastly paid tribute to Sandy's mothering abilities and praised her for the "bright, self-confident children" she had reared.[21] They stayed close to these grandchildren, and the boys spent several summers at the Teton ranch as campers and counselors. In June 1976 Doug married Naomi Allred, from Fountain Green in Sanpete County. She was a graduate of Snow College, a trained beautician, and a returned Netherlands missionary. Lowell called her "choice" and a compatible spirit in the family.

Doug and Naomi became the parents of two musically gifted daughters, Carrie, born in 1978, and Delyn, two years younger, who began taking piano lessons from Merle at an early age. With each semi-weekly visit, Naomi brought enough home-cooked food for two meals, a more-than-even swap, Merle declared. Naomi would later minister to Lowell and Merle for five hours a day, and after Merle's death would continue to help Lowell.

Merle was delighted to see Doug enter the teaching profession, since he had always shown an aptitude for it. She cherished a letter from his first principal that praised his teaching ability and expressing appreciation for his personal qualities.[22] Not surprisingly for a Bennion, Doug had workaholic tendencies, and Merle fretted about that. During his career at Granger High he continued studying for a master's degree in history. Doug's own view was that it took him a long time to settle into a career. "I floated in and out of the university," he recalled. Lowell accepted his indecision philosophically but "took me aside after my mission and said, 'I don't care what you decide to do—if it's a mechanic, then be the best mechanic you can.'"[23]

Doug's interests also ran to politics. In 1980 he ran for the House of Representatives in Utah's District 29. His brochure pictured him with Scott Matheson with Doug saying, "Let me work for you." By then he had worked in the Democratic party for twelve years and had been a teacher for sixteen.

Stephen Don served a mission to Scotland, married Marjorie Hopkins of Vernal, and completed his undergraduate degree at the University of Utah in political science, where he served in student government and joined Lambda Delta Sigma. Marjorie, with a degree in elementary education and child development, taught for two years. Steve became the third of Lowell and Merle's children to choose education as a career, earning a master's degree from Cornell University in public administration and a doctorate in higher education administration from the University of Wisconsin at Madison, where his grandfather, Milton Bennion, had studied. Steve served for ten years in the administration of the University of Wisconsin where he was also bishop of the LDS ward.

In the early 1980s Steve served a term as associate commissioner for planning in the Utah system of higher education, then was appointed president of Snow College in Ephraim, Utah, from 1982-89. This college had hired Lowell back in 1934; except for Apostle John A. Widtsoe's negotiations, Steve might have grown up there. In November 1989 he was inaugurated as president of Ricks College, near Rexburg, Idaho, succeeding Joe J. Christensen, the same man who had succeeded Lowell at the institute.

At the ceremony Henry Bennion Eyring[24] quoted from the pioneer diary of John Bennion, the ancestor he shared with Steve: "We expect to start a school here in a few days of a dozen scholars and as many more as we can get. The Lord's word is to us, schools, meetings, righteousness, Zion."[25]

President Gordon B. Hinckley, then first counselor in the church's First Presidency and an East Millcreek neighbor, delivered the inaugural address and charge to the president, nostalgically describing Steve's childhood friendship with his own son, Richard, in East Millcreek: "Here is a man," he summarized, "whose childhood had much of what . . . ought to be experienced by every child . . . the touch of the warm earth in the spring, the scowling frown of adversity, the contagious laughter of a small boy having a wonderful time, the toil of the scholar, the satisfaction of laurels honestly won, the burdens of financial struggle, the love of family, the peace of service to fellow men and to God."[26]

Lowell, like his father before him, had always warned his sons away from church employment. He appreciated the irony that Steve, in taking over the church's oldest continuous junior college, now stood near the pinnacle of the Church Education System. Apostle Hinckley's graceful compliment to the new president's parents was heart-warming: "Both are well educated. . . . They have emphasized with the children the importance of education. But with the emphasis, they have taught that education is to equip one the better to serve one's fellowmen and most certainly not to walk with pride or ostentation."[27]

This branch of the Bennion tree produced five children: Steven Don Jr., Jeffrey Hopkins, Mark Daniel, Brian Colton, and Kathryn. Brian died at age three in his bed of an unknown cause and was buried next to Laurel in the family plot. Lowell spoke at the funeral in a heartrending repetition of their own loss. Hermana Lyon, recovering from cancer and worried about some "troubling symptoms" of Ed's, recorded the occasion in her diary: "May 9—Went to Colonial Mortuary. Lowell in tears, Merle looked stricken. I did not look at little Brian—too sad. . . . Lowell . . . had to write [his talk] and read it because he couldn't trust himself not to break down." Summarized Hermana, "I have never heard him give a better talk."[28]

In this speech Lowell gave Steve and Marge permission to mourn. "You have every reason . . . to shed tears unashamedly [for] this beautiful child, this choice spirit, this lovable son and brother. . . . Because of a little child's innocence, a parent's love is deep and tender, unmarred by conflict, disappointment, or failure. . . . Where shall we go for comfort, to find peace, when our dreams are shattered, our ties broken?" He recalled the paradoxical comfort that came to him and Merle from Uncle Mark Paulson, after

Laurie's death. He and Zoe had lost two small sons. "Don't try to understand why this has happened because you never will." Still, Lowell preached hope. "One cannot judge from a human, mortal perspective. Like Job of old, we who believe in God must put our trust in Him. . . . Man proposes; *life* disposes. . . . We must keep on proposing, planting our crops even though the weather may destroy them. . . . We have no choice but to act with purity of motive, do the best we can, and leave the harvest to one who knows better than you or I."[29]

These accomplishments and sorrows were the normal, even predictable, patterns of family life, but Howard Wayne, their fourth son, followed a different path. The Bennion-Colton emphasis on education intimidated Howard, who "never liked school very much." Howard inherited his mother's love of beauty, however, and his father's devotion to ranch life. He loved the horse given to him by Uncle Len Folsom. Lowell's attempts to turn Howard into an athlete met with little success. Attempts to teach him to work did succeed. As each brother departed, Howard took over their chores. In his handwritten "Memories" Lowell appreciatively described Howard's artistic talents and sensitivity to the needs of others.[30]

During the Vietnam War, Howard followed his brothers' examples and joined the reserves. Two days after high school graduation, Howard and forty or so others were shipped to Fort Polk, Louisiana, for basic training. Howard remembered that it was "hotter than Hades" but "a good experience for me . . . . I was real religious there."[31] Lowell sent airfare so Howard could take the entrance exam to the University of Utah.

At age nineteen Howard had the traditional Mormon boy's interview with his bishop about serving a mission. His bishop sent in the papers, but Howard could not bring himself to embark. He called it off twice. Then on his third try, after Merle had purchased missionary clothing and scriptures, Howard told the bishop the mission was off. "I can't go." Howard had finally accepted the fact that he was homosexual. The bishop urged him to tell his father. Howard had broken the news to Merle without naming the reason. She was, Howard recalled, "crushed, but I think she expected that I wouldn't go." Certainly the two earlier failed attempts had prepared her for a third refusal.

But to Lowell, Howard told the full truth, news that caused Lowell to burst into tears. "I've never seen him cry like that," said Howard. "Not before, not since. It just crushed him." At first Lowell advised Howard not "to tell your mother. She won't be able to handle it."[32] Howard retreated to the Wilson ranch where he worked for two years, returning to Utah and a suicide attempt. When Merle arrived at his bedside in hospital, she told him, "I've always known it." "She didn't shed a tear," marvelled Howard. "She just accepted it."[33]

Homosexuality was an issue few families in the 1960s and 1970s were prepared to deal with, much less an orthodox Mormon family. Nothing in their experience, and nothing in Howard's childhood and adolescence, seemed to explain this fact. With characteristic determination, Lowell and Merle learned what they could about Howard's "lifestyle" and encouraged him to finish his degree. After he began working as an orderly at LDS Hospital, a doctor acquaintance told Merle, "Howard should have been a doctor, or at least a nurse because . . . he has more perception than any of the nurses about what is best for patients and a lot more than many of the doctors."[34]

This was encouraging news, and Lowell urged Howard to work toward an RN degree. But even though he took a full load at the university while working full time, Howard felt he "wasn't accomplishing anything," and he spiraled into depression. The family supported the advice of Howard's psychiatrist that he should move away.

Howard chose to work in a hospital in Oahu, Hawaii, where Merle and Ellen visited him. By the time he returned to Utah, confidence in his own identity was strong, and finally in the 1980s he and a partner built a home on his father's property and entered into a business relationship in a successful gift and card shop in Salt Lake City.

In the 1970s Howard's bishop and stake president (Howard was living in another ward) convened a church court—supposedly in an effort to simply "clean up the records," as Lowell saw it. Howard had been living quietly with a partner for several years, not attending church, not calling attention to himself in ward or community. He was profoundly touched when his father called with the words, "I want to testify. Will you pick me up?" Knowing that his father did not endorse his lifestyle, Howard was moved to tears by Lowell's defense: "How can you judge this young man? You don't know him." Howard was excommunicated, but he felt strengthened by his father's love.[35]

Merle accepted the dilemmas of Howard's path as she searched for understanding. In her oral history she said, "I've had to accept [Howard's lifestyle]. I've shed many tears and spent years of worry, but I've had to get over that."[36]

In the 1980s Lowell responded to an interviewer's question: "Did your University life give you more time with your family?" He admitted that his career had kept him from living a private life. "You know, I was active in the Church and invited to weddings of children of students and had former students come to see me about their problems. So I haven't had a private life anytime that I recall."[37]

The family adjusted to his absences, each in his or her own way. Doug recalls that his father promised in his final year at the institute that "he would spend more time with his family," but that "he just wasn't around."[38]

Ellen Jean, seventeen years younger than Ben and six years younger than Howard, concluded that the gap between her and Howard and their elder brothers meant that she and Howard were really their parents' second family. Ellen was not close to her oldest brothers until she herself was mature enough to become their friend. As the cherished answer to her parents' prayer for a daughter, she felt no need to compete.

She appreciated that Lowell was inordinately proud of her ability as a pianist and her good grades in school, but she sometimes resented Lowell's unassailable reputation. "Everybody in my entire life has said, 'Do you know how wonderful your father is?'" she commented wryly.[39] But she was able to come to terms with Lowell's divided attention. "Bless his heart," she said, "you know he loves you." She recognized Lowell's "huge heart" and believed that he knew "his family will make it," while the needy were at greater risk and therefore needed his attention more. Lowell's pride in Ellen is evident in a letter to Bill Moran when Ellen was eighteen: "Ellen is very bright, tall, attractive, mature, and a lot of fun for me—calls me everything from 'Cutie,' and 'Phony,' to 'Father.'"[40]

On August 20, 1976, Ellen married Neil Hirschi Stone, a next-door neighbor described by Lowell as a "mature, able, and gentle young man"[41] who had been permanently injured in a high school skiing accident. Using a wheelchair for mobility, Neil modeled cheer and courage. He had graduated from the University of Utah and was working in his father's industrial supply business. When Ellen told Merle that she might marry Neil, Merle, knowing the challenges involved in dealing with paraplegia, said mildly, "You are going to have to give that a lot of thought." Ellen shot back, "I have!"[42]

Lowell and Merle wrote that the young couple was "supremely happy."[43] Neil enjoyed Ellen's "noisy vitality and creativity," having learned to tolerate her fifteen birds, forty-three plants, and two dogs.[44] Lowell wrote fondly of his youngest child: "She has fine ethical values, good insight into people's feelings and needs, and is gifted with imagination."[45] After their wedding they built a house on the lot next to their parents. Daughter Lindsay was born on June 4, 1978, followed by Jacob on July 6, 1982—two "miracle" children.

Their life together would be punctuated by suffering as Neil's kidneys failed and he fought for health. On July 5, 1989, Neil gave up his long battle with kidney disease. Eight years on dialysis—administered by Ellen three times a week—and an unsuccessful kidney transplant. For fourteen years "everything [Ellen] did and everything she planned was planned around him," Merle said. When it became clear that Neil's health was failing, Ellen finished her bachelor's degree with a teaching certificate that secured a job at Horizon Elementary School in nearby Murray. This career supported her children and allowed her to spend summers with them.

In 1975 Lowell's mother, Cora Bennion, who had been living with Maurine and Len Folsom, had to be moved into a nursing home. "It was terrible to put her there," said Len, "but she never complained." Six months after her one hundredth birthday and four days after she was admitted to the home, she died. "She had her wits about her till the end," said Maurine.[46]

The family gathered to celebrate Cora's productive life. "She had been so devoted to her family and to Father in his years of suffering and physical impairment that I feared she might be at a loss when he died," Lowell wrote. "But Mother took charge of her life—read books, undertook new projects in Relief Society, spent two days a week at the temple as an ordinance worker, ironed and mended for family members." Her one extravagance was the purchase of a small organ, "which she loved along with her guitar." She could have afforded more. Milton had sold the family home in Forest Dale to Len, who remodeled it into apartments, including one for the retired couple. He then invested the money for Cora so that "she was better off financially when she died than she had been at Father's death."[47] In the lively and even heated discussions of the Bennion clan, Cora was an interested listener and a calming influence, wrote Lynn Bennion. "She died as she had lived, a serene and devoted disciple of Christ."[48]

This period was also a time of suffering for the Ed and Hermana Lyon family. Hermana's intermittent cancer returned in the summer of 1978. It turned out to be simply a reaction to her medication; but Ed too was ill. After a five-hour operation to "remove an obstruction in the colon," the verdict was cancer. Hermana was so crushed she could write only, "They can do nothing for him. Words can't describe my feelings."[49]

Ed's cheerful grit did not leave him. "I'm not through yet," he announced. During that summer, as he recovered from the first operation, he and Hermana read the recently-published biography of Spencer W. Kimball, written by son Edward and grandson Andrew. It was comforting to read the candid record of sorrows, fears, and seemingly endless illnesses, including a bout with cancer.

After three operations Ed asked his sons to "pray for his release." On September 20 he was well enough to sit with Hermana at a hospital window admiring both the view over the city and his wife, "You're beautiful." He fell asleep about noon, and then, about 8:30 that evening, he "just slipped away."[50]

The funeral service was held in the institute, scene of Ed's and Lowell's heyday. The chapel filled to overflowing as a seemingly endless line filed past the casket by the fireplace. Second son, John Lyon, offered the family prayer before the casket closed over the beloved face. A Scottish piper led the coffin to the grave.

Davis Bitton, assistant official LDS church historian and a close friend, celebrated Ed's energy and love of life. He quoted Ed: "I was never bored in my life!"[51] Lowell paid moving tribute to their long companionship. "I could never get enough of his company," he said. Ed's "stock of tales" enlightened not only the institute classes but also their study group, which would turn to Ed when discussion lagged. Proudly Lowell reminded the mourners that Ed's was not a simple faith but one that had been tested through studies of comparative religion and sound historical scholarship. He had loved Joseph Smith and modeled his life after the teachings of Jesus Christ. Tenderly Lowell described Ed "as ready to meet his maker as anyone I have ever known" and closed with his faith in the hereafter: "Surely a universe that can create the likes of T. Edgar Lyon has also the power to preserve him."[52]

Ed's death marked the rending of lives seamlessly woven together. Merle said of the Lyon marriage: "There was never a couple who loved each other more."[53] After Hermana's death the children found a sheaf of love poems that Ed had written to her for special occasions.[54] Hermana struggled against her sorrow, weakened by her own cancer. For the next two years Lowell and Merle called on her regularly, inviting her to university lectures and study group meetings. Hermana recorded in her diary a tender visit from Lowell who encouraged who her "to talk. He brought me some vegetables, apples, and oranges. He's a great person. I am blessed."[55] Just two weeks before her death she and Merle prepared their Relief Society lessons together. When she died on June 8, 1980, Lowell and Merle were doubly bereaved. In talking with Ted and Cheryl Lyon, Merle said, "You know how wonderful she was—brilliant really. . . . She could explain things so much better than I could. She had a better perception of things. I came away feeling uplifted just from being around her."[56]

Lowell and Merle were comforted later in June 1980 by a family reunion with their children, during which they were summoned by telephone to the home of Bill Boyd, a counselor to their stake president. Such a summons usually meant a church calling. An hour later Lowell and Merle returned to clamorous excitement.

"Talk about curiosity!" remembered Merle.

After peppering their parents with questions, the family concluded that a mission call must be imminent. Merle finally closed the speculation by saying, "Yes, we have been called on a sort of mission that we can't talk about right now."

A few days later in sacrament meeting stake president Joel

Garrett announced Lowell as the new bishop of East Millcreek Twelfth Ward amid audible gasps of delight. Lowell, now nearing his seventy-second birthday, was well past the age of most bishops. The calling astonished him, as he had never aspired to such offices, but he was comforted to think that church president Spencer W. Kimball had approved it.[57] Lowell had never refused a church calling. Ironically, recalls Merle, "he turned down some [callings] for me. When he was on the high council, he told them I couldn't take a stake MIA calling because of our small children."[58]

Geographically, the ward was smaller than Bishop Woodruff's old Forest Dale Ward, and demographically it was a "good cross-section" of Saints. Built on a foundation of "old-timers" like the Hinckleys, Tanners, Osguthorpes, Eccles, Geigles, Drages, and Bennions themselves, it expanded through a dynamic mix of younger families in upscale subdivisions whom Kent Murdock, second counselor and a lawyer, described as "good people, very solid people. We don't have wealthy people, only constant people. . . . not flashy and not given to highs and lows."[59] First counselor Tom Pike, a businessman and singer, had long viewed the Bennion family as integral to the fabric of the ward. "Most people kind of thought that maybe [being a bishop] had gone by the boards for him," said Pike.[60] Lowell stepped into the office without groping for direction. As at the institute he wanted the sacrament meetings to be Christ-centered, and he wanted ward members to be service-centered.

Sacrament meetings did come close to real worship services in a phenomenon Murdock and Pike characterized as a "lovely rejuvenation of the ward." Lowell's philosophy of meetings sprang from his "great reverence for the Savior." Consequently he "stressed that people needed to speak about the gospel," commented Murdock. "We encouraged missionaries to do more than give travel descriptions. . . . Lowell asked people to speak about one idea, well illustrated, and to draw from the scriptures and their own personal experiences." He also "sought out the people who hadn't been in the limelight."[61] He insisted that announcements and business be kept to a minimum, that all three bishopric members downplay their own personalities. All-music programs for Easter and Christmas wove powerful emotional and spiritual experiences for the ward, lovingly and diligently prepared. "We didn't want just good tries," observed Murdock. "We really wanted excellent work."[62]

Lowell depended on his younger counselors for assigned paperwork and administrative duties. Working with a "strong cadre of clerks," they quietly gave Lowell the freedom to concentrate on service, counseling, and worship.[63]

Lowell began by asking the ward's teenagers to commit one morning a month to serving the needy, coordinating with adult leaders. "We paid a great deal of attention to the widows and to those who were lonely. Lowell knew them all," recalled Murdock.[64] Knowing needs outside the ward boundaries from his work on the Community Service Council, Lowell expanded horizons of service.

"In a quiet way we visited everyone in the ward," Murdock said. Unlike some bishops who acted like "organized bulldogs" with dogmatic personalities, Lowell's approach radiated kindness, love, and inviolable respect for the agency of the individual. "Lowell taught me that you can't really help anybody do anything if they don't want to," Pike commented. "But Lowell was always available. And he would just quietly appear on your doorstep with a loaf of bread,"[65] sometimes of his own making. "It made all the difference in the world to . . . think about people first, instead of programs and institutions," summarized Pike.[66]

Paradoxically, such service led to more independence in the lives of members. Lowell was always willing to talk with any officer or teacher struggling with a calling or perplexed about an issue, but he communicated immense trust in their ability to solve their own problems. Murdock, who would become bishop himself, saw that ward members learned that "all roads do not lead to the bishop." Instead, "they sought the inspiration of the Lord and their hearts were opened to the people they served."[67] Without fanfare or frustration, ward members began meeting their own and others' needs.

In his three years as bishop Lowell never held a church court, instead supporting efforts at repentance. "I had one man who did something and repented," he recalled. "Why haul him off to court if he's confessed and repented? I turned another case over to the stake."[68]

With Lowell's release in June 1983, the ward honored Lowell and Merle, staging an emotional "This is Your Life" program that left them tired but grateful. Merle, who had continued to teach cultural refinement lessons in Relief Society, joyfully adding the new tasks of the bishop's wife, summed up the experience: "It was a nice three years."[69]

In the church and in the community Lowell's Christian standards were the same. In 1982 when he addressed the fledgling B. H. Roberts Society, an organization formed by a group of Mormons interested in addressing contemporary social and Mormon issues, he preached a stirring sermon on the social gospel: "Feed My Sheep: An Unfulfilled Social Agenda." "There are several thousand elderly, two-thirds of them women—in the Salt Lake valley, who have neither spouse nor children," he said soberly. "They face old age, disabilities, insecurity, fear of assault and death—alone. There are those who object to government housing for these folks. That is acceptable if the church and its organized groups or other volunteers would fill the gap." Though the church does a "pretty good job of caring for some of the needs of our members . . . in my judgment, we do not do nearly enough." He warned, "Latter-day Saints have no greater mission than to relieve suffering . . . to feed the master's sheep."[70]

According to listener Robert Vernon, "Lowell established himself as the conscience of the community in that one speech."[71] Peggy Fletcher, publisher of *Sunstone* magazine, subsequently enlisted volunteers for food drives to supply the Community Services Council's Food Bank. Similarly motivated, Eugene England, now an English professor at Brigham Young University, organized a "Food for Poland" drive to provide food and medicine during the dark days of the Solidarity movement.

Interspersed among these activities were frequent award ceremonies. In fact, Lowell's honors were coming so fast Merle was having trouble storing the plaques, medals, statuettes, and other gifts bestowed on him almost monthly. Lowell seldom enjoyed these occasions. Richard Winters, who succeeded Lowell as director of Community Services Council, ruefully noticed that receiving an award "just devastates the man." When the Freedom Foundation at Valley Forge named him one of their heroes, Winters accompanied Lowell to the ceremony. "You've never seen a guy so miserable in your life!" The other honorees had exercised physical courage in saving lives. Lowell was cited for "what he has done all his life—no jumping-in-the-river heroic event, just day after day doing little things that make a difference."[72]

He felt more comfortable, however, with an honorary doctorate from the University of Utah in 1982. Ten years before he had received his university's Distinguished Alumnus Award for his "devoted service as inspirational mentor and intellectual conscience to thousands of students representing many ethnic groups, religious faiths, political persuasions and professional backgrounds."[73] University of Utah president David P. Gardner lauded Lowell's "lifetime of service as an inspiring teacher, a trusted counselor, and a compassionate community leader, for his unselfish dedication to the advancement of civil rights and equal opportunity, for his deeply rooted ethical idealism and his unceasing quest for ultimate human values, and his countless contributions to the well-being of others." The degree of Doctor of Humane Letters, *honoris causia,* was presented by Lowell's longtime friend, Boyer Jarvis.

Lowell saw himself primarily as a catalyst for others who aspired to feed the sheep. He worked with university, community, and church citizens who wanted to integrate altruism with career and family duties.

During the summer of 1984 Merle joined Pat Jarvis's art tour through Germany and France, revisiting scenes from her early marriage. During this nostalgic trip she received a lonesome letter from Lowell: "I quite enjoyed a few days alone, but miss you much of late. . . . Glad to have you remember our romantic days in Paris. Why not revive them again? Have a good time and come back on two feet."[74]

Unfortunately, she came back in a wheelchair. She had fallen en route to an airport, fracturing her arm and wrenching her back. And Lowell had just been diagnosed as needing a proctectomy for a nonmalignancy. Their mini-honeymoon thus became joint recuperation. And Lowell had developed other symptoms. For some time he had felt a trembling in his capable hands. His eager stride was slowing to a shuffle, and chronic shoulder pain was worsening. The diagnosis—Parkinson's disease and ruptured shoulders—shocked them and forced them to face the implications of their years: Lowell was seventy-six, Merle almost seventy-eight.

Help was close at hand. Lowell and Merle had deeded their land to their children, a lot for each with Steve's share in the garden plot. When Ellen and Neil built their home on Ellen's lot in 1976, they roughed out an easy-access garden-level apartment for Lowell and Merle, finishing it in May 1986. It was bounded by Ellen's well-tended yard and Lowell's large garden, with a view of two mountain ranges. A cozy space, compact and easy to care for, it included room for Lowell's study and space for Merle's piano and organ. As live-in grandparents, they were a boon to Lindsay and Jacob.

Since Howard had inherited the lot with the old family home, he proposed to build a house on it. He showed Lowell and Merle plans for a spacious Spanish-style home that could rise on the basement of the old, complete with a swimming pool. Chagrined at the thought of tearing down a usable house, Lowell wondered, "Can't you just fix up the old place?"[75]

Howard pointed out that the old place needed so much renovation that building anew would be more practical. His plans intrigued Merle, centered as they were on a view of Mt. Olympus. Howard promised to salvage the "nice, dry basement" for Lowell's book storage. On the day the wrecking crew arrived, Lowell and Merle watched. Suddenly Ellen rushed past them and into the house. She had remembered a built-in "stuck drawer" that had never yielded to her curiosity. This time she pried it open, calling out, "Look, Father, your missionary diary!" The valuable document accompanied some fine black and white photographs of Ellen's older brothers as children, posing with their young parents before the mountain backdrop.

Forlornly Lowell mused that the house of his marriage had met the same fate as the house of his childhood. Less sentimentally, Merle, the housekeeper, laundress, and cook in that old farmhouse, pointed out that where the Forest Dale home had given place to a freeway, the inconvenient old house was replaced by a work of art. Howard's lifelong love of the outdoors manifested itself in a beautiful flower garden.

That same year both Lowell and Merle felt well enough to accept an invitation from Laurie Newman DiPadova, now a stake Relief Society president in Albany, New York, to speak at her stake's Relief Society conference—a rare opportunity for Merle to be invited as co-speaker. She found it satisfying to address the women entirely in verse on the subject of some of her favorite women: Mary, the mother of Jesus; the biblical Ruth who knew the "true meaning of love"; Golda Meir, "fiercely nationalistic"; Elizabeth Barrett Browning, a poet in love with her husband; and the reclusive Emily Dickinson. Lowell gave his address the same title as his book, *The Things That Matter Most.* According to DiPadova, the stake president commented that the "spirit of Christ had descended on the large group of women."[76]

DiPadova was surprised by Merle's "boundless energy and interest" in touring the scenic countryside. ("She wouldn't even wait for the car to stop to start taking pictures.") Merle's appetite for life was "a great inspiration to us all," she added, particularly to "so many women, say, in their forties or so who think life is finished."[77]

Back home Lowell maintained a full schedule at the Community Services Council, but the staff began to notice his physical problems. How long, they wondered, could he keep it up? Lowell's old friends were worried too. Louis Moench, for instance, noticed that Lowell's back trouble "didn't keep him from lifting quadriplegics and paraplegics in and out of their wheelchairs. . . . We'd go to his house for study group and [find that] a lot of people had their driveways shoveled by him, but he didn't get to his own—and fell on it."[78]

His focus ever on daily service, Lowell showed his usual uncomplaining grit and soldiered on.

NOTES

1. Merle C. Bennion, interviewed by Mary L. Bradford, 25 Jan. 1990.

2. Merle Colton Bennion, Oral History, 68.

3. Lowell L. Bennion, "Memories," 118, photocopy in Bradford's possession.

4. Merle Colton Bennion, Oral History, 68.

5. Ibid., 68.

6. Ibid., 68.

7. Ibid., 70-71.

8. Some members were Steve and Hilda Inkley, Brigham and Betty Madsen, Charles and Vivian Monson, Sam and Elly Thurman, Jack and Peggy Adamson, and, after Jack's death, Roald Campbell.

9. Lowell L. Bennion to Laurie Newman, 4 Dec. 1971, photocopy in Bradford's possession.

10. Members included Mel Thayne, Wendell Adams, Jack and Peggy Adamson, Bob and Francine Bennion, Carma and Ed Brown, Harriet and Leonard Arrington, Dixie and Caryle Hunsaker, Wanda and Dale LeCheminant, Barbara and Larry Lewis, Marti and Dennis Lythgoe, Maureen Ursenbach Beecher and Dale Beecher, Eileen McKean, Linda and Jack Newell, Kay and Ted Packard, Helen and Stuart Poelman, and Neil and Ellen Bennion Stone.

11. Ramona Adams, interviewed by Mary L. Bradford, 12 Feb. 1988.

12. Merle Colton Bennion, Oral History, 81.

13. Marjorie Pay Hinckley, interviewed by Mary L. Bradford, 19 July 1988.

14. Lowell L. Bennion, "Memories," 117.

15. Douglas C. Bennion, interviewed by Mary L. Bradford, 18 Oct. 1987.

16. Gary B. Peterson and Ben Bennion, *Sanpete Scenes* (Eureka, UT: Basin/Plateau Press, 1987).

17. The J. B. Jackson prize awarded annually by the Association of American Geographers for the best book in popular human geography.

18. Sherry Bennion, *Equal to the Occasion: Women Editors of the Nineteenth-Century West* (Reno: University of Nevada Press, 1990).

19. Douglas C. Bennion, interviewed by Mary L. Bradford, 18 Oct. 1987.

20. Lowell L. Bennion to Elmo and Frances (Morgan), 20 June 1961.

21. Douglas C. Bennion, conversation with Mary L. Bradford, 28 May 1990.

22. Merle Colton Bennion, Oral History, 55.

23. Douglas C. Bennion, interviewed by Mary L. Bradford, 18 Oct. 1987.

24. Eyring, former president of Ricks College and church Commissioner of Education, became a member of the Quorum of the Twelve Apostles in April 1995.

25. Henry B. Eyring, *Inauguration* (n.p.: Ricks College, 5 Nov. 1989), 4, in Bradford's possession.

26. Gordon B. Hinckley, in ibid., 6.

27. Ibid.

28. Hermana Lyon, Diary, 9 May 1978, Lyon Collection, archives, Historical Department, Church of Jesus Christ of Latter-day Saints, Salt Lake City, Utah; typed notes in Bradford's possession, 2.

29. Lowell L. Bennion, "Brian Colton Bennion," typewritten speech, 9 May 1978, photocopy in Bradford's possession.

30. Lowell L. Bennion, "Memories," 132.

31. Howard W. Bennion, interviewed by Mary L. Bradford, 15 Feb. 1988.

32. Ibid.

33. Ibid.

34. Merle C. Bennion, interviewed by Mary L. Bradford, 25 Jan. 1990.

35. Ibid.

36. Merle Colton Bennion, Oral History, 85. Twenty years later Lowell wrote the foreword to a collection of personal and professional essays on same-sex orientation for Mormons. In his steady voice he pointed out that "homosexuality is complex in origin. Some . . . believe there is evidence to support the conclusion that a genetic or biological basis contributes . . . If this is true, it explains why homosexuals find change to be difficult, and it obliges us to evaluate anew our attitudes towards gays and lesbians" (in Ron Schow, Wayne Schow, and Marybeth Raynes, eds., *Peculiar People: Mormons and Same-sex Orientation* [Salt Lake City: Signature Books, 1991], xii).

37. Lowell L. Bennion, Oral History, 180.

38. Douglas C. Bennion, interviewed by Mary L. Bradford, 19 May 1989.

39. Ellen Jean Bennion Stone, interviewed Mary L. Bradford.

40. Lowell L. Bennion to Bill Moran, 9 Oct. 1970, photocopy in Bradford's possession.

41. Lowell L. Bennion, "Memories," 133.

42. Merle C. Bennion, interviewed by Mary L. Bradford, 17 May 1989.

43. Ibid.

44. Lowell L.Bennion, "Memories," 134.

45. Lowell L. Bennion, Oral History, 121.

46. Maurine Bennion and Leonard Folsom, interviewed by Mary L.

Bradford, 13 Oct. 1987.

47. Lowell L. Bennion, "Memories," 100.

48. Milton Lindsay Bennion, *Recollections of a School Man: The Autobiography of M. Lynn Bennion* (Salt Lake City: Western Epics, 1986), 27.

49. Hermana Lyon, Diary, 18 July 1978.

50. Ibid., 25 July; 9, 29 Aug.; 17, 19, 20 Sept. 1978.

51. Davis Bitton, "In Memoriam: T. Edgar Lyon (1903-1978)," *Dialogue: A Journal of Mormon Thought* 11 (Winter 1978): 11. Three years later Leonard J. Arrington and Davis Bitton coauthored *Saints Without Halos* (Midvale, UT: Signature Books, 1981). One chapter, devoted to T. Edgar Lyon, honored the "many remarkable individuals who have devoted years of their lives to the seminary and institute program—Franklin L. West, Lowell L. Bennion, Wyley Sessions, George S. Tanner, George Boyd, Ed Berrett, and many others—but no one who knew him would deny that T. Edgar Lyon's energy and devotion as well as his breadth and versatility were unexcelled. His was a unique contribution to the improvement of Latter-day Saint education" (153).

52. Lowell L. Bennion, "Reflections on T. Edgar Lyon: A Tribute Given at His Funeral," *Dialogue: A Journal of Mormon Thought* 11 (Winter 1978): 13.

53. Merle C. Bennion, Oral History, 83.

54. Joseph Lynn Lyon, interviewed by Mary L. Bradford, 26 Sept. 1990.

55. Hermana Lyon, Diary, 2 Apr. 1979.

56. Merle C. Bennion, interviewed by Ted and Cheryl Lyon, 6 Jan. 1989, transcript in Bradford's possession.

57. Merle C. Bennion, interviewed by Mary L. Bradford, 21 June 1991.

58. Merle C. Bennion, interviewed by Mary L. Bradford, 2 Feb. 1988.

59. Kent H. Murdock, interviewed by Mary L. Bradford, 18 May 1988.

60. Thomas G. Pike, interviewed by Mary L. Bradford, 9 May 1988.

61. Kent Murdock, interviewed by Mary L. Bradford, 9 May 1988.

62. Ibid.

63. Thomas G. Pike, interviewed by Mary L. Bradford, 9 May 1988.

64. Kent Murdock, interviewed by Mary L. Bradford, 9 May 1988.

65. Ibid.

66. Thomas G. Pike, interviewed by Mary L. Bradford, 9 May 1988.

67. Kent H. Murdock, interviewed by Mary L. Bradford, 8 May 1988.

68. Lowell L. Bennion, interviewed by Mary L. Bradford, 10 May 1988.

69. Merle C. Bennion, interviewed by Mary L. Bradford, 17 Sept. 1990.

70. Lowell L. Bennion, "Feed My Sheep: An Unfulfilled Social Agenda," address to the B. H. Roberts Society, 1982, photocopy in Bradford's possession.

71. Robert Vernon, interviewed by Mary L. Bradford, 11 Feb. 1988.

72. Richard K. Winters, interviewed by Mary L. Bradford, 11 Aug. 1992.

73. "Five Receive Honors at Founders' Day Banquet," *University of Utah Review,* Feb. 1971, 1. The other four were Gordon B. Hinckley, Virginia F. Cutler, James E. Hogle, and David W. Evans.

74. Lowell L. Bennion to Merle C. Bennion, 17 Sept. 1984, photocopy in Bradford's possession.

75. Howard W. Bennion, interviewed by Mary L. Bradford, 15 Feb. 1988.

76. Laurie DiPadova to Ellen Bennion Stone, 16 Aug. 1986, photocopy in Bradford's possession.

77. Ibid.

78. Louis Moench, joint interview with Louis and Mavonne Moench, conducted by Mary L. Bradford, 13 Feb. 1988.

CHAPTER 15

THE LOWELL L. BENNION COMMUNITY SERVICE CENTER (1978-94)

In some ways I'd like to retire and spend my time reading and writing and gardening, and visiting the sick and the afflicted.

—LOWELL L. BENNION

On October 9, 1986, Merle and Lowell attended "The Triumph of the Spirit," a public roundtable discussion sponsored by the B. H. Roberts Society to honor Lowell. Unknown to either, Emma Lou Thayne had planned a surprise as part of the celebration.

Thayne, among many, felt the time had come to end the seventy-eight-year-old Lowell's struggles with his battered pick-up with its manual shift and jammed windows. She asked her brother, Rick Warner, owner of a Ford franchise in Salt Lake City, to provide at his cost a small stationwagon Escort with power steering and windows. As word of the gift spread, money began arriving from all over the country. Some called in the night or drove to Thayne's door with checks, asking anxiously, "Am I too late? I want to be in on this."[1] The station wagon had a rear door that folded down for hauling and room still for Merle to ride in comfort in the front seat. Decorated with an enormous red ribbon, it appeared in Lowell's driveway the night of the B. H. Roberts Society meeting with a card from the donors—500 of them.

The B. H. Roberts night was a festive evening of tribute. Lowell and Merle sat with the crowd, a few rows from the front. On the stand Emma Lou Thayne joined Leonard Arrington, who acted as master of ceremonies, Marion D. Hanks, Elaine Smart, and Sterling McMurrin in recalling, with humor and eloquence, their lives with the Bennions. They passed the hat for the Community Services Council. Jack and Linda Newell, editors of *Dialogue: A Journal of Mormon Thought,* announced an annual prize for the Lowell L. Bennion Essay in Christian Living; and Arrington made a heartwarming announcement in the name of Chase Peterson, president of the University of Utah:

> The University of Utah is proposing to the Board of Regents the establishment of the Lowell Bennion Community Service Center on the Campus. President Peterson said the center will acknowledge the life and work of Lowell and is being funded through a substantial gift of an anonymous donor and will advocate the ideas, skills, and satisfactions of community service. The center will assist in matching volunteer opportunities for students and others on campus, cooperating with community agencies and campus units in identifying and assessing volunteer placements, build relationships with community agencies, develop courses and forums for teaching the civic values of community service, sponsor training for volunteer users, sponsor conferences, promote community service values, sponsor student tutoring at local schools, collect and distribute food donations, and work with the elderly and the handicapped.[2]

This announcement culminated several months of negotiation among university officers, staff, and Lowell. Earlier in 1986 Anthony W. Morgan, Lowell's nephew and vice president at the university for planning and budget, had asked Lowell to meet with him about an idea he shared with his friend, Richard Jacobsen.

Jacobsen, a stalwart supporter of Lowell's boys' ranch who later participated in purchasing it, had observed a successful community services program at Stanford University near Jacobsen's home in Palo Alto, California.[3] The two men envisioned a similar component at the University of Utah, devoted to Lowell's brand of volunteerism.[4] This idea echoed an escalating interest in community service among other universities, including the Campus Outreach Opportunity League (COOL) founded by two Harvard graduates and headquartered in Minnesota. As Jacobsen later put it: "The political activism of the '60s followed by a more apathetic and inward turning bent in the '70s eventually gave way to a genuine concern among university students and faculty for the welfare of the local, national, and global communities of which they were a part."[5]

The group voted to "keep Lowell's legacy alive while he's still alive," as Norm Gibbons expressed it.[6] They suggested that the center be housed in the student union building in the student services side of administration. After presenting the idea to the president, the student senate, and the regents, they began interviewing for a director.

Plans coalesced with remarkable speed during the spring of 1986. An anonymous donor gave start-up money, and other funds began flowing. Morgan was amazed. "When you propose new programs," he explained, "it is hard to get people to take enough interest to make necessary decisions. But that was no problem here. I didn't have to explain or defend anything." When he called members of the institutional council and the board of regents, the responses were enthusiastic.[7] Jacobsen declared, "The idea seemed to catch fire throughout the University. . . . Everywhere we found enthusiastic support for a Community Service Center in general and great love and admiration for Dr. Bennion in particular."[8]

Despite these fast-forming plans, Morgan recalled that Lowell balked at granting formal permission to use his name. Even after a special visit focused on that problem, Morgan left wondering, "Do we have the go-ahead or not?" Lowell, incurably modest, was struggling with the concept of having something named after him. "Donors usually have no hesitancy about suggesting that things be named after them," Morgan recalled, but "one of the few times I ever heard Lowell criticize another person was when that person wanted his name on something."[9]

Finally in a meeting of the advisory board Lowell offered to "leave the room while you decide." But they had already decided. They unanimously voted to move ahead with the Lowell L. Bennion Community Services Center. "Lowell never did sign anything," Morgan smiled. He simply acquiesced.[10]

Deseret News columnist Dennis Lythgoe observed, "It isn't often that a person's philosophy of life is embraced and institutionalized while he is still living."[11] University president Chase N. Peterson commented, "That is what the Bennion Center and the university are all about—educated idealism."[12]

By June 1987 the center defined its purposes:

> To seek to honor the life of Lowell Bennion, to develop in young adults

> an early awareness and commitment to community service, to arouse in the larger community a heightened sense of civic responsibility, to seek out and assist in the meeting of community needs, and to provide action-learning experiences and opportunities for program participants to acquire increased knowledge, skills, and abilities basic to enlightened community service.[13]

The mission statement was adopted on September 14, 1987:

> The Lowell Bennion Community Service Center seeks to involve university students, faculty, alumni, and staff in service to the communities in which they live—local, national, and global. Inspired by the enduring example of Lowell Bennion, whose life-long devotion to the well-being of others has guided both his personal and professional affairs, the Center engages in identifying community needs, exploring possible solutions, and, particularly, offering enlightened and human service. The Center promotes understanding of the nature of human communities, the benefits of voluntary cooperative effort, and the rewards found in the relief of suffering or the banishment of ignorance and fear. In a society of material plenty, those who participate in the Center's activities and projects will find meaning through community service and pleasure in the improvement of life around them.[14]

L. Jackson Newell was the primary author of this mission statement which proved "a very useful tool for defining the purpose of the Center and informing others of what we intended to accomplish."[15] It was clear from the outset that although most of its founders were Mormon, the new organization would be aggressively ecumenical, action oriented, and open to anyone who felt a call to serve.

The first advisory board included: a representative of the Associated Students of the University of Utah; Richard Jacobsen; Lowell; Marion D. Hanks; Lowell's friend Edith Shepherd; Keith Whisenant, past president of Community Services Council; Isabel Jensen, CSC board member; Ted L. Wilson, former mayor of Salt Lake City and director of the Hinckley Institute of Politics at the university; Grethe B. Peterson, community activist and wife of the university president; and Andrew Peterson, dentist and board president (later called to the LDS Quorum of the Seventy in 1995). Ramona Adams and Norm Gibbons were ex-officio members.

In September 1987, still breathless from the speed at which the project had come together, university administrators interviewed prospective directors. The top name on their list was also Lowell's favorite—Irene S. Fisher, executive director of Utah Issues Information Program, Inc., since 1981. Tony Morgan recalled, "Our greatest [question] in setting up the center was 'Is there anyone who can carry on Lowell's philosophy and work?'"[16] They soon realized that Fisher had many of the same qualities.[17]

In her letter of application the forty-eight-year-old Fisher declared, "I share the values of community service and higher education which I have seen Lowell Bennion live so fully." A native of South Dakota, a Methodist, and educated as a schoolteacher, she had been in Utah for seventeen years. Fisher spearheaded public issue and legislative campaigns to improve conditions for low-income families, the disabled, and the elderly, including minorities, refugees, single parents, and children. She had received eleven awards for service to children, women, and the entire community and been president of the League of Women Voters of Salt Lake City. Lowell had worked beside her on many joint projects and was impressed with her direct, compassionate methods, and quiet efficiency.

Utah Issues, a private, non-partisan, and non-profit corporation founded in 1973, addressed the causes of poverty statewide.[18] Even though it lost funding, Fisher revived it as a respected voice for low-income Utahns. Lowell-like, she said, "I believe in the importance of government funding to meet human needs, and I've seen some of its limitations. . . . Now I'd like to see what the capacity is through individual community service."[19] She operated with the philosophy that "service must be included with education and professional service to lead a full life."[20] Hired by the university on October 21, 1987, she reported to work on November 16. The student *Chronicle* reported that the Bennion Center "doesn't even have its phone hooked up, has no organized crew of volunteers, and doesn't officially open until today, but that isn't stopping Irene Fisher." Fisher had learned that twenty-six residents of the Sugarhouse Adult Living Center were about to be evicted because the Salt Lake County Board of Health was shutting down the hopelessly neglected facility. The newspaper story included a photograph of Tony Morgan and Jack Newell painting and spackling a room as part of the Bennion Center's first project.

Volunteers, alerted by word of mouth, and board members materialized at the "dirtiest place you've ever seen" for a five-weekend rehabilitation project. The students "put on their masks and took the carpet up and painted the walls and revitalized something that was supposed to be pulled down." The project was "Lowell all the way," exulted Gibbons. "He would take the worst and clean it up and make it good, a human soul or a facility."[21] Gibbons photographed the event for what would become an ongoing pictorial history of the center. Fisher thought of the refurbishing project as just "a contribution to get [the Bennion Center] off the ground. But people were so taken with it that we went back five Saturdays with different groups of students, two shifts, and then we sponsored an open house for residents and volunteers at Christmas."[22]

The new volunteer corps adhered closely to Lowell's time-tested method: Ask a group of students to contribute one Saturday morning a month to a service project. Involve the volunteers in planning the project. Give the volunteer committee ownership of the project. Work toward a tangible result to make the experience rewarding. And "top off the occasion with good food."[23]

Patrick McCabe, administrative assistant to ASUU president Jacque Morgan, attended Bennion Center Advisory Board meetings and described the first formal project of the new Volunteer Corps. On December 19 "about 40 to 50 students participated by delivering holiday food parcels to dozens of elderly and home-bound people. Meeting and talking to these people put a face on the problems of the elderly poor."[24]

That was just the beginning. McCabe recalled his first year's involvement at the center as "one of the happiest years of my as yet rather short life. We created a wonderful atmosphere of camaraderie and friendship. We were having so much fun, it often felt like the final scenes of *It's a Wonderful Life*."[25]

When the center officially opened its doors in January 1988, it already had two major service projects under its belt and was primed for more. At the open house a videotape of Lowell being interviewed by Emma Lou Thayne introduced the legend to a new generation.

Administratively Irene Fisher encouraged experimentation.

McCabe praised her "special ability to support and encourage while not requiring that it be done in just one way, and to allow people to make decisions as well as mistakes."[26] Thanks to this style and serendipity, the center spent its first year doing projects, figuring out rules, policies, and procedures as it went along. McCabe observed, "I believe waiting to develop a structure until after we had accomplished a good deal saved us from a lot of worry about just the right way to do things. . . . Just as good university planners pour the sidewalks to new buildings after seeing where students make their own paths, the Bennion Center did not impose an organization structure until after we thought one might be helpful."[27]

"Our goal is to impact the lives of students profoundly enough while they're here that they will spend a lifetime involved in the community, many of them as leaders," Fisher said when she was interviewed in 1990. She believed in letting students struggle with projects, to learn by devising their own strategies. "Reflection time" was built into each project, allowing student project leaders to ponder together on their experiences and share their outcomes. This component provided good learning opportunities with a chance to review mistakes in a supportive climate.[28] She remembered how Lowell had fashioned work at his boys ranch. "They worked in the morning and talked at night. We play together and we enjoy each other. We see we can keep working with each other even when we disagree about the way we view experience. Finding common ground is an important part of the Bennion Center."[29]

Projects in 1988 included doing yard work for the elderly, sorting sixty tons of food at the Food Bank, and painting Girls' Village, a non-profit shelter for court-referred teenage girls. These projects attracted good publicity for the fledgling center. Chase and Grethe Peterson hosted the volunteers for breakfast at the president's mansion. Fisher could see that the corps, composed of one-Saturday-a-month volunteers, "meets the need for those who don't have a lot of time to give but want to do something. Some liked it so much they volunteered for more. This is Lowell's style."[30]

Salt Lake City's Rotary Club agreed to fund seven student internships, the first set selected on February 28, 1988.[31]

The internships paid a modest amount toward tuition but not enough to make the internship attractive for monetary reasons alone. Interns worked twenty hours per week as the center's staff, and each devised a project, either short-term or long-term. In the spring 1988 quarter alone one student created an adult literacy action program, recruiting twenty-five other students to tutor for a year. Another organized volunteers in a drug rehabilitation program. A third recruited companions for the elderly. A fourth organized the center's first annual Community Service Action Week in April. A fifth created a partnership with the Lowell Elementary School in the avenues neighborhood of Salt Lake City. The Lowell School was selected—not because of its name (for poet James Russell Lowell)—but because it was "not quite so troubled" that its needs outpaced students capabilities. It also had a "gung-ho" principal who loved volunteers.[32]

A moving—and substantial gesture of support—came during an unforgettable ASUU student assembly during the first year of operation, 1987-88. The ASUU had about $85,000 in its Special Project Fund, and McCabe hoped to raise $50,000 more. The original donor had agreed to match contributions up to $200,000. McCabe lobbied everyone on the Special Funds Project Committee and the proposal passed.[33]

The ASUU assembly was the next hurdle, and Bennion Center representatives received a few minutes on the agenda to make their proposal. "It was like the state legislature," Fisher described, "everybody talking among themselves and paying no attention. When it was our turn, Lowell walked up." An uncharacteristic hush fell over the room. "Lowell spoke briefly about the need for people to be involved, and you could have heard a pin drop." It took only a few moments to vote. "They gave the Bennion Center their entire gift of $50,000. It was astounding. Students just don't do that!"[34] Once more Lowell's presence alone was a powerful message.

By design the Bennion Center staked out separate turf from the Community Services Council, although the two cooperated cordially. "The council would try to use placements from the center with a clear understanding that they were separate entities," Morgan explained.[35] Several students were attracted to Lowell's Community Services Council work, especially the food bank, the

Ouelessebougou-Utah Alliance, and the Befriending Program. "If you think about it," Fisher declared, "there are people on this campus with every kind of skill. Art, drama, everything, we have a lot to offer anybody. We can tailor-make any program for a day, a week, a year, whatever it takes."[36]

She and her crew formulated projects in the racially mixed central city with Head Start and other daycare centers. "Students could see the diversity." Fisher hoped to bring minority youth a widened view of the world as well as widening the world view of the volunteers.[37]

In that first year University of Utah faculty also became involved. When Provost James Clayton convened a meeting of forty professors, Fisher was stunned: "It's not easy to get faculty to come," but "almost everyone we invited came." Clayton pointed out that candidates for tenure are judged not only on research and teaching but also on service. The university was prepared to prove that it rewarded service, and the Bennion Center could be the perfect vehicle to fulfill that requirement. Small discussion groups met, and a faculty advisory group formed. The faculty developed courses combining service and learning, some faculty receiving funding through annual Lowell Bennion Public Service Professorships. Each summer since 1990 the center placed two or three students in fellowships in Washington, D.C., Seattle, and Boston to work in service projects.[38]

In January 1992 the university announced the Service Learning Scholars Program designed to reward students who enrolled for fifteen hours of service-learning courses, performed 400 hours of volunteer work, and completed a special integrative project. The Bennion Center Faculty Advisory Committee designates which classes meet the criteria for service learning courses by combining "academic content with related, altruistic work in the community." A faculty advisor oversees volunteer hours and sits on a supervisory committee that directs a project, which relates to the students' course work and volunteer experience.[39] These students are recognized at commencement and honored at an awards banquet.[40] This concept, developed by Bennion Center team leaders Andrea Pinnock, Janice Ugaki, and Valerie Arango in cooperation with ASUU leaders and the Bennion Center leaders, received federal funding through the newly created Commission on National and Community Service.[41] Lowell was still on the advisory board, meeting monthly and approving these projects.

Also in 1988 Grethe B. Peterson, a member of the Bennion Center Advisory Board, suggested that the Bennion Center respond to the plight of the homeless. McCabe then directed a "Campaign for the Homeless," beginning with a dinner for campus leaders, who assisted in recruiting volunteers to help conduct a summer school funded by the Salt Lake City school district for children living at the homeless shelter. A few small newspaper ads produced "an overwhelming response." The college students were "excited about the school and responsible in fulfilling their commitments. The summer school teachers were fantastic. They gave the children a lot of needed structure and support and were creative in tapping the talents of the volunteer tutors."[42] They also organized a legal outreach program for the homeless with Utah Legal Services and the University of Utah Law School and a project where blankets were donated and distributed to the homeless. Volunteers served meals at St. Vincent de Paul and Salvation Army shelters.

The Bennion Center provided significant energy throughout the state. The work of the center was divided between volunteer staff members and interns. The center got a permanent secretary, and the office moved into 101 Olpin Union Building, where it is still housed.

Irene Fisher thoughtfully pinpointed one reason for the center's success. By focusing on service and bridge-building—prime "Lowell Bennion values"—it sidestepped the Mormon/non-Mormon tension that affected many other arenas and activities on campus. "Some of the students feel that the Bennion Center may be the only place on campus where they don't have to worry about that."[43]

During the center's first two explosive years Fisher and the burgeoning student leadership group organized a topical resource library with information about every volunteer agency in the state. "If a student wants to help the disabled, he can look up every group dealing with the disabled and check them out," explained Fisher.[44] She hired Terri Busch, a skilled secretary with an "amazing capacity to relate to all manner of people in the most upbeat way."[45] Even people from off-campus began calling the center for help, and Brigham Young University reorganized its student government as a service organization. According to Eugene England, who was on the Restructuring Committee at BYU, this change was inspired, in part, by Lowell's writings. Utah's universities and colleges organized the Serving Utah Network (SUN), with the Bennion Center working in partnership with various campuses.

At the end of 1988 the Bennion Center reported 5,450 volunteer service hours with over 500 volunteers for its first year. By the end of its second year hours had quadrupled to over 21,000 with 1,400 volunteers. By 1994 the center was averaging 100,000 hours with 5,000 volunteers a year.

Projects spanned an intriguing range. One newsletter asked, "Who spent the night of August 28, 1989, sleeping in the park between the Myton, Utah, City Hall and the Three-Legged Dog Saloon? Answer: Sixteen community service volunteers from the U. of Utah."[46] They were conducting the first rural community service project in northeastern Utah. After consultation with Myton city council members, the students painted city hall and several houses, hauled junk out of an elderly woman's yard, and "groomed a park" during their two-day stay.[47] After "tasting Myton's unique culture," swimming, and eating dinner with citizens, the group reported that they learned two lessons: more community participation would make the townspeople feel ownership for the project, and the project should be geared to meet long-term needs.

They then took action to insure long-term involvement. They wrote a successful grant proposal to the Kellogg Foundation and hired a full-time rural projects coordinator. Myton, Oakley, Clarkston, and the Ute and Navajo reservations became project partnership sites. Over the next two years more than 300 students, faculty, staff, and alumni participated in projects that reached out to include these rural communities. "The work ranged from cutting wood and rounding up sheep for elderly Navajos to painting and providing ramps for wheelchair accessibility," recalled Rick Van De Graff, project coordinator. "Students also taught in schools, did CPR training, and built, painted, and stocked a small library." It was a particular triumph that this project reached across school boundaries to involve students and staff from Weber State University, Brigham Young University, Salt Lake

Community College, and "schools as far away as New York City and Los Angeles."[48]

In parallel activities they brought Ute and Navajo students to campus to see the university as a possibility.[49] Interest was so high that "when they posted their spring break trip to Navajo country this year [1992]," commented Irene Fisher, smiling, "seventy-five people signed up in three days.[50]

The rural projects were far from restricted to Native American concerns, however. Projects stretched from Moab to Tooele. By 1991 fifty-two student leaders were overseeing projects that interfaced with thirty-six community agencies.

By 1991 the center had connected with Project Prohimo which originated with biology professor David Warner from Palo Alto, California. He had tried to bring health care together with local people to administer it, but no one had the time to be trained, except for disabled people—and he saw no disabled person over the age of twenty. Warner decided to train the disabled and, in the process, made a wonderful discovery: While becoming health-care givers, the disabled became more self-sufficient, lived longer, and promoted health for others. By 1991 Warner's book, *Where There Is No Doctor,* was used in forty countries.[51]

Intrigued, a group of Bennion Center volunteers traveled to Ajoya, Mexico, to help construct a therapy building. The wheelchair-bound residents had already made bricks and laid them as high as they could reach. The volunteers raised the walls, returned to Utah to scrounge medical supplies, and, shortly after Christmas 1991, loaded three vehicles with old wheelchairs, braces, walkers, and other supplies and headed south. On the way a shocking rollover accident killed student leader Dan Wendelboe and injured three other students. One was hospitalized with a head injury.[52]

"On that trip we really learned that everyone can be a giver and everyone can be a receiver," Fisher said. "There we were, affluent Americans, taking down these supplies. With the accident, in a split second we became receivers. A pig farmer with his truck full of pigs was the first person to happen by. People did so much to help us."[53] Speaking at Wendelboe's funeral, Lowell praised the young man. "This is the way I'd like to die—in the harness," he said.[54]

Each Christmas Fisher presents Bennion Center student leaders with a personal copy of Lowell's book, *The Things That Matter Most.* "I wish he would present them personally," she lamented, "but he is so modest, he doesn't realize how significant it would be for the students."[55] She measured the impact Lowell had on others by the sheer numbers of people who came up to her after her talks to groups about the center and told her, "Lowell is my friend." She smiled, "He can't possibly be a close personal friend to that many people, but they see him that way. He has somehow touched them."[56]

Another touchstone experience that quickly passed around the office occurred when Dave Angulo innocently picked up the office phone during the summer of 1992. The elderly lady on the other end had grown frustrated trying to get the telephone number for a university department from the campus switchboard. "But I knew that any center that bore Lowell Bennion's name will help me," she said trustingly.[57]

Speaking to the student leaders at the Bennion Center in September 1991, Lowell praised their "concrete projects" like "trying to help kids succeed in school or teaching the illiterate to be literate, or the hungry to be fed." But he also encouraged them to meet the intangible needs for acceptance, productivity/creativity, self-esteem, and purposefulness in life. "When you are going to clean up a yard for a widow," he suggested, "you should be conscious of her basic psychological needs. Show her a lot of love and attention and accept her. Get her talking. Let her know that you have a high regard for her."[58]

The work of the student volunteers changed lives for people in the community, including those of the volunteers themselves. Bill Crim, president of the Associated Students of the Bennion Center in 1990-91, described how cold he became on the freeway after just five minutes of helping a woman jump-start her car. Then while serving lunch at the St. Vincent de Paul Center, he was overcome with grief and shame when he saw a little girl, who had been waiting outside in the lunch line with her father and brother, weep with pain as the heat brought feeling back to her cold-numbed hands. "Where is she [now]?" he wrote. "What, if anything, is protecting her from this freezing wind. . . . We cannot rest."[59]

Crim, a freshman in mechanical engineering, attended the inauguration of U.S. president George Bush as an intern to a Utah

Congressman. The opulence of the inauguration contrasted with "the deprivation on the streets" sent him home to change his major to political science. He answered an ad in the *Chronicle* to tutor homeless children. As a junior, he became project director working with the Salvation Army and St. Vincent de Paul's food for the homeless project. In February 1993 he began working full time for Utah Issues, Irene Fisher's old job, and was also master of ceremonies at a party of 300 celebrating the fifth anniversary of the Bennion Center.[60]

Leslie Warner, Associated Students of the Bennion Center president for 1992-93, developed new sensitivities when a Bennion Center summer fellowship took her to Boston and the Women's Lunch Place for homeless and poor women and their children. She was surprised and hurt that people were so frequently angry at her when she was only trying to help them, then realized: "People in situations requiring a service from others are always waiting, and they get tired of it. . . . I realized that many people didn't have the energy to wait any more." Rather than withdrawing in hurt or blaming the women, Leslie began thinking about ways to "remedy situations so people didn't have to wait so much."[61]

A 1991 survey showed that Bennion Center volunteers were almost evenly divided between men and women. Most said they would "likely" or "very likely" remain involved in community service after graduation. Most lived off campus. Majors ranged from biology to graduate economics to Spanish, from single students to a busy mother who still felt that community service was essential. Most of them had done more than one service project: Ouelessebougou projects, soup kitchen, subbing for Santa, youth mentoring, work on the Navajo reservation, or working on the spouse abuse shelter in Moab. A significant number had volunteered with other organizations as well—a week in Appalachia with the Overseas Development Center, three months in Ghana, building houses with a Christian group in Baja California, and working with the Peace Corps in Colombia.[62]

As administrators, Irene Fisher and her staff were determined to create a community of caring within the center for the students and staff. All major decisions, especially if they involved controversy, needed to be made by consensus not by majority rule. This commitment to the concept of "community" was tested during the 1990-91 school year.

After two years of delivering food to AIDS patients, the students decided they wanted to do more. They suggested education and prevention campaigns on campus. First, Aids Project director Bradley Weischedel and his small group of volunteers studied AIDS and its incidence on college campuses. Next they learned the consensus process from Quaker and other resources. "They all felt there was a problem and they shouldn't duck it, just because it was hard," commented Fisher.[63] Then they met with all of the Bennion Center student leaders, trying to reach agreement on the role the Bennion Center should play in AIDS education and prevention.

At first, Fisher said, groups split off and talked among themselves, reinforcing their own beliefs and opinions. Gradually they realized that no consensus could be reached until they talked to people who disagreed with them.[64] It became clear that distributing condoms on campus—even if accompanied by information listing such options as abstinence and monogamy—was a controversial point with some students. After a brainstorming process, the students decided that the center could educate on campus without distributing condoms randomly. "The process was absolutely powerful," Fisher said.[65] It forced students who cared about the Center and the issue of AIDS to listen to and acknowledge the importance of diverging views. It forced people to question their own views. And it showed the students that solving community problems by consensus requires hard work.

In 1993-94 the Befriend the Elderly Project placed sixty volunteers with individuals in their houses or nursing homes. The director, Christina Bailey, matched students who met once a week to visit and help with chores, sponsoring a Valentine Party in one of the nursing homes. Kevin Hammond, Monthly Elderly Project director, organized yardwork and house cleaning. The once-a-month Saturday project is now a weekly service in the spring and fall. Students also worked with the disabled and the homeless.[66]

The center continues to shoulder some big dreams while still possessing the breadth of spirit to match it. Emma Lou Thayne, in an evocative essay about the Bennion Center, wrote:

> To find the Bennion Center at the University of Utah is not easy. For

the newcomer, it is a circuitous route from the parking lot into the Union building, down steps to the bowling alley. Inquire at the candy bar. No one knows. Finally someone points. Through the cafeteria. Out the other end. A hallway. Turn a corner. In the distance, a sign "Bennion Community Services Center." And an arrow. Another door—two. Through the right one. To Irene Fisher. . . . She is smiling—of course. . . .

Late on a Wednesday, after 4, most cubicles are empty, three computers and a typewriter are still. . . . Gray, neutral, functional what's left. But the air is charged like the inside of a head about to explode with an idea.

The seven cell-like cubicles of the student leaders are radically different. One is "stacked with stacks, a mug, a candy wrapper, a phone half-hidden by papers, notes thumb-tacked to the walls." A second is "shipshape as a Franklin planner, names of volunteers printed on red rectangles, large, orderly on a wall across from neatly stacked red plastic trays on a desk to organize each organizer's assignments.

"Both do the job," Irene smiles. "Just differently."

A typical volunteer brochure of "Choices" from winter quarter 1992 offered thirty-two different projects, including the Campus AIDS project, "Decency Principles/Poverty Reduction," and Youth Monitoring. Each description ends with a time commitment: "2 to 3 hours one morning per week" or "must commit to an academic year, approximately 4 to 5 hours per week." When a volunteer expresses an interest in a project, his or her name goes into the project director's pigeon-hole with the promise of a phone call within three days.

Where is Lowell in this center that bears his name? There are visible signs of his presence. The office walls are decorated with a montage of photos of Lowell—as a boy, a missionary, a father, a teacher. On one wall is a sign-up list to drive Lowell on his weekly visits to elderly friends. It's a first-name list—"not Dr. Bennion, not Brother or Mister Bennion. Lowell."

But in the very air are the values Lowell shaped his life around. A "Good on Ya" panda holds a scroll in his stuffed arms. It is awarded by the staff to the member who embodies the nine values that they themselves felt represented the center: initiative, open and honest communication, idealism, integrity, humor and fun, commitment, creativity, plurality, and community. It's not a bad legacy.[67]

NOTES

1. Emma Lou Thayne, interviewed by Mary L. Bradford, 22 Oct. 1987.

2. Leonard J. Arrington, reading statement of Chase N. Peterson at the B. H. Roberts Society, 9 Oct. 1986; original audiotape in possession of Emma Lou Thayne, copy in Bradford's possession.

3. Richard Jacobsen, "Bennion Center Beginnings," *Reflections on the Lowell Bennion Community Service Center* (brochure), not paginated; photocopy of page proofs dated 15 Jan. 1993 in Bradford's possession.

4. Ibid.

5. Ibid. Attending the meeting were Normand Gibbons, Dean of Student Affairs and Service; Ramona Adams, Associate Dean of Student Affairs and Services; Jacque Morgan, President of the Associated Students of the University (ASUU); Brooks Amiot, ASUU Vice President; and L. Jackson Newell, Dean of Liberal Education.

6. Normand Gibbons, interviewed by Mary L. Bradford, 19 July 1988.

7. Anthony Morgan, interviewed by Mary L. Bradford, 10 Feb. 1988.

8. Jacobsen, "Bennion Center Beginnings," n.p.

9. Anthony Morgan, interviewed by Mary L. Bradford, 10 Feb. 1988.

10. Ibid.

11. Dennis Lythgoe, "Connections: U.'s Bennion Center Is a Fitting Tribute," *Deseret News*, 18 Aug. 1988, C-1.

12. Quoted in ibid.

13. "Mission Statement," Lowell Bennion Community Service Center, June 1987, copy in Bradford's possession.

14. "Mission Statement," *The First Five Years of Serving: 1987-1992: Reflections on the Lowell Bennion Community Service Center* (brochure), 15 Jan. 1993, n.p.; copy in Bradford's possession.

15. Patrick McCabe, "The Bennion Center's Early Years," *Five Years of Serving, 1987-1992*, n.p.

16. Anthony Morgan, interviewed by Mary L. Bradford, 10 Feb. 1988.

17. Normand Gibbons, interviewed by Mary L. Bradford, 19 July 1988.

18. *Meet Utah Issues: Seeking Permanent Solutions to Poverty in Utah*

(brochure), n.d., 1, in Bradford's possession.

19. Irene S. Fisher, interviewed by Mary L. Bradford, 13 July 1988.

20. Ibid.

21. Normand Gibbons, interviewed by Mary L. Bradford, 19 July 1988.

22. Irene Fisher, interviewed by Mary L. Bradford, 13 July 1988.

23. Lowell L. Bennion, "How to Motivate Volunteers," n.d., handwritten list in Bradford's possession.

24. Patrick McCabe, "The Bennion Center's Early Years," n.p.

25. Ibid.

26. Ibid.

27. Ibid.

28. Irene S. Fisher, interviewed by Mary L. Bradford, 13 July 1988.

29. Ibid.

30. Ibid.

31. McCabe, "The Bennion Center's Early Years," n.p.

32. Ibid.; Irene Fisher, interviewed by Mary L. Bradford, 13 July 1988.

33. McCabe, "The Bennion Center's Early Years," n.p.

34. Irene S. Fisher, interviewed by Mary L. Bradford, 19 Sept. 1990.

35. Anthony W. Morgan, interviewed by Mary L. Bradford, 10 Feb. 1988.

36. Irene Fisher, interviewed by Mary L. Bradford, 19 Sept. 1990.

37. Ibid.

38. Irene Fisher to Emma Lou Thayne, 14 Sept. 1992, photocopy in Bradford's possession.

39. "New U. Program Will Bring Service into Curriculum," *Deseret News*, 14-15 Jan. 1992, B-6.

40. *The First Five Years of Serving*, n.p.

41. "New U. Program Will Bring Service into Curriculum," B-6.

42. McCabe, "The Bennion Center's Early Years," n.p.

43. Irene Fisher, interviewed by Mary L. Bradford, 5 Feb. 1990.

44. Ibid.

45. McCabe, "The Bennion Center's Early Years," n.p.

46. *The Lowell Bennion Community Service Center Bulletin*, no. 2, autumn quarter 1989, 2.

47. Rick Van De Graff, "Experience in Rural Communities," *Reflections on the Lowell Bennion Community Service Center* (brochure); photocopy of page proofs dated 15 Jan. 1993 in Bradford's possession, n.p.

48. Ibid.

49. Irene Fisher, Interviewed by Mary L. Bradford, 11 Mar. 1992.

50. Ibid.

51. Ibid.

52. Ibid.

53. Ibid.

54. As quoted by Irene Fisher, ibid.

55. Ibid.

56. Ibid.

57. David Angulo, "Lowell's Influence," "The Bennion Center's Early Years," n.p.

58. Lowell L. Bennion, "Excerpts from Speech to Bennion Center Student Leaders," *The First Five Years of Serving*, n.p.

59. Bill Crim, "An Epiphany in the Cold," in *The First Five Years of Serving*, n.p.

60. Emma Lou Thayne, "Arrivals," 20 May 1993, 3-4, typescript in Bradford's possession.

61. Leslie Warner, "Summer Fellow," *The First Five Years of Serving*, n.p.

62. "Bennion Center Volunteer Questionnaire," cover letter by Irene Fisher and Mark C. Hampton, Oct. 1991; copy of survey and summary of selected responses in Bradford's possession.

63. Irene Fisher, interviewed by Mary L. Bradford, 11 Mar. 1992.

64. Ibid.

65. Ibid.

66. *Annual Report, Lowell Bennion Community Service Center, 1993-94*,

8, 101 Olpin Union, University of Utah, Salt Lake City, Utah. As of 1993 the Bennion Center's operating budget was about $300,000. The university contributed space, heat, light, and salary for one. The rest of the money comes from endowment interest, individual gifts, foundation and corporate contributions, and a major federal grant. The original endowment goal had been $1.25 million; but both needs and response had been so great, it stood at $2.5 million in 1993, with $1.5 million still needed. See Irene S. Fisher, "The Bennion Center's Financial History and Needs," *Reflections on the Lowell Bennion Community Service Center* (brochure), n.p.; photocopy of page proofs dated 15 Jan. 1993 in Bradford's possession.

67. Thayne, "Arrivals."

CHAPTER 16

THE TEACHER'S VOICE

(1978-92)

I'm not a literary man, but I believe in trying to teach fundamental ideas and principles in language that's understandable.

—LOWELL L. BENNION

Lowell's circle of influence expanded through his writing. He never described himself as anything more than a "weekend writer," but he had enjoyed the process ever since his student days. In critiquing Lowell's "robust" dissertation, sociologists Laurie DiPadova and Ralph Brower praised Lowell's "direct and readable style and integration of themes from disparate Weberian writings."[1] They also marveled at his ability to elucidate Weber's "formidable and forbidding style that was also written in a foreign language." The ability to move to the heart of an argument, rendering it accessible to the general reader, was Lowell's hallmark. Perhaps he had learned both process and style from his father. A 1938 letter from his father advised him:

> Don't fuss overmuch as you go about language and literary details. Get your first draft written as you have opportunity to write undisturbed for an hour or two, preferably two. Then when you have got your ideas on paper, revise and revise and seek editorial criticism. If at any time you have opportunity to indulge in writing but don't get the "spirit" or have constipation of ideas, take to reading or physical exercise and let further writing wait until your thought moves as fast as your fingers can put it down.[2]

The first phase of his significant writing for LDS readers began almost as soon as the institute doors opened at the University of Utah in 1935 when he wrote instructional manuals for youth and adults in church education, including Sunday school and MIA courses. Between 1935 and 1968 he wrote fourteen manuals, some of which were excerpted in later manuals and/or reprinted. Dozens of other lessons supplemented these, including a series of eight visiting teaching messages printed by the *Relief Society Magazine* for 1948; twelve teaching supplements for James E. Talmage's *Jesus the Christ* for adult Gospel Doctrine lessons in 1963-64; and twelve "teaching insights" published in *The Instructor* in 1967. During the early 1960s Lowell published an article in almost every issue of *The Improvement Era* and *The Instructor.* He wrote individual lessons included in other manuals and thoughtful articles in *The Improvement Era.* Some manuals were printed in hardback to sell in church bookstores.

Lowell's bibliography includes thirty books and study manuals and more than one hundred essays. He wrote competent works on philosophy, religious, social and personal ethics, sociology, scripture, history, practical living, education, world religions, and politics. Philip Barlow, in his study on *Mormons and the Bible,* analyzed Lowell's influence: "When the publicity surrounding his social action and the fact of his rarely paralleled leverage with four decades of college students are combined with the impact of his writing, it is doubtful that more than a handful of modern figures have wielded greater enduring influence on major sectors of Mormondom."[3]

Lowell's former student, Brigham Young University English professor Eugene England, in a perceptive introductory essay to his compilation of Lowell's writings, described Lowell's voice as "rather rough and homey, quite informal, and unself-conscious, even when delivering an eloquent talk to an LDS General Conference on preparing for happy marriage. He is completely fearless, almost old-fashioned, outspoken against unchastity, drugs, intellectual pride, materialism, and prejudice—and willing to be heard and published anywhere."[4]

Lowell's first book, *The Religion of the Latter-day Saints,* was a course for institutes first published in 1938 and reprinted in 1940, 1941, and 1965. It became a popular general discussion of LDS theology for anyone seeking a succinct explication of Mormon doctrine. Organized into sections on "Mormon Doctrine and Philosophy," "The Restored Church of Christ," and "Joseph Smith and the Restoration," the book closed with a "unit" called "Unfinished Business" in which he introduced an idea he would develop throughout his life and his career:

> Man all too frequently idealizes the past and daydreams about the future. Seldom does he live in the present—building on the past and for the future. . . . The only part of life man actually has under control is the present. True, the past is gone and in one sense unchangeable. Yet man is daily adding to the past. . . . Past events take on new significance as they become a part of the larger whole.[5]

He expanded concepts from this book in his 1955 Sunday school manual, *Introduction to the Gospel.* In addition to a brief description of the organization and history of the LDS church, he examined the LDS concepts of God, human nature, revelation, and salvation through Jesus Christ. The section on "Characteristics of the LDS Way of Life" described attitudes toward the body, the mind, marriage and family, government, economics, worship, and contained an analysis of Mormonism's place among other churches and religions.

It was easy to teach from this manual, but the manual also led to deeper analysis of church doctrines and personal faith. It allowed students and teachers alike to freely express and explore their faith. Though many works had been written about Mormonism, few had achieved such a simple yet strong structure. Reprinted in the 1960s, this centerpiece has been translated into several languages and still circulates briskly in used bookstores. Dale LeCheminant, a teacher at the Salt Lake City institute from 1962-93, learned that the publishers were going to shred stacks of *Introduction to the Gospel.* He drove to the warehouse and loaded his station wagon, thereafter awarding copies to his students at graduation.[6]

In 1956 Lowell wrote *Teachings of the Old Testament* as a Sunday school manual, also published in hardback by Deseret Book. In 1959 he organized his popular courses for college students into *Religion and the Pursuit of Truth,* also published by Deseret Book. This work related the "search for truth" to the provinces of knowledge, science, philosophy, art, everyday life, and religion, delineating their harmonies and dissonances for the thinking student. Reading it, students could retain their religious faith while studying their chosen fields.

During the decade after leaving the institute, Lowell heard that an unidentified church authority had placed his name on a list of writers banned from writing for official church magazines. Lowell had no idea where the ban originated, but he first heard of it when a staffer on a church magazine asked him to prepare an article and then shamefacedly informed him that it had been refused. An editor finally told him of the list.

Lowell tested the ban only once. In 1983 he spoke in a Salt Lake City ward on the same program with then-apostle Ezra Taft Benson. After Lowell's sermon on "grace," Benson commended him and said, "The church ought to read that. You write it up and send it to me." He did, only to receive word from Benson's secretary that it could not be published.[7]

In the late 1970s he decided to write the first of his "little books" about his lifelong beliefs, private musings, and meditations. He arranged its publication himself with Bookcraft. After that, Deseret Book Company and Bookcraft published his next seven books. Hard-backed but almost pocket-sized, they were easy to carry—in the hand and in the mind—and became steady sellers among LDS books during the 1980s and into the 1990s. A college-age sales clerk at Deseret Book store in Salt Lake City told the author recently, as she was purchasing two copies of *Legacies of Jesus,* "I love this book. It makes me feel good about myself."

Countless readers who never met Lowell personally have treasured his manuals, books, articles, and then his "little books" because they delineated a plan of action, a blueprint for living that seemed paradoxically noble but within the grasp of both "mainstream Mormons" and educated people of all faiths. His voice was plain, never "preachy," informal yet deepening his essential themes of a practical, ethical religion. Lowell's direct style avoided both academic language and esoteric arguments in favor of topics that repeated and expanded on themes that he had expounded his entire adult life. In his "little books," Lowell typically incorporated the classical principles of unity with an easy-to-remember format of naming and expounding on principles in sets of three or four. As in all his other writings, teaching, and speaking, he stressed the development of a single idea, with all supporting materials establishing that single point. He disliked the extreme use of the "proof-text" method of studying scripture one chapter or verse at a time, without context or larger plan.[8] Using an outline form, he adopted a style that was long on process, short on didactic answers. He often couched his conclusions with diffidence and introduced them with "in my opinion." Though informal, he was never slangy or blunt. His writing grew naturally from the same ground that nourished his speeches and courses. He used personal examples only to make a larger point, often with a quietly wry humor. While claiming, "I am not a theologian," he described his goal as:

> To deal with the fundamental issues in theology, as well as the ethical and moral aspects of the gospel. . . . In the institute years my goal was to make theology functional rather than abstract. And if any change has occurred since then, I think it's that I've laid greater stress on the ethical dimensions of religion. . . . I have tried to combine the basic Mormon faith in man and Christ and in God, stressing that as an underlying foundation, and then moving on to justice and mercy and the Beatitudes and Ten Commandments.

He summarized: "I've been interested in bringing Christian living together with Christian faith, not just taking either one alone. I think they reinforce each other and both are badly needed."[9]

According to Philip Barlow's definition of theology that goes beyond "a study of God and beliefs about God" by stressing an examination of how we might best live our lives in the light of the Judaeo-Christian tradition," it seems that Lowell *was* a theologian.[10] His writing reflected the Aristotelian concept that rhetoric moved people to action.[11] He did not aspire merely to sponsor good feelings. Rather he hoped to move readers to action in communities, churches, families, and individual lives. At best, his writings also moved readers to a deeper understanding of themselves. All of Lowell's works are strong on ethics, logic, and persuasion. They all grew out of confrontation and consultation with students and colleagues, family and friends, with great religious books as his on-going consolation. All his life he explicated the Old and New Testaments and the Mormon scriptures, read

Buddhist, Hindu, Islamic, and Taoist holy works, and often referred to his early mentors—Schweitzer, Goethe, Kant, and Weber. Intellectuals and scholars found his works authentic, as did the less educated church member looking for inspiration. He also made clear his respect for non-Christian thinkers and leaders.

A short essay called "The Weightier Matters," first published in *Sunstone* in 1978 and reprinted in 1988 in the BYU off-campus student newspaper, *Student Review*, is an example of Lowell at his persuasive best. Eugene England chose it for the first essay in his collection because "it is an excellent introduction to the values of his life and writing—and one of the very best essays written by anyone in our time."[12] It captured in "just a few paragraphs Lowell Bennion's central theme and the spirit of his central contribution to twentieth-century Mormonism."[13]

The essay set the stage by introducing the reader to a "little lady of seventy-five in a two-room shack." Heated by a coal range with a gaping hole, the house also has a hole in the ceiling and inoperative plumbing. Widowed with no family nearby, she lives on a monthly social security check of $173. Yet "less than a block away stands an LDS chapel where the faithful meet regularly to praise God, to take upon them the name of Jesus Christ, and to discuss the Lord's poor in priesthood quorums. A few miles to the east other Saints live in luxurious homes with many bedrooms and multiple bathrooms."

Lowell followed this vivid introduction with guilt-inducing statistics on the number in the Salt Lake Valley who are living well below the federal poverty level and asked, "How can these conditions exist in Zion?"[14] Reminding the reader that similar conditions were found in ancient Israel, he quoted the Old Testament prophet Amos who cried, "Woe to them that are at ease in Zion," and commented: "The greatest modern convenience is the ability to insulate against the poor—to assume either that there are no poor nearby or that some church or government program will take care of them."

Two other examples of the poor in the midst of Zion follow: one a well-educated widow who is not in need financially but is sitting in her comfortable home "nearly blind." Once a "voracious reader" she now "sits alone hour after hour in a dark room reviewing her life, trying to keep her mind from slipping." Friends and neighbors visit only occasionally. "Yet Latter-day Saint youths in the surrounding area have time for skiing, shows, concerts, television and other events." He lists the many activities available to youth, with practically no time allotted to service projects. "Our time and means are desperately needed, not only to build human relationships but also to save the health and lives of the poor in our midst." His conclusion quotes the wrath of Amos and the condemnation of Jesus: "Woe unto you, scribes and pharisees, hypocrites! for ye pay tithes of mint and anise and cumin, and have omitted the weightier matters of the law, judgment, mercy, and faith: these ought ye to have done, and not to leave the other undone."[15]

The concept for Lowell's "little books" gestated in the fall of 1976 when he was the concluding speaker at the annual Boston Stake Education Week, a two-day conclave that attracted about a thousand Latter-day Saints in New England. The audience was sprinkled with Lowell's former students, but most in attendance had never met him.

Lowell enjoyed this opportunity to distill his major values into a single speech, organizing around "life in two worlds:" the "objective" world of natural law, and the internal, subjective world. In the first, he said, "I don't feel very important. I have to adapt to nature and adjust to the laws and forces of nature. I don't have a lot of influence with my fellow man." In apposition to this world was a subjective realm of individual values, where each can carve a creative niche. In the first world we try to "get somewhere." In the second we try to "be someone." He then sketched a "pyramid of values" with footings of health and economic adequacy. "The economic side of life is as grammar to language." Health is based on "sane optimism." He encouraged people to sharpen their sensory awareness, describing his own song of gratitude to Mount Olympus, the beauty of his Teton ranch at sun-up, and the "lightning and thunder [that is] the thrill of being part of nature." He referred to "non-verbal communication" between husband and wife and the need to "touch, touch, touch."

The next step on the pyramid was human relationships. "In my work I have a lot to do with blacks, with Chicanos, with American Indians. I am on committees with them—Chinese, Japanese, Polynesians, common folks, poor folk, 'big shots.' I have dealings with all kinds of people." Such experiences had taught him to value "the quality of human relationships" as "the most important thing in life." He called for integrity and love in such relationships. "Don't love me so you will get to heaven." Such a motive discloses that "you love heaven" most. "Love me because I am a human being or because it is in your nature to love."

Near the top of the pyramid Lowell placed creativity. Since men and women are born in the image of a creator, they need to create. Motherhood, he said, is a great creative act. "I told my wife that one thing I envy her is that I can't bear a child. I wish I could. She said, 'I wish you could, too.'" Anyone, however, can "help another human being or spark his mind . . . to play a creative role."

Faith cemented the pyramid. "I believe Joseph Smith entered the sacred grove and found his God and built a very close and wonderful relationship with him." Latter-day Saints often feel they know *about* God through Joseph Smith, but to really *know* God, each must find "our own sacred grove." Lowell closed this sermon with a favorite paraphrase from Montague: "Religion is the faith that the things that matter most in life are not ultimately at the mercy of the things that matter least."[16]

From his seat on the stand, Dennis Lythgoe, chair of the event, noted the rapt expressions of the listeners, the hush in the air. Afterward people approached Lowell almost hesitantly, reverently. Former students agreed he had lost none of his vigor as teacher and speaker. Strangers felt drawn to him as if he had focused on them within the crowd. Seventeen years later Finnish immigrant Mimmu Sloan remembered how she felt both mesmerized and galvanized. "I was on the edge of my seat. He seemed to be speaking only to me. He changed my life." Lowell inspired her to search for the best way to serve in the community. She settled on work with mentally ill and abused women.[17]

So many requests for copies of the speech poured in that Lowell decided to print it in a pocket-sized book, in collaboration with a designer and an editor. The idea of self-publishing came to him after he learned he had been banned from the official church magazines.

Lowell titled the first "little book" that grew from the Boston speech, *The Things That Matter Most*. Keith Eddington designed it.

His son Ben and friend Emma Lou Thayne helped edit the text, and Thayne wrote the foreword. Describing Lowell's teaching style, she said he entered the classroom "head first, twinkling like a boy with adventure on his mind. . . . His face, handsome, ruddy with expectation, was always turned toward us, ahead of the stride that never seemed to keep up with the impulses that persuaded it." Lowell dedicated the book to Merle as "speller par excellence" and credited the Boston Saints for its motivation. He had discussed his reading of Montague's *Belief Unbound* with Sterling McMurrin who had studied with Montague in the 1940s. Montague had coined one of Lowell's favorite definitions of religion: "It's the faith that our highest human values have cosmic support, that we're not alone in our pursuit of truth, beauty, and goodness or integrity, love."[18]

Readers welcomed this gift from Lowell that could so easily be shared with others. Some were disappointed, however, that many of his warm, homely examples did not survive the speech's translation into print. At least one reviewer, Susan B. Taber, confessed herself bewildered and "disappoint[ed]" by the image of the pyramid: "Should not faith . . . be the basis of the pyramid? Are economic sufficiency and health necessary to our achievement of love, integrity, faith, or learning?"[19] She suggested the circle as a more appropriate image since Lowell's values supported and complemented one another.

Lowell's affection for his book was apparent: "Whenever I need pepping up, I get it out and re-read it," he commented in the 1990s.[20] Its warm reception encouraged him to write nine successors, published by Deseret Book Company and Canon Press during the next decade. Each explicated a religious theme from scriptural to social. The themes sometimes coincided with the topics being studied in LDS church courses, and many saw the books as supplemental manuals, especially adaptable since each short chapter developed only one idea.

The little books expanded on themes from manuals, articles, and speeches throughout his life: Jesus Christ as teacher and savior; the scriptures as guides to personal conduct; and personal essays on his deeply held beliefs. Each carried talismanic aphorisms that his students and other readers cherished: "I believe in a personal God—an intelligent, sentient person who is concerned with human beings, who is seeking to achieve his purposes in their lives. . . . I believe man is enough like God—created in his image—that he can know in some measure the character and will of God."[21] Lowell's search for wholeness permeates his writings. Analysis gives way to synthesis. Belief in God or in any other verity comes through total life experience, not through one visionary, show-stopping revelation, but through the daily search for truth and understanding.

Lowell's is a faith anyone could aspire to, a faith based on personal prayer and study, a reasoned and reasonable faith requiring that the mind be as much engaged as the emotions. Though he had himself been healed by the power of prayer, been "confirmed in some very important decisions of my life," and felt reassured by "what I believe to be the witness of the Holy Spirit," he noticed that since these experiences were apart from "customary human experience," they were subject to emotional misinterpretation. Declaring himself "not a mystic by nature" and therefore preoccupied with practical service and ethics, he affirmed,

> I have had experiences that enable me to treat the experience that mystics report of God with due respect and with the conclusion that they lie in the realm of possibility. . . . The basic values and principles that Jesus and the prophets taught are true, that is, that they give meaning and fulfillment to life. I have witnessed their fruits in the lives of my fellowmen. I have experienced in a modest way the fruits of gospel living. I also know from my own experience and by observing the consequences of violating the qualities of life Jesus taught. Jesus said, "Believe me for the very works' sake."[22]

In other words, Christ himself preached an action-oriented religion.

Unlike those whose faith in God is shaken by the actions of men and women, Lowell found that his contact with others only strengthened his faith: "I have known men and women and children whose brilliance of mind, fine qualities of integrity and love, or masterful creations of art are such that it is easier for me to believe they are from God, partakers of his nature, than it is to believe that they have their ultimate origins in impersonal forces. Man leads me to God even as the latter helps me to keep faith in man."[23] This God-centered humanism nourished the roots of his optimistic outlook on life.

Indeed, Lowell's mature faith was almost beyond threat. He declared that even without faith in God, the human values of freedom, integrity, love, and beauty would be worth following. And in such action was the profoundest source of his faith: "My sense of [God's] reality and of communion with him is strongest when I too—in my limited way—try to do justly, and to love mercy, and to walk humbly with [my] God (Micah 6:8)."[24] Lowell candidly noted that a major hindrance for devoted Christians is "the perception . . . that every line of the Bible except for mistranslation is divine." He thought it more important to uphold the character of God than the inerrancy of scripture and so rejected any interpretation of God as partial, unforgiving, hateful, or vengeful.[25]

Lowell returned to Micah as the basis for his 1988 essays, *Do Justly and Love Mercy: Moral Issues for Mormons.* After defining personal and social morality, he dealt succinctly with capitalism, women, wealth, sexuality, "the sanctity of Life"—abortion, capital punishment, war—personal and impersonal authority, the relation of religion to politics, and the meaning of "liberal." He dedicated the book to his father in a citation that might well be applied to himself: "To Milton Bennion, my father/Socratic teacher, ethical philosopher/Christian saint."

One of Lowell's touchstones was Albert Schweitzer's philosophy: "I cannot but have Reverence for all that is called life. I cannot avoid compassion for everything that is called life. That is the beginning and foundation of morality."[26] In Lowell's words,

> I am pleading for us to cultivate a basic reverence for life, to nurture a feeling about the sanctity of life which would include the animal kingdom, the unborn child, the criminal, and the men, women, and children of all nations. The ill, the hungry, the diseased, and the illiterate are also manifestations of God's great gift of life. Each individual, no matter what his or her circumstances, merits our reverence. People are the work and the glory of God—the most important things on earth. Our reverence for God is inseparably linked with a basic regard for the sacredness of life itself.[27]

Like Schweitzer, Lowell believed that "this idea of kindness toward humans and all creatures is now recognized as part of true civilization."[28] Lowell was opposed to hunting for sport, and he walked a sensible and sensitive path on abortion:

> Several medical situations justify abortion: to preserve the mother's life or health when the fetus is dead, or when the unborn child has such severe mental and/or physical handicaps that no meaningful life he or she will experience is possible. . . . No woman who is pregnant as the result of rape or incest should be required to deal with the psychological trauma of the pregnancy and birth in addition to the trauma of the rape or incest itself.

But "casual abortion," he believes, is "a serious wrong. . . . The creation of a longed-for human life is one of the great experiences of our existence."[29]

Lowell opposed capital punishment and war—though he stopped short of outright pacifism, regretfully accepting the need of nations to be ready to defend themselves.[30]

As to women's issues, Lowell admitted that "men have dominated recorded history" for reasons he did not fully understand. He guessed that women's childbearing duties and the generally superior physical strength of men have kept men from realizing the "profound satisfactions . . . of family life in favor of more public challenges and achievements."[31] Drawing on his experience in working with men and women over the years, he observed no differences in the quality of their contributions that he could ascribe to gender. While women and men are not "identical," they are "equal in their talents and potentiality in almost every field. . . . Women can do everything men can do and . . . men can do everything women can do allowing for the obvious differences in physical strength and in engendering, conceiving, giving birth to and nursing a baby."[32]

His reverence for the role of mothers in his own life kept him from endorsing a modernist feminism that he thought might demean motherhood, a role he considered close to divine. But his years at the institute had taught him that women had an equal need to excel at something besides their religious and physical roles. By founding Lambda Delta Sigma as a "co-ed" organization in a time when such groups were unheard of, he demonstrated his belief that a wholesome interaction between sexes encouraged full development of character. His habitual use of "man" to signify "humankind" did not, even unconsciously, communicate sexism. He espoused a whole-hearted political devotion to the ideals of equality in society because he trusted women and men to make wise choices. People might differ on the best methods for obtaining equality, but they should agree on the "rightness of the goal."

Reviewing Lowell's most recent little book, *The Legacies of Jesus*, Eugene England observed:

> This continues his series of little volumes of humane, sensible, eclectic thinking about Mormon scriptures and theology. . . . Bennion sees in Jesus Christ the supreme expression of his own Mormon Christian faith: an emissary from God sent to show us by example what God is like and to heal and move us to be god-like, that is, . . . to love and be loved, to be free and creative, to find joy. He finds the four basic teachings of Jesus to be humility, integrity, love, and faith, and those are for him the central Mormon values.

England continues: If "orthodoxy" means being

> focused on the great central ideas and values of a group then it seems to me that [Mormon orthodoxy] means being committed to the optimistic view of life, to faith in Christ and his Atonement as sufficient and powerful to save us from ignorance and sin, to a liberal concept of the nature of humans and of God and to a conservative moral life, based in reason and committed service. If so, then Lowell Bennion is still the most orthodox modern Mormon writer.[33]

Lowell's holistic philosophy could be published in a single volume, but he chose to convey his views one theme at a time. His habit of mind was to pick certain verities and look at them again in each decade. As a reviewer put it, "He has lived trying to dovetail the aspects of his life into a whole. No wonder, then, that each essay and sermon here seems to call up others."[34]

Lowell's decades as a teacher crystalize within the prism of his little books. He extracted the main theme, then allowed it to penetrate and radiate within the mind. His apt, almost spare illustrations awakened in the reader that which was already within. The books, like their author, are guides to self-knowledge. As England argues, Lowell created an essential Mormon methodology.

Like Goethe, Lowell formed his values early and articulated

them in simple, strong language that stood up to the wear and tear of life. His little books were not published to enhance his reputation but to complement his values and ideas. "Integrity and love complement each other," he said, "love presupposes integrity, and integrity needs love to guide its power and influence."[35]

Lowell's high-selling status was recognized by the company that published most of his little books. In January 1990 Deseret Book Company honored Lowell with a special award, carrying this citation, "The writings of few authors have such profound influence on their readers as those of Lowell L. Bennion, and Deseret Book is pleased to honor him this year for his numerous books published through the years."[36]

Reviewing Lowell's collected essays, critic Jerry Johnston captured Lowell's spare, direct style:

> In his essays and other non-fiction writings, Lowell L. Bennion has done what LDS novelists have been trying to do for decades. He sounds the universal themes in Mormonism that link the culture with the rest of society and humanity at large. . . . And though Bennion did make his major mark as a teacher in the Salt Lake Institute of Religion and later, as a humanitarian, it will likely be through these writings that he'll be remembered. . . . As an LDS writer, Bennion may not only be the conscience of his culture but also its "Great Communicator." His thinking is sophisticated, but his vocabulary would test out on a sixth-grade level—a fact that would probably please him. Bennion doesn't want you to read between the lines, he just wants you to read the lines.[37]

Lowell never lost the teacher's voice that he had developed so early. When he left the institute in 1962, he stepped into a larger world where his opinions and views were sought, where he was in heavy demand as an "itinerant preacher." His sermons were cherished, he was in demand at funerals, missionary farewells, civic gatherings, study and service groups, and high school commencements. Lowell accepted as many invitations as he could, managing a full schedule of workshops, debates, keynote speeches, and radio discussions. At the University of Utah's memorial service for John F. Kennedy in 1963, Lowell offered the benediction. His Christmas sermons were popular throughout Utah and beyond.

His belief that brotherly and sisterly love extended to all religions and to those without any organized church expressed itself in a conference called, "Two Days Abroad at Home: A Look at Diversity." In 1977 the Utah Endowment for the Humanities sponsored this conclave of 200 clergy, poets, politicians, playwrights, journalists, and futurists exploring how diversity could provide breadth and harmony. Lowell's view was that "persons without faith in God can have true values, respect for fellowman, love, integrity, freedom and creativity." He urged Utahns to "try to love and understand persons in poverty and those with other than white complexions."[38] The core of Mormonism, he affirmed, is "humanism in the context of faith. . . . All men are brothers, capable of eternal progression towards a life of increasing self-fulfillment. Our goal is to live in harmony with the moral laws of the universe, the greatest of which is brotherly love."[39]

In addition to his civil rights stand, he thought through the equally volatile and still unresolved issue of equality for women. In 1975, as the Equal Rights Amendment went before state legislatures for ratification, the Utah Senate favored passage with thirty-six yes votes. When the LDS *Church News* editorialized against the amendment, the yes votes dropped more than half. Prominent Mormons who had favored the Equal Rights Amendment suddenly fell silent or opposed it.

Irene Fisher, president of the League of Women Voters, was fairly new to Utah and not a Mormon. Her group decided that it would be wise "to get the most responsible Mormon possible . . . and Lowell's name came up repeatedly."[40] He agreed to speak at a press conference in the governor's conference room in the state capitol on January 22, 1975, in a meeting sponsored by the ERA Coalition of Utah and chaired by Fisher. In his statement, Fisher remembered, Lowell "didn't directly advocate the ERA" but gave a reasoned appeal for legislators to maintain their free agency and think for themselves. In the emotional turbulence surrounding this issue, Lowell's reminder of principle "was an eminently rational thing to do," she said.[41]

In this, as in every other issue, Lowell maintained a compassionate, people-centered stance. He could speak to people at all walks of life, to rank and file, "ordinary" people as well as highly educated "intellectuals." In fact, he avoided such terms as "ordinary" and "intellectual." He emphasized faith by study and experience; he shied away from speculation and fantasy, declining to elaborate the unknown in favor of "the things that matter most." What mattered most to Lowell was the service he could perform for others, whether aiding a student in her thinking, strengthening a seeker in his faith, or painting a widow's house.

NOTES

1. DiPadova and Brower, "A Piece of Lost History: Max Weber and Lowell Bennion," *American Sociologist* 23 (Fall 1922): 38.

2. Milton Bennion to Lowell L. Bennion, 18 Mar. 1938, photocopy in Bradford's possession.

3. Philip Barlow, *Mormons and the Bible* (New York: Oxford University Press, 1991).

4. Eugene England, "Introduction: The Achievement of Lowell L. Bennion," *The Best of Lowell L. Bennion, Selected Writings, 1928-88* (Salt Lake City: Deseret Book Co., 1988), xi.

5. Lowell L. Bennion, *The Religion of the Latter-day Saints* (Salt Lake City: Department of Education, LDS Church, 1940), 285.

6. Dale LeCheminant, interviewed by Mary L. Bradford, 3 Feb. 1988.

7. Lowell L. Bennion, Oral History, 178.

8. Philip Barlow to Mary L. Bradford, 2 Mar. 1992.

9. Lowell L. Bennion, Oral History, 142.

10. Philip L. Barlow, "Wanted: Mormon Theologians, No Pay, Great Benefits," *Sunstone*, Nov. 1993, 37. This article evaluates theological entries in the *Encyclopedia of Mormonism: The History, Scripture, Doctrine and Procedure of the Church of Jesus Christ of Latter-Day Saints* (New York: Macmillan Publishing Co., 1992), 4 vols.

11. See W. Ross Winterowd, *Rhetoric & Writing* (Boston: Allyn and Bacon, 1965), xi.

12. England, "Introduction," xxv.

13. Ibid., 3.

14. Lowell L. Bennion, "The Weightier Matters," in *The Best of Lowell L. Bennion*, 4.

15. Ibid., 5.

16. Lowell L. Bennion, "The Things That Matter Most," *The Best of Lowell L. Bennion,* 29-40. The quotation from William Pepperell Montague is paraphrased from *Belief Unbound* (New Haven, CT: Yale University Press, 1930), 123-24.

17. Mimmu Sloan, interviewed by Mary L. Bradford, 28 Mar. 1993.

18. Lowell L. Bennion, Oral History, 201.

19. Susan B. Taber, "The Things That Matter Most," *Sunstone Review* 1, no. 1.

20. Lowell L. Bennion, interviewed by Mary L. Bradford, 17 May 1990.

21. Lowell L. Bennion, *I Believe* (Salt Lake City: Deseret Book Co., 1983), 5.

22. Ibid., 8.

23. Ibid., 6.

24. Ibid.

25. Philip L. Barlow to Mary L. Bradford, 2 Mar. 1994.

26. Quoted on the dust jacket of *Reverence for Life: The Words of Albert Schweitzer,* comp. Harold E. Robles (San Francisco: Harper, 1993).

27. Lowell L. Bennion, *Do Justly and Love Mercy: Moral Issues for Mormons* (Centerville, UT: Canon Press, 1988), 67.

28. Robles, *Reverence for Life,* 1.

29. Lowell L. Bennion, *Do Justly and Love Mercy,* 63.

30. Ibid.

31. Ibid., 31.

32. Ibid., 32.

33. Eugene England, "Books for Mormons," *This People,* Spring 1991, 60.

34. Jerry Johnston, "Bennion Earned His Say—and Says It Eloquently," *Deseret News,* 22 Apr. 1990, E-4.

35. Lowell L. Bennion, *The Things That Matter Most,* 43.

36. Announcement with citation, Deseret Book Co., 18 Jan. 1990, copy in Bradford's possession.

37. Johnston, "Bennion Earned His Say—and Says It Eloquently."

38. "UEH Sponsors Conclave," *Salt Lake Tribune*, 1977, 2, 1, undated newspaper clipping in Bradford's possession.

39. Ibid.

40. Irene Fisher, interviewed by Linda Sillitoe, 13 July 1988, notes in Bradford's possession.

41. Ibid.

EPILOGUE

Lowell Bennion has the rare distinction of becoming a legend in his own time, a legend that has led to increasing awards and honors. His appreciation has always been tinged with embarrassment: "If you publicly give credit for good things done, it diminishes the act of kindness."[1] When pressed, however, he admitted that the resurrection of the Teton Boys Ranch and the founding of the Lowell Bennion Community Service Center gave him the greatest satisfaction. To see his goals, his ideals, and his creations extended through younger hands in both community and church settings was the true honor.

For Lowell's eighty-fifth birthday, the Bennion Center hosted a work party at the university under Irene Fisher and Eugene England. The morning of service included visits to five local widows who had their yards weeded, pruned, and cleaned. Lowell himself visited too, with the workers congregating at the Alumni House for lunch and speeches from Irene Fisher, Douglas D. Alder, Marion D. Hanks, and Laurie Newman DiPadova. Hanks honored Lowell as a teacher and leader: "As a leader, he taught many the way of appreciation, which is the element that may be missing in much of civilization, a leader who taught us understanding, and a way of action, of love."[2]

The year 1988 was a time of ending and beginning. Lowell lessened his hours at the Community Services Council and saw the Bennion Center at the University of Utah take wing. Moving through his seventies and eighties, Lowell enjoyed a remarkable synthesis among the various aspects of his life. When age and diminishing health compromised his effectiveness, he persisted with the determination and the energy of a much younger man.

Increasingly, he and Merle stood on the shore, bidding farewell to those departing for a next life whose existence they never doubted. Between 1988 and 1990 they lost six close relatives. Lowell's institute secretary and Merle's sister, Ethel C. Smith, died in a nursing home. At her funeral Lowell paid tribute to Ethel as Merle's earliest companion and the "memory of the institute." Next Lowell's oldest sister, Claire B. Jones, passed peacefully away in her ninety-first year after returning home from Relief Society. Only days later Leonard (Len) Folsom, Maurine's husband, also succumbed. Maurine followed her husband in the fall of 1991.

In October 1990 Merle and Lowell mourned the passing of Bill Moran and joined in a memorial service in his honor at Salt Lake City's Unitarian Church. During a time of open response Merle paid tribute to the "gentle man who was also a gentleman, . . . a friend in capital letters from beginning to end." Lowell pronounced the benediction: "Father, we pray that we will not mourn his passing as much as we rejoice in our association with him over the years."[3]

Honors accumulated around Lowell's head. In December 1989 Lowell and Merle flew to Washington, D.C., where he was declared one of the "Most Caring People in America" by the national Caring Institute. The impressive program at the Senate Office Building also honored such community benefactors as the founder of Habitat for Humanity, founders of fifty centers for Attitudinal Healing to support ill and disabled children and adults, and the first woman elected to the tribal council of the Navajo Nation.[4] Reacting to the award, Dick Winters rejoiced, "They threw away the mold after Lowell Bennion. He's one of a kind. Lowell's friends in Utah must be proud for him receiving this Caring Institute honor. Lowell is too humble and too selfless to be proud for himself."[5]

The Caring Institute was a foundation established in 1985 by former senator from Utah Frank Moss and two brothers from Price, Utah, Val and Bill Halamandaris. The Halamandaris brothers, professionals in home health care and hospice programs, were searching for ways to increase compassion for others. Following Schweitzer, they believe: "Example isn't the best way to teach. It's the only way." The awards honor "examples of the kinds of people we thought we should all try to be."[6]

In 1990 Bill Halamandaris published *Profiles in Caring* about America's most caring people. Lowell appeared in a chapter, "Saint on Earth," that emphasized Lowell's three basic values: "One is to love life and accept other people; the second is to be creative and productive; and the third is to have a feeling of worth."[7] In *Faces of Caring: A Search for the 100 Most Caring People in History*, published the following year by Val Halamandaris, Lowell's picture with a page on his life was included in the panoply that also honored Jesus Christ, Goethe, Gandhi, Schweitzer, and Einstein.[8]

Always uncomfortable in the public spotlight, Lowell relaxed and expanded contentedly in the private glow of his family circle. When he celebrated his eighty-third birthday in July 1991, it was with a family reunion—this time a three-pronged party for three generations that included a hike in the canyon for the able-bodied, a swimming party at Howard's pool, and a picnic at Wheeler Farm. It was a time for basking in successes—personal, shared, and vicarious. The family circle had been broken by death and divorce, but it had regrouped itself stoutly—all of the children and grandchildren successful in their own ways. Each had inherited the Bennion independent streak and love of the land, plus Merle's appreciation for beauty. It seemed to her they had grown closer as they grew older.

In a letter to Laurie DiPadova, Ben analyzed his family circle:

> The clearest sign of Lowell and Merle's individuality may lie in the utter diversity of their children. No two of them resemble each other, either physically or socially. We vary greatly in complexion, height and weight, and personality. The parents have produced a staunch Republican and a liberal Democrat. They have set high standards for us but have never compelled any of us to conform to their norms. . . . They themselves differ as much as their children, making me . . . wonder what drew and held them together. Dad, a product of Salt Lake, has always yearned for the country; Mom, an orphan from the country, has always clung to the city. Yet they have developed strong bonds of respect and affection.[9]

At summer commencement 1991 Brigham Young University awarded Lowell and Merle a joint honor: a presidential citation for service presented by President Rex E. Lee. Handsome portraits of them appeared in the program, with the warm tribute:

> The Bennions' writings and example, particularly their humane emphasis and integrity, continue to influence thousands. For instance, as students at BYU decided a few years ago to disband their student government and form in its place, BYUSA, an association completely devoted to service, one important influence was Lowell's writings and example. And through the Lowell Bennion Community Services Center, established in his honor at the University of Utah, over five hundred students give volunteer service each quarter. All over the world, former students, readers of Lowell's books and essays, and observers from all walks of life continue to be moved by the Bennions' example toward Christ-like quality and consistency in their own thinking and living. For the power of that example and in the hope it will long continue, Brigham Young University is pleased to present Lowell L. and Merle Colton Bennion with the Presidential Citation and Medallion.[10]

Their family table at the banquet that night, with all their children and their spouses represented, personified many of their happiest moments. At that point even the memory of that old wound, inflicted in 1962 when the doors of the institute closed behind Lowell, held no sting. Steve, whose appointment as president of Ricks College brought him into close contact with the general authorities, reported that he had asked "among the Brethren what the feeling was" about his father. He was told, "Never heard anything but good things," and "Your father did more in one day than some do in a lifetime" to help the poor.[11]

Another signal honor came in February 1992, as Utah state senator Scott Howell stood to introduce SCR10, a concurrent resolution of the legislature and the governor. A noisy undercurrent died out as Lowell slipped in and sat down on a bench in the front of the chamber. The senators, their staffs, and the audience in the gallery above focused on the modest figure as Howell pronounced the first of a series of rolling whereases—"WHEREAS Lowell L. Bennion's life reflects an uncommon depth of commitment to the ideal that lasting happiness is unattainable without learning to love to serve. . . . "[12]

Howell summarized Lowell's life. The "whereases" mentioned countless hours of personal service and a philosophy of life centered on love, integrity, and creativity. "I had the great pleasure of growing up near Dr. Bennion," said Howell, "and he had a significant impact on my life." He quoted Lowell, "We get pleasure from a good show or from a party or a ball game, but real happiness comes from what is inside us—our thoughts and our values, the basic human values of life." Howell described Lowell's influence on thousands of lives through teaching, counseling, and volunteer service. During all three careers he had organized and coordinated services for the needy. His twenty books and scores of articles attested to a life of the mind focused on action. His boys ranch in the Tetons carried on these same values, providing a place "where city boys could learn how to work."

> WHEREAS Lowell L. Bennion is one of the great examples of unselfish service and the fulfillment it can bring to those who serve, and his life sets a standard of giving to which all Utahns can aspire:
>
> NOW, THEREFORE, BE IT RESOLVED that the Legislature of the state of Utah, the governor concurring therein, honor Lowell L. Bennion for what his life teaches all Utahns about the difference one person's service can make in the lives of all of us and illustrates the joy his life exemplifies as he has given of himself to others.[13]

Five other senators eagerly took the floor. One had sat in Lowell's classes, another had served with him on task forces, a third had sent his son to Lowell's ranch. A fourth honored Lowell's humor, his love of the land, his humanity. They celebrated his marriage to Merle Colton Bennion with its six children, fifteen grandchildren, and three great-grandchildren.

As applause echoed through the chamber, Lowell characteristically sought to share the limelight: "I get credit for a lot of things other people do. Most of the things that have been mentioned I've done with colleagues, great colleagues. I do believe that the most important thing in the world is *people*—and we need to think of the things we do in terms of people."

Looking back on their lives, Merle and Lowell felt much gratitude and few regrets. Known for saintly sweetness, Merle was also spunky. Steve enjoyed telling about the time he asked her for advice on the selection of a mate. She replied, "Why don't you go ask your father? He did a better job than I did."[14]

Lowell's and Merle's health slowly failed. A hernia operation sent Merle to the hospital. Then in 1993 she developed congestive heart failure, requiring that she be connected to an oxygen machine at home.

Lowell gave no quarter to his Parkinson's disease as it slowly robbed him of strength and sureness. In June 1991, when he addressed institute student leaders at Utah State University, former CES colleague Ken Godfrey, area director of institutes, noticed the changes inflicted by the disease: "He had two scabs on the left side of his face caused by a recent fall. His right arm shook unless he rested it on the podium. His left arm could not be raised high, and he struggled to turn the pages of his talk. He is very thin, and he walks with a kind of stoop. He has large bags under his eyes, but he wears no glasses, has no hearing aid." However, Godfrey added, "His mind is still keen." Lowell's speech, "Life Is Meaningful to the Extent That It Has Purpose," had a "Christ-like charm and the students were captivated by his insights and eloquence."[15]

In 1985 an interviewer asked Lowell, "How do you view suffering—physical, mental, or emotional suffering? What's its purpose in life?" Lowell's answer reflected his sturdy practicality: "I haven't suffered that much, but I think there's more human suffering then we need in order to develop human values, to teach us the meaning and value of life, compassion for other people. . . . Some people are exposed to suffering beyond any possible value to them." Thanks to Mormon doctrine, "I don't have to blame God for all the human suffering that goes on in the world. I ascribe part of it to man's eternal free agency and part of it to the eternal nature of the elements and the laws of nature. So my idea is let's do everything we can to eliminate and minimize suffering, not just sit back and say it's for [our] good."[16]

Both Lowell and Merle were willing to face the inevitability of their own deaths. In a letter to another student following the death of her husband, Lowell wrote: "Socrates said that no harm could come to a good man in death. For either death is the best night's sleep a person may have, or he goes to a place where justice reigns, and you can talk with great people who have preceded you in death. Believe in the second alternative."[17]

Merle often awakened in the night, short of breath and with questions on her mind. "Is death painful? Will someone be there to welcome me on the other side? My parents, my grandparents, my daughter?"[18] But these occasions lessened until she was finally able to say, "I feel at peace now. I am ready for whatever comes. I have faith."[19]

A few days after their sixty-sixth anniversary, Merle's labored breathing sent her to bed. A few nights later, on September 23, 1994, she died quietly in her sleep with her family nearby.

Seven days later, on September 30, the East Millcreek Stake Center was filled to capacity as family and friends celebrated Merle's life. Howard Bennion opened the meeting with a heartfelt prayer; Steven Bennion spoke an eloquent biographical eulogy; Emma Lou Thayne spoke for Merle's many friends; and Lindsay Stone represented her grandchildren. Merle's favorite singers, Tom and Ellen Jeanne Pike, were accompanied by Merle's favorite pianist, daughter Ellen. Lynn Bennion's talented daughter, Rebecca B. Glade, also sang. Bishop David Poulsen represented the East Millcreek 12th Ward, and his wife, Adrienne Poulsen, pronounced the benediction. Merle's grave was dedicated by son Doug at Wasatch Lawn Memorial Park near the grave of little Laurel. It was announced that the Lowell Bennion Community Service Center at the University of Utah would honor Merle at a "Merle Bennion Service to the Elderly Day" on October 15, 1994.

In 1993, when a newspaper columnist asked him what he would choose as an epitaph for his own tombstone, Lowell answered with his favorite scripture: "What doth the Lord require of thee, but to do justly, and to love mercy, and to walk humbly with thy God?" (Micah 6:8)[20] Lowell's faith in an afterlife posited no elaborate schemes of a bureaucratic heaven. "I don't believe that heaven is just a glorified version of this life. I leave it open. I trust in God."[21]

NOTES

1. As quoted in Jan Thompson, "Humanitarian Faces Embarrassing Praise," *Deseret News,* 7 Dec. 1989, B-1.

2. Marion D. Hanks, quoted by Dennis L. Lythgoe, in "Praise for Bennion Comes Straight From the Heart," *Deseret News,* Thursday, 19 Aug. 1993.

3. Transcript of Bill Moran Memorial Service, Unitarian Church, Salt Lake City, 22 Oct. 1990, photocopy in Bradford's possession.

4. "Caring Awards Go to 'Best of the Best,'" *USA Today,* 7 Dec. 1989.

5. As quoted in Thompson, "Humanitarian Faces Embarrassing Praise," B-1.

6. "The Caring Award: A Hand for Those Who Give," *The Plain Truth,* Aug. 1993, 10.

7. Bill Halamandaris, *Profiles in Caring* (Washington D.C.: Caring Publishing, 1991), 29.

8. Val J. Halamandaris, ed. and comp., *Faces of Caring: A Search for the 100 Most Caring People in History* (Washington, D.C.: Caring Publishing, 1992), 89.

9. Lowell L. "Ben" Bennion to Laurie N. DiPadova, 28 Apr. 1986, photocopy in Bradford's possession.

10. "Presidential Citation," Summer Commencement Exercises, Brigham Young University, One Hundred and Sixteenth, Thursday, 15 Aug. 1991, 8, printed program in Bradford's possession.

11. Steve D. Bennion, interviewed by Mary L. Bradford, 26 Sept. 1990.

12. "Resolution Saluting Lowell L. Bennion," by Scott N. Howell, SCR No. 10, filed 23 Jan. 1992, 1.

13. Ibid.

14. Quoted in Lythgoe, "Bennion's Lifetime of Quiet Service," E-1.

15. Kenneth Godfrey to Mary L. Bradford, 31 Jan. 1991.

16. Lowell L. Bennion, Oral History, 211-12.

17. Lowell L. Bennion to Mary Lythgoe Bradford, 18 Dec. 1991.

18. Merle C. Bennion, Conversation with Mary L. Bradford, 15 May 1994.

19. Merle C. Bennion, Conversation with Mary L. Bradford, 4 June 1994.

20. Dennis L. Lythgoe, "Epitaphs," *Deseret News,* 1 Jan. 1993, C-1.

21. Lowell L. Bennion, conversation with Mary L. Bradford, 27 May 1990.

APPENDIX A

Lowell L. Bennion's Writings

Copies of most of the following items are housed in the archives of the Lowell Bennion Community Services Center, University of Utah.

1. "Diary." Handwritten letters and entries in leatherbound volume, LDS mission in Germany, 18 Oct. 1928-23 May 1931.
2. *Max Weber's Methodology.* Paris: Les Presses Modernes, 1933.
3. *What About Religion?* Salt Lake City: General Boards of the Mutual Improvement Association of the Church of Jesus Christ of Latter-day Saints, 1934.
4. "Supplement to the M Men-Gleaner Manual, chapters 4-6." *Improvement Era* 37 (Nov. 1934): 689.
5. "Religion and Life in the World." *Millennial Star* 100 (24 Feb. 1938): 114-16, 125.
6. "The Meaning of God." *Millennial Star* 100 (Mar. 1938): 165-66.
7. "How Can a Man Be Saved." *Millennial Star* 100 (21 Apr. 1938): 242-44.
8. "Whence Religion." *Millennial Star* 100 (23 June 1938): 386-88.
9. "How God Speaks to Man." *Millennial Star* 100 (13 Oct. 1938): 642-43.
10. Review of *Life of Christ* by Hall Caine. *Week-day Religious Education* 3 (June 1939): 27.
11. "Teaching Religion by Word of Mouth." *Week-day Religious Education* 3 (Dec. 1939): 7-10.
12. *Youth and Its Religion.* Salt Lake City: General Boards of the Mutual Improvement Association of the Church of Jesus Christ of Latter-day Saints, 1939.

13. *Contributions of Joseph Smith.* A series of radio talks, with William E. Berrett and T. Edgar Lyon. Salt Lake City: Deseret Book Co., 1940.

14. *The Religion of the Latter-day Saints: A College Course.* Salt Lake City: LDS Department of Education, 1939; rev. and enl., 1940; 2d ed., 1965.

15. *The Church of Jesus Christ.* Salt Lake City: Deseret Sunday School Union Board, 1941.

16. *Today and Tomorrow.* Salt Lake City: Church of Jesus Christ of Latter-day Saints, 1942.

17. "The Fruits of Religious Living in This Life." *Improvement Era* 44 (Apr. 1941): 208-209. Reprinted in 73 (Nov. 1970): 90-93.

18. Eight-part series of visiting teaching messages: "Christ's Example." *Relief Society Magazine* 32 (July 1945): 436; "Charity Suffereth Long and Is Kind," 32 (Aug. 1945): 502; "Charity Envieth Not," 32 (Sept. 1945): 570-71; "Charity Vaunteth Not Itself, Is Not Puffed Up," 32 (Oct. 1945): 628-29; "Charity Doth Not Behave Itself Unseemly," 32 (Nov. 1945): 699; "Charity Rejoiceth in the Truth," 32 (Dec. 1945): 771-72; "Charity Hopeth All Things, Charity Endureth All Things," 33 (Jan. 1946): 60-61; and "Charity Never Faileth," 33 (Feb. 1946): 132-33.

19. *Trail Builder Lessons.* Salt Lake City: Primary Association of the Church of Jesus Christ of Latter-day Saints, 1948.

20. "Joseph Smith—His Creative Role in Religion." Joseph Smith Memorial Lecture, 18 Dec. 1948.

21. *The Church of Jesus Christ in Ancient Times.* Salt Lake City: Deseret Sunday School Union Board, 1951.

22. *Goals for Living.* Salt Lake City: Church of Jesus Christ of Latter-day Saints, 1952, including other materials for lessons; pp. 227-456 in 1962 ed.

23. "Practical Mormonism." No. 11 in *BYU Speeches of the Year.* Provo, UT: Brigham Young University, 1953. Given 5 Nov. 1952.

24. *Teachings of the New Testament.* Salt Lake City: Deseret Sunday School Union Board, 1953. Reprinted in hardback, Deseret Book Co., 1956.

25. *An Introduction to the Gospel.* Salt Lake City: Deseret Sunday School Union Board, 1955. Reprinted 1964.

26. *An Introduction to the Gospel: Teacher's Supplement.* Salt Lake City: Deseret Sunday School Union Board, 1956.

27. "How Shall We Judge One Religion As 'Better than Another'?" Unpublished address, Humanities-Social Sciences Seminar, University of Utah, Salt Lake City, 7 Feb. 1956.

28. "But the Greatest of These. . . ." Baccalaureate address, University of Utah, 3 June 1956.
29. "Life Eternal." Theme Lesson for *M Men-Gleaner Manual, 1957-58.* Salt Lake City: Church of Jesus Christ of Latter-day Saints, 1957, 142-49.
30. "Toward a Happier Marriage." Address given at Priesthood Session, LDS General Conference, 5 Apr. 1958. Published in *One Hundred Twenty-eighth Annual Conference* (Salt Lake City: Church of Jesus Christ of Latter-day Saints, 1958), 83-87; *The Instructor* 93 (June 1958): 166-69.
31. "How Can We Increase Reverence?" *The Instructor* 93 (July 1958): 212-13.
32. *Introduction to the Book of Mormon and Its Teachings.* Provo, UT: LDS Department of Education, 1959.
33. *Religion and the Pursuit of Truth.* Salt Lake City: Deseret Book Co., 1959. Reprinted 1968.
34. *Developing Abilities and Skills in Leadership (As a Preparation for Missionary and Other Church Service).* Salt Lake City: Church of Jesus Christ of Latter-day Saints, 1959.
35. "What It Means to Be a Latter-day Saint." No. 15 in *BYU Speeches of the Year.* Provo, UT: BYU Extension Publications, 1964. Given 4 Feb. 1959.
36. "Pursue Truth in Sincerity and Love." No. 5 in *BYU Speeches of the Year.* Provo, UT: BYU Extension Publications, 1960. Given 14 Oct. 1959.
37. "Teacher Helps" for *Spiritual Values of the Old Testament,* by Roy A. Welker. Salt Lake City: Mutual Improvement Association General Boards, 1960. Three to five pages of outlined teacher aids by Bennion after each chapter, making up thirty lessons.
38. "In the Sweat of Thy Face." *Improvement Era* 63 (Aug. 1960): in the "Era of Youth" insert, 2-5.
39. *Six Fundamentals of Good Teaching and Leadership.* Salt Lake City: Mutual Improvement Association General Boards, 1961.
40. *Training for Church Service and Leadership.* Provo, UT: LDS Department of Education, 1962. Reprint of *Six Fundamentals* as instructor manual for teacher training.
41. "Cultivating Love in Marriage." In *Handbook for Young Marrieds, 1962-63.* Salt Lake City: Mutual Improvement Association of the Church of Jesus Christ of Latter-day Saints, 1962, 89-101.
42. "The Working Wife." In *Handbook for Young Marrieds, 1962-63.* Salt

Lake City: Mutual Improvement Associations, 102-11. Reprinted in *Young Marrieds Manual 1964-65.* Salt Lake City: Mutual Improvement Associations, 153-63.

43. "The Sabbath in the Home." In *Handbook for Young Marrieds, 1962-63.* Salt Lake City: Mutual Improvement Associations, 152-60.
44. "Thou Shalt Love . . . Thyself." *Improvement Era* 65 (Apr. 1962): 248-49; 277-80.
45. Baccalaureate address, Weber College, 27 May 1962.
46. "Where Is Goodness." *The Instructor* 97 (July 1962): 226-29, 250.
47. "Honesty—From Idea to Action." *The Instructor* 98 (Mar. 1963): 92-93.
48. "The Joy of Teaching." Address to Deseret Sunday School Union Conference, 7 Oct. 1962. Published in *The Instructor* 98 (Apr. 1963): 124-25.
49. "Morality." Unpublished keynote address for Religion in Life Week, Salt Lake City Institute of Religion, 23 Feb. 1962.
50. Twelve teaching supplements to accompany James Talmage, *Jesus the Christ,* text for Gospel Doctrine class of the Sunday School, 1963-64; published in *The Instructor:* "Our Study of *Jesus the Christ,*" "The Quality of One's Faith," "Greatness in the Kingdom of Heaven," and "A Controversial Figure" (97 [Nov. 1963]: 406-10); "The Light of the World," "And the Truth Shall Make You Free," "Blindness," and "Who Is My Neighbor?" (97 [Dec. 1963]: 436-39); "Versatility in Gospel Living" (98 [Jan. 1964]: 38-42); "The Parables of Jesus" (98 [Feb. 1964]: 80-83); "Slow to Learn" (98 [Mar. 1964]: 120-24); "Render unto Caesar . . . And unto God" (98 [Apr. 1964]: 164-67); "The Last Supper" (98 [May 1964]: 196-201); "Jesus before Pilate" (98 [June 1964]: 242-47); "Teachings of the Resurrected Christ" (98 [July 1964]: 285-87); "Christ on the Western Hemisphere" (98 [Aug. 1964]: 322-25); "In Search of Truth" (98 [Sept. 1964]: 368-71); and "Jesus the Christ to Return" (98 [Oct. 1964]: 408-11).
51. "What Is Man? (A Mormon View)." Unpublished address to an Interfaith meeting, Salt Lake City, 2 Dec. 1963.
52. *Teacher's Manual for Jesus the Christ by James Talmage.* Salt Lake City: Church of Jesus Christ of Latter-day Saints, 1964. With Chauncey D. Riddle. 176.
53. "The Liberal and Conservative View in Mormonism." Debate with Chauncey D. Riddle, Brigham Young University, 28 Mar. 1963. Audiotape and 23-page transcript.
54. "The Art of Casual Conversation." In *M Man-Gleaner Manual, 1964-*

65. Salt Lake City: Mutual Improvement Associations of the Church of Jesus Christ of Latter-day Saints, 1964, 121-26.

55. "Death and Life Hereafter." Address to Interfaith Dialogue, Salt Lake City, 19 Oct. 1964.

56. *Fundamentals of Leadership*. Salt Lake City: Mutual Improvement Association General Boards, 1965.

57. "Accepting Students." *The Instructor* 100 (Feb. 1965): 68-69.

58. Series on "Teaching Insights" called "Jesus, the Master Teacher": "Jesus Taught People," *The Instructor* 100 (May 1965): 194-95, 197; "Jesus Loved People," 100 (June 1965): 240-41; "Jesus Taught Principles, Not Rules," 100 (July 1965): 284-85; "Jesus Taught Positively," 100 (Aug. 1965): 326-27; "Jesus' Use of Words," 100 (Sept. 1965): 376-77; "Jesus' Use of Illustrations," 100 (Oct. 1965): 406-407; "Jesus—Master Artist in Proverb and Parable," 100 (Nov. 1965): 448-49; "Jesus Taught with Singleness of Purpose," 100 (Dec. 1965): 494-95; "Jesus Made Men Think," 101 (Jan. 1966): 26-27; "Jesus Kindled the Imagination," 101 (Feb. 1966): 66-67; "Jesus Taught for God, Not for Himself," 101 (Mar. 1966): 106-107; and "Jesus Lived What He Taught," 101 (Apr. 1966): 146-47.

59. "Religion and Social Responsibility." *The Instructor* 100 (Oct. 1965): 388-91.

60. "And Always Remember Him." *The Instructor* 101 (Oct. 1966): 382-83.

61. "For by Grace Are Ye Saved." *Dialogue: A Journal of Mormon Thought* 1 (Winter 1966): 100-104.

62. "There Is a Law." *Improvement Era* 70 (Jan. 1967): 6-10.

63. Twelve "Teaching Insights" published in *The Instructor* as a series running January 1967-February 1968: "The Outcome," 102 (Jan. 1967): 23; "Adapting the Gospel to Human Nature," 102 (Feb. 1967): 83; "The Glory of Man," 102 (Mar. 1967): 117; "Singleness of Purpose," 102 (Apr. 1967): 156; "Discipline," 102 (May 1967): 187; "Teaching: Giving or Quickening?" 102 (June 1967): 223; "How Does the Teacher Learn to Ask a Thought-provoking Question?" 102 (July 1967): 294; "I Don't Know," 102 (Aug. 1967): 307; "Inspiration," 102 (Sept. 1967): 370; "Relationships," 102 (Oct. 1967): 401; "Religion and Morality," 102 (Nov. 1967): 440, 443; and "Simplicity," 102 (Dec. 1967): 495.

64. "Forgive Thyself." *Improvement Era* 70 (Oct. 1967): 12-15.

65. "The Mormon Family in a Changing World." *Dialogue: A Journal of Mormon Thought* 2 (Autumn 1967): 41-42. (Guest editor's introduc-

tion to special issue on the Mormon family.)

66. "This-Worldly and Other-Worldly Sex: A Response." *Dialogue: A Journal of Mormon Thought* 2 (Autumn 1967): 106-108. A reply to "Three Philosophies of Sex, Plus One," by Carlfred Broderick.

67. "Teaching Ideas and Persons." Address delivered to the College of Family Living faculty, Brigham Young University, 19 Sept. 1967. Published in *Family Perspective* 4 (Fall 1969): 5-12.

68. *Scriptures of The Church of Jesus Christ of Latter-day Saints.* Salt Lake City: Deseret Sunday School Union Board, 1968.

69. Review of David Brewer's *The Mormons.* In *The Religious Situation: 1968.* Boston: Beacon Press, 1968, 547-54.

70. "Use the Scriptures." *The Instructor* 103 (Feb. 1968): 91.

71. "Seek Ye Wisdom." Address to priesthood session of LDS General Conference, 6 Apr. 1968. Published in *One Hundred Thirty-eighth Annual Conference* (Salt Lake City: Church of Jesus Christ of Latter-day Saints, 1968), 94-99; and *Improvement Era* 71 (June 1968): 90-94.

72. "Drugs: Their Use and Abuse." *Improvement Era* 71 (Oct. 1968): 18-22.

73. "The Place of the Liberal in Religion." Address at Salt Lake Institute of Religion, 28 Feb. 1969. Published as a pamphlet LDS Student Association.

74. "Seek Learning . . . by Study and by Faith." *Improvement Era* 72 (Apr. 1969): 5-7.

75. "Gracious Partners." *The Instructor* 104 (June 1969): 191."The Church and the Larger Society." *The Carpenter* 1 (Summer 1969): 64-72.

76. "My Memories of President David O. McKay." *Dialogue: A Journal of Mormon Thought* 4 (Winter 1969): 47-48.

77. "What Should Be the University Policy with Respect to Student Violence?" Panel presentation, Great Issues Forum, University of Utah, 25 Feb. 1970; audiotape, Special Collections, Marriott Library, University of Utah.

78. "The Gift of Repentance." *Dialogue: A Journal of Mormon Thought* 5 (Autumn 1970): 61-65.

79. "The Fruits of Religious Living in This Life." *Improvement Era* 73 (Nov. 1970): 90-93. Reprinted from 44 (Apr. 1941): 208-209.

80. "A Black Mormon Perspective." Review of *It's You and Me, Lord!* by Alan Gerald Cherry. *Dialogue: A Journal of Mormon Thought* 5 (Winter 1970): 93-94.

81. "Question and Answer." *New Era* 1 (Jan. 1971): 11. Answer to "How can I develop enthusiasm to magnify my present church calling when I'm honestly not all that excited about it?"

82. "Religion and the Social-political Order." Address at Tucson Institute of Religion, 17 Mar. 1971. First in annual Henry Eyring Speaker Series.

83. "Prejudice." Unpublished essay, spring 1978.

84. "Faith and Reason: Carrying Water on Both Shoulders." *Dialogue: A Journal of Mormon Thought* 6 (Spring 1971): 110-12.

85. "Faith and Reason: The Logic of the Gospel." *Dialogue: A Journal of Mormon Thought* 6 (Autumn 1971): 160-62.

86. "Situation Ethics." Unpublished essay, 7 Nov. 1971.

87. *Husband and Wife.* Salt Lake City: Deseret Book Co., 1972, reprinted in 1976.

88. *Looking Towards Marriage.* Salt Lake City: Deseret Book Co., 1972.

89. *On Being a College Student.* Salt Lake City: Deseret Book Co., 1972.

90. "Learning by Study and Faith." *M Men-Gleaner Manual.* Salt Lake City: Church of Jesus Christ of Latter-day Saints, 1972, 56-61.

91. "Question and Answer." *New Era* 2 (Feb. 1972): 34-35. Answer to "What does 'Love thy Neighbor' mean?"

92. "Overcoming Our Mistakes." Devotional Address at Salt Lake Institute, 14 Apr. 1972. Published in *New Era* 2 (Nov. 1972): 12-16.

93. "Faith and Reason: Religion and Morality." *Dialogue: A Journal of Mormon Thought* 7 (Summer 1972): 90-93.

94. "I Dare You to Believe—in Jesus Christ." Devotional address, Salt Lake Institute of Religion, 20 Apr. 1973. Published as a booklet by the LDS Student Association.

95. "The Uses of the Mind in Religion." An Address at Phi Kappa Phi Honors Banquet, Brigham Young University, 12 Apr. 1973. Published in *Brigham Young University Studies* 14 (Autumn 1973): 47-58.

96. "Three Loyalties in Religion." *Dialogue: A Journal of Mormon Thought* 9 (Spring 1974): 62-65.

97. "Question and Answer." *New Era* 4 (July 1974): 11. Answer to the question, "I think I have a strong inferiority complex. If I wait long enough, will it go away?"

98. Address, Governor's Prayer Breakfast, 21 Apr. 1976.

99. "Latter-day Saints as a Subculture: Our Survival and Impact upon the American Culture." Panel presentation, convention of the Association of Mormon Counselors and Psychotherapists, Salt Lake City.

Published in *AMCAP Journal*, Fall 1976, 22-24.

100. *The Things that Matter Most.* Salt Lake City: Bookcraft, 1978.
101. "The Weightier Matters." *Sunstone* 3 (Jan.-Feb. 1978): 28-98. Reprinted in Brigham Young University student off-campus newspaper, *Student Review,* 23 Feb. 1988, S2.
102. "Reflections on T. Edgar Lyon: A Tribute at His Funeral." *Dialogue: A Journal of Mormon Thought* 11 (Winter 1978): 12-13.
103. "A Response." Reply to "Priesthood and Philosophy," by E. E. Ericksen, an address reprinted from 1948. *Sunstone* 4 (July-Aug. 1979): 13.
104. "Challenges in Change," Address to the BYU Women's Conference, 10 Feb. 1979.
105. "A Response." Reply to "Knowing, Doing and Being: Vital Dimensions in the Mormon Religious Experience," by Arthur R. Bassett. Paper presented at the Sunstone Theological Symposium, Aug. 1979. Published in *Sunstone* 4 (Dec. 1979): 68.
106. "Jesus and the Prophets." *Dialogue: A Journal of Mormon Thought* 12 (Winter 1979): 96.
107. *Jesus the Master Teacher.* Salt Lake City: Deseret Book Co., 1980.
108. "The Hebrew Prophets." *Sunstone* 5 (July-Aug. 1980): 41-42.
109. "A Response." Reply to "The Mormon Christianizing of the Old Testament," by Melodie Moench Charles. Paper presented at the Sunstone Theological Symposium, Aug. 1980. *Sunstone* 5 (Nov.-Dec. 1980): 40.
110. *Understanding the Scriptures.* Salt Lake City: Deseret Book Co., 1981.
111. "So—You're Going To Get Married." Pamphlet. White House Conference on Children and Youth, Dec. 1981.
112. "From the 'Golden Days' of My Youth." In *Turning Points.* Salt Lake City: Bookcraft, 1981, 37-40.
113. *The Essence of Love.* Salt Lake City: Bookcraft, 1982.
114. "My Odyssey with Sociology." Address, Utah Sociological Association, Weber State University, 5 Nov. 1982.
115. *I Believe.* Salt Lake City: Deseret Book Co., 1983.
116. "Thoughts for the Best, the Worst of Times." *Dialogue: A Journal of Mormon Thought* 15 (Autumn 1983): 101-104.
117. *The Book of Mormon, A Guide to Christian Living.* Salt Lake City: Deseret Book Co., 1985.
118. "Reflections on the Restoration." *Dialogue: A Journal of Mormon Thought* 18 (Autumn 1985): 160-67.

119. "Learning to Live with Yourself," Devotional address, Salt Lake Institute of Religion, 4 Jan. 1985.
120. "To Serve, Then Teach," *Dialogue: A Journal of Mormon Thought* 19 (Fall 1986): 51.
121. "Faith and Reason: Three Essays." In *Dialogue: Personal Voices: A Celebration of Dialogue,* ed. Mary L. Bradford, 95-110. Salt Lake City: Signature Books, 1987.
122. "What It Means To Be a Christian." Address given at Washington, D.C., Sunstone Symposium, June 1987. Published in *Sunstone* 11 (July 1987): 5-7.
123. "Caring: Share Yourself This Holiday Season." *This People* 8 (Holiday 1987): 18.
124. *The Unknown Testament.* Salt Lake City: Deseret Book Co., 1988.
125. *Do Justly and Love Mercy: Moral Issues for Mormons.* Centerville, UT: Canon Press, 1988.
126. *Legacies of Jesus.* Salt Lake City: Deseret Book Co., 1990.
127. "Faith and Knowledge," *Sunstone,* Dec. 1991, 15-18.
128. Untitled and unpublished statement, protest rally against the death penalty, 23 July 1991.

129-30. Two compilations of essays, as yet untitled, will be published by Apen Books in 1996.

APPENDIX B

HONORS

I. Membership on Community Boards

1. The Salt Lake County Hospital Advisory Board (1954-59)
2. Utah Association for Mental Health Board and President (1950-55)
3. Member, Advisory Council of Salt Lake Community Mental Health Services (1962-72)
4. Chair, Conciliation Committee, subcommittee of Governor's Civil Rights Commission (summer of 1965).
5. Member, Crossroads Urban Center Board (1970s)
6. Shriners Hospital Volunteer Board (1970-75)
7. Board of Editors, "Common Carrier," *Salt Lake Tribune* (ca. 1970-71)
8. Founding member, Salt Lake County Commission on Youth Education (1970s and 1980s)
9. Utah Power and Light Advisory Council (1972-75)
10. Utah Housing Coalition (1972-74)
11. Member, Norman Anderson Foundation Board (1978-89)
12. Member, Steering Committee on State Division on Aging (1979-88)
13. Member of the Board, Salt Lake County Association for Retarded Citizens (1979)
14. Chairman, Salt Lake County Youth Shelter board
15. Member, Utah State Board of Family Services (1979)
16. Department of Education Advisory Council, University of Utah (1979-88)
17. Chairman, first interagency Homeless Committee (1983)
18. School of Social Work Advisory Council, University of Utah (1985-90)

II. *Awards*

1. Master M-Man Award, awarded by the Young Men's Mutual Improvement Association of the LDS church (1952-53)
2. Honorary Life Member Award, Utah Parent Teacher Association (Oct. 1962)
3. Distinguished Alumnus of the University of Utah (Feb. 1972)
4. The Distinguished Service to Humanity Award, Association of Mormon Counselors and Psychologists (1981)
5. Honorary doctorate, University of Utah (1982)
6. Award, American Society of Public Administration (1983)
7. The Good Samaritan Award, Utahns Against Hunger (1985)
8. "The Triumph of the Spirit," An Evening Honoring Lowell Bennion, B. H. Roberts Society (Oct. 1986)
9. Book of Golden Deeds Award, National Exchange Club (1986)
10. Establishment of the Lowell L. Bennion Essay in Christian Living Award, editors of *Dialogue: A Journal of Mormon Thought* (Oct. 1986)
11. Beehive Hall of Fame (Jan. 1987)
12. Lowell Bennion Community Service Center, University of Utah (Nov. 1987)
13. Richard D. Bass Award for Distinguished Service by a Utahn in the Humanities (Apr. 1988)
14. Committee on Aging, LDS Social Services (1988-present)
15. Outstanding Citizen of the Decade Award, Salt Lake County Commissioners (Feb. 1989)
16. Good Samaritan Award, Collegium Aesculapium (Association of LDS Physicians) (Mar. 1989)
17. Freedom's Foundation at Valley Forge Award for American Heros (Feb. 1989)
18. Retirement picnic, Wheeler Farm, sponsored by Community Services Council (16 June 1989)
19. Honored as One of Hundred "Most Caring People in America," by the Caring Institute, Washington, D.C. (Dec. 1989)
20. Deseret Book Service Award (18 Jan. 1990)
21. Presidential Citation and Medallion for Service, awarded jointly to Lowell and Merle Bennion, Brigham Young University (15 Aug. 1991)
22. Concurrent Resolution of the Legislature and the Governor Honoring Lowell L. Bennion for His Life of Devotion to the Values of Service,

Love, and Self Worth and the Powerful Influence His Life and Example Have Had on the Communities of Utah and the Citizens of the State, SCR No. 10 (Feb. 1992)

23. Cited in Val Halamandaris, ed., *Faces of Caring: A Search for the 100 Most Caring People in History* (Washington, D.C.: Caring Institute, 1992).
24. Citation of Merit, Salt Lake Rotary Club (23 June 1992)
25. "Lowell Bennion: A Life Worthwhile," television documentary, written and produced by Louise Degn; narrated by Bruce Lindsay; KSL-TV (2 Sept. 1992)
26. "A Morning of Service to Elderly People," service project honoring Lowell Bennion's eighty-fifth birthday, sponsored by Friends of Lowell Bennion, Lowell Bennion Community Service Center, and the Community Services Council (7 Aug. 1993)
27. Dedication of the Lowell and Merle Bennion Community Services Building, 24 Jan. 1995, at 1025 South 700 West, Salt Lake City, Utah. See "Groups Christen New Food Bank, Honor Volunteer," by Nancy Hobbs, *Salt Lake Tribune,* 25 Jan. 1995, B-2.

APPENDIX C

INTERVIEWS

Unless otherwise indicated, the following interviews and oral histories regarding Lowell L. Bennion and Merle C. Bennion were conducted by Mary L. Bradford and recorded on audio cassette tapes (transcriptions are indicated). They are listed in alphabetical order according to the last name of the interviewee.

1. Adams, Romona. 12 Feb. 1989, Salt Lake City (transcription).
2. Anderson, Lavina Fielding. Interviewed by Linda Sillitoe.
3. Archuletta, Archie. Interviewed by Linda Sillitoe, 22 Aug. 1988.
4. Arrington, Leonard. 23 May 1988, Salt Lake City (transcription).
5. Bennion, Douglas Colton. 19 May 1989, Salt Lake City.
6. [Stone] Bennion, Ellen Jean. 22 May 1989, Salt Lake City (transcription).
7. Bennion, Howard Wayne. 15 Feb. 1988, Salt Lake City (transcription).
8. Bennion, Lowell Colton "Ben" and Sherry Cox Bennion. 7 May 1988, 4 sides, Salt Lake City (transcription).
9. Bennion, Lowell L. 29 Sept. 1985, taped speech at funeral of Leo Lythgoe.
10. ____________. Interviewed by Robert Miller.
11. ____________. Interviewed by Fred Buchanan.
12. Bennion, Lowell L. and Merle. 13 Feb. 1988, Salt Lake City (transcription).
13. ____________. 9 Aug. 1988, Salt Lake City (transcription).
14. ____________. 10 Aug. 1988, Salt Lake City (transcription).
15. ____________. 19 Sept. 1989, 4 sides, Salt Lake City (transcription).
16. ____________. 25 Jan. 1990, Salt Lake City (transcription).

17. ____________. 2 Feb. 1990, Salt Lake City.
18. ____________. 17 Sept. 1990, Salt Lake City (transcription).
19. ____________. 22 Sept. 1990, Salt Lake City.
20. ____________. "Ranch, Arizona, Scrapbooks," 22 Sept. 1990, Salt Lake City.
21. ____________. 20 June 1991, Salt Lake City.
22. ____________. 21 June 1991, Salt Lake City (transcription).
23. Bennion, Merle. May 1987, 4 sides, Salt Lake City (transcription).
24. ____________. 2 Feb. 1988, Salt Lake City (transcription).
25. ____________. 3 May 1988, Salt Lake City (transcription).
26. Bennion, Mrs. Milton and her sister Mrs. Edwin Bennion, in Utah State Historical Society, Salt Lake City; interviewed by Desla Bennion.
27. Bennion, M. Lynn and Kathryn Snow. 14 Oct. 1987 (transcription).
28. Bennion, Steven Don. 30 Nov. 1988, Arlington, Virginia (transcription).
29. ____________. 26 Sept. 1990, Salt Lake City (transcription).
30. Bennion, Vaughn Lindsay. 9 Feb. 1988, Salt Lake City.
31. Bennion, Grant Madison and Marjoris Ralph. 14 May 1989.
32. Bennion, Ione. 12 Oct. 1988, interviewed by Alice Smith.
33. Bennion, John and Sylvia. 11 Feb. 1988, Salt Lake City.
34. Berrett, William E. 5 May 1987 (transcription).
35. Boyd, George T. 4 Feb. 1988 (transcription).
36. Boyd, George with David Whitaker, 14 Mar. 1989, Brigham Young University, Provo, Utah.
37. Bradford, M. Clive. 16 Feb. 1990.
38. Bradford, Stephen L. 15 May 1988, Pasadena, California.
39. Bradshaw, Afton Bradford. 16 Feb. 1990.
40. Bridgeforth, Ruffin. Interviewed by Linda Sillitoe, 6 Sept. 1988.
41. "Brother B. and Sister Smith." Interviewed by mail with Darline Anderson, 19 Sept. 1988, Los Angeles.
42. Buchanan, Frederick J. 9 Feb. 1988, Salt Lake City.
43. Canning, Ray. 14 July 1988, Salt Lake City (transcription).
44. Cannon, Angus S. 6 July 1988, Provo, Utah (transcription).
45. Cannon, Paul B. 14 July 1988, Salt Lake City.
46. Cardon, Bartley. Interviewed by Gigi Doty, Dec. 1990, Tuscon, Arizona.
47. Cassity, Yvonne. 1990, interviewed by Marie Jones, Alaska.

48. Chamberlain, Burt. 20 Apr. 1991, interviewed by mail.
49. Clayton, James L. 18 July 1988, Salt Lake City.
50. Colton, Eleanor Ricks. 24 Aug. 1989, Bethesda, Maryland.
51. Colton, Hugh. 7 Mar. 1987, interviewed by Eleanor R. Colton.
52. Cutler, Garr. 30 June 1990, Eugene, Oregon.
53. DiPadova, Annie Laurie Newman. 12 Nov. 1990 (transcription).
54. Dunn, Paul. 22 Mar. 1989, Salt Lake City (transcription).
55. Erickson, Louise Livingston and Ed. 23 Aug. 1988, Provo, Utah.
56. Fisher, Irene. 13 July 1988, Salt Lake City; interviewed by Linda Sillitoe.
57. ____________. 19 Sept. 1990, Salt Lake City (transcription).
58. Fletcher, James C. 15 Mar. 1991, McLean, Virginia (transcription).
59. Folsom, Maurine Bennion and Leonard. 13 Oct. 1987, Salt Lake City (transcription).
60. Frobes, Virginia. Interviewed by Linda Sillitoe, 19 Sept. 1988.
61. Gibbons, Normand. 19 July 1988, Salt Lake City (transcription).
62. Godfrey, Kenneth. Spring 1987, Logan, Utah.
63. Gray, Darius. Interveiwed by Linda Sillitoe, 1 Feb. 1991.
64. Haglund, Elizabeth. 3 Feb. 1990, Salt Lake City (transcription).
65. Hancock, Eva. Interviewed by Linda Sillitoe, 15 Sept. 1988.
66. Hanks, Marion D. 22 Mar. 1989, Salt Lake City (transcription).
67. Hinckley, Marjorie Pay. 19 July 1988, Salt Lake City (transcription).
68. Handley, George. No date, Berkeley, California.
69. Henry, Alberta. Interviewed by Linda Sillitoe, 6 Sept. 1988.
70. Jarvis, Pat and Boyer. 15 July 1988, Salt Lake City (transcription).
71. Johnson, Charles. 19 Sept. 1990 (transcription).
72. Jones, Claire Bennion. 14 July 1988, Salt Lake City
73. Jones, Rheim. No date, tape recording.
74. Keefer, Theodore (Ted). 21 Dec. 1988, Salt Lake City; interviewed by Linda Sillitoe (notes only).
75. Kenney, Don. No date, phone interview, Springfield, Virginia (notes only).
76. Kimball, Edward and Bea. 10 May 1988, Provo, Utah (transcription).
77. Landa, Esther. Interviewed by Linda Sillitoe, 22 Oct. 1988.
78. Landsdowne, Carole. 29 May 1988, Arlington, Virginia (transcription).
79. Lecheminant, Dale. 3 Feb. 1988, Salt Lake City (transcription).

80. Leonard, Florence. Interviewed by Linda Sillitoe, 20 Dec. 1988; and by Mary L. Bradford, 8 Oct. 1989 (notes and transcript in Bradford's possession).
81. Lindsay, Richard N. 13 July 1988 (transcription).
82. Littke, George. 25 Feb. 1988, Pasadena, California.
83. Lyon, James F. 10 Mar. 1989, San Diego.
84. Lyon, Joseph Lynn. 26 Sept. 1990, Salt Lake City (transcription).
85. Lyon, Lawrence and Conna Reeder, 14 June 1990, Monmouth, Oregon (transcription).
86. Lyon, Theodore E., Jr. (Ted) and Cheryl, interviewing Lowell L. Bennion and Merle (transcription).
87. Lyon, Theodore E. (Ted). 6 May 1988, Logan, Utah (transcription).
88. Lythgoe, Dennis L. 16 Apr. 1989, Arlington, Virginia; 27 Sept. 1989, Salt Lake City.
89. Lythgoe, Thomas M. 27 Sept. 1989, Salt Lake City.
90. MacArthur, Mary Ellen. 25 Feb. 1988, Pasadena, California.
91. Mauss, Armand. 17 Apr. 1989.
92. Maxwell, Neal A. 26 Sept. 1989, Salt Lake City (transcription).
93. McKeen, Eileen Bennion. 23 Aug. 1988, Salt Lake City; provided books on Bennion family history.
94. McMurrin, Sterling M. 9 Feb. 1988, Salt Lake City.
95. Meheles, Persis. Interviewed by Linda Sillitoe, 16, 19 Sept. 1988.
96. Moench, Mavonne and Louis. 13 Feb. 1988, Salt Lake City (transcription).
97. Moran, William and Olive B. 10 May 1989 (transcription).
98. Moran, William. Aug. 1990.
99. Moran, William. Diary segments relating to Lowell L. Bennion from 1935-40, spoken into tape by Mary L. Bradford
100. Morgan, Frances Bennion and Elmo. 22 May 1989, Walnut Creek, California (notes only).
101. Morgan, Anthony. 10 Feb. 1988, Salt Lake City (transcription).
102. Murdock, Kent. 8 May 1988, Salt Lake City (transcription).
103. Nebeker, Lora Bennion. 22 Mar. 1989, Salt Lake City.
104. Parkinson, Preston. 19 Sept. 1989, Salt Lake City.
105. Payne, Albert. 12 May 1987, Provo, Utah (transcription).
106. Pike, Thomas. 9 May 1987 (transcription).
107. Pingree, Timothy. "Memories of the Boys Ranch," 16 Sept. 1990.

108. Poulsen, Orlene Jones. Interviewed by LaRee B. Aldous, Salt Lake City.

109. Rogers, Tom and Merriam. 16 Aug. 1988, Provo, Utah (transcription).

110. ________. 15 Feb. 1988, Provo, Utah (transcription).

111. Schmidt, Alice and Duwayne. 14 Feb. 1988 (transcription).

112. Schmidt, Brian. Feb. 1988 (transcription).

113. Schmidt Family on the Ranch—Tracey, Jeff, Rod, Heather, Heidi. 14 Feb. 1988.

114. Shepherd, Edith F. Feb. 1988. (transcription).

115. Shirts, Cozette and Garry. Interviewed by mail.

116. Sloan, Mimmu. 28 Mar. 1993.

117. Smith, Whitney and Alice. 20 Sept. 1989.

118. Stark, Helen Candland. 19 Feb. 1990 (notes only).

119. Tanner, Obert C. 10 May 1989, Salt Lake City (transcription).

120. Thayne, Emma Lou. 14 July 1988, 22 Oct. 1989, Salt Lake City.

121. Vernon, Robert. 9 Feb. 1992, Salt Lake City.

122. Ward, Dolly Lindsay. 4 Apr. 1989.

123. West, Roy. Oral History Tape at LDS church archives, 20 Sept. 1990; portions read into tape by Mary L. Bradford.

124. Williams, J. D. 18 Feb. 1988, Salt Lake City (transcription).

125. Woodruff, Ashael D. 5 Dec. 1988.

126. Winters, Richard. Mar. 1988 (transcription).

127. __________. Aug. 1991.

128. Wise, Rolland. 21 Mar. 1990, Arlington, Virginia (transcription).

INDEX

A

Adam, and Eve, 67, 132-34. *See also* science and religion
Adams, Ramona, 226, 234, 235, 289, 314
Adamson, Jack, 199, 223
Africa, 277-78
Alder, Douglas D., 111, 166, 349
Alpha Chapter, 73
American Society of Public Administration, 268
Anderson, Darline, 116
Anderson, Edward O., 99
Angulo, Dave, 323
Arango, Valerie, 319
Archuleta, Robert (Archie), 267, 276
Argus, LDS yearbook, 90
Arrington, Leonard J., 169, 185, 253-54, 311
artificial insemination, 94
Aspen Grove (Utah), 77
Australia, 10
Aztec Club, 289

B

B. H. Roberts Society, 303, 311-12
Bailey, Christina, 325
Ballard, Melvin J., 29, 67
Ballif, John, 64
Bangerter, Norm, 279
Barlow, Philip, 335
Becker, Howard, 53
Beecher, Maureen, 289
Beehives, 29
Beeley, Arthur, 31, 41, 121
Befriend the Elderly Project, 319, 325
"Befrienders," 271
Belnap, Olive, 89
Bennett Motor Company, 99
Bennett, Bonnie, 287
Bennett, David, 226
Bennion Creek, 7
Bennion Teton Boys Ranch. *See* Teton Valley Boys Ranch
Bennion, Adam S., 14-15, 64, 127, 131, 136, 139, 142
Bennion, Allfred, 10
Bennion, Brian Colton, 294
Bennion, Carrie, 292
Bennion, Christian Douglas, 292
Bennion, Claire, 11, 13-14
Bennion, Cora Lindsay (mother), 3, 9, 10, 12-15, 120, 298-99
Bennion, David Sterling, 292
Bennion, Delyn, 292
Bennion, Douglas Colton (son), 77, 94, 96, 119, 171, 188, 198, 288, 291, 292, 297, 355

Bennion, Edwin, 10
Bennion, Eliza, 10
Bennion, Ellen (daughter). *See* Stone, Ellen Bennion
Bennion, Frances, 12, 16
Bennion, Grant Madision, 12, 15, 32
Bennion, Hattie, 8
Bennion, Heber, 10
Bennion, Howard Wayne (son), 98, 119, 188-89, 288, 295-97, 304, 355
Bennion, Hugh, 35
Bennion, Ione Spencer, 15
Bennion, Israel, 32
Bennion, Jeffrey Hopkins, 294
Bennion, John, Jr., 3, 5, 8, 226, 293
Bennion, John, Sr., 4
Bennion, Katherine Ellen Snow, 15
Bennion, Kathryn, 294
Bennion, Laurel Colton (daughter), birth and death, 50-51, 295
Bennion, Lindsay, 206
Bennion, Lona, 292
Bennion, Lorilynn, 291
Bennion, Lowell Colton ("Ben") (son), 64, 68, 77, 86, 94, 96, 110, 119-20, 171, 188, 288, 291, 339, 351
Bennion, Lowell Lindsay, family background, 3-16; childhood and adolescence, 3, 15-21; education of, 9-10, 17, 19-20, 31-32, 47-49, 52, 71, 227-28; courtship and marriage of, 32-41; mission, 32-41; marriage and family life, 25, 30, 32, 33, 91-92, 94-95, 119-20, 121; work at LDS Institute, University of Utah, 55-175; work at Teton Valley Boys Ranch, 188, 197-219; work at University of Utah, 13, 161, 163, 164-65, 171, 183-84, 223, 224-238, 304; work at Community Service Council, 265-86; founding of Lowell L. Bennion Community Service Center, 312-26, 349; retirement, 278-80
Bennion, Lowell Lindsay, and church callings, 118, 301-3; and David O Mckay, 33, 64-65, 92, 93, 106, 117, 121, 126, 127, 133, 136, 137, 142, 157, 160, 163, 165-66, 168, 174, 136, 138-39, 166-67, 215; and *Dialogue,* 253; and Ernest L. Wilkinson, 129-30, 131, 135, 136, 142-44, 155, 156, 163-65, 172-73, 187-88, 246; and Joseph Fielding Smith, 56, 78, 92, 131, 133-37, 138, 142, 156, 157, 165, 250; and LDS correlation, 244, 245; and Mark E. Petersen, 94, 131-36, 157, 165; and politics, 47, 49, 231-34, 237, 246-50, 275-76, 345; and senior citizens, 271, 274-75, 319, 325; and travel, 10, 40, 41, 45-49, 52, 53, 188-92, 233; and women's issues, 70, 90-92, 95, 116, 207, 253, 342-43, 345
Bennion, Lowell Lindsay, his intellectual influences and reading: *Bhagavad-Gita,* 192; Brooks, Van Wyck, 68; Buddha, 40; Chaucer, 29; Dante, 40; Goethe, 40, 228, 343; Hamilton, Edith, 68; James, William, 21; Kant, Emmanuel, 228; Milton, John, 8; Pappini, 38; Schiller, 40; Schweitzer,

Albert, 51, 192, 341-42; Scott, Walter, 29; Shakespeare, 29, 68; Spencer, Herbert, 36; Weber, Max, 8, 9, 52-53, 56, 227-28, 229;

Bennion, Lowell Lindsay, on abortion, 342; on birth control, 67, 92; on blacks and priesthood, 93-94, 131-33, 165, 167, 230-31, 245-47, 248-49, 250, 252-53, 254-58; on Book of Mormon, 71-72, 118; on capital punishment and war, 342; on civil rights, 245, 251-52, 274, 345; on courtship and marriage, 77, 90-92, 95, 253; on free agency, 64, 67; on fund raising, 276-77; on gardening, 69, 96, 183, 192-93; on higher biblical criticism, 31, 74-75; on hobbies, 20, 192-93; on homosexuality, 295-97; on Jesus Christ, 67, 111-12, 175; on science and religion, 31, 49, 132-34; on scriptures, 70; on study groups, 288-89; on teaching, 69-70, 112-17, 276

Bennion, Lowell Lindsay, his speaking and writing: 87, 118-19, 331-44; church ban against, 334; his style, 331, 334-36, 344; *An Introduction to the Gospel*, 111; *Do Justly and Love Mercy: Moral Issues for Mormons*, 341; "Great Issues" television series, 226; his "little books," 339-41, 343-44; his only poem, 193; *Introduction to the Book of Mormon and Its Teachings*, 118; *Introduction to the Gospel*, 333; Joseph Smith Memorial Lecture, 99; *Legacies of Jesus*, 334, 343; *Religion and the Pursuit of Truth*, 118, 333; *Religion of the Latter-day Saints*, first institute text written by, 87, 332-33; *Teachings of the Old Testament*, 333; *Things That Matter Most*, 323, 337-39; "Weightier Matters," 336-37; *What About Religion?*, 69; *Youth and Its Religion*, 87

Bennion, Margaret, 12, 16

Bennion, Marjorie Hopkins, 293

Bennion, Marjorie Ralph, 16

Bennion, Mark Daniel, 294

Bennion, Mary Bushel, 6, 9

Bennion, Mary Turpin, 6, 11, 17

Bennion, Maurine, 11, 14, 120

Bennion, Merle Colton (wife), 13, 27, 157, 184, 230, 236; and boys ranch, 199, 207; and children, 49-51, 95; and institute dismissal, 183; and travel, 42, 188-89; church work, 289-90; early life, 25-31; education, 29-30, 68, 189-90, 287-88, 289; married life, 33-34, 95, 286-91; death, 355

Bennion, Milton (father), 3-12, 17, 31, 64, 86, 96-97, 120-21, 341

Bennion, Milton Lindsay (Lynn), 12, 14, 65, 74, 77, 78, 79, 299

Bennion, Naomi Allfred, 292

Bennion, Richard Lindsay, 292

Bennion, Ricky, 211

Bennion, Samuel O., 14

Bennion, Samuel Roberts, 3, 5, 6, 9

Bennion, Sandra Peterson, 292

Bennion, Sherilyn Cox, 110, 188, 291

Bennion, Steven (son), 94, 96, 119, 171, 183, 188, 198, 206, 210, 213, 214, 288, 291, 293, 352

Bennion, Steven Don, Jr., 294
Bennion, Teddy, 32
Bennion, Vaughn Lindsay, 12, 16, 211
Bennion, Wayne Lindsay, 12, 15, 20, 97, 291
Bennion, Zina, 11
Benson, Ezra Taft, 126, 157, 334
Benson, Merle, 182
Benson, Steve, 182
Bentley, Joseph T., 189
Bernhisel, John M., 7
Berrett, William E. ("Ed"), 128, 131, 137, 150, 155, 156, 157, 158, 160-61, 162-63, 165, 167, 172, 182, 184, 186, 187-88
Berry, Hannah, 7
Birch, Esther Ann, 8
Bird, Richard L., 226, 267
birth control, 67, 92
Bitton, Davis, 299-300
blacks and priesthood, 93-94, 131-32, 165, 167, 230-31, 245-47, 248-49, 250, 252-53, 254-57; and David O. McKay, 93, 165-67; and Mark E. Petersen, 132; change of policy, 257-58. *See also* Genesis Group.
Blaesser, Willard, 140, 141, 144, 145
Boas, Franz, 11
Book of Mormon, 21, 36, 71-72
Boyd, Bill, 300
Boyd, George T., 106-7, 131, 134, 136, 138, 186, 201
Boyd, Maurine, 138
Boyden, John, 232
Boyer, Pat, 210
boys ranch. *See* Teton Valley Boys Ranch
Bradford, Lyle, 29
Bradford, Stephen, 207, 208, 212
Brady, Rodney, 110
Branch Agricultural College, 55
Brewer, David, 251, 252
Briand, Aristide, 47
Bridgeforth, Ruffin, 254, 256. *See also* Genesis Group
Brigham Young University, 31, 64, 126, 167, 321, 351-52
Brower, Ralph, 331
Brown, Hugh B., 142, 144, 145, 156, 157, 162, 163, 165, 169, 250
Buchanan, Fred, 115, 169-70, 199, 202, 226
Buehner, Karl, 17
Buehner, Otto, 17
Burton, Alma, 183
Busch, Terri, 320
Bush, Lester E., Jr., 93, 253
Bushel, Mary, 5
Butler, Nicholas, 11

C

Calder, Vera, 42
Callis, Charles A., 56, 67
Camp, Richard Cecil, 27
Camp, Sara Jane Glenn, 27
Campus Outreach Opportunity League (COOL), 312
Canning, Ray, 163, 171, 225-26, 255
Cannon, Angus, 18, 20, 35
Cannon, Antone, 75
Cannon, Cavendish, 39
Cannon, Floyd, 37
Cannon, George Mousley, 18, 20
Cannon, George Q., 18
Cannon, John B., 55
Cannon, John M., 11, 17
Cannon, Marian Morris, 18
Cannon, Paul, 68
Cannon, Sally, 73

Cannon, Zina Bennion, 17
Cannon-Hinckley dinner group, 289
Cardon, Irena, 76
Caring Institute, 350
Carlsen, Harold J. ("Hap"), 36
Castleton, Elaine M., 114
Catheral, Susannah, 7
Catholicism, 37
Catmull, Joseph, 226
Cattell, M. McKean, 11
Chamberlain, Burt, 200, 201
Chamberlain, Joy, 200, 201
Chamberlin, Ralph, 31
Chamberlin, William Henry, 74
Chaplin, Charlie, 36
Chase, Daryl, 75
Chicago World's Fair, 10
Christensen, Joe J., 155-56, 157, 158, 161, 172, 186, 293
Christian Action Ministry Academy (CAM), 230-31
Christian Science, 27
Church Commission of Education, 64, 65
Church Education System, 55-175, 181-82
civil rights, 245, 251-52, 274, 345. *See also* blacks and the priesthood
Civilian Conservation Corps, 54-56
Clark, J. Reuben, 4, 31, 78, 87, 92-93, 120-21, 127, 134
Clayton, James, 319
Collett, Flora Colton, 28
Colton, Alice, 70
Colton, Charles Henry, 26
Colton, Don Byron, 26, 35
Colton, Eleanor, 211
Colton, Ethel, 28
Colton, Flora Elsie, 26
Colton, Frank Edwin, 26
Colton, Hugh Wilkens, 26, 27
Colton, Lela Merle, 27
Colton, Lewis Lycurgus, 26, 28
Colton, Lula Camp, 26
Colton, Lula Ethel, 27
Colton, Merle. *See* Bennion, Merle Colton.
Colton, Mildred, 27
Colton, Nancy Fern, 26
Colton, Nancy Wilkens, 25
Colton, Roland, 27, 28
Colton, Roy, 26
Colton, Sterling Driggs, 25
Colton, Sterling LeRoy, 26
Colton, Warren, 26
Colton, Zora Maria, 26
Columbia University, 11
Community Service Action Week, 318
Community Service Council, 235-36, 257-81, 312, 318
Cook, Barbara Redford, 202
Cook, John, 110, 202
Cooper, Effie Lenore, 8
Cooper, Hannah Turpin, 8
Cooper, Lyle, 281
Cornwall, Lyle, 16
Cox, Sherilyn. *See* Bennion, Sherilyn Cox
Crim, Bill, 323-24
Crossroads Urban Center, 266, 267
Cummings, Horace H., 65

D

Darley, Roy, 287
Delta Phi, 187
Der Sterne, 50
Dialogue: A Journal of Mormon Thought, 253, 312
DiPadova, Laurie Newman, 229-30, 254, 305, 331, 349, 351
Driggs, Eva, 11

Driggs, Howard, 11
Driver, Johnie, 251
Dudley, Jeanne, 272
Duncan, Adam, 251
Dunn, Paul H., 186, 187
Dunyon, Joy F., 128, 131, 136, 138
Durant, Will, 20, 36
Dwyer, Father, 67
Dykstra, Daniel, 140, 161

E

East High School, 29
East Millcreek Twelfth Ward, 245, 301
Eastern States Mission, 54
Eddington, Keith, 280
Eisenhower, Dwight D., 126
Elderly and Handicapped Services, 270
Emerson Ward, 34
Emerson, Noreen, 287
Emery, Alfred C., 235
England, 3, 7, 10
England, Eugene, 113, 119, 253, 303, 321, 332, 336, 343, 349
England, Kathy, 207
Ensign, 244
Ericksen, E. E., 14, 74, 108, 121
Erickson, Carol Lee Gale, 287
Ethiopia, 278
Evans, John Henry, 67
Evans, Richard L., 142, 144, 157, 160, 244
Eve, and Adam, 67, 132-34
evolution. *See* science and religion
Eyring, Henry, 133, 136, 172, 293

F

Farmer Jack, 272
Farr, Melissa, 77
Fellows, George Emery, 31, 41
Fisher, Irene, 315-317, 320, 324, 349
Fitzgerald, John W., 255-56, 275
Fleming, Frances, 250-51
Fleming, Monroe, 250-51, 254
Fletcher, James C., 225, 226-27, 231, 232, 235
Fletcher, Peggy, 303
Folsom, Elry Leonard, 14
Folsom, Leonard, 119, 298, 350
Folsom, Maurine, 298, 350
"Food for Poland," 303
Forest Dale (Utah), 6, 11, 12, 17-18, 30, 267
Forest Farm House, 18
Fort Douglas, 226-27
France, 10
Frazier, Sid, 205
Freedom Foundation (Valley Forge), 303
Frobes, Virginia, 224, 225, 227, 231, 232, 233, 235, 236
Frost, Henry, 227
"Functional Fashions," 270-71

G

Garden Grove (Iowa), 6
Gardner, David P., 238, 304
Garrett, Joel, 300
Genesis Group, 254, 274. *See also* blacks and priesthood.
Germany, 10, 35, 41, 53, 191
Gibbons, Norman, 214, 313, 314
Ginn and Company, 15
Glade, Rebecca Bennion, 355
Granite Junior High School, 15
Grant, Heber J., 64, 77, 87
Gray, Darius, 254, 274
Greene, J. Thomas, 235, 267
Guadalupe Center, 267

H

Haenle, Max, 45, 189
Haglund, Elizabeth, 112, 224, 227,

233, 234, 238, 276
Haglund, Richard, 267
Halamandaris, Bill, 350, 351
Halamandaris, Val, 350, 351
Hammond, Harlan, 109
Hammond, Kevin, 325
Hancock, Eva, 236, 257, 267, 273
Handley, George, 208
Hanks, Marion D., 106, 107, 181-82, 251, 278, 311, 314, 349
Harrison, Conrad B., 267
Hart, Edward L., 69, 70, 91
Henderson, W. W., 74
Henry, Alberta, 268, 273
higher biblical criticism, 31, 74-75
Hill, Alberta, 267
Hill, George R., 121
Hinckley Institute of Politics, 232
Hinckley, Gordon B., 156, 157, 254, 293
Hinckley, Marjorie, 287, 289
Hitler, Adoph, 45-46
Holland, 10
homosexuality, 295-97
Hope, Len, 251
Howell, Scott, 352
Huber, Kenneth, 37
Huefner, Steven, 197
Huish, Agnes, 34
Hunter, Howard W., 157
Hutchinson, Bill, 214-15

I

"I Know That My Redeemer Lives," 29
Improvement Era, 244
Inoway, Rita, 273
Instructor, 244
Israel, 190-91
Italy, 10
Ivins, Antone, 97

J

Jacobsen, Richard, 213, 312, 314
Jacobsen, Rosebud, 244
Jacobsen, Susan, 213
Jacobsen, Ted, 213
James, William, 21
Jarvis, Boyer, 210, 223, 304
Jarvis, Pat, 190, 304
Jensen, Isabel, 314
John Birch Society, 232-33
Johnson, Charles, 269, 276
Johnson, Richard, 69
Johnson, Wesley, 253
Johnston, Jerry, 344
Jon Huntsman Center, 226
Jones, Claire B., 350
Jones, Mildred, 188
Jones, Paul, 68, 188
Jones, Rheim, 73
Jones, William Lunt, 13
Jordan River, 6, 8
Joseph Smith Memorial Lecture, 99
Juilliard School of Music, 14
Junior League, 267
Juvenile Instructor, 12

K

Kayser, Anna, 52
Kearsley, Art, 204
Keefer, Theodore E. ("Ted"), 269, 272
Keller, Karl, 253
Kellog-Briand Pact, 7
Kemmerer (Wyoming), 30
Kimball, Camilla Eyring, 109
Kimball, Edward L., 76, 119
Kimball, LeVan, 76
Kimball, Spencer W., 157, 301
King, David S., 67
Klopfer, W. Herbert, 114
Korean War, 109
Kreisler, Fritz, 14

L

Lambda Delta Sigma, 73, 76, 79, 88, 90, 110, 111, 162, 183, 186, 187, 342
Lambert, A. C., 74
Lambert, Libbie, 290
Landa, Esther, 267-68
Larson, LeGrand, 199
Latter-day Saint Students Association (LDSSA), 187
LDS Business College, 29, 30
LDS Church Commissioner of Education, 55
LDS Church School System. *See* Church Education System
LDS College, 10
LDS High School, 19-20, 25, 30
LDS Institute, University of Utah, 55-175
League of Nations, 47
League of Women Voters, 267, 315
Leavitt, Jackie, 281
Leavitt, Mike, 281
LeCheminant, Dale, 186, 249, 333
Lee, Harold B., 127, 131, 150, 156, 157, 160; and correlation, 187, 243-44
Lee, Rex, 351-52
Leonard, Florence, 271, 279
Leviathan, 35, 42
Lincoln, Abraham, 26
Lindsay, Emma Bushel Bennion, 9
Lindsay, Gordon, 214
Lindsay, Joseph Shanks, 9
Lindsay, Kathleen, 214
Lindsay, Mary Elizabeth, 11
Lindsay, Richard, 211
Lindsay, Susan, 207
Liverpool (England), 4
Livingston, Louise, 88
Lloyd, Wesley, 75
Los Angeles (California), 138
Lowell Bennion Public Service Professorships, 319
Lowell Bennion Study Group, 289
Lowell L. Bennion Community Service Center, 312-26, 349
Lowell L. Bennion Essay in Christian Living (*Dialogue* award), 312
Ludlow, Daniel, 244
Lyman, Richard R., 77
Lyon, David, 79
Lyon, Hermana Forsberg, 54, 79, 91, 159, 162, 169, 174, 224, 294, 299, 300
Lyon, James, 79, 182, 211
Lyon, John, 79, 299
Lyon, Laurie, 79
Lyon, Lynn, 201
Lyon, T. Edgar, 54, 76, 79, 85, 91, 100, 105, 106, 107, 129, 131, 135, 136, 139-40, 150, 155, 156, 157, 159, 161, 169, 171, 182, 183, 184-85, 190, 201, 211, 232, 299-300
Lythgoe, Dennis, 229, 313

M

Madsen, Brigham, 255
Madsen, Gordon, 215
Mair, Debbie, 270
Marcum, Dale, 204, 205
Matheson, Norma, 277
Matheson, Scott, 266
Maxwell, Neal, 161, 163, 168, 172, 186, 223, 224, 227, 235
McCabe, Patrick, 316
McKay, David O., 92, 93, 106, 117, 121, 126, 127, 133, 136, 137, 142, 157, 160, 163, 165, 168, 174; and Ernest Wilkinson, 138-39, 166-67; and Lowell

Bennion, 64-65, 136; and Ray Olpin, 144-45; and Utah Boys Ranch, 215; death, 186, 257; marries Lowell and Merle, 33; on blacks and the priesthood, 93, 165-66
McKay, Llewellyn, 142, 144
McMullin, Dix, 215
McMullin, Keith, 281
McMurray, Frank, 11
McMurrin, Natalie, 230
McMurrin, Sterling, 223-24, 230, 232, 253, 255, 256, 311-12, 339
Meheles, Persis, 272-73
Merrill, Joseph F., 75, 86
Middlemiss, Claire, 144
Millennial Star, 244
Miller, Clinton, 88
Milton Bennion Memorial Foundation, 121
Moeller, Hero, 45
Moench, Louis, 68, 192, 306
Moench, MaVonne, 68
Mona (Utah), 26
Monson, Charles, 189
Monson, Diane, 253
Monson, Thomas S., 254
Moore, Ardith, 73
Moose Creek Lodge, 199-200
Moran, Bill, 37, 68, 75, 77, 86, 89, 97-98, 224, 297, 350
Morgan, Anthony W., 312
Morgan, Elmo R., 16
Morgan, Frances B., 77
Morgan, Jacque, 316
Morgan, Kent, 206
Morgan, Tony, 315
Mormon History Association, 253
Moscow (Idaho), 55
Mosher, Emma, 202
Moss, Frank, 350
"Most Caring People in America" award, 350
Moyle, Henry D., 131, 142, 156, 157, 158, 160
Mukai, Bob, 251
Mulder, William, 190
Murdock, Kent, 301, 302
Mutual Improvement Association, 69, 118

N

NAACP, and Mormon church, 250
Nabors, Charles, 251
Nauvoo (Illinois), 3, 5, 185
Nauvoo Restoration, Inc., 185
Neff, Branson, 198
Neff, Sherman, 68
Neilsen, Alfred C., 139
Nelson, Eric, 201
Nelson, Lowry, 253
Nelson, Richard, 200, 201, 213
New Zealand Mission, 10
Newell, L. Jackson, 312, 314
Newell, Linda, 312
Nigeria, 246

O

O'Dea, Thomas, 227
Oaks, Dallin H., 186
Olpin, A. Ray, 130, 136, 138, 140-41, 142, 143-45, 156, 157, 158, 159-60, 161, 163, 165, 168, 223, 224, 226
Omega Chapter, 73
organic evolution. *See* science and religion
Orr, Eugene, 254
Ouelessebougou-Utah Alliance, 270, 277-78, 319

P

Pack, Fred J., 133
Pack, Frederick G., 31

Packer, Boyd K., 138, 140, 155, 160, 164, 254
Palestine, 10
Papanikolas, Helen Z., 274
Park, John R., 9
Parry, Robert A., 203, 207
Parson, Talcott, 227
Patton, Michael J., 235
Payne, Albert, 112, 139-40, 201, 211
Peters, John Durham, 197
Petersen, Mark E., 131-37, 157, 165; and Joseph Fielding Smith, 135-36; on artificial insemination, 94; on blacks and priesthood, 131-32
Peterson, Andrew, 314
Peterson, Chase N., 312, 313
Peterson, Gary B., 291
Peterson, Grethe B., 314, 320
Peterson, Henry, 31
Peterson, Joseph, 31
Peterson, Kathy, 214
Peterson, Steve, 214
"Piano Wire Murders," 212
Pike, Ellen Jeanne, 355
Pike, Tom, 301, 355
Pinnock, Andrea, 319
Pioneer Trails State Park, 18
Pleasant Hours Club, 18
plural marriage, 5, 37
Poelman, Stuart, 257, 258
Poulsen, Adrienne, 355
Poulson, George Melvin, 28
Pratt, Orson, 10
Pratt, Parley P., 10
Price, Allen, 206
Price, Jerry, 213
Progressivism, 11
Project Prohimo, 322
PTA Congress, 226
Pugh, Don, 277, 278
Pugh, Lorin, 213

R

Rampton, Calvin L., 251
Redford, Barbara, 110
Relief Society Magazine, 244
Relief Society, 13, 28, 187, 244
Reorganized Church, 35
Rich, Wendell, 139
Richard D. Bass Achievement Award, 279
Richards, LeGrand, 157
Richards, Stephen L., 67, 97
Ricks College, 68, 130, 186, 198, 213-14, 254, 293
Ricks, Eleanor, 112
Riddle, Chauncey, 246-249
Rogers, Lewis, 189
Romero, Mike, 267
Romney, George, 245-46
Romney, Marion G., 131, 157
Romney, Thomas, 72
Rubin, Jerry, 232
Russell, James E., 11

S

Salt Lake City School District, 15
Salt Lake Community College, 322
Salt Lake County Commission on Youth, 266
Salt Lake County Division of Aging, 274
Salt Lake County Hospital Board, 266
Salt Lake Food Bank, 270, 271-72
Salvation Army, 272
Schmidt, Alice, 202-3
Schmidt, Brian C., 205, 209, 210, 211, 214
Schmidt, DuWayne, 116, 170, 202-3
Schmidt, Heidi, 206
Schmidt, Jeffrey, 205, 213
Schmidt, Rodney, 204
Schwendiman, Glenn, 68, 70

science and religion, 31, 49, 67; and Joseph Fielding Smith, 132-34.
Serving Utah Network (SUN), 321
Sessions, J. Wyley, 55, 72
Sharp, Luella Ferron, 30
Shepherd, Bob, 201
Shepherd, Edith F., 201, 244, 314
Shepherd, Gary, 229
Shepherd, Gordon, 229
Shirley, Mack, 213
Shirts, Cozette, 188, 199-200
Shirts, Garry, 115, 188, 199-200
Silver, Madelyn, 278
Simpson, Robert L., 267
Smart, Elaine, 269, 311
Smith's Food King, 272
Smith, Aseneth, 42
Smith, Elwin, 54
Smith, Ethel Colton, 54, 106, 350
Smith, George Albert, 70, 99, 100, 106
Smith, Hyrum, 6
Smith, Joseph F., 42
Smith, Joseph Fielding, 56, 78, 131, 134, 137, 138, 142, 156, 157, 165; and David O. McKay, 136; and Mark E. Petersen, 135-36; on birth control, 92; on blacks and priesthood, 250; on Henderson-Snell papers, 74-75
Smith, Joseph, 5, 21, 67, 67, 99, 134, 256
Smith, Lynn, 213
Smith, Whitney Winslow, 35, 70
Snell, Heber, 74, 253
Snow College, 55, 56, 74, 183, 293
Snow, Helen, 68
South Africa, 165
Spann, Othnar, 49
Spellman, Mildred, 29
Spencer, Ione, 33, 42
Sperry, Sidney, 75, 253
St. Vincent DePaul, 272
Stanford University, 15, 65
Stapley, Delbert L., 157
Stewart School, 15, 32, 86, 95
Stewart, John J., *Mormonism and the Negro,* 167
Stone, Ellen Bennion (daughter), 120, 207, 287, 288, 291, 297-98, 304
Stone, Jacob, 298
Stone, Lindsay, 298, 355
Stone, Neil Hirschi , 298
Stucki, Richard, 203
Student Review, 336
Students for a Democratic Society, 233
Sugar House Bank, 30
Summerhays, Margaret Lindsay, 109
Sunstone, 303, 336
Swann, Verna, 69
Sweeney, Lawrence P., 267
Swenson, Russel, 75
Swiss-German Mission, L., 32
Syria, 10

T

Taber, Susan B., 339
Tadje, Fred, 35
Talmage, James E., 10, 133
Tanner, George, 72
Tanner, Grace Adams, 68, 95
Tanner, Obert C., 68, 73, 95, 174-75, 183, 202
Taylor, Harvey L., 186
Taylor, John, 7
Taylorsville (Utah), 7, 8
Teton Mountain Leadership Institute, 213-14
Teton Valley, 183
Teton Valley Boys Ranch, 12, 197-215, 349

Thayne, Emma Lou, 191, 289, 311, 316, 325-26, 339, 355
Thayne, Mel, 191
Thomas, Elbert D., 31, 40
Thomas, George, 64
Thompson, Noleen, 201
Thompson, Veda, 201, 207
Tingey, Dale, 155
Toele (Utah), 97-98
Topaz (Utah), 268
Trade Technical College, 270
Tufts, James H., 11
Tuscon (Arizona), 76, 79
Tuttle, Theodore, 138, 164

U

Udall, Stewart, 76, 253
Ugaki, Janice, 319
Uinta Basin, 26
Uintah Stake Relief Society, 28
Uintah-Ouray Reservation, 26, 27
United Airlines, 16
United Way, 269-70
University of Arizona, 76
University of California, Berkeley, 13, 14, 65, 74, 106
University of Chicago, 11, 65, 75
University of Deseret, 9
University of Erlangen, 41
University of Utah Counseling Center, 224
University of Utah Foreign Student Advisory Council, 224
University of Utah KUED, 226
University of Utah Marriage and Family Counseling Bureau, 224
University of Utah Marrott Library, 226
University of Utah Park Building, 183
University of Utah Research Park, 226
University of Utah School of Education, 11
University of Utah Service Learning Scholars Program, 319 (U of U)
University of Utah Student Affairs Committee, 224
University of Utah Student Behavior Committee, 234
University of Utah Student Welfare Fund Board, 224
University of Utah Study Abroad, 190, 233
University of Utah, 11, 13, 14, 15, 16, 40, 64, 161, 163, 164-65, 171, 224-38, 304; appointment of Lowell Bennion, 167, 223, 227-28, 231; establishment of Lowell L. Bennion Community Service Center, 312
University of Utah, LDS Institute. *See* LDS Institute, University of Utah
University of Washington, 71
University Sunday Night Group, 288
University Ward, 64
Utah Agricultural College, 14
Utah Association of Mental Health, 266
Utah Boys Ranch, 214-15
Utah Center for the Prevention and Control of Juvenile Delinquency, 171, 225-26
Utah Educational Review, 12, 31
Utah Endowment for the Humanities, 274, 345
Utah Executive Commission on Civil Rights, 251
Utah Independent Living Center, 270
Utah Issues Information Programs, Inc., 315, 324
Utah Legislature, Lowell Bennion honored by, 353
Utah Mother of the Year, 13, 120
Utah Peace Officers Association,

226
Utah Power and Light Company, 272
Utah State Agricultural College, 13, 65, 87
Utah State Board of Family Services, 266
Utah State Prison, 274
Utah State University, 15
Utahns Against Hunger, 266
Utes, 26

V

Van De Graff, Rick, 321
Verdross, Victor, 48
Vernal (Utah), 26, 27
Vernon, Robert, 303
Vetterli, Richard, 159
Victor (Idaho), 202
Voegelin, Eric, 48
Voluntary Action Center, 270
Von Schelting, Alexander, 53

W

Wainwright, Esther, 5
Wales, 7
Warner, David, 322
Warner, Leslie, 324
Warner, Rick, 311
Weber State Universtiy, 321
Weber, Max, 8, 9, 52-53, 56, 227-28, 229
Weeks, Francis, 202
Weimar Republic, 36
Welch, Robert, 232
Welling, Yvonne, 88, 91
Wells, Emmeline B., 28
Wendelboe, Dan, 322
West Valley City (Utah), 7
West, Franklin, 65, 73, 74, 76, 78, 79, 87-88, 99, 100, 106, 126-28, 129, 138
Whisenant, Keith, 277, 280, 314
Widtsoe, John A., 35, 45, 48, 55, 63, 65, 67, 92, 133
Widtsoe, Leah Dunford, 45, 48
Wilkinson, Ernest L., 130, 142-43, 155, 156, 160, 161, 163-65, 168-69, 172-73, 246; and campaign for U. S. Senate, 173-74, 186; and Church Education System, 126, 128-29; and David O. McKay, 137, 138-39; and Franklin West, 127; and Joe Christensen, 155-56; and junior colleges, 126-27, 130; and Ray Olpin, 140, 159-60; and University of Utah Institute, 129-30, 131, 135, 136, 143-44, 163-65, 170-71, 172-73, 187-88; death of, 186; on blacks and priesthood, 166-67
Williams, Cozette, 115
Williams, J. D., 232, 237, 251
Wilson, Grant, 198, 199
Wilson, Guy C., 19
Wilson, Mark, 198, 199
Wilson, Sharol Duffin, 198
Wilson, Ted L., 314
Winters, Mary Nebeker, 279
Winters, Richard K., 276, 279, 303, 350
Winterton, Bonnie Lauper, 287, 289
Wise, Roland V., 266, 268
Wood, J. Karl, 128
Woodruff, Wilford, 7, 134
Woodruff, Elias Smith, 18, 35
World War I, 17
World War II, 88-98

Y

Young, Brigham, 6, 7, 8, 18, 26, 27, 134

Young, John W., 18
Young, Kimball, 53
Young, Levi Edgar, 67
Youth Correlation Comimttee, 244

Z

Zucker, Louis, 68

About the Author

Mary Lythgoe Bradford is a writer, editor, and teacher. She graduated from the University of Utah with degrees in education and English. She then taught English literature and grammar at the University of Utah, Brigham Young University, and Amer-ican University. She has also consulted and taught writing, editing, and speech to government agencies over a twenty-year period. She has edited *Dialogue: A Journal of Mormon Thought*, two book-length collections of essays, and numerous books and reports for firms and individuals. She is the author of an autobiographical compilation of personal essays as well as numerous articles, essays, reviews, and poems. Her husband Charles H. Bradford died in 1991. She is the mother of Stephen Lythgoe Bradford, Lorraine Bradford Gravallese, and Scott Charles Bradford, and the grandmother of seven. She lives in Arlington, Virginia.